WordPress®

IN DEPTH

Bud Smith and Michael McCallister

800 East 96th Street
Indianapolis, Indiana 46240

WORDPRESS® IN DEPTH

Copyright © 2010 by Pearson Education, Inc.

ISBN-13: 978-0-7897-4275-9

ISBN-10: 0-7897-4275-6

Library of Congress Cataloging-in-Publication Data:

Smith, Bud E.

   WordPress in depth / Bud Smith and Michael McCallister.

     p. cm.

   ISBN-13: 978-0-7897-4275-9

   ISBN-10: 0-7897-4275-6

   1. WordPress (Electronic resource) 2. Blogs—Computer programs. 3. Web sites—Design—Computer programs. I. McCallister, Michael. II. Title.

   TK5105.8885.W66S65 2010

   006.7'52—dc22

                             2009049995

Printed in the United States of America

First Printing: February 2010

Trademarks

Warning and Disclaimer

Bulk Sales

Que Publishing offers excellent discounts on this book when ordered in quantity for bulk purchases or special sales. For more information, please contact

> **U.S. Corporate and Government Sales**
> **1-800-382-3419**
> corpsales@pearsontechgroup.com

For sales outside of the U.S., please contact

> **International Sales**
> international@pearson.com

Associate Publisher
Greg Wiegand

Acquisitions Editor
Michelle Newcomb

Development Editor
Todd Brakke

Managing Editor
Kristy Hart

Project Editor
Jovana San Nicolas-Shirley

Copy Editor
Karen Annett

Indexer
Lisa Stumpf

Proofreader
Julie Anderson

Technical Editor
Paul Chaney

Publishing Coordinator
Cindy Teeters

Cover Designer
Anne Jones

Compositor
Nonie Ratcliff

CONTENTS AT A GLANCE

CONTENTS

ABOUT THE AUTHORS

Bud Smith wrote his first book for Que about buying computers fifteen years ago—and had to do his online research for it using dial-up Internet. Since then, he's lived and worked in Silicon Valley; London, England; Auckland and Christchurch New Zealand; and San Francisco, and written a dozen more books. And he does most of his online work at broadband speeds—except when he's using the Web on his cell phone, which is slower than his old dial-up modem. Bud runs a WordPress-based blog at gvDaily.com.

Michael McCallister is devoted to the idea that technology need not be feared, and can be mastered by anyone. He has been writing about technology in general, and open source software in particular, for the whole of the twenty-first century, and part of the last century too. He tries to help build the open source community, from which derives WordPress and so much else that is good, true, and pure in life (the parts of life that run on computers, anyway). While Bud has moved hither and yon, Michael has lived the relatively boring, stable life in the central United States (Milwaukee, Madison, and Boulder). Michael has been running "Notes from the Metaverse" on WordPress since 2006, now at www.michaelmccallister.com.

DEDICATION

Bud dedicates his portion of the book to the open source community, pioneers in what threatens to become the "new normal": doing what you like, because you like to do it, to help other people, not because someone told you to.

Michael echoes Bud's thoughts, and further dedicates his portion of the book to Jeanette, who puts up with so much.

ACKNOWLEDGMENTS

We would like to acknowledge the help and support of our excellent acquisitions editor, Michelle Newcomb; our dedicated and tireless technical editor, Paul Chaney; and our patient and personable development editor, Todd Brakke.

WE WANT TO HEAR FROM YOU!

As the reader of this book, *you* are our most important critic and commentator. We value your opinion and want to know what we're doing right, what we could do better, what areas you'd like to see us publish in, and any other words of wisdom you're willing to pass our way.

As an associate publisher for Que Publishing, I welcome your comments. You can email or write me directly to let me know what you did or didn't like about this book—as well as what we can do to make our books better.

Please note that I cannot help you with technical problems related to the topic of this book. We do have a User Services group, however, where I will forward specific technical questions related to the book.

When you write, please be sure to include this book's title and author as well as your name, email address, and phone number. I will carefully review your comments and share them with the author and editors who worked on the book.

Email: feedback@quepublishing.com

Mail: Greg Wiegand
         Associate Publisher
         Que Publishing
         800 East 96th Street
         Indianapolis, IN 46240 USA

READER SERVICES

Visit our website and register this book at informit.com/register for convenient access to any updates, downloads, or errata that might be available for this book.

Introduction

WELCOME

We're glad that you've purchased, or are considering the purchase of, this book. WordPress, in its various forms, is amazing blogging software. It's also an amazing project, a shining example of human collaboration, a great example of open source at work, a fascinating business, and much more.

In less than a decade, WordPress has become the most important tool around for blogging, which itself is the channel for one of the great uncensored, unedited, unrestrained outpourings of creativity in human history. WordPress blogs often serve as a home for breaking news or insightful comments that affect other media. As such, WordPress is important to people who don't like blogs or who don't even like computers.

WordPress is a serious and tremendously flexible tool—and also a framework for creating more tools. WordPress blogs include some of the biggest websites around, as well as spur-of-the-moment creations that attract a few posts, perhaps a few comments, and then go the way of the dodo.

Along with the blogs themselves, one of the amazing things is the power of blogs as a network, referring to each other, with blog entries and comments forming a mesh—well, a web, actually—of comment, criticism, and encouragement. (Even a criticism can serve as a form of encouragement, inspiring a blogger to answer a complaint or to post a better entry next time.)

Another powerful feature of blogs in general, and WordPress blogs in particular, is the strong community that's formed around them. That's partly because of the popularity of WordPress blogs and partly because of the open source nature of WordPress software. The WordPress community seamlessly intermixes reaction to blog postings with advice and help on technical aspects of running a blog. It's often hard to tell where one ends and the other begins, but that's part of the fun.

Why This Book?

This book is, of course, *WordPress In Depth*, and the *In Depth* part means something.

There are a few things that any book about WordPress should seek to do. It should seek to explain the different forms of WordPress—primarily the two versions called WordPress.com, a kind of sandbox for easy blogging, and WordPress.org, in which you more or less build your own sandbox, then blog in it.

A book about WordPress should show you how to use either version to get up and running with your blog as quickly as possible. And, for WordPress.org users, it should show you how to install your blog software quickly and easily.

An *In Depth* book, though, does even more. So we show you how to create your own themes and plug-ins in WordPress.org—and how to use upgrades in WordPress.com to get some of the power of WordPress.org for only a small amount of money per month.

WordPress is a framework as well as a tool. It allows you to take advantage of graphics, video, audio, HTML, CSS, PHP, and more. (Don't worry if you don't know what all of this means; we explain it as we go along.) We cover a great deal of this in the book you hold in your hands.

We explain your choices at each step of the way thoroughly, giving you perspective lacking from the voluminous but disorganized online resources that exist for various versions of WordPress.

Our hope is that we've provided a complete, coherent, useful resource. The WordPress universe is so vast that no one can cover all of it in one place. But our aim has been to cover the core of the two main WordPress versions so you can spread your wings and fly. Then you can take advantage of other WordPress resources, such as the WordPress community, to help you catch an occasional updraft and soar even higher.

In writing this book, we sought to be concise, accurate, interesting, elegant, and (occasionally) funny. A few words on each of these goals might be appropriate here.

By concise, we have worked to keep our explanations as brief as possible—but no briefer. That is, we don't assume you know much coming in. The book tries to provide all the "salmon ladders" needed so you can swim upriver with confidence, eventually arriving at your goal.

Accurate should speak for itself, but much of the explanatory material we found about WordPress in our research for this book is sadly inaccurate. Part of this is because WordPress has so many versions. As it's upgraded, old information hangs around, and even updated versions don't always fully reflect current reality. And some of it is just lack of care. We tried to be careful and up-to-date to make this book accurate.

A special note about versions: This book is going to press just as Version 2.9 is being completed. We've used a very late beta version of 2.9 for some screenshots. Please excuse any minor differences that result from changes in the final version of 2.9 or additional updates after this book is published.

We also sought to make this book interesting. You, the design of your blog, the words, the images and more that you put into it, and the ways in which you extend it are the main source of interest in the use of this book, of course. However, we have tried to help by using examples and references that are up-to-date, not trivially simple, and relevant to the topic at hand.

To write elegantly is even harder than writing interestingly. Each of us, though, brings years of past experience, as well as ongoing current work, in conveying detailed and sometimes difficult information in a useful way. We hope that we've managed a turn of phrase here, a trick of organization there, that make you feel that you're in the hands of people you can trust as you seek to get the most of WordPress.

Which brings us to funny. We doubt anyone will, to put it bluntly, bust a gut cracking up, or roll on the floor laughing, over any of our meant-to-be humorous asides. A wry smile from you here and there might be the best we achieve. However, a little bit of humor reminds us of our shared humanity, which can be reassuring when things get difficult, and makes learning easier as well.

In all of this, we try to reach relative beginners, intermediate users, and experts. The way in which each such audience uses the book might differ, but the goal of being useful to each and every one of you remains. We believe we've achieved it.

How Our Book Is Organized

We've divided the book into four parts. Each builds on the previous ones.

The first three parts are usable by both WordPress.com and WordPress.org users. Only in Part IV, "Building Your Own WordPress Installation," do we address WordPress.org users exclusively. This is intended to help users of both kinds of WordPress. WordPress.org users sometimes use WordPress.com for specific projects, and often end up serving as unpaid, informal support for WordPress.com users as well.

This is different from the practice in many other WordPress books and online resources, which mash WordPress.com and WordPress.org together. We believe that this just confuses people and increases the burden of informal support on the more knowledgeable users.

Don't worry if you feel like an unpaid tech support person for a WordPress.com user; at some point, your student might mature and "graduate" to WordPress.org. Then you get to serve as unpaid, informal support for them in their new role as a WordPress.org user instead!

With all that in mind, here's a brief description of each major part of the book:

Part I, "Getting Started with Your Blog," handles the naming of parts of different WordPress versions and introduces the WordPress community. We also compare WordPress with a popular alternative, Blogger, and introduce WordPress hosting options. We then describe getting your blog started and introduce the rich topic of domain name options for your blog. Finally, we describe the theme, header, and widget options available to WordPress.com users. (And, in much richer form, to WordPress.org users.)

In Part II, "Running Your Blog," we go through actually running your blog—the heart of using WordPress. This is where you learn how to create a post with links and formatting and publish it. Then, we step you through putting posts in categories and using tags. WordPress sometimes uses the same words a bit differently than anyone else, and categories, in particular, are an example of this. We finish by showing you how to extend your blog with static pages and polls and how to use statistics.

Some blogging tools start running out of gas at this point, but WordPress is just getting going. Part III, "Taking Your Blog Further," shows how you can add graphics, which requires paying some attention to issues like copyright as well as the mechanics of actually getting the graphic into your blog post. We then go on to describe how to add audio or video to your blog, whether you're a WordPress.com user, in which case, each requires the purchase of an upgrade, or a WordPress.org user, in which case you should know if your host charges extra for the bandwidth needed to serve a popular audio, or especially, video file.

Part IV is where we take you into the WordPress features exclusive to WordPress.org. This part begins with a description of installing and upgrading the WordPress software. We then take you through choosing from existing themes and plug-ins for your blog and, finally, show you how to use CSS to build your own theme or PHP to create your own plug-ins. You don't have to learn the languages from scratch; in fact, many excellent WordPress blogs have been built through tweaks to existing code, which you can learn through a bit of reading (ahem) and trial and error. No, that's not part of the "funny" we said we tried to add to the book.

Part V, "Appendices," begins by taking you through using WordPress.com versus WordPress.org in so much depth that you can probably even explain it to your boss after reading this. We then describe the WordPress online documentation in some detail, as it's a fantastic resource, but sometimes causes as much wasted time as joy.

Conventions Used in This Book

Special conventions are used throughout this book to help you get the most from the book and from WordPress.

Text Conventions

Various typefaces in this book identify terms and other special objects. These special typefaces include the following:

Type	Meaning
Italic	New terms or phrases when initially defined
Monospace	Information that appears in code or onscreen
Bold monospace	Information you type

All book publishers struggle with how to represent command sequences when menus and dialog boxes are involved. In this book, we separate commands using a comma. So, for example, the instruction "Choose Edit, Cut" means that you should open the Edit menu and choose Cut.

Key combinations are represented with a plus sign. For example, if the text calls for you to press Ctrl+Alt+Delete, you would press the Ctrl, Alt, and Delete keys at the same time.

Special Elements

Throughout this book, you'll find Notes, Tips, Cautions, Sidebars, and Troubleshooting Notes. Often, you'll find just the tidbit you need to get through a rough day at the office or the one whiz-bang trick that will make you the office hero. You'll also find little nuggets of wisdom, humor, and lingo that you can use to amaze your friends and family, not to mention make you cocktail-party literate.

 tip

We specially designed these tips to showcase the best of the best. Just because you get your work done doesn't mean you're doing it in the fastest, easiest way possible. We show you how to maximize your WordPress experience. Don't miss these tips!

 **note**

Notes point out items that you should be aware of, but you can skip them if you're in a hurry. Generally, we've added notes as a way to give you some extra information on a topic without weighing you down.

 **caution**

Pay attention to cautions! They could save you precious hours in lost work.

We Had More to Say

We use sidebars to dig a little deeper into more esoteric features, settings, or peculiarities of WordPress. Some sidebars are used to explain something in more detail when doing so in the main body text would've been intrusive or distracting. Sometimes, we just needed to get something off our chests and rant a bit. Don't skip the sidebars, because you'll find nuggets of pure gold in them (if we do say so ourselves).

 ### Something Isn't Working

Throughout the book, we describe some common trouble symptoms and tell you how to diagnose and fix problems with WordPress. These troubleshooting notes are sure to make your life with WordPress a bit easier.

GETTING STARTED WITH YOUR BLOG

IN THIS PART

GETTING STARTED WITH WORDPRESS

What Is WordPress?

WordPress is the leading blogging tool, period. It's popular with rank beginners, mainstream bloggers, business bloggers, and pros. People use it to post their thoughts for a few friends—and to reach hundreds of thousands of people a day.

WordPress is notable for several reasons. The backbone of all WordPress blogs is free, open source software. Michel Valdrighi developed the original software, called *b2\cafelog*; he's now a contributing developer to WordPress. The current WordPress software first appeared in 2002 as a new version or "fork" by Mike Little and Matt Mullenweg, now the most visible leader of the WordPress community.

Matt founded Automattic in 2005. Automattic is the business behind WordPress.com, the free, hosted version of WordPress, and Akismet, the spam blocker built for WordPress.

WordPress is the jewel in the crown of the blogging world. Other blogging tools tend to be less capable, less popular, more limited, more expensive, or a combination of these. Only WordPress has the combination of ease of (initial) use, power, flexibility, and low cost that have made it the leading tool for blogging.

There are three keys to WordPress's power: its multiple versions, its user community, and its status as a free or low-cost tool.

WordPress Versions in Brief

You might have noticed that there are actually multiple versions of WordPress. The question as to the difference between WordPress.com and WordPress software, supported by the WordPress.org website, is initially confusing to a lot of people. The difference, though, is easily explained, and a big part of WordPress's power.

WordPress comes in three versions, each covered in this book. The versions are as follows:

- WordPress.com, a website that hosts a wild profusion of customers' blogs. Automattic, the company that owns the WordPress software and brand, hosts this site. WordPress.com bloggers and their visitors only "pay" by having occasional text ads displayed on the blogs, or pay a small annual fee to have their site be ad free. You can put a wide variety of content in your WordPress blog, but customization is limited to setup options, scores of canned themes, and existing widgets—sidebar tools that give additional options to site visitors.

- WordPress software, supported by the WordPress.org website. You can download the WordPress software yourself and install it on your own website, find a web host who allows you to install WordPress on their site, or use a specialized WordPress hosting service in which the host sets up and maintains the software for you. As a WordPress software user, you can borrow or buy additional themes and plug-ins and use them on your blog, as well as create your own.

- WordPress MU, for multiuser. WordPress MU is the version of the software that runs WordPress.com. You can use it to create your own hosting network, within an organization (for an intranet or extranet), or when hosting public-facing blogs.

We explore just how to get the most out of WordPress in all its versions throughout this book, though WordPress is so deep that further books could easily be written.

One interesting aspect of the structure of WordPress offerings is that the company, in classic technology style, chooses to "eat its own dog food." Automattic, the company behind WordPress, uses WordPress MU to run the WordPress.com website. Any improvements they make for their own use are made available to users as well—and improvements requested by users immediately impact Automattic in its daily use of its own software.

WordPress was originally developed by bloggers wanting a tool to blog with. Today, Automattic continues this tradition—all its activities feed back into the development of better tools and services for blogging.

The WordPress Community

Many technology products claim to be at the center of a vibrant community of users, developers, and others. In WordPress's case, it's actually true.

Blogging naturally creates a sense of community among participants, bloggers, and blog readers alike. In the case of WordPress, the community extends to the developers. Bloggers themselves, creators of tools for bloggers, users of blogging for company communications—the WordPress community is rich and varied.

There is a plethora of blogs, podcasts, and, of course, books focused on WordPress in all its versions. WordCamps are more or less impromptu gatherings, with WordPress bloggers gathering in one city or another, usually on a Saturday, to meet one another and discuss issues.

WordPress users contribute a great deal to the software. Most WordPress support resources are created and maintained on a voluntary basis by people sharing solutions to problems they themselves encounter in trying to use the software. For WordPress.com users, resources offered as part of the software, such as themes and widgets, are contributed by developers who might not be professionals at all, just generous enthusiasts.

Support and shared resources are most extensive for the WordPress software available from Wordpress.org. WordPress.org is not a version of WordPress, as many people seem to think; it's the nonprofit community that provides the great bulk of support for WordPress software. However, bowing to widespread usage, we refer to using the WordPress software directly as "using WordPress.org" at some points in this book.

Part of the strength of WordPress comes from its status as open source software. Any user of WordPress software can change it. Just as important, due to the strength of the WordPress community, any user of the WordPress software can describe a change they need made—and, very often indeed, some other WordPress user will make the change for them.

The change can then get picked up and used by dozens, hundreds, or thousands of WordPress software users. Eventually, the best changes are rolled into the WordPress core—the version of WordPress software Automattic releases to a waiting world. Each new release is the base for further innovations.

As you'll see in this book, the WordPress resources you can get for free are tremendous. In fact, one of the things you might end up paying for if you take your WordPress blogging further is an expert to help you weigh the plusses and minuses of the free resources so you can choose which ones to use!

What Does It Cost You?

Automattic is focused only on WordPress. Automattic, though, is much like its wider-ranging cousin, Google, in an interesting way: Both companies have found a way to provide a hugely popular set of services while exercising a very light touch on customers' experiences and wallets.

WordPress was introduced in 2003—a surprisingly recent introduction, given Automattic's current strong leadership position. WordPress was first made publicly available (as downloadable software) just before a competing tool suddenly raised the rates it charged bloggers. A large number of existing and new bloggers moved over to WordPress, largely because so much of what it offered was and is free. The software improved in step, largely due to contributions from the community, and the rest is history.

WordPress is free to use for the vast majority of its users. Yet Automattic is profitable, while offering a virtually free service to its direct "customers"—bloggers who use WordPress—and to the end user, people who visit blogs. Automattic's ability to find a way to pay its bills while interfering so little with its users of all types is a big part of its appeal. It has also committed that services that are free today will continue to be free in the future.

The only payment that you have to make to Automattic to use WordPress is that free blogs hosted on WordPress.com sometimes carry Google AdSense ads—context-sensitive ads that are intended to add value to a site by being relevant while generating revenue, paid by the advertiser when users click on ads. Ads run infrequently—but with more than a billion pageviews a month on WordPress.com, they are still likely to generate significant revenue for Automattic.

Ads don't run at all in the following conditions:

- If the WordPress site visitor is using the Firefox browser

- If the visitor is logged in to their own WordPress account; many visitors to blogs have an account so they can comment on WordPress blogs that allow it

- If the visitor has linked into your site from another WordPress-powered blog

These exceptions don't cover most users most of the time, so ads have a chance to run on most site visits. It does mean most of us bloggers don't see the extent to which our site visitors are, or aren't, afflicted with ads on our sites. Apparently, ad displays are still relatively rare.

You also pay for premium features. A page from the list of premium services, current as of this writing, is shown in Figure 1.1. You can see the current version of available upgrades; from within your WordPress blog, choose Dashboard, then click the Upgrade link under Upgrades in the left column.

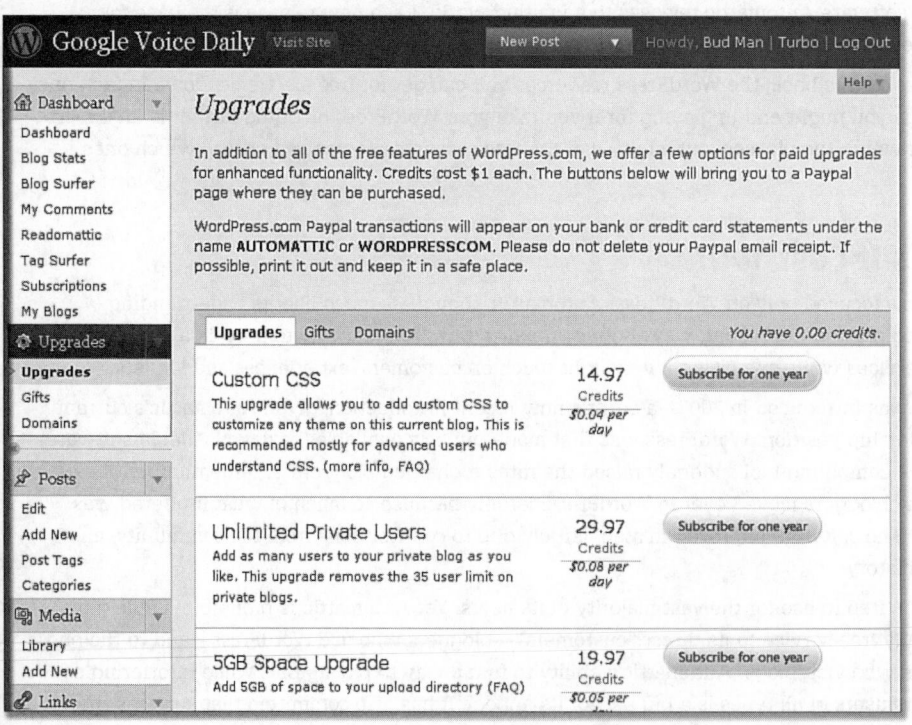

Figure 1.1
WordPress upgrades add capabilities to your blog, for a price.

One premium service many of us might consider is going ad free, which costs about $30 per year. It's said that most WordPress.com site visitors never see an ad, but some bloggers don't want any ads to appear on their blogs, ever.

Other bloggers find any ad, or specific ads, so inappropriate that paying to prevent them makes sense. For example, a nonprofit or government organization won't want to show ads, or a company might be concerned that competitors' ads could appear on its site.

 **note**

Unfortunately, paying WordPress.com to go ad-free does not allow you to put in your own ads. To do that you need to host a blog with the WordPress.org software.

The most visible service for many of us is the charge for getting your own domain name, which currently costs about $15 per year. This is double or more the price you would pay for registering a domain on your own without hosting, but it includes Automattic's costs for supporting the external domain, some of the hosting services that non-domain-owning WordPress bloggers get for free, and probably some profit.

You can also pay for additional storage for text and graphics beyond the 3GB allowance you get for free. You have to pay for at least one such chunk of additional storage to have WordPress host even the most minor chunk of audio; the current charge is $20 per year for the first such chunk.

You have to pay a separate charge of about $5 per month for WordPress video streaming support, though you can work around this with third-party hosts such as YouTube. All of these hosting-related options are described in Chapter 10, "Adding Upgrades, Audio, and Video."

WordPress allows you to customize the *style sheets* for your WordPress.com blog; that is, the code that gives sites their look and feel, in the form of *CSS*, or Cascading Style Sheets, which are described in Chapter 12, "The WordPress Toolkit: Themes." The cost of customizing your style sheet is currently about $15 per year.

If you maintain a private blog, you're limited to 35 users for free, which is usually plenty for testing and small groups. If you want to go large and serve a wider audience with a private blog, you can add an unlimited number of private users for about $30 per year.

There's a paid version of Automattic's tool, PollDaddy. Created and improved to make hosting polls easy (and free), the paid version removes the PollDaddy branding and allows unlimited questions per survey.

Automattic developed Akismet, a spam solution for WordPress blogs. Akismet is said to do an excellent job of stopping comment and trackback spam, which we explain in more detail later in the book. If you maintain a corporate blog or run a network of blogs, you have to buy a license for Akismet, which costs $50 per month or more. There's a bit of a Robin Hood aspect to this, with only the better-off users having to pay for a service that protects all WordPress bloggers from spam.

Automattic also charges for access to their Support Network for WordPress. If you pay for this support, the WordPress development team gets involved in fixing any problems you may have. Charges for this service start at about $2,500 per year. Again, there's a Robin Hood aspect here, as the problems that are resolved for the minority who pay are also resolved for the majority who don't.

WordPress.org hosts a list of third-party web hosting providers who pay a fee to be listed. These are referral links, so Automattic gets a commission from sales.

Automattic also makes money by hosting blogs through WordPress VIP Hosting. This is an exclusive service for big name customers and well-supported startups; you have to apply to join. CNN's Political Ticker site is one of their customers; the Official NFL Blog is another. Pricing begins at $500 per month per blog. We don't discuss WordPress VIP Hosting as a separate topic in this book.

So the summary of charges for most users is as follows: Google AdSense ads on your site, which is not a direct cost; domain name fees; additional or audio storage; specialist video storage; super-PollDaddy. If you had your own domain name and one chunk of extra storage, for either graphics and audio or for video, you'd still be paying less than $100 per year.

Large sites might pay for these services plus others: Akismet for corporate blogs and blog networks, Support Network access, listing as a WordPress software host, and WordPress VIP Hosting. The charges here can easily be thousands of dollars per year, but the people paying these fees have many choices, including hiring people and buying equipment and software to do it themselves.

The free or very low-cost services that most users enjoy contribute to the willingness of many WordPress users to contribute to the WordPress community. In turn, all this community work helps keep the costs to Automattic of routine operations for WordPress low. The result is a virtuous circle that benefits all involved.

The impression most people, including long-time participants in the WordPress community, have is that Automattic keeps costs free as far as possible, and as low as they can in most areas where they do charge. There might or might not be a soak-the-rich aspect to a few of the charges for big sites, but only for customers who have plenty of capability to analyze the fees and decide whether the charges are a good value for them.

It's hard to make a case that Automattic is charging anything like what it could get if short-term profit or revenue growth was its main goal. WordPress's early success was significantly due to a competitor trying to monetize the asset they had in the form of bloggers dedicated to their platform. When the charges went up, though, the asset—that's people like us—went elsewhere. It seems Automattic keeps this in mind and works hard to avoid the same fate.

What does this mean for you? You can go very far indeed with free WordPress services and online support, and a lot farther with a few investments in, for example, a domain name, an independent hosting service, and a few learning resources, including books like this one. If you then really want to go large, the sky's the limit, and you might have to invest a lot more money—but only after you've reached a point where you are likely to be able to afford it, and to have many other options as well.

What If You Want to Make Money?

WordPress.com has a strongly noncommercial ethos. As such, most of its bloggers don't seem to mind that they aren't allowed to integrate their own Google AdSense ads, multiple Amazon links (which can generate revenues), and other money-generating add-ons. Such ads, and much more, are available via plug-ins or custom coding if you run WordPress software on your own host and such blogs have a non-WordPress.com domain name.

This stance seems to make sense for WordPress.com users who don't have their own domain names. If your blog is at *yourname*.wordpress.com, you're getting just about everything free, and users are probably expecting a WordPress blog. WordPress and the community might well have a legitimate interest in keeping the associated look and feel relatively ad free.

The gray area seems to be for those of us who have paid for a custom domain name. Such a blog seems more "mine," from the blog owner's perspective, and the blog's character might be such that ads would be more or less appropriate. Yet ads are still banned.

To be fair to Automattic, ads on blogs are generally not very lucrative. Most blogs don't get much traffic, and the mood inspired by most blogs seems to be more reflective rather than actively commercial. So, for most blogs, allowing ads might cause a lot of damage to the user experience without generating much revenue.

Even if you were to do relatively well with your advertising, it takes a lot for the money to add up to much. You might get 5 cents, for example, every time a user clicks a Google AdSense ad on your site. If your click-through rate on the ads were as high as 5%, which is considered very good indeed, your average payment would be a quarter of a penny per pageview on your blog. To make $10 a month, you'd need 4,000 pageviews a month—more than 100 per day. To make $1,000 a month, you'd need 400,000 pageviews per month.

Still, the prospect of at least paying for a morning cup of coffee from blogging profits entices many people to ask Automattic for help on the advertising front. The management continues to tease us with hints that AdSense ads, or at least Amazon partner program links, might be available soon; but as of this writing, nothing. Until then, this book seeks to make it as easy as humanly possible for you to upgrade to using the WordPress software and adding plug-ins and custom code, including revenue-generating options, yourself.

Who Is WordPress For?

If you're still deciding whether to use WordPress for your current and future blogging needs, you'll want to know who it's best suited for. If you've already committed to it for now, you'll still want to know this so you can get the most out of WordPress, and decide how long to stick with it.

Blogger as a Worthy Alternative

Let's begin by pointing out that there is one type of user for whom WordPress might not be the very best option: those who put an absolute priority on simplicity and are not very interested in growing their blog or their blog's impact over time.

If this describes you, a couple of other platforms besides WordPress are worth considering. The main competitor to WordPress among beginning bloggers is Blogger, now owned by Google. Blogger is all about making blogging dead easy, launching beginners with what is literally a 1, 2, 3 approach to getting a blog going (see Figure 1.2).

 tip

WordPress makes it easy to import blogs from several competing platforms, including Blogger.

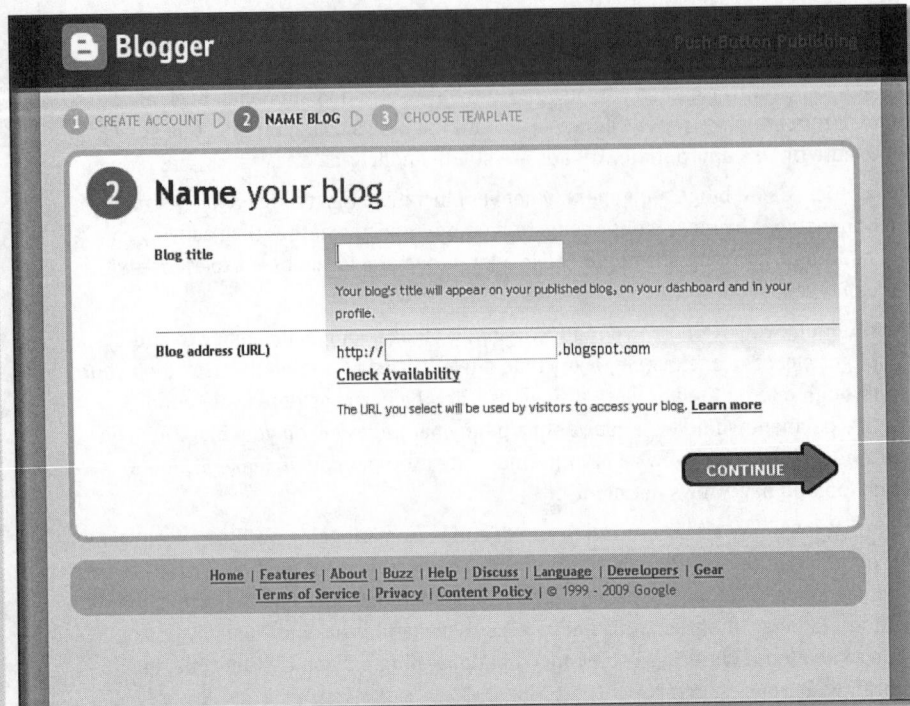

Figure 1.2
Blogger
makes start-
ing a blog a 1,
2, 3 process.

A simple example of a feature that Blogger doesn't support is *categories*, "buckets" that group related posts. WordPress makes it easy to define categories and put your posts into categories, which both bloggers and blog visitors find very useful and powerful. However, it takes a bit of focus and work to understand, use, create, and maintain categories. By not offering categories at all, Blogger makes your blogging life easier, if poorer.

Blogger does allow you to edit the CSS, which is where many layout decisions are made, without paying or moving to a hosted solution. It also allows Google AdSense ads, as you might expect from a Google-owned blogging platform.

Features change, and some differences between platforms are as much a matter of style as substance. However, it seems fair to say that Blogger emphasizes simplicity over extensibility. There's no open source aspect to Blogger, and no Blogger community to support that. You can get your own domain name with Blogger, but you can't download your own copy of

 tip

If you want to see a detailed comparison of blogging platforms, try searching on key magazine-style sites such as PCmag.com, CNET, and LifeHacker. One specific, regularly updated comparison we found is on TopTenReviews at http://blog-services-review. toptenreviews.com/.

It's worth doing such research for your own purposes. It's a necessity to do such research, and share your findings, if you're looking for a blogging solution for a business or other organization, which will affect a number of people and will need sign-off at several levels.

the Blogger software to host yourself. There's certainly no Blogger MU to allow multiple users to run from a core installation of Blogger software.

WordPress is, as we said earlier, deeper than Blogger and most competing options. Getting started with it can take more time and focus than with Blogger. There are certainly more options in WordPress to both empower and, potentially, confuse you. This book provides answers to most of your early questions, helping you cut through the clutter of online help and related resources.

WordPress User Case Study 1: Beginners

Though it's not the very simplest alternative, beginners use WordPress.com every day to start new blogs. Many other people use the WordPress software from Day 1, giving up the simplicity of WordPress.com for the power of the WordPress software.

WordPress.com requires no investment of money and only a modest investment of time and energy. In return, it offers benefits that millions of beginners have found compelling:

- **Low barriers to entry**—There's no large, single cost of money, time, or learning needed to start with a blog on WordPress.com.

- **Large support resources**—Support for WordPress is very impressive: free online help, meetings, and third-party resources. Because WordPress has different forms and does so much, it can take a bit of digging to get an answer to your specific question. This book, in itself a third-party support resource, should help bridge the gap.

- **Legs**—The depth of WordPress.com alone matches up well against many other platforms, and the availability of WordPress software, a large network of WordPress hosts with varying support options, WordPress MU, and more, means that you'll be able to take your blog as far as you want it to go.

Who might be beginning a blog? Although there are "a thousand stories in the naked city," as the poem says, it's worth considering some of the purposes different beginning bloggers might have in mind.

Personal Journals

The word *blog* means *web log*, and a blog today still often serves as a personal journal or online diary. This is a fine and fully legitimate purpose for blogging, even though blogging has also become a tool of professional journalists, corporate communicators, and others with skills, training, and resources. Citizen bloggers have often bested the professionals on many fronts. Personal journals are valuable in and of themselves, and provide a training ground that can take you a long way.

The goal of a personal journal is more about self-expression than how many people read it. In fact, having readers might almost seem beside the point at first. Such journals, though, might gradually become part of a loose online community of bloggers with some degree of shared interests.

WordPress is well suited to personal journals. The ease of starting a WordPress blog, the lack of up-front costs, and the extensive community that users tend to encounter soon after joining WordPress—it feels like joining, not just using, WordPress—are very supportive of this kind of blogging.

Personal Journalism

Growing up reading comic books, or watching Superman movies, many of us envied Clark Kent, "mild-mannered reporter for the Daily Planet," almost as much as we did Superman, the Man of Steel. Being a reporter has long appealed to many of us who weren't one, though in these days of cutbacks in newspapers and magazines, the dream has dimmed a bit.

Blogging allows people to jump onto the spectrum of journalistic roles at all sorts of different points, from occasional commentary on local issues to full-time advocacy of a point of view, backed by professional-level reporting accompanied by insightful commentary.

Personal journalism is satisfying for a while as a solo activity, but of course, it soon requires some degree of readership to make sense. So bloggers of this bent are usually looking to grow their reader base.

WordPress.com is an excellent match for this kind of blogging. It's easy enough to make getting started quick and convenient, but deep enough to scale as posts accumulate. Built-in category support and the ability to easily connect to other, related blogs via *trackbacks* and *pings* (notification tools described in Chapter 4, "Creating Your First Post") are among the many features of WordPress that support this often very serious, even driven, kind of blogging.

The built-in statistics in WordPress are a gift for this kind of blogging. You don't have to do any extra work at all to get good, useful, up-to-date statistics on visits to your blog.

A blog run by one of the authors (Smith), Google Voice Daily, is of this type. The blog tracks news and opinion about Google Voice, a telephony-related service from Google that has received its initial release only in the United States—and has been in the news frequently since. Figure 1.3 shows traffic for the blog in a period in the first two weeks of its life. The traffic chart is right in the Dashboard—you can't miss it, which is perfect for those of us starting out.

The biggest concern a proto-journalist might have with WordPress.com is the lack of ways to make money. However, as I mentioned previously, it usually takes most of us a lot of time and effort to get the kind of pageviews that might help pull in even a few dollars a month of revenue. WordPress allows you to get started with a very easy platform, and draw on a very supportive community, until you reach the level of productivity and popularity at which an upgrade to using WordPress.org, as described in the second half of this book, makes sense.

 tip

When trying to calculate what your blog might be worth, remember that a penny per pageview is an excellent result for a typical blogger. At that (high) rate, 1,000 pageviews is worth $1. So until you're up around 100,000 pageviews per month—$100 per month at this rate of return—you're not even potentially losing enough money by staying ad free to offset the expense and hassle of using WordPress.org instead of WordPress.com.

Figure 1.3
WordPress puts your stats in the Dashboard, right where you can see them.

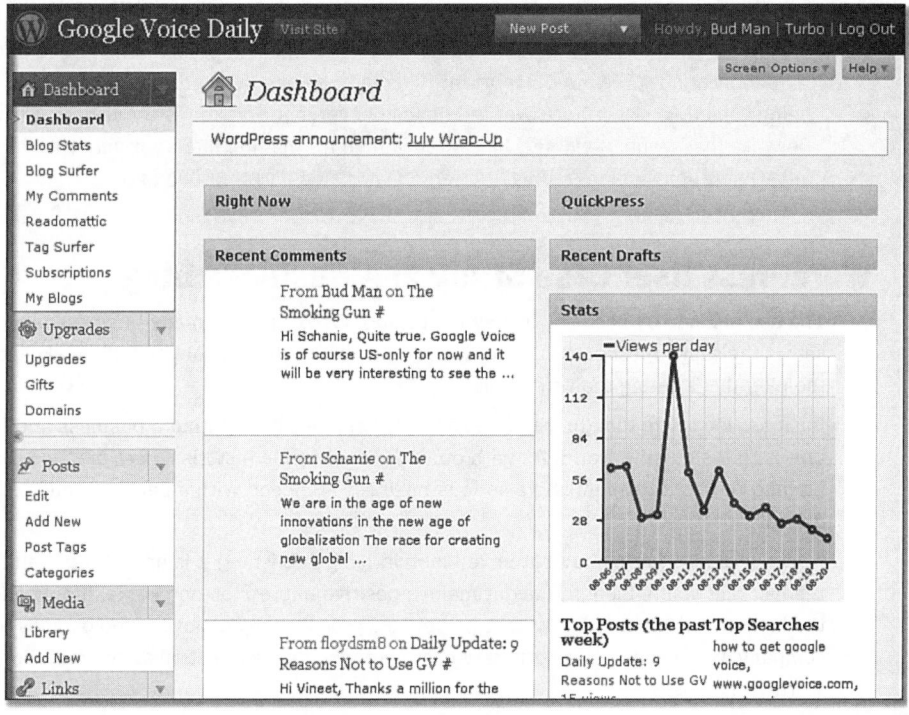

Blogging and the Rest of Your Life

One of the huge changes that social media of all types is causing—be it blogs, Facebook, Twitter, as well as online reports of various types that might mention one's name—is that we all leave an increasingly large trail online. Blogging makes what might have been a spotty sketch into a very rich portrait indeed.

Unfortunately, as you blog, you have to consider the impact of what you write on all aspects of your life. You might talk about how a company messed up your weekend with poor customer service—only to have your spouse apply there for a job. Your worries about the impact of having a child on your life might be read by that same child years later. And so on, and so on.

WordPress's advantages of categorization, search-engine friendliness, and reliability might not seem completely benign when a future employer digs up more information about you than you ever realized you were revealing.

Continued...

Etiquette and common sense for how to handle these new realities are still evolving. Unfortunately, many hiring departments take a draconian approach: one risqué photo on Facebook = no job. For now, the most important rule might be simply to consider everything you write as being copied, in skywriting, over the heads of everyone you know—or will meet in the future. Because that's what it will feel like when you go for that job interview with the company whose advertising you so eloquently criticized on your blog a year or two ago.

WordPress User Case Study 2: A Business Blog

The use of blogs by business is only increasing. Why? I'm sure many business bloggers ask themselves the same question as the clock ticks past midnight and they're still awake, adding a post to the blog that's eating their free time!

Business blogging, though, can be extremely valuable, both within a business and for communication with the outside world. As with our individual online histories, best practice is still evolving. Finding the right tone, mixing a serious business approach with a personal touch, can be all too difficult.

A business blog has somewhat mixed motivations. Publishing it is important in and of itself. Just the fact that you're blogging might make a positive impression on people. If only one person reads the blog in a given month, but that person is a prospective employee who decides to join the company as a result, or a disgruntled customer who gets a question answered, then the blog is worthwhile.

Businesses usually, however, want to build up traffic. So company blogs are usually promoted in other communications, such as on the company's permanent website.

This is where one of WordPress's truly distinguishing capabilities comes in. This is the ability to easily create not only posts—typical blog posts, which appear with the newest one first—but pages, static web pages that contain reference and other information.

WordPress is one of the few blogging tools that lets you use the posting interface to create pages, treats pages as being just as important as posts, and even lets you make a static page the front page of your blog, which instantly makes it feel more like a traditional website.

Along with WordPress's strong growth path from WordPress.com to WordPress.org, which gives you just about unlimited customization potential, pages and other WordPress features make it hard to beat as a tool for business blogs.

A business blog can be for building up a personal brand as well as the brand of an established business. One of the authors (McCallister) keeps a WordPress blog mostly about open source technology, shown in Figure 1.4. His blog gets and keeps him involved with an ever-shifting group of ~~fellow nerds~~ kind, wise, and, by coincidence, unusually attractive people who share his particular interests.

The Metaverse blog demonstrates several benefits of online communities. In normal conversation, one's passionate interest in open source tools would be met by incomprehension from most people. On one's blog, though, where people come either because of prior knowledge of the blog and its topic, or through online search, an interested audience who can discuss the various tools intelligently is ensured.

Figure 1.4
McCallister
never meta
verse he
didn't like.

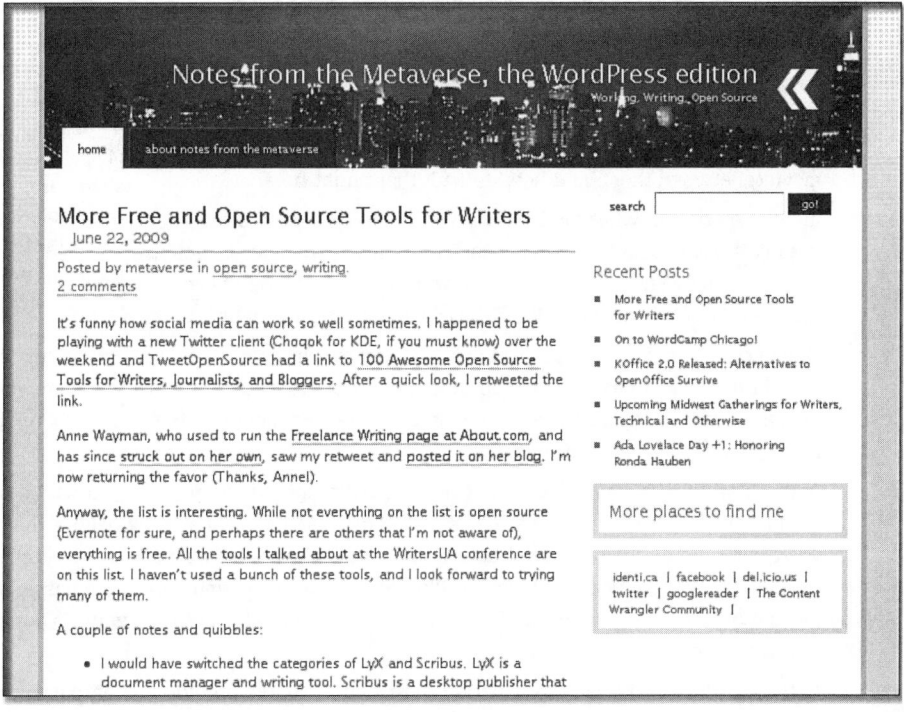

The ability to connect to the like-minded can go even further. The Metaverse blog gets syndicated on Planet SUSE, a community of open source fans. (You might not have previously known that you live on Planet SUSE, but trust us, you do.)

You can use WordPress to build up your own community, too. One small example is the Tag Surfing tool. *Tags* are words or brief phrases that allow you to label your blog for search. The Tag Surfing tool allows you to find blogs that share the same tags you do. Chances are, you'll be amazed what you find.

Computer Literacy and Blogs

Both of the authors of this book tend to blog on computer-related topics. As you might expect, the online world is rich indeed in information and opinion on all sorts of topics related to computer technology, which of course includes WordPress itself.

However, don't be put off if this doesn't describe you. Bloggers have a huge range of interests. WordPress meets the needs of people who have everything from a passionate interest in computer technology to no interest at all. WordPress is a tool; what you use it for is up to you.

WordPress Hosting Options

Now it's time to definitively answer the question as to whether you should start out on WordPress.com or with your own copy of the software from WordPress.org. You need to know not only which option to choose, but also when someone might consider moving between them, and how difficult that might be.

 tip
A true salmon ladder is a series of pools placed in a rising ladder alongside dams, so salmon can work their way up from their journey's start in the sea to their spawning grounds upstream.

In our experience, what most people want is to be able to start with WordPress.com because it's easier and less expensive to get started with it. They also want to know, however, that they have the option to easily move to WordPress software if they want.

One of our main concerns in this book is to create what we call a "salmon ladder" for you as a WordPress user: an easy transition from the sea of WordPress.com users, where you can start your blog and learn blogging skills, to the more rarefied, challenging, but ultimately rewarding environment of WordPress software users.

In the first three parts of this book, Chapters 1 through 10, we provide you with a power user's guide to WordPress.com. This will seem strange to some because they believe that any power user will quickly go directly to using the WordPress software. This isn't so; many people create quite extensive, and very popular, blogs on WordPress.com. They don't want the hassle and expense of moving to WordPress software. They might move eventually, but they want to get the most out of WordPress.com before they do.

In the fourth part of this book, Chapters 11 through 15, we provide you with a complete guide to the additional features you have access to with the WordPress software from WordPress.org, including how to create your own themes and plug-ins. This supports those who move from one to the other, as well as those who start out with the WordPress software from the beginning.

Throughout the book, we provide information about how to make the most of each environment.

So if you're wondering if it's OK to start out in WordPress.com, even if you suspect (or even know) you'll need full WordPress software in the future, the answer—from our own efforts and those of a wide range of people who have done it—is "Yes." Yes, WordPress.com is the best choice to start out in if you think you might need the full power of WordPress software later. And yes, it is easy to move your blog—including all the content, categories, and links—to WordPress software.

It's also OK to start out directly on WordPress.org. You need to be ready to either pay a host extra to handle most of the hassles for you or take the time to learn how to do it yourself. In either event, you'll be in a very powerful environment in which you can make your WordPress blog fully your own.

If you already decided to work with WordPress.org, you can still use this book from beginning to end. Start in Chapter 11, "Installing and Upgrading WordPress Software," to learn how to find a host and set up your blog. Then you can go straight through the book, from Chapter 2, "Starting Your Blog Right," forward. You'll just have more choices at each point.

Making the Move

We describe the process of transferring a blog from WordPress.com to using the software from WordPress.org in detail in Chapter 11. However, you might want a brief summary of the process here so you can understand whether it's truly easy.

It is. Every WordPress.com blog has a Tools area in the Dashboard. The Tools area has an Export option, alongside an Import option.

Choose the Export option. WordPress creates a file on your computer's hard disk with the entire content of your site, including all posts, comments, categories, tags, static pages, and custom fields. If there's more than one author on your blog, you can export content per author, or for all authors.

Record your API key. This is sent to you by email when you first create your WordPress.com blog and is also available on the Profile page of your blog, under My Account.

Now set up your WordPress software, as described in Chapter 11. To populate your new WordPress blog, simply go to the Dashboard. Choose the Import option. Your WordPress.com site's contents will populate your WordPress software blog.

That's it! Oh, and you might want to make sure the transfer proceeded correctly, and that you have your API key. Then add links from the old blog to the new one, so no one gets confused....

Comparing WordPress.com with WordPress Software

What do you get in WordPress.com—and what are you missing out on by not starting immediately with WordPress software?

The key features of WordPress.com are as follows:

- Free hosting

- Automatic backup, software upgrades, and security

- Easy setup

- Choice from more than 70 themes

- Dozens of widgets to choose from

However, you have a very limited ability to customize your blog beyond the existing customization options, themes, and widgets— which are themselves limited in what they can do. The existing options don't include ways to monetize your blog, and you pay extra if you want to block ads that some of your visitors will otherwise see.

If and when you want to go to WordPress software, you'll have to do the following:

- Find a host and start paying.

- Download and install the WordPress software—unless you pay for your host to maintain WordPress for you.

 tip

Not everything that's available in WordPress.com is automatically available in WordPress software. For instance, up-to-date blog stats—one of the most powerful features of WordPress.com—is not automatically available in WordPress software. You need to install a plug-in called "WordPress.com stats" and enter your API key from your former WordPress.com site.

- Import your blog from the file you previously exported.

- Choose from a much wider range of themes, tweak an existing theme, or create your own theme.

- Reinstall any widgets that you previously used if your theme supports widgets (or replace them with plug-ins).

- Choose from a wide array of plug-ins, tweak existing plug-ins, or create your own plug-in.

Table 1.1 sums up the advantages and disadvantages of each platform.

Table 1.1   WordPress.com Versus WordPress.org

		WordPress.com	WordPress.org
Setup	Free hosting	✓	X
	Easy setup	✓	X
	Automatic backup, software upgrades, and security	✓	Extra cost
Extensions	Choose from existing themes	Limited to 70+	✓
	Create your own theme	X	✓
	Avoid Automattic ads for users	Extra cost	✓
	Choose from existing widgets	✓	✓ (many themes)
	Choose from existing plug-ins	X	✓
	Create your own plug-ins	X	✓
	Run your own ads	X	✓ (via plug-ins)

Naming of Parts

One of the most confusing aspects of the WordPress.com versus WordPress software choice for many people is the wording used to describe it. WordPress.com is often referred to as a *hosted solution*. WordPress.org is called a *self-hosted solution*, even though most WordPress software users don't actually host it themselves. Confused? You aren't the only one!

WordPress.com is a website where Automattic, the owners of WordPress, offer free hosting of a WordPress blog for anyone who wants it.

The key point, if you decide to use the WordPress software directly, is that hosting is your responsibility. You might pay a third party to handle the responsibility for you, but it's no longer up to Automattic. From their point of view, you're self-hosting, even if you're paying a third party to do it. Self-hosting really means "hosting by someone other than Automattic, somewhere other than on WordPress.com."

The most important point, when choosing how to get started, is that starting in WordPress.com gives you a chance to get up and running with a WordPress blog quickly and easily. You don't incur any penalty for deferring the move to WordPress software. Many blogs go on for years without ever moving from WordPress.com.

When you do make the move to WordPress software, you'll actually be much better educated and more experienced with blogging, allowing you to make the most of the more capable, but more costly, platform.

Other Ways to Create an Online Presence

Increasingly, people and businesses both have an opportunity to use a variety of social media—and what feels increasingly like an obligation to have multiple points of presence online.

For instance, if you're a professional, you might find that your colleagues are all on LinkedIn. If you're a businessperson seeking to hire recent college graduates, you might find your target audience expects you to have a Facebook page.

Twitter allows you to send out an endless stream of messages, called *tweets*, to your subscribers, called *followers*. You—whether that's "you" as an individual, or "you" as an organization—might be deemed cool, not cool, or somewhere in between depending on whether or how you use Twitter. Facebook updates are also handled in a Twitter-like manner now, and you can even use the two services together.

As a business, you probably need a traditional website more than you need a blog. A blog is a "nice to have"—if you do it right, a very "nice to have," but still optional—whereas at least a basic website is a must-have.

WordPress can remove the either/or nature of this dilemma. You can use WordPress as a full-fledged content management system that can create a traditional website with excellent built-in blogging capabilities. You can also use your blog as a home or reference point for all your social media interactions.

The point is not that you shouldn't have a blog; it's that the days when having a blog was, by itself, enough to make your online presence both complete and "cool" have passed. Be ready to use what you learn from blogging to establish a presence elsewhere in the online world as needed.

2

STARTING YOUR BLOG RIGHT

"The beginning is the most important part of any work."
— Plato

Creating Your Blog

WordPress might look complex when you're beginning a blog. If you're using WordPress.com, there are fewer options, but some are still on the advanced side. If you're using WordPress software, there are additional options. The ones that have to do with blog setup, posting blog entries, and hosting concerns are somewhat mixed together. Yet the options that *are* important from the beginning make a big difference in having a trouble-free and enjoyable experience in blogging with WordPress.

We're happy to help make the setup process easy. This chapter highlights the opportunities available and shows you how to overcome any difficulties. This chapter is focused on WordPress.com; for setting up the WordPress software from WordPress.org, see Chapter 11, "Installing and Upgrading WordPress Software."

We'll keep it as simple as possible, but as you know, the World Wide Web is a big stage. Most of what goes on attracts relatively little attention, but something as simple as an offhand comment about a celebrity or a domain name that incorporates a trademarked term can lead to court action. WordPress equips you to play with the big boys and girls, if that's your desire. So, we need to point out some hazards along the way to help avoid problems, even if these seem rather remote. These problems are like potholes—they're not a problem unless you drive through one. We'll help you dodge problems.

If you use this chapter step-by-step through the setup process, you'll avoid potential hassle and rework later and get your blog off to a strong start. You can rush through this chapter if you want, get your blog up and running, and come back and review the settings later. However, until you do, you'll find yourself with some unanswered questions about why your WordPress blog works the way it does.

As you go through setup, there are four categories of things that you want to get right as early in your blog's life as possible:

- **Setup options**—WordPress asks you a number of questions as you first start your blog or blogs. Some of these can be changed later; others can't. Spending just a bit of time to get these settings right can help you avoid regrets.

- **Settings**—WordPress has dozens of options divided among a number of headings in an area called Settings. Most people make at least a halfhearted effort to get settings right when they start using a new program or web service (or a new car, for that matter). In WordPress, that's a really good idea. We show you how to move expertly around the Settings area, bending WordPress to your will.

- **Other options**—WordPress has a number of options outside the Settings area that are important to review during setup, all mixed in with options you won't worry about until later, if ever. In this chapter, we point out the ones that matter.

- **Themes**—WordPress offers over 70 themes to choose from and gives you a couple of different ways to customize themes, but unfortunately, none of the customization options are free. We guide you through the options to help you get the most bang for your buck (or for no bucks).

 note

You might notice a lot of bullets and short, punchy instructions in this chapter. We don't mention every setting, only the ones you need to pay attention to for most setups. This is part of our effort to guide you through a very wide array of choices as intelligently and efficiently as possible. We keep explanations to just the facts to get you through setup as quickly as possible, with the best results.

Easy Does It

Blogging has been promoted as a great way to make money. We're not so sure. It's definitely a worthwhile adjunct to other activities that make money, but actually generating profits directly from a blog is very difficult for most people, most of the time.

With this in mind, we suggest you think about everything except making money at first. Set up your blog carefully and let it find its own purpose through your first few weeks or months of posts. Gradually improve your blog until it looks good, works well, is interesting, and has lots of visitors. Then consider whether it can potentially generate revenue, and how to do so without putting people off. It's all too easy to kill the goose—to drive away your site visitors and step on any "buzz" you had going—without ever producing any golden eggs.

How Many Visitors Do You Want?

If someone were to ask you what kind of blog you want, you would probably start talking about your blog's topic. However, in setting up your blog, the type of blog you want has to do with how widely you want your blog to be read:

- **You, me, them, everybody**—You want to build up the number of users as fast as you can to promote a cause, to change minds, or to lay the groundwork for making money. WordPress is built to efficiently do this.

- **Only people you publicize it to**—You can tweak your WordPress settings to keep your blog off of search engines and out of automatically generated links. People will still be able to visit your blog, but they'll have to find out about it from you or people whom you've told about it.

- **Only people you name**—WordPress allows you to keep your blog private, only usable by people you specifically name as users. These users have to sign in before they're allowed on your blog. You can have up to 35 users for free; above that ceiling, you have to pay a flat fee to add an unlimited number of users. This is great for creating a private blog for a club or a small company. It's also good for protecting a blog from public exposure while you get it just the way you want it.

Decide now how public you want your blog and be ready to make your settings choices to fit. To summarize the privacy settings in advance, the relevant settings are as follows:

- **Search engines**—In the blog setup screen, described later and shown in Figure 2.2, turn off search engine access.

- **Discussions**—In the Discussion Settings for your blog, described later and shown in Figure 2.6, you can make people register with WordPress.com to comment, or you can let people who aren't registered comment.

- **Blog Visibility**—In the Privacy Settings for your blog, described later and shown in Figure 2.8, set your Privacy Settings to be visible to everyone, including search engines; to block search engines, but allow normal visitors to see your blog; or to only be visible to users you choose.

- **Related links**—In the Extras subpanel of the Appearances menu, described in the next chapter, hide related links. (Many people prefer this option to be off even if they aren't keeping their blog particularly private.) This also keeps your links from showing up on other people's blogs.

Playing the Domain Name Game

WordPress names your blog's domain—its web address—using the following formula: *blogname*.wordpress.com. Depending on what you choose as *blogname*, this is not a terrible domain name. The WordPress name is quite well respected even outside the WordPress community; within it, having a domain name of this type identifies you as a member of a large and overwhelmingly friendly club.

Many of us, though, have ambitions that only a custom domain name, of the form www.*blogname*.com, can fulfill. WordPress makes it easy to add a custom domain name at any point in your ownership of your blog, charging about $15 per year for the privilege. We describe the considerations in choosing a domain name and signing up for one in Chapter 10, "Adding Upgrades, Audio, and Video."

You might want to look at Chapter 10 now and make a decision about a domain name for your blog even before you sign up. This is because your blog's domain name is part of its identity from Day 1. There are several domain name-related options you need to consider.

Starting with a Custom Domain Name

Starting with a custom domain name right from the beginning establishes a strong identity for your blog that doesn't change (unless you change your mind about the domain name later; WordPress makes changing easy to do).

gvDaily.com, which belongs to one of the authors (Smith), is the fourth name that blog had in its first four months of existence. The initial name for your blog can always be changed.

Adding a Custom Domain Name Later

You can always start with a free domain name, in the form *blogname*.wordpress.com, and upgrade to a custom domain name later. Even so, the initial name of your blog matters—and, optimally, the user-determined part of the initial wordpress.com domain name is the same as the central part of the eventual custom domain name. For instance, if you want to have a WordPress-based website called www.xavier.com, you will want your initial blog name to be xavier.wordpress.com, so the move to the custom domain name is as smooth as possible. (People will search for "xavier" to find your blog after you move it, for instance, and having the new domain name include "xavier" gives them the best chance of finding it.)

Given that other sites will link to your site early on, via pings, trackbacks (see Chapter 3, "Creating Your Blog's Look"), and explicit links, and that these links are the foundation for strong rankings on Google and other search engines, you want these links to be going to your long-term domain name as soon as possible. Friends and admirers will also bookmark your site the first time they visit it, if they like it a lot.

This is an argument for deciding on and buying your custom domain name sooner rather than later, so you don't punish your friends and admirers—and the search engines, as well as their users—by inflicting a change on them after your original domain name has started to become embedded in the Web. If you do everything through WordPress, it will do its best to keep your traffic coming to you across a change, but no one and no software is perfect, especially when it comes to the tricky subject of search engine optimization.

Back in the early days of Silicon Valley, there was a harsh saying for the need to decide early whether to adopt a new technology breakthrough: "Get on the train or die." (*Die* was shorthand for *miss out*, or perhaps suffer a business loss, rather than anything more serious.) If you're seriously considering getting a custom domain name in the long run, you and your site visitors might be best served if you do it sooner rather than later.

Using a WordPress.com Domain Name Forever

As we just mentioned, having a WordPress.com domain name, in the form *blogname*.wordpress.com, is not all a bad thing. With this kind of domain name, though, whatever success your blog achieves will always reflect at least as much on WordPress as on you.

For a personal blog, a blog for a hobby, or a blog for an interest group, this is not necessarily a bad thing. If you're an enthusiastic WordPress user who wants to encourage others to blog along with you, along with the other specific interests you're blogging about, having WordPress in your domain name is actually a good thing.

There's no harm in deciding for the long term—it doesn't have to be forever—to begin with and keep a domain name in the *blogname*.wordpress.com format. Once you make this decision, the *blogname* part of the domain name becomes rather important.

WordPress.com has literally millions of blogs. Once someone starts their blog with a given *blogname*, they keep *blogname* forever, even if they later upgrade to a custom domain name or stop using their account. So you need to choose your *blogname* carefully. It sets your blog apart, and must be unique. It's also your first choice for a custom domain name if, somewhere down the road, you do decide to make the move away from a WordPress.com domain name.

You might want to try your ideas for *blogname* out before you start the sign-up process for your WordPress account. Just start up a Web browser and enter *blogname*.wordpress.com as the domain name. See if it takes you to a live site or to a message that the domain name is not found. If the domain name is not found, you should be able to sign up for it during the WordPress sign-up, and you'll be off and running, with an important decision already made.

What's the Worst That Can Happen?

Domain name pirates are called that because they use dubious tactics to get money or Internet traffic—which they can use to make money—away from what might be seen as the legitimate owners. If your WordPress blog starts to take off, you might want to consider registering one or more relevant domain names as a defensive move, even if you don't intend to rename your blog.

Let's say you create a wonderful blog called alaskapolitix.wordpress.com, attracting every web user in Alaska and millions of other people as well. People start visiting several times a day, taking your updates as an RSS feed, and your posts attract scores of thoughtfully written comments. Do you think some domain name pirate, seeing this, might just register the domain name www.alaskapolitix.com, closing off that growth path to you—and attracting traffic that legitimately should be yours? You betcha.

Signing Up

Although WordPress makes it easy to add other authors to your blog, if you're creating a blog that will be a group effort, you might want to let other people use your username and password in some kind of a pinch. So consider creating a username and password that you don't mind sharing with someone else if some kind of minor blogging emergency occurs.

If you want updates from the blog to go to a group of people, consider setting up a custom email address that you can automatically forward to a group of people concerned with the blog. If you're doing this for work, school, or some other organization, do it in such a way that you can comfortably hand it off to someone else when you're ~~canned~~ promoted from your job or when you ~~are expelled~~ graduate from your school.

Creating a WordPress Account

Follow these steps to sign up for a WordPress account:

1. Visit WordPress.com.

2. Click the Sign Up Now link. The Sign Up page opens, as shown in Figure 2.1.

3. Enter the username you want to use. You can use the same username to create many blogs. Many people have a standard username they reuse for many different kinds of online services. However, if you'll be sharing your username and password with others, you might want to consider using something friendly to a group instead.

4. Enter your password. Your password must be at least four characters, letters and numbers only. WordPress displays a strength rating for your password based on how long and how "random" it is, for instance mixing letters and digits in a hard-to-predict pattern.

 tip

Consider taking a moment to visit the "Delete Blog" section of this chapter before signing up. It's a useful reminder that WordPress, unlike most such services, will never delete the account you create when you sign up. You can stop using the account, and you can create a new one (but not associated with the same email address), but you can never get rid of this one. So choose your username and other options carefully, as you might be living with them for a long time.

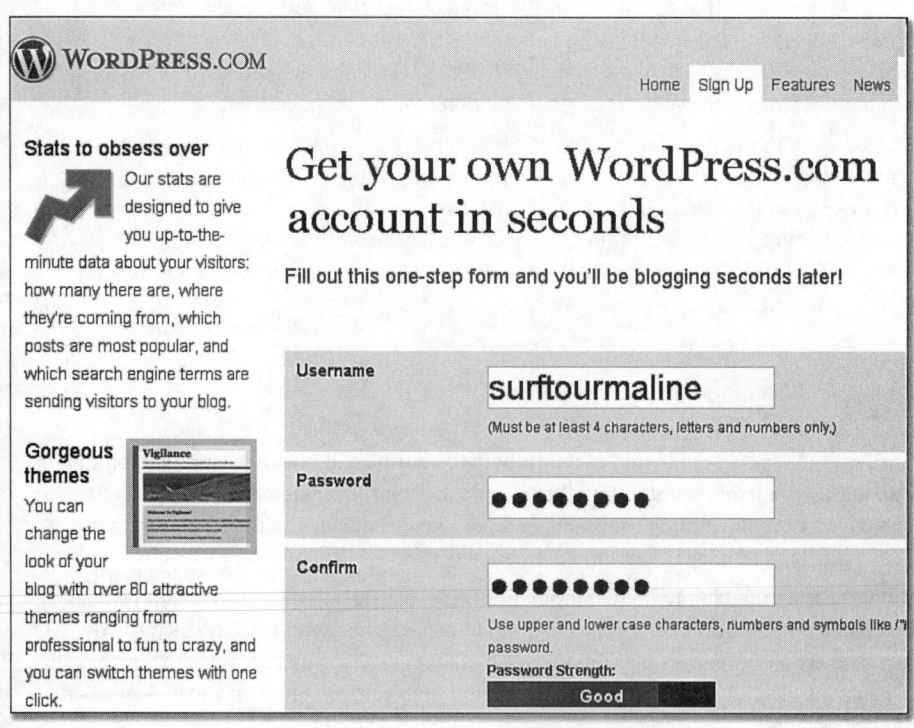

Figure 2.1
WordPress sign-up ties up an email address.

5. Confirm your password by reentering it.

6. Enter your email address. This is the email address to which updates about the blog will come, so be sure to enter it correctly. Also, realize that you are connecting this account to one of your email addresses—and that you can't delete the account, ever. So if you're planning to create more than one WordPress account, think carefully about how you'll associate email addresses with them. If the WordPress account is for work or other organizational purposes, consider having your organization create a dedicated email account for it.

7. Check the Terms of Service check box. Click the link to read the terms.

8. Choose the option, Gimme a blog!, not the other option, Just a Username, Please. Contributors to your blog and even visitors to WordPress sites that only allow signed-in WordPress users to comment may choose to only create a username, not a blog.

9. Click Next. Your account is created.

Creating Your Blog

After you create your WordPress account and click Next, you arrive at an unnamed screen, shown in Figure 2.2, which is where you actually create your blog. Unlike your WordPress account, which can't be deleted, you can delete the blog in the future if you want. However, if you delete the blog, the blog name will then be made permanently unavailable to anyone, including you.

 caution

WordPress blog passwords are prized among various kinds of hackers, so choose a strong password, and consider changing it every few weeks to protect your account.

note

If you're doing this for work purposes or toward building a business, consider reading the terms of service carefully, or even getting a lawyer to review them, before proceeding. The terms of service for WordPress are quite restrictive, especially when it comes to using your blog for commercial purposes (that is, to make money), a common goal in creating a blog. If your purposes are explicitly commercial, consider starting with the WordPress software and WordPress.org from the beginning.

About the Example

We use several blogs in this book as examples. The specific sample blog created for this book is a blog for surfing at the famous (to people who live in the neighborhood, at least) Tourmaline Surfing Park in Pacific Beach, San Diego, California. Pacific Beach is about an hour's drive north of the border with Mexico, just south of the famous beach at La Jolla Cove and the well-known racetrack at Del Mar.

Figure 2.2
The Surf
Tourmaline
blog is born!

You can also navigate to this screen if you already have a WordPress account but not a blog, or already have a blog and want to create a new one. Just log in to your account, visit the Dashboard, and choose the option to create a blog.

Here's how to create a blog, either immediately after you've created your WordPress account, or in the future:

1. Enter your blog domain in the form *blogname*.wordpress.com. The blog domain cannot be changed, so think carefully about the choice, as described previously in the section on domain names. Your blog name will be rejected if it is the same as the name of an existing WordPress blog.

2. Enter the blog title. This can be changed any time, but should be a variation of the blog name from the URL, rendered into normal English, capitalized correctly, and so on.

3. Specify the language you want to use for the blog's content. Shortcuts to English, German, French, Italian, Brazilian Portuguese, and Bahasa (used in Indonesia) can be found at the top of the scrolling list. Below that short list, you can choose from a total of more than 130 languages. You will be able to change the authoring language used for administering the blog in WordPress later—which will usually, but not always, be to the same language as the blog's content—but you need to complete the setup in English first.

4. Here's a very important check box: Would You Like Your Blog to Appear in Search Engine Listings? It's checked by default. If you want to keep your blog private, either permanently or at least in the short term, uncheck this box.

5. Review your entries. When you're ready, click the Signup button. This sends an activation email to the email account you specified during sign-up. You're given the opportunity to update the profile shown on your blog—your first name, last name, and a bit about yourself. The information will be available in the administrative parts of your blog, and the theme you choose for your blog might or might not display it.

6. After a few minutes, find the email and click the link to activate your blog. (If clicking the link doesn't work, cut and paste the URL shown in the link into the address bar of a browser.) This activates your account.

7. WordPress sends you another email message with login instructions. Keep this email; it contains valuable links and your API key for your blog. Your API key is one of those things that you don't need often, but when you do need it, you need it badly. (You can also retrieve it from your Profile, which you access via a link from your WordPress Dashboard.)

Taking Advantage of Resources

Many of us have grown unused to saving URLs and so on, figuring we can retrieve anything needed through web search, a search of our email Inboxes, and so on. This is not true for WordPress. The software is so deep in its various forms that it's sometimes hard to find just the right information that you need to get something done. This means it's worth preserving useful WordPress links when you do find them.

Note that some of the URLs in the welcome note are specific to the blog you've just created; others are generic, available to anyone and applicable to any WordPress blog.

Both types of URLs given in the email are likely to be quite useful; they're shown in Table 2.1 for easy reference.

Table 2.1 Handy WordPress.com Links

Blog-Specific URLS	
Write a new post	http://*blogname*.wordpress.com/wp-admin/post-new.php
Change your blog's settings	http://*blogname*.wordpress.com/wp-admin/options-general.php
Choose another theme	http://*blogname*.wordpress.com/wp-admin/themes.php
General WordPress URLs	
Beginner's questions	http://support.wordpress.com/getting-started/
Frequently asked questions	http://support.wordpress.com
Submit questions or comments	http://support.wordpress.com/contact/
Akismet spam filter	http://akismet.com/

Changing Initial WordPress Settings

Entire books could be written about settings in WordPress.com and WordPress.org; however, this is *WordPress In Depth*, not *WordPress Settings In Depth*, so we don't want to do that. Instead, we're going to gallop through the many settings for WordPress.com here and highlight only the ones that really make a difference, at setup time and beyond. Settings specific to WordPress.org are covered in Chapter 11.

In this section, we highlight options that affect your entire blog rather than specific parts of it. Most of these settings are under the actual Settings menu, which contains nine subpanels: General, Writing, Reading, Discussion, Media, Privacy, Delete Blog, OpenID, and Domains. We also cover Ratings settings and the Post by Email option here.

This tour serves two purposes: to help you get your blog set up correctly for getting started, so "wrong" settings don't drive you crazy, and to begin familiarizing you with WordPress settings so you know where to go when you want to change something later. Even if you don't remember the location of a specific setting, having gone through these pages, you can come back to them and find the setting in which you're interested.

 tip

For help on specific fields in WordPress screens, start your search with the Help link that appears on every WordPress administration page, or access the WordPress Codex directly at codex.wordpress.org.

General Settings

The appropriate values to choose for many of the General Settings for WordPress are self-evident. For instance, the email address to use for administration is set when you create the blog, as described earlier in this chapter, and can be changed when needed.

Among the General Settings, as shown in Figure 2.3, the following settings are the ones for which we can provide some pointers for getting the most out of WordPress:

 caution

Many onscreen dialog boxes for various kinds of traditional and web software now avoid any kind of Save button, but WordPress uses them. On all the Settings pages, click the Save Changes button, or you're likely to lose your changes.

- **Blog Title and Tagline**—Most of the blog themes you will choose from (see the next chapter) will display these fields. The title should be pithy and easy to remember; the tagline should be friendly and explain the blog's area(s) of focus. Review them regularly as your blog progresses. Many blogs change their focus over time, adding or dropping topics as needs and interests of bloggers and site visitors change. If your blog's focus changes, its title and tagline should change, too.

- **Timezone**—The time in WordPress blogs is not automatically updated to match daylight savings time. You have to change the Timezone setting in a way that is, in fact, incorrect to get the correct time to show during daylight savings periods. To get your UTC time zone, visit www.time.gov. During daylight savings periods, adjust one time zone to the east during daylight savings time periods. The Timezone setting helpfully gives you the current time for the selected time zone, so you can compare it with your time.

This flaw in WordPress is important to be aware of, as having the time be off by an hour is potentially confusing to you and your blog visitors. Set a reminder to yourself to "spring ahead and fall back" by an hour with your WordPress Timezone setting as needed to reflect the actual current time.

 tip

If your audience is mostly military, from any country, your choice of time format is clear. This is also one audience who really hates it if you don't change the time zone to reflect daylight savings time changes. You don't want people with artillery and tanks to hate your blog, do you?

- **Date Format**—If you ever expect to have a foreign visitor to your site, use either of the first two date formats, with the sample dates given as August 20, 2009 and 2009/08/20. Both these formats are clear as to which is the month and which is the year, though the first is clearer. Avoid the latter two formats, with the sample dates given as 08/20/2009 and 20/08/2009. Americans and many others put the month first and the day number second; Europeans and many others put the day number first and the month second. You're bound to confuse someone with either of these potentially confusing formats, so stick to the first two.

- **Time Format**—Similar to the Date Format, Americans and others use times with AM and PM, and Europeans and others use the format that Americans call military time, such as 23:41. Use the format that suits most of your audience best, though AM/PM time is more easily understood by military time users than military time is understood by civilians.

Figure 2.3
Take care, even the General Settings have a few pitfalls.

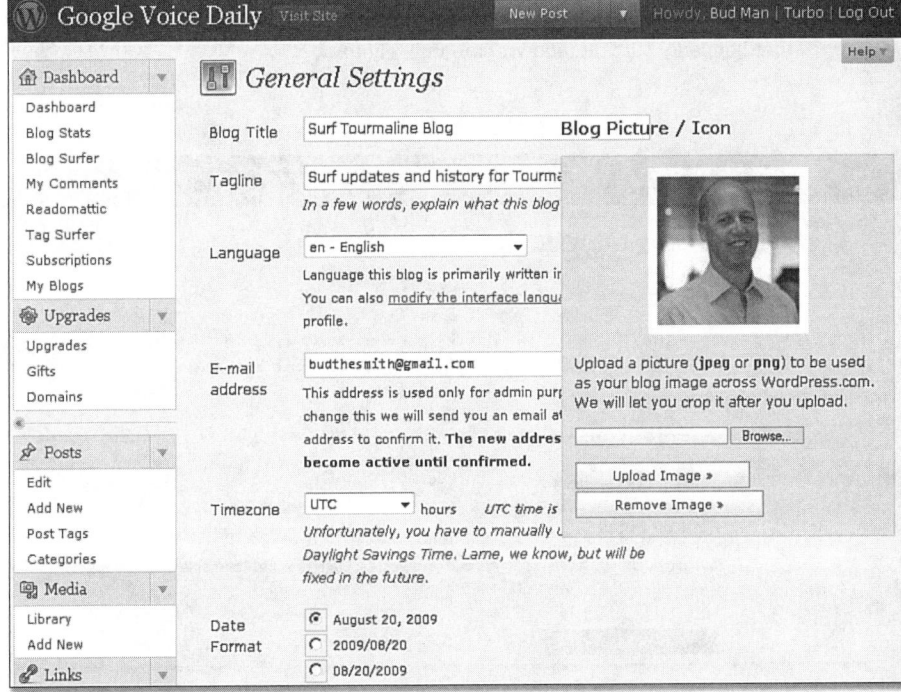

Writing Settings

Writing Settings, shown in Figure 2.4, affect what happens when you write posts and pages. There are only a few Writing Settings, though they can be important:

- **Size of the Post Box**—This is the depth of the main post box on the Dashboard page. Making the post box taller pushes some options below it off the page, without getting you more width, the real missing element. We suggest ignoring this one and doing most of your work in Full-Screen mode, which is reached via a toggle button at the top of the post box. (This toggle button is, ironically, inaccessible unless you make the window quite wide.)

- **Formatting**—The WordPress Should Correct Invalidly Nested XHTML Automatically check box is one of those "gotcha" settings that might contribute to problems without your ever knowing why. If you leave it unchecked, which is the default setting, WordPress allows incorrect XHTML to remain in your posts and pages. That can cause display problems in browsers that, reasonably enough, prefer their XHTML to be nested validly. You're not likely to remember, when the occasional user complains of an intermittent problem, that you left this check box unchecked.

  If you check the box, problem solved: The invalidly nested XHTML will be corrected. However, some plug-ins might now have problems, if you use WordPress.org software and use plug-ins. We could tell you to remember this setting in case that happens, but you (and we) are unlikely to.

 **tip**

In these Settings descriptions, we only address the settings that are tricky or particularly important. We leave out obvious (to us) or obscure settings. (No offense intended, we realize that such settings can become important and nonobvious in some situations. It's just that we haven't run into all of them, or can't spare the space to cover them.) For settings not covered here, we refer you to the onscreen Help in WordPress.

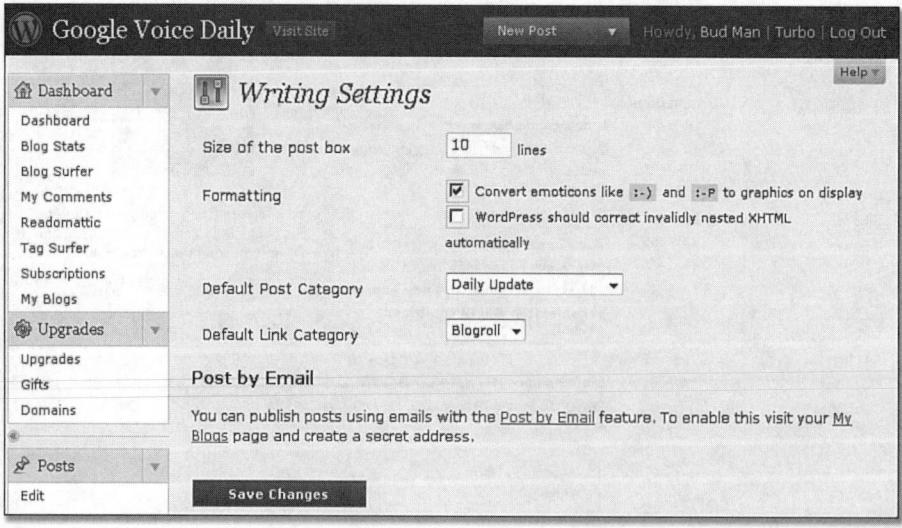

Figure 2.4
Writing is your main activity in WordPress, so get the settings right.

- **Default Post Category and Default Link Category**—New posts and new links are automatically assigned a category when you create them. This only matters if you are remiss in categorizing all your posts and links yourself. When you create your categories, come back to this link and change the settings so the default is either the most-used category or a nicely renamed "catchall" category. ("Uncategorized" and "blogroll," two of the default wordings, are such ugly names, don't you think?)

Reading Settings

Usability is a funny thing. It's easy to ignore what life is like for customers or users—in this case, your blog visitors. The trouble is that, if you ignore them in setting up your blog, they might return the favor and ignore you when it comes to visiting.

Reading Settings, shown in Figure 2.5, get little attention, but they might affect your blog visitors' experiences of your blog as much as, say, the theme, which we all agonize over. Think carefully about these settings up front, and don't be afraid to return to them later and experiment to find out what works.

Figure 2.5
Reading is the main activity of your site visitors and RSS subscribers, so make it easy for them.

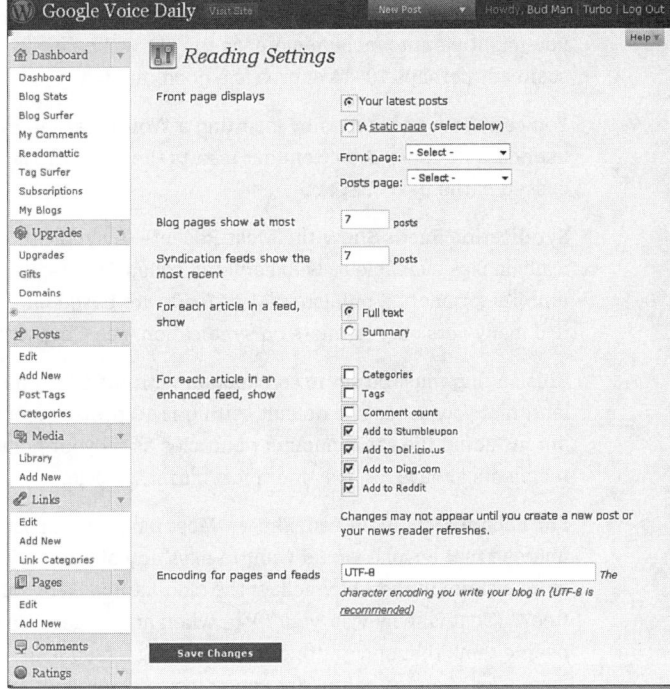

Here are suggestions for key Reading Settings:

- **Front Page Displays**—You can choose to display your latest posts, as with most blogs, or a static page. You should only change this, in our humble opinion, if you're completely converting your blog to a standard website, and have done the hard work to make it a good standard website. (This is hard to accomplish in WordPress.com; you might need to move to WordPress.org to pull it off.) If you change to a static front page prematurely, you might end up with the worst of both worlds: a boring blog because the front page doesn't change much, embedded in a badly designed website!

- **Blog Pages Show at Most**—This setting has to be used in conjunction with showing the full text of a post or just the summary. If you're showing full posts, and the posts are on the long side (as with gvDaily.com, for one example), then 10 posts—the default—is probably too much. The average person can remember 4–7 things in short-term memory and tends to get bored with lists longer than this, so consider limiting yourself to 7 full posts on the front page. If you use summaries, you might want to include more, as the list will be easily scanned; perhaps 10–14 entries is a good number.

 tip

A reader-friendly approach to the front page of your blog is to have your front page host the full most recent article and summaries for previous articles. Then readers can see what's on your mind at the moment and also scan previous postings for anything else interesting they might have missed. The easiest way to make this happen is to use the More tag in all posts but the current one. When you write a new post, leave it More free, but insert a More tag in the post that was previously newest. Your readers are likely to love this approach.

You can show summaries by inserting a WordPress tag in your posts called More that makes the user click for more. A button that inserts the More tag is available in the Edit Post page, discussed in the next chapter.

- **Syndication Feeds Show the Most Recent**—A syndication feed is a file that WordPress automatically makes available to web services, called *feed readers*, that bring the content of sites into a uniform format and publish it. Most feeds are based on RSS, Really Simple Syndication, which has many versions; for more on syndication, see Chapter 9, "Adding Graphics to Your Posts."

This setting must be set in conjunction with the next one, as you might be concerned with the length of your feed. The default setting is 10 posts; other settings you might want to consider are including the same number of articles as on your home page, or including one post, so feed recipients always get just your most current article.

- **For Each Article in a Feed, Show**—Most bloggers choose to show full texts because we can't imagine that anyone would want to miss any of our sterling words. However, people who want more visitors to their blog follow the old dictum, "Why buy a cow when you can get the milk for free?" (That is, why visit your blog, when an RSS feed delivers complete postings for free?) Most people think that only putting summaries in a feed is annoying, so you should only do it if you have a lot of added value—for you or visitors—on your site. Because most WordPress.com blogs are noncommercial, the assumption is that you'll include full posts in your feed, as you're not losing anything financial by doing so. (And really interested readers might visit your blog anyway, to see what else you have to say.)

■ **For Each Article in an Enhanced Feed, Show**—You can choose what to show in an enhanced feed, which anyone who takes an RSS feed of your blog has the option to subscribe to. The enhanced feed can include a count of comments (tempting the feed recipient to add their own), categories and tags used, and links to add the article to Del.icio.us, Digg, or StumbleUpon, popular sites for people to share interesting blog postings.

We're not sure if the categories and tags are all that interesting to feed recipients, and the comment count is likely to be quite low when the feed goes out, which will actually discourage people from visiting to comment. So you might consider leaving these fields out, but including the Del.icio.us, Digg, and StumbleUpon links so people can indicate their interest in your post by sharing it with others on their favorite sharing sites.

Discussion Settings

Comments and links between blogs are part of the very essence of blogging. So we recommend that you encourage them—but manage them as well.

Usability is a concern for commenters, as they are not only users, but users trying to help make your blog more interesting and lively by adding their own thoughts. So make things as easy for commenters as you can.

The Discussion Settings page, shown in Figure 2.6, is the wordiest, and has the most options, of any WordPress Settings page. Hang in there—it's worth taking the time to go through this one carefully and assign settings you can live with.

These are key Discussion Settings and our recommendations for them:

■ **Attempt to Notify Any Blogs Linked to from the Article**—This causes a notification, called a ping, to go to blogs you post to. Pinging slows down posting, but is vital. Other blog authors often check these notifications carefully and can then link back to you in return, widening your potential audience. The gvDaily blog run by one of the authors (Smith) often links to a dozen other blogs in a single posting, and the posting process still only takes a few seconds, so we recommend you enable this option. This notification setting can be overridden for each article.

■ **Allow Link Notifications from Other Blogs**—As with link notifications going out to other blogs, this is a vital kind of traffic for building up your blog. Allow it to appear unless the notifications become too voluminous or you encounter other problems. This setting can also be overridden for each article.

■ **Allow People to Post Comments on New Articles**—The number of blogs that should not allow comments is, in our humble opinion, very limited. Allow comments unless you have a very good reason not to; and if you do ban comments, don't expect to receive as much traffic for your blog. This is the final setting that can be overridden for each article.

■ **Comment Author Must Fill Out Name and Email/Users Must Be Registered and Logged In to Comment**—Requiring commenters to register or declare their details sounds like a good idea at the time, but can be quite disruptive of individual comments and of spontaneous exchanges of comments among visitors. Avoid requiring these steps if possible.

- **Email Me Whenever: Anyone Posts a Comment/A Comment Is Held for Moderation**—These options are a good idea. If you aren't holding comments for moderation, as we recommend, email is your first line of defense. Be ready to keep an eye on your email traffic and move in quickly if a comment is over the top. This setting is also helpful in case some comment spam sneaks by Akismet.

- **Before a Comment Appears: An Administrator Must Always Approve the Comment/Comment Author Must Have a Previously Approved Comment**—These are also tempting controls. We recommend you leave them turned off unless you experience problems.

- **Hold a Comment in the Queue If It Contains X or More Links**—The idea here is to hold comments for moderation if they contain more than a certain number of links, as comment spam is often full of links. The default setting for this option is two or more links, but we recommend you consider setting this to three or more, as it's reasonable to think a legitimate commenter might easily link to one other blog for comparison, then have a link in their signature file as well. (Even this might seem a bit spammy to you, but you can consider it on a case-by-case basis as the emails come to you with comments.)

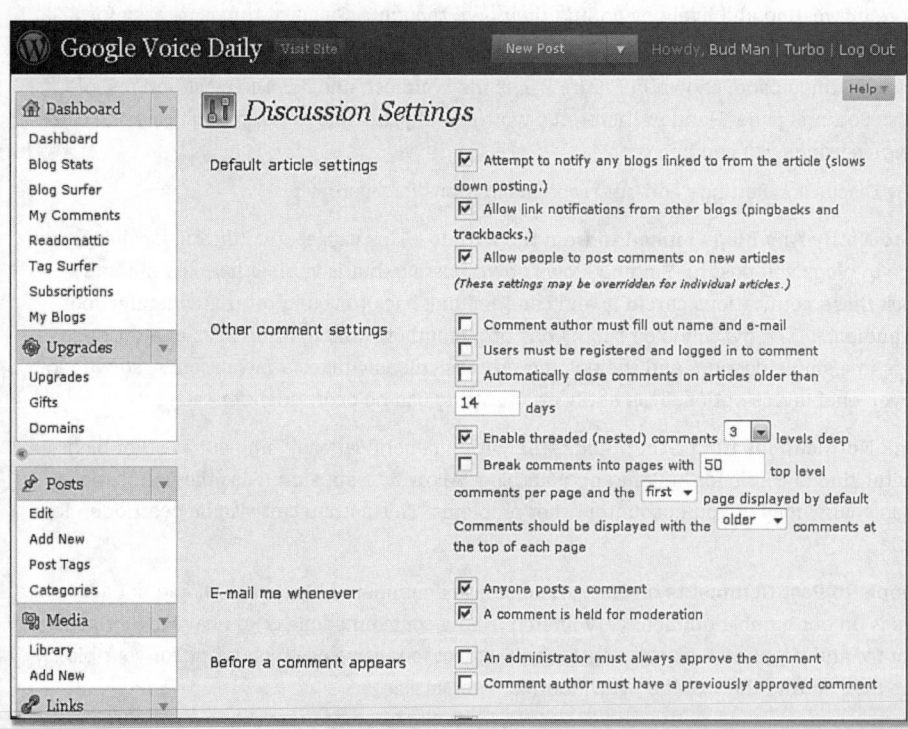

Figure 2.6
Comments are like oxygen for your blog; encourage them.

In addition to the settings listed here, we recommend you use two additional settings only with care. You're allowed to create lists of words that either cause a comment to be held in the moderation queue or that simply list it as spam, which deletes the comment immediately. Not a very nice thing if it happens to legitimate commenters!

We can all think of possible words for such lists, but you might be better to leave this to the experts at Akismet until you have specific problems. Then you can put words in these lists to address the problems you're having.

WordPress also includes options relating to avatars. Having a picture next to a comment really livens it up, so we suggest you allow avatars; keep the rating at G (why would someone have a suspect avatar?); but leave the avatar field blank for commenters who don't have one.

Stopping Spam and Scams

As we mentioned earlier in this chapter, the ability to comment on blog entries is part of the very definition of what makes a blog. However, comments can be inappropriate, mean, cruel, outright obscene, or even—horror of horrors—comment spam, comments that are only placed there to advertise something for sale or lure people into a scam.

The good people who run WordPress rightly recognized comment spam as an existential threat to blogs and developed Akismet, an excellent spam blocker that WordPress users all benefit from— most of us for free, as described in Chapter 1, "Getting Started with WordPress." So you don't have to worry too much about seeing spam in your blog.

However, all those real people out there who are mean, obscene, and so on can still be a worry! We recommend that you keep a close eye on comments—that is, that you have all comments emailed to you so you can respond quickly to problems—until you get a handle on what kind of comments your site attracts.

This might keep you busy, but it will improve the tone of your blog, without interfering with the commenting process for users.

Media Settings

As we've mentioned, *Word*Press is a very good name for this software and covers how most people use it. You'll distinguish your blog, though, if you use images and perhaps other media as well.

Media Settings, shown in Figure 2.7, are an important part of making it easy for you to use images in your blog posts. (They don't affect audio and video at all.) We discuss the use of images extensively in Chapter 5, "Taking Posts Further."

It's best to use relatively small images in WordPress. People expect blogs to load quickly. If you have, for example, seven posts on your home page, each with an image, the images need to be fairly small in file size for the page to load quickly.

WordPress gives you predetermined image size settings for thumbnail-, medium-, and large-sized images. In many cases, you'll grab an image at a size you like, or size the image yourself. In these cases, you'll display it at the original resolution.

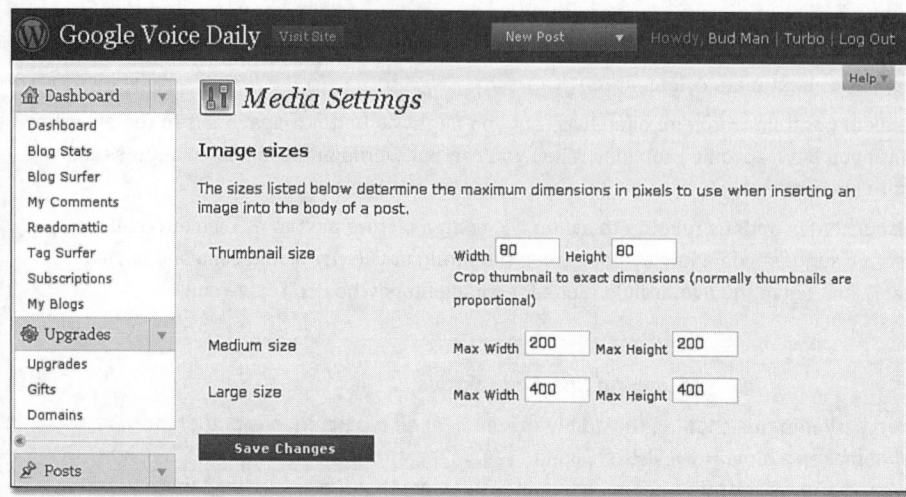

Figure 2.7
Make it easy
to use
images in a
hurry.

These are maximum sizes; your image will be resized proportionally. The larger dimension (either width or height) will be set to the predetermined size, and the smaller dimension will be resized to keep it in proportion to the larger size.

You only use the established sizes when you haven't gone to this extra work and want a quick-and-dirty way to get the image to a size that will fit well in your blog post. The default media settings in WordPress are too large for most people's purposes and for the goal of creating a fast-loading home page. We recommend that you reduce the settings, as described here:

- **Thumbnail Size**—The thumbnail size you're given as a default is 150 x 150. In professional web publishing, a thumbnail—for instance, an image of a person's face—is typically about half that length and width. So set your thumbnail size to, say, 80 x 80 pixels. This is great for a face shot to use as reference to a mention of a person in your blog.

- **Medium Size**—We've found, in using images in our own blogs, that an image about half the width of the blog's middle column allows us to flow text beside it with good effect. A typical theme allows a column width of about 400–500 pixels. Because your blog will not always be displayed at full width, you should go for the low end of this range, and set the medium-size height and width to 200 pixels.

- **Large Size**—The most sensible large size for a picture is the full width of your blog's main column. For most themes, this is about 400 pixels or a bit more. A height of the same size makes sense. This allows you to have text above and below the picture without it looking odd within your blog.

Nothing here stops you from using larger pictures—or pictures of any size. The established settings are there for convenience. It makes sense for them to be at a size that's a good fit for your blog.

Privacy Settings

The WordPress Privacy Settings, shown in Figure 2.8, are limited to three options for a single choice: Blog Visibility. This setting can completely change how you use your blog:

- **I Would Like My Blog to Be Visible to Everyone, Including Search Engines (Like Google, Sphere, Technorati) and Archivers**—This is the usual setting; in fact, anything else is somewhat inimical to the spirit of blogging! You might be tempted to avoid this setting during the early days of your blog, if you have a list of improvements you'd like to make. However, high search engine rankings are built up gradually, so you should allow search engine visits very early on.

- **I Would Like to Block Search Engines, But Allow Normal Visitors**—This sounds like a comfortable choice, but with this option, only people who know about your blog directly from you, or from other visitors to it, will visit—and then perhaps only occasionally. So only choose this option if you're willing to have an audience made up only of friends and family.

- **I Would Like My Blog to Be Visible Only to Users I Choose**—You can have your blog be limited only to specific, named people who you choose. This is a great option for sites under development or, for instance, an internal company site.

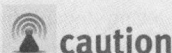 **caution**

Administering who can sign into different kinds of web or internal company intranet sites is a big business worth billions to the few companies that have mastered it—Microsoft, IBM, and Google among them. (Apple, for instance, large as it is, doesn't have a corporate-scale solution of its own.) Think twice before you take on the job of managing a large group of users for a private blog.

Figure 2.8 Privacy is important, but an easy choice for most.

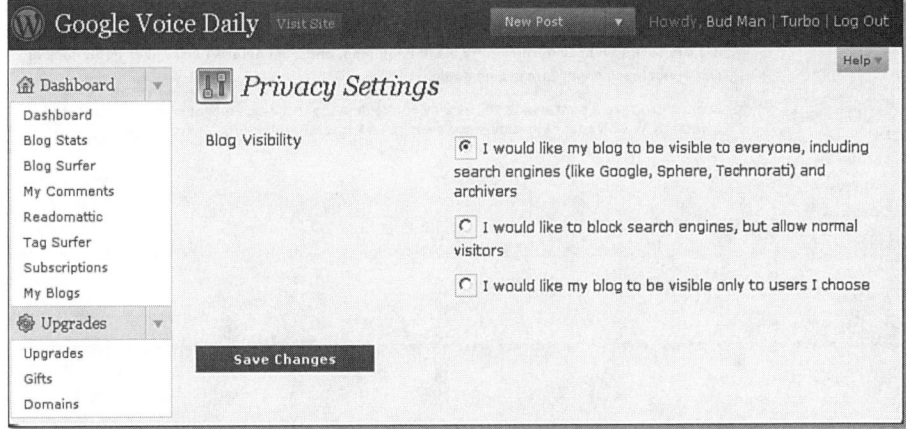

Delete Blog

You're not likely to be deleting your blog so early on, but it's worth knowing what the options are—and aren't—in case you consider doing so in the future.

The Delete Blog options are shown in Figure 2.9. Note the following:

- **Deleting a blog is permanent**—You can never get it back. The WordPress name, in the form *blogname*.wordpress.com, is permanently disabled. Any domain name you've purchased, however, can be reused.

- **Deleting isn't for getting rid of entries or transferring ownership**—The Delete Blog screen provides links to information or support for solving such problems.

- **Deleting doesn't free up your account name**—You can use your account name to create multiple blogs, but you can't get rid of your account name. It also permanently ties up an email address of yours for WordPress purposes; you can't use the same email address for another WordPress account, though you can change WordPress accounts to use different specific email addresses.

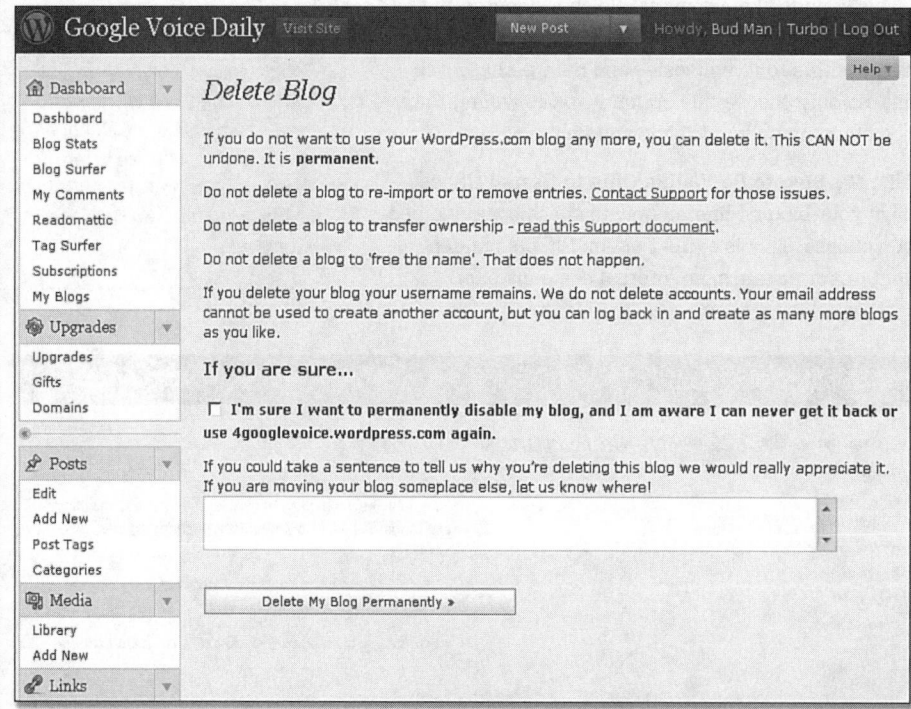

Figure 2.9
Deleting doesn't do all you might be hoping for.

WordPress asks you, if you do delete your blog, to let them know if you are taking it somewhere else—and where to, which is, as the Brits say, a bit cheeky. This is to help WordPress know how to improve, but you don't have to tell them unless you want to.

Other Settings Subpanels: OpenID and Domains

OpenID is an identity standard that allows you to use a unique URL, such as your blog's domain name, to log in to a wide variety of sites. You can use your blog's domain name, in the form *blogname*.wordpress.com, as an OpenID. WordPress will authenticate you. You can use the OpenID Settings subpanel to list trusted sites, which you can then log in to more quickly.

WordPress is an OpenID provider, but you can't use your OpenID to log in to WordPress itself.

The Domains Settings subpanel allows you to buy and use domain names. WordPress makes this really, really easy—so easy that one of us (Smith) has gone through four domain names for the same blog in four months! Despite the ease of doing it, there's a lot to think about, so we discuss this topic, and this subpanel, in full in Chapter 10.

 tip

If you're logged in to your WordPress account, and visit another WordPress blog that requires logging in to comment, you don't need to log in again; comment away! The same is true for your users.

WordPress Settings Not in the Settings Menu

There are only two important WordPress settings that are not handled either during sign-up or in the Settings menu, as covered in this chapter so far. Those are ratings of blog posts and comments and the ability to post by email.

These settings are, like the setup and Settings menu options described up to this point, very good things to try to nail during setup—and to know about from the beginning so you have an idea of how to modify them later if needed.

Ratings Settings

The Ratings Settings are found in a subpanel of the Ratings menu on WordPress Administration pages (see Figure 2.10). Here are the things you can allow users to rate, and the options for each:

- **Posts**—You can allow users to rate blog posts by yourself and other authors. You can also specify whether to use a five-star rating, as on Amazon.com and other sites, or a Nero rating—thumbs up or thumbs down. You can customize the style of stars or thumbs, the layout and font, the color, and more. (Most themes don't let you choose fonts and so on, so it's almost a bit annoying that you can choose them for ratings!)

  For the font and color, you can choose Inherit to use colors determined by your theme. This is the safest and easiest choice, but you can certainly try others. You can also customize the labels that go with various numbers of stars and so on. And you can put the rating above each blog post, which might attract readers, or below it, which makes more sense, as the reader then has a chance to form their own informed opinion first.

  We recommend that you start out by allowing ratings, especially for posts; like comments, they're an additional participatory element in your blog. However, if you find they conflict with the content and feel of the blog as it evolves, or if too few people use them to be worthwhile, you can change or remove them later.

- **Pages**—You can extend the ratings options set for posts to pages as well, and position the ratings above and below each page. Unlike posts, though, your site visitors don't necessarily expect to be able to rate each page. Ratings are potentially a good way to get feedback for your pages. You might conclude, though, as we do, that your blog visitors expect you to have the pages in good shape and stable, and be just as happy not to be asked to rate them.

- **Comments**—You can further extend the ratings options set for posts to comments, so people can rate one another's comments. As a specific example, Amazon.com allows people to rate comments for helpfulness, though they mix five-star ratings for books with Nero ratings for whether a rating and comment about a book are helpful or not. WordPress only allows you to use star ratings or Nero ratings, not to use each for different purposes.

Although allowing people to rate comments makes more sense to us than having them rate pages, it still seems both complicated and potentially discouraging to your commenters. Also, you don't have the option, which you might well want, of having the finely tuned five-star ratings for posts and Nero ratings for comments. So we recommend you also leave this option turned off, unless you want to create a real free-for-all feeling around your comments.

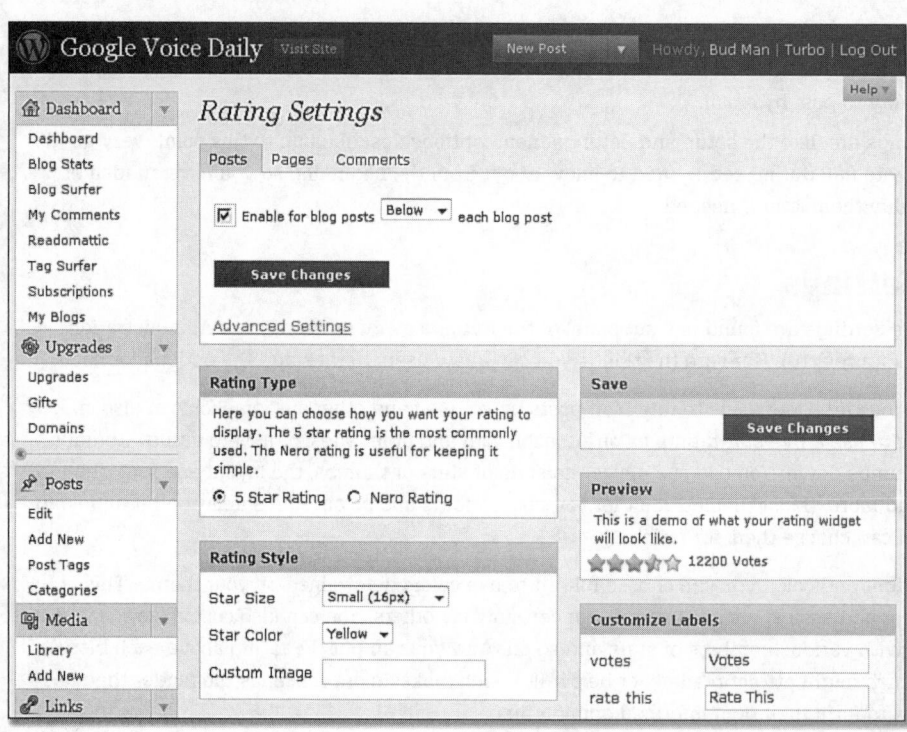

Figure 2.10
Let your users rate to their hearts' content.

Ratings have both a substantive element—your blog has a different feel depending on what you do and don't allow to be rated—and a subjective one relating to how the ratings look. Make the substantive choices now, and take an initial stab at the appearance. However, be ready to come back and modify the appearance of ratings in keeping with the choices you make for your blog's theme, as described in the next chapter.

Post by Email Settings

The Post by Email setting is set differently from any of the other settings described in this chapter, but it belongs with the others here because it's something you'll want to consider setting right at the beginning of your blog's life.

The Post by Email setting can be very useful—or problematic, as described here. These days, there is an alternative. If you have a smartphone, you might be able to download an app for it that enables you to do at least basic WordPress blog management on the go. As of this writing, apps are available for the iPhone/iPod touch and for BlackBerry. See WordPress.com for links to such apps, or search for "WordPress" in the app store or equivalent for your smartphone to find alternatives. These apps do not require that you have the Post by Email setting turned on, though you can use an app sometimes and Post by Email other times.

How to Post by Email

To change the Post by Email setting, go to the Dashboard area in the upper-left corner of the administration part of your site. Click the My Blogs link.

You'll see the name of your blog within a table with columns for different settings. Under the Post by Email setting, you'll see an Enable button.

To turn on Post by Email, just click the Enable button. A "secret" email address will appear. Hover your mouse over it to see options, as shown in Figure 2.11.

 tip

Don't let your "secret" email address be a secret from you when you need it most! Write it down someplace where you'll have access to it when you're away from your computer, as you might want to post to your blog from a smartphone, a borrowed computer, and so on. You'll need to have the "secret" address with you to do this.

Figure 2.11
Post by Email, if you're brave enough.

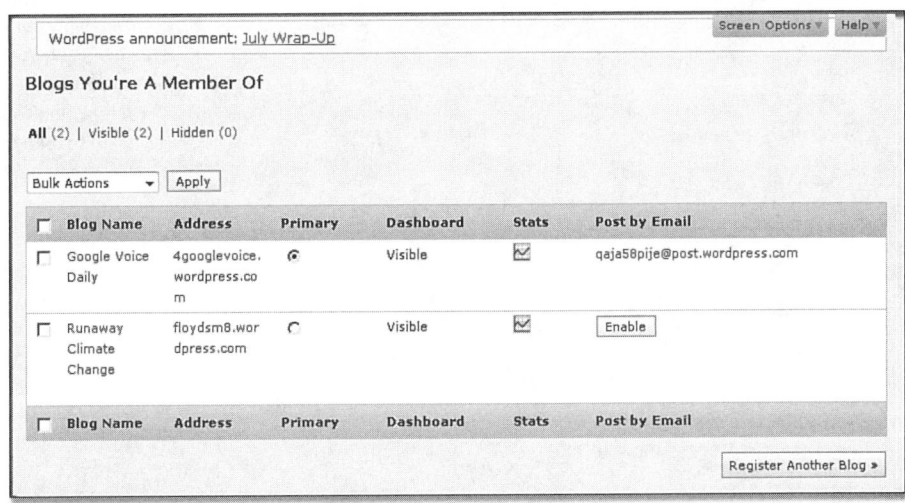

Why Not Post by Email?

In addition to the ease of accidentally sending email to your Post by Email address, there's also the common phenomenon of sender's regret, which applies to all email, but many times over to blog posts. (Remember that in Chapter 1, we suggested you consider a blog post to be skywriting in the sky above your home town—and your employer's, and your family members', and….) It's very easy to find yourself wishing, with all your heart and soul (and perhaps your paycheck as well), that you hadn't emailed in a blog posting, beginning mere milliseconds after you clicked the Send button.

You can, of course, delete or modify a blog posting after you put it up. However, the main use for Post by Email is for those times when you don't have access to the WordPress posting interface. So it might be a long time before you can fix an error—or even notice it!

This concern brings up the related topic of a syndrome that could be called publisher's aphasia, which makes errors invisible in draft form, but screamingly obvious after publication. The quick turnaround possible with blogs militates against the worst cases, except when you're able to post remotely without reviewing the post on the blog straight afterward, as happens with Post by Email.

 caution

Some email interfaces make it very easy to send email to the wrong address. For instance, they suggest a destination based on the first couple of letters you type. This makes it very, very easy to accidentally post a work or personal email message on your blog, or to accidentally send a blog posting to an email contact.

If this is a concern for you, consider not enabling the Post by Email setting, or being very careful how you send emails if you do use it. Accidentally sending a nasty comment about your boss to your blog instead of to your best work friend could be a career-limiting move.

 tip

You can generate a different Post by Email address, or delete the current one, at any time. Just mouse over the Post by Email address in the My Blogs screen and the options will appear, as shown in Figure 2.11. Use this capability, for instance, to share the Post by Email address with someone, then change to a different email address when you want to take the option away from that person.

3

CREATING YOUR BLOG'S LOOK

You've Got the Look

Most WordPress blog users never do much with their blog's look. Most
WordPress.com users pick a safe-looking, existing theme from among
the 70-plus choices without really understanding what they're getting.
Even WordPress software users, with many more choices, tend to make
a quick choice from among a relatively small subset of the available
themes, some free, some paid for.

Many themes have a similar look so your blog visitors always know, for
better or worse, that they're on a WordPress blog. This is okay when
you're starting out, for blogs with a WordPress.com domain name, or if
you desire to be strongly identified as part of the WordPress community.
However, you might want a more customized look, either right from the
beginning or later on.

In this chapter, we show you how to use the options available for
WordPress.com blogs to begin with a more distinctive look or improve
the look of your existing blog. We also take you through the available
widgets so you can make informed choices, enhancing your blog.

In later chapters, beginning in Chapter 10, "Adding Upgrades, Audio,
and Video," we show you how to use the additional options made possible through WordPress.com upgrades, or by moving to WordPress software, to take your blog—both its look and functionality—as far as you
want to go.

Introducing Themes

Themes are a critical part of your WordPress blog. The theme determines not only the look of your blog, but also much of its functionality.

A theme is a mix of a visual look for your blog—a visual design—and a container for specific functionality, what many web designers would call a template.

Because they include both look and feel functionality, WordPress themes are powerful, but also a bit dangerous, as they can allow you to make big mistakes on your page. A theme that isn't properly constructed can be "blown out" by some kinds of content, distorting the web page containing the blog.

For this reason, Automattic offers 70-plus carefully selected themes from which WordPress.com users can choose. Even this limited number of choices is overwhelming for most people, who don't necessarily understand all the implications of what they're choosing. Most people quickly choose a safe-looking theme and get down to what most of us think a blog is all about: writing posts.

The most popular theme for WordPress blogs is called Kubrick, the name of the director of *2001: A Space Odyssey* and other films. Kubrick is the default theme for WordPress.com blogs. It's shown in Figure 3.1.

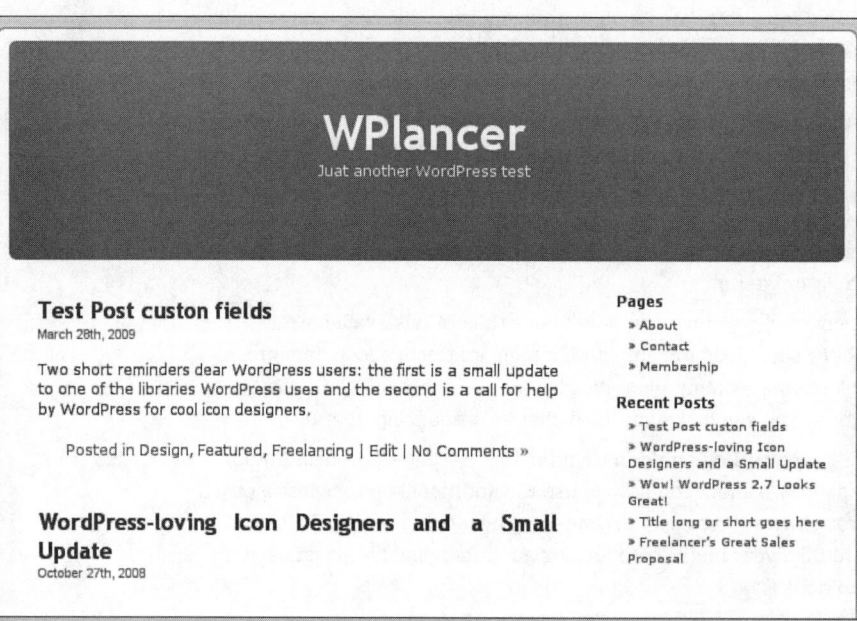

Figure 3.1
Kubrick is a safe choice for your cyberspace odyssey.

WPlancer
Juat another WordPress test

Test Post custon fields
March 28th, 2009

Two short reminders dear WordPress users: the first is a small update to one of the libraries WordPress uses and the second is a call for help by WordPress for cool icon designers.

Posted in Design, Featured, Freelancing | Edit | No Comments »

WordPress-loving Icon Designers and a Small Update
October 27th, 2008

Pages
» About
» Contact
» Membership

Recent Posts
» Test Post custon fields
» WordPress-loving Icon Designers and a Small Update
» Wow! WordPress 2.7 Looks Great!
» Title long or short goes here
» Freelancer's Great Sales Proposal

Users of WordPress software have many, many more choices: choosing from about a thousand free themes directly available from the WordPress.org Free Theme Directory; choosing from many other free or paid-for themes; starting with an existing theme and tweaking it; or creating a more or less entirely new theme. Many WordPress software users are not that different from WordPress.com users, though, and quickly choose a safe, relatively popular theme, whether paid for or free.

The tendency to choose quickly is unfortunate because choosing an appropriate and yet distinctive theme can make a blog stand out. Choosing a theme with the right look and functionality almost certainly makes more difference to the impact of your blog than wordsmithing an overly long post to within an inch of its life (and to the limits of your blog visitors' patience), which is how most of us tend to spend our blogging time.

So whether you're just getting started, and wanting to be distinctive from the beginning, or looking to improve your existing blog, use this chapter to help you choose a theme and other appearance-related options to make your blog great.

 note

This chapter is limited to free options available in WordPress.com blogs. It's worth understanding these, though, even if you're a WordPress software user and have more options. In later chapters, we show you how WordPress.com users can buy an upgrade to tweak their theme, and how WordPress software users can do just about anything they want. With these options, you'll have a chance to blow out a web page yourself!

What to Look for in a Theme

Because you can't change WordPress.com themes without paying for an upgrade to WordPress software (as described in Chapter 11, "Installing and Upgrading WordPress Software"), every aspect of a theme has to be exactly right for you to effectively use it. This can lead to some difficult choices, for instance when a theme with just the right colors doesn't allow needed widgets (add-ins that go in a theme's sidebar or sidebars).

How should you choose a theme? Most of us do it like how we buy a car, by personal preference, with an emphasis on looks and a nod to functionality.

Your blog will have a life of its own, though. Although you're responsible for it, you'll find that it develops its own personality, especially if you get lots of comments.

So your theme needs to have a look that fits not only you but the contents of the blog itself, as well as the visitors you want to attract and retain. It also needs functionality to support what your blog visitors want to do.

As you choose your theme, think about your blog's purpose and its users. Make choices that work for them, not just for your personal preferences.

The 70 or so themes available on WordPress.com can be divided up by several important features that really make a difference: colors, columns, fixed or flexible width, whether widgets are allowed, and other features (that is, functionality).

People are very visually oriented, and colors are visually compelling and affect us emotionally. This means that most theme choices are strongly affected by color. However, color is the easiest thing to change with a Cascading Style Sheets (CSS) tweak, and might, within limits, be less important to your website visitors than many other aspects of your theme.

 tip

WordPress offers a filter that allows you to specify what you want in your theme and select just the themes that fit. So, once you've thought through the options, you can more easily narrow down to the themes that offer just what you want.

So we recommend that you narrow down your choice of themes by other aspects; then, from among the otherwise acceptable themes, choose the best look in terms of color. If you choose by color first, you'll probably miss out on other aspects of your theme and functionality that could be much more important to you in the long run.

That said, we still cover colors first because that's how the filter works.

Colors

In the Feature Filter, the colors you can select are Black, Blue, Brown, Orange, Pink, Purple, Silver, Tan, White, Dark, and Light. (The last two options, Dark and Light, are descriptors of the overall color scheme rather than specific colors.)

To give yourself more choices, rather than looking only for the colors you like, think more about what colors you don't want. Include all the colors that are at least somewhat acceptable to you. Remember that color names are imprecise; your Brown might be someone else's Tan; their White might be your Silver.

Also, be open to surprises—even a dash of pink might not be too amiss in a theme that has everything else you need.

Focus on readability. There's a reason that the vast majority of what we read, onscreen and off, is black text on a white background: The contrast makes reading easier. If your blog is easy to read, it's likely to get more and longer visits.

This consideration is even more telling on a computer. Reading on a computer screen, which is low resolution and backlit (rather than restfully lit by reflected light), is harder than reading print. Black text, of a large enough size, on a white background eases your site visitors' struggles.

In using the Themes filter (described later), leave the color choices unchecked at first. Use them to narrow down your choice after you have all, or at least most, of the other things you want.

Is White on Black in Your Future?

A minority of sites have always used white on black because it looks sort of cool, though often in an intimidating and harsh way. Concerns about saving energy have led to other sites adopting white on black as well—having large areas of dark background means less energy is used.

Now a new kind of screen, called an organic light-emitting diode (OLED) screen, is about to come into view (sorry for the pun). OLED screens are eco-friendly in that they use fewer environmentally unfriendly materials, but they also use disproportionately more power to display white than black versus previous screen types. This not only affects power consumption, which so many are concerned about, but also has a noticeable effect on battery life, which is sure to get the attention of more road warriors.

As OLED adoption accelerates, expect to see more white-on-black designs in the near future. If you join the trend, or even want to lead it, try to find designs that are relatively readable (for instance, using a larger font size) and less intimidating.

Number of Columns

Columns are a critical aspect of page design—just look at a few magazines and newspapers to see how important columns are. The number of columns does a lot to determine just how useful and interesting your blog is.

Remember that most people come to your blog to see your posts. You might also want to offer a lot in addition to that, but your posts need to be front and center.

In our experience, a two-column layout gives you the power of a main column for your blog posts and the flexibility of an additional column for widgets. A three-column layout (or even more columns) is likely to cheat the space available for your blog post.

In a two-column layout, you should have a wide column for blog content and a narrow column, called a sidebar, for widgets.

Some themes cleverly use more than one column for blog content. However, this is usually a bad idea on the Web, for two reasons:

- Because page length and width aren't fixed, the column layout can shift, making reading difficult. This is especially true for screen-reading software that visually impaired people use.

- Because the screen is (even) lower resolution than a newspaper page, reading narrow columns of text is difficult; somewhat wider columns, perhaps a bit narrower than the width of this page, are easier to read.

Note that both of these concerns go to readability. It's easy to pick a theme that looks cool to you and to visitors when they first arrive at your blog, but that actually makes it hard to read your posts. Visitors tend to be quick to leave and slow to return, though they might not understand just why.

 caution

More and more devices display web content, such as netbooks, smartphones, and other noncomputer platforms. People often read wordy content on the move, even downloading a favorite web page or blog in advance of, for example, a train trip. Blogs are a great fit for this kind of web use, so a small but growing proportion of your blog visitors might be using small, or even tiny, screens. Complex layouts are hard to read on smaller screens and are likely to be slow to render as well, making your blog hard on your visitors indeed. No one is likely to tell you they're having a problem, either; they'll just spend their time on other blogs, and you won't know why. So choose an easy-to-use layout from the beginning.

Fixed-Width or Flexible-Width Columns

We tend to like fixed-width columns for reading for usability reasons. Even with only two columns, the blog content and widgets in the additional column are going to want a fairly large amount of space, so having flexible-width columns doesn't buy you that much in terms of actual flexibility.

For an example of the perils of flexible-width columns, as well as three-column layouts, look no further than the WordPress Add New Post page where you'll be spending so much of your time as a WordPress blog owner. You will very commonly want to be writing a post in one web browser window while having a document or web page open next to it. This is theoretically possible on most computer screens, including the evermore common widescreen laptop (with a typical resolution of 1280×800).

However, the flexible-width columns in this page don't really let you do much unless the page is quite wide. Here's what happens at various web browser window widths:

- **1000 pixel window or wider**—All features available; no visual degradation of page layout.

- **Window 884-1000 pixels wide**—Crucial central editing area and buttons partly covered by the right column.

- **Window 884 pixels wide or less**—Blowout! (See Figure 3.2.) Graphics and text in the middle column are forced down into the editing area.

The layout of the page in Figure 3.2 leaves you no useful additional screen area on a 1280-pixel wide screen and just barely fits on another common laptop resolution, 1024×768. Although the flexible-width columns seem to give you flexibility, they actually just tempt you to narrow the window below the point where the editing area really works.

Ironically, the solution to this problem is to switch to Full-Screen mode for editing, and then narrow the window to use it alongside another document or web browser window. Unfortunately, the button that turns on Full-Screen mode is one of the first ones to be covered over by the right column when you narrow the window.

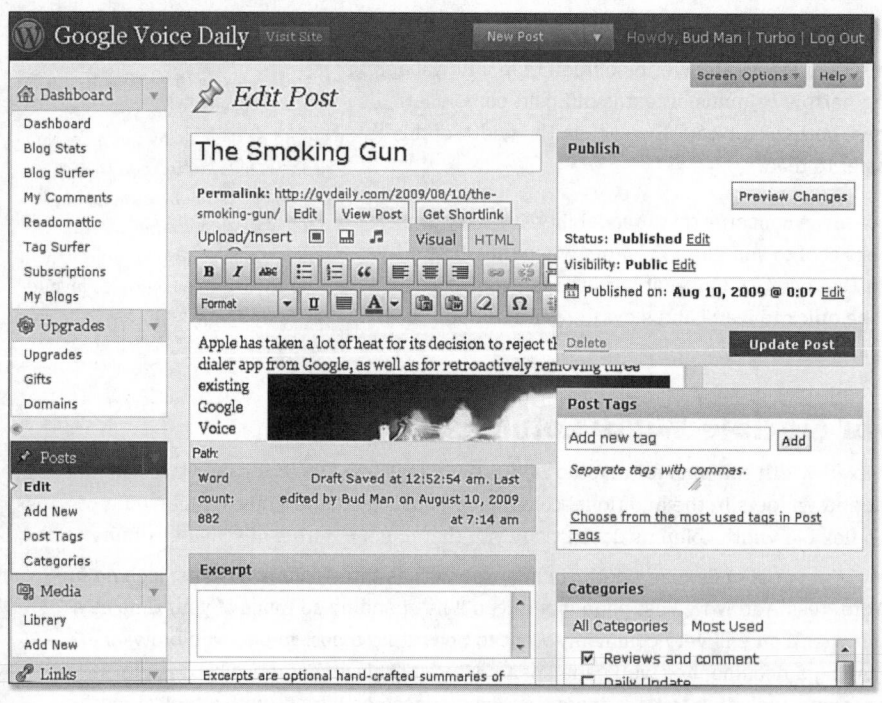

Figure 3.2
Minor blowouts can happen even in the best-planned pages (see center, under "Permalink").

The upshot of this brief case study is that you should think about how your blog visitors are going to use your blog, and then choose your theme accordingly. Blog content is inherently flexible in its space requirements—does your theme encourage your blog to be used flexibly?

Although we all think that our blog visitors have absolutely nothing else to do than give full attention to our blog, they might be visiting it while waiting for a file to download, while watching a video clip, or as a reference for an email or document they're writing. A theme that gracefully adjusts to sharing the screen can be a big plus.

Widgets and Other Features

Widgets are small pieces of code that drive the content of small boxed areas you put in a sidebar of your blog. Widgets can do many things, such as provide links to your most recent posts, provide links to pages in your blog, show recent posts from another blog, and so on. In Figure 3.3, shown later in this section, the Archives, Categories, and Blogroll areas in the sidebar are all widgets.

Whether widgets are allowed in a theme is a crucial feature for you as a reader of this book. Later in this chapter, we tell you how to choose from among available widgets. In Chapter 9, "Adding Graphics to Your Posts," we show you how to modify certain widgets using HTML. However, to take advantage of the power of widgets, you need a theme that accommodates them.

Fortunately, nearly all of the themes available through WordPress.com support widgets. Some have more interesting widgets preinstalled than others. However, with this book in hand, you'll be able to find the additional widgets you need and install them, so all you need in a theme is basic support for widgets, which is nearly always present.

A few WordPress.com themes are additionally customizable as to their colors or even their number of columns or other theme options. Themes with this kind of flexibility are very promising for your blog, allowing you to redesign your blog's look within a theme; investigate them carefully among your options.

Many themes have custom headers, meaning you can put any image in the top area. In a negative sense, you need this flexibility if the theme you favor has, for example, dolphins in it, but your blog is about how to crush large rocks with bulldozers. If it's a custom header, just replace the dolphins with rocks and bulldozers and you're off.

In a positive sense, custom headers give you a helpful element of flexibility without making you play designer too much. Although you can only take this so far—your custom header can't clash strongly with the rest of the blog's look—it's a very nice stepping-stone into changing the look of your blog without having to pay for a CSS upgrade or leave WordPress.com behind entirely before you're ready.

Microformats are special HTML codes that denote specific kinds of data, such as addresses. If this is important to you, choose one of the few themes that support microformats, or use a CSS upgrade or the WordPress software to support it yourself.

Right-to-left (RTL) text support is a crucial issue for bloggers who work in languages that use RTL scripts such as Arabic, Hebrew, Urdu, and others. Ideographic languages such as Chinese and Japanese can be written left-to-right, right-to-left, or top to bottom—often all mixed on the same page! This is clearly recognized as an important issue by Automattic, the owners of WordPress, as all of the themes available in WordPress.com have RTL text support.

As an example of some of these points, Figure 3.3 shows the Google Voice Daily blog belonging to one of the authors (Smith). The blog is functional enough, and uses the traditional blue fade found in the WordPress default theme, Kubrick, and many others. It does include a (slightly) customized header, at least.

Figure 3.3
Google Voice
Daily is a bit
clunky.

Should You Change Your Theme with CSS?

You can customize the theme in use by your current blog using CSS. (Cascading Style Sheets are an offspring of HTML, the original language of web pages. CSS allows you to change your web page in a more organized and structured way than HTML ever could.) However, to modify CSS in the WordPress.com environment is an extra-cost add-on, for which the current charge is about $15 per year.

Should you do this? If you're skilled in both CSS and actual design—meaning, you can create a decent look, and have the technical skills necessary to implement it—then yes, the CSS upgrade is a good deal. You get all the advantages of WordPress.com plus, for a low price, a custom look as well.

Ironically, the CSS upgrade is also good if your CSS skills are very limited, and there's a theme you like that has just one or two elements in it that you can't stand. You can make the minor tweaks to fix the theme, or get someone else to help you, and have a theme you love and all the advantages of WordPress.com for a low cost. (Though paying $15 per year just to, for example, get rid of a banana might seem a bit annoying.)

See Chapter 12, "The WordPress Toolkit: Themes," for information on making small changes to themes using CSS.

If you want to make more extensive changes, though, or have new ideas for what a theme can do or be like, but don't have strong skills in both CSS and graphic design, you're probably better off using the WordPress software available from WordPress.org.

Using WordPress software gives you the option of using a far wider range of free themes—nearly 1,000 at this writing, as shown in Figure 3.4. You have access to many additional themes that are paid for. Choosing from this far greater range of options enables you to start off with a theme much closer to what you want. From there, you're completely free to modify themes, and you become involved in a community that will support you every step of the way.

See Chapter 11 for information on making the move to WordPress.org.

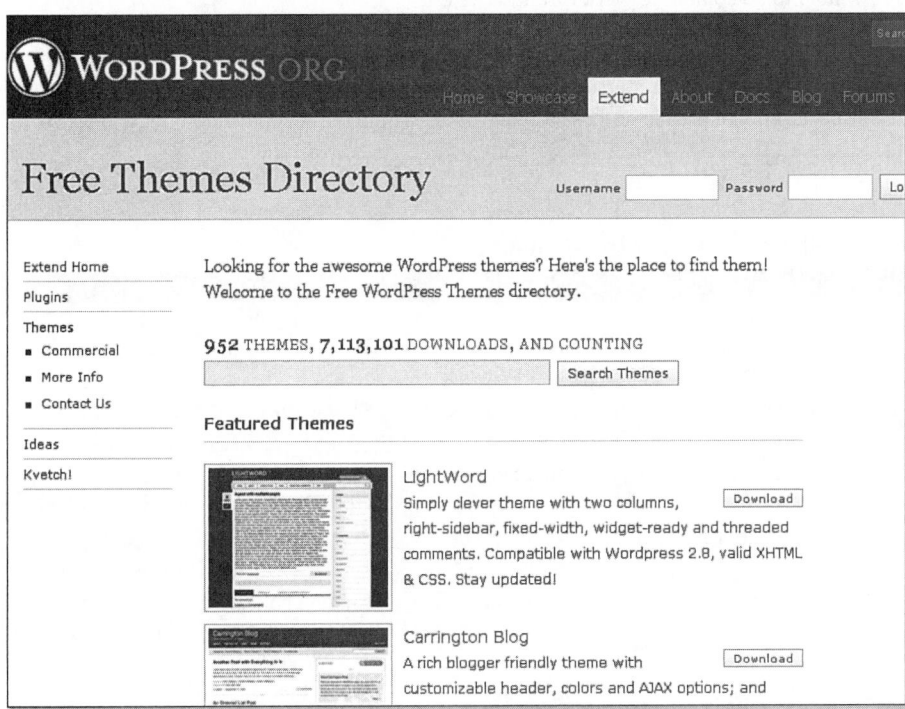

Figure 3.4
Free themes give WordPress.org users a great deal of freedom.

Listing the Themes

The number of themes on offer is overwhelming for most people. If you're serious about themes, though, you need to be able to compare the existing themes to get an idea of what's offered and help you focus on the themes that have the key features you need.

If you're considering buying the CSS upgrade for WordPress.com to tweak a theme, or working in WordPress software, you want to know which theme has the right structure to serve as a starting point for your own work.

To assist, we've summarized the currently existing themes in WordPress.com for you in Tables 3.1 through 3.4. The tables summarize the themes as follows:

- **Table 3.1**—Themes with one, three, or four columns, including themes that offer a choice as to number of columns.

- **Table 3.2**—Themes with two flexible columns.

- **Table 3.3**—Themes with two fixed columns and a custom header, a highly desirable feature for semicustomizing your blog.

- **Table 3.4**—Themes with two fixed columns and no custom header. (Customizing the header is one of the easier things to do if you're willing to do some CSS work through the CSS upgrade or by using WordPress.org.)

tip

Automattic occasionally adds a new theme to those available for WordPress.com users. To see new additions, search for "new theme" on the Wordpress.com blog at http://en.blog. wordpress.com.

These tables should give you a great starting point for choosing an initial theme, or one to change to. You can also see additional details of most themes, including full-size screenshots, in this article:

http://ourtimes.wordpress.com/2007/04/29/choosing-a-wordpresscom-theme/

Table 3.1 Themes with One, Three, or Four Columns

Name	Description	Columns/Width	Other Features	Colors
Sandbox	CSS selectors	One, two, or three, flexible L & R sidebars	Microformats Theme options	White
DePo Masthead	Classy	One or Three, fixed	Theme options	Black, red, white, light
Ambiru	Calm, relaxing	One, fixed	Custom header 500×225	Green, white, light
ChaosTheory	For WordPress.com	One, fixed		Black, dark, blue
Day Dream	Narrow	One, fixed	Custom colors Custom header Theme option	Blue, white, light,
Monotone	Photo blogging theme	One, fixed	No widgets Custom colors Photo blogging	
Spring Loaded	Fresh, clean	One, fixed Right sidebar		Green, seasonal
Andreas04	Two sidebars on right	Three, flexible Right sidebar		Light
Andreas09	Sidebars on L & R	Three, flexible L & R sidebars	Custom colors	White, light
Garland	Flexible	Three, flexible L & R sidebars	Custom colors	
Fadtastic	Double the widgets	Three, flexible Right sidebar	White, blue, light, green	
Digg 3 Column	Digg-like	Three, fixed L & R sidebars	Custom header 904×160	
Grid Focus	Grid-aligned	Three, fixed Right sidebar	Blavatar	White, light

Name	Description	Columns/Width	Other Features	Colors
Twenty-eight Thirteen	Minimalist	Three, fixed Right sidebar		White, light
Fjords04	Split custom header	Four, fixed Right sidebar	Custom header 900×200	
Neo-Sapien	Photo header	Four, fixed L & R sidebars	Custom header	Black, red, dark

Table 3.2   Themes with Two Flexible Columns

Name	Description	Columns/Width	Other Features	Colors
Girl in Green	Journal-style	Two, flexible Right sidebar		Green, dark, black
Rounded	Unique navigation	Two, flexible Right sidebar		Brown, green, white
Rubric	Clean	Two, flexible Right sidebar	Custom header 215×150	White, light
Sandbox-10	CSS canvas	Two, flexible Left sidebar	Microformats	White, light
Shocking Blue Green	Light and flexible	Two, flexible Right sidebar		Green, blue, white, light
Silver is the New Black	Clean	Two, flexible Right sidebar		Silver, white, light
WordPress Classic	Asking for custom CSS	Two, flexible Right sidebar		White, light, green

Table 3.3   Themes with Two Fixed Columns, Custom Header

Name	Description	Columns/Width	Other Features	Colors
Benevolence	Simplistic	Two, fixed Left sidebar	Custom header 700×225	White, light
Black-LetterHead	Minimalistic	Two, fixed Right sidebar	Custom header 760×200	Black, dark, orange
Blix	Tried and true	Two, fixed Right sidebar	Custom header 690×115	Green, white, light
ChaoticSoul	Based off old website	Two, fixed Right sidebar	Custom header 760×151	Dark, black
Connections	Super classy	Two, fixed Right sidebar	Custom header 741×142	Green, light
Contempt	Pro version of Kubrick	Two, fixed Right sidebar	Custom header 760×200	Blue, white, light

Table 3.3 Continued

Name	Description	Columns/Width	Other Features	Colors
Cutline	Minimalistic	Two, fixed Right sidebar	Custom header 770×140	White, light
Freshy	Page navigation	Two, fixed Right sidebar	Custom header	White, light
Greenery	Fresh and clear	Two, fixed Right sidebar	Custom header 740×171	Green, white, light
Iceburgg	Holiday theme	Two, fixed	Custom header 790×150	Seasonal, blue, white, light
K2-lite	Clean	Two, fixed Right sidebar	Custom header 780×200	Blue, white, light
Kubrick	Default WordPress theme	Two, fixed Right sidebar	Custom header 760×200	Blue, white, light
MistyLook	Page navigation	Two, fixed Right sidebar	Custom header 760×190	White, light
Neat!	Stylish	Two, fixed Right sidebar	Custom header 700×200	Blue, white, light
Ocean Mist	Category navigation	Two, fixed Right sidebar	Custom header 736×229	Blue
Pool	Tabbed page navigation	Two, fixed Right sidebar	Custom header	Blue, white, light
PressRow	Journalistic	Two, fixed Right sidebar	Custom header 770×200	White, light
Prologue	Inspired by Twitter	Two, fixed Right sidebar	Custom header Front page post form	Blue, white, light
Redoable Lite	Slimmed-down	Two, fixed Right sidebar	Custom header 730×180	Dark, black, red
Regulus	Versatile	Two, fixed Right sidebar	Custom colors Custom header Theme options 730×140	
Sapphire	"Apple" feel	Two, fixed Right sidebar	Custom header 740×180	Blue, white
Tarski	Two spots for widgets	Two, fixed Left sidebar	Custom header 720×180	
Vigilance	Search friendly	Two, fixed Right sidebar	Custom colors Custom header Theme options	White, red, light

Table 3.4   Themes with Two Fixed Columns, No Custom Header

Name	Description	Columns/Width	Other Features	Colors
Albeo	Light and colorful	Two, fixed Right sidebar	No widgets	Pink, blue, yellow, white, light
Almost Spring	Light and simple	Two, fixed Right sidebar		Green, white, light
Banana Smoothie	Adorned with a banana	Two, fixed Right sidebar		Yellow, light
Dusk	Flowers	Two, fixed Right sidebar		Dark
Emire	Professional	Two, fixed Right sidebar		Green, dark
Fauna	Flower header	Two, fixed Left sidebar		Green, white, light
Fleur De Lys	Classic	Two, fixed Left sidebar		White, brown, light
Flower Power	Screams "personality"	Two, fixed Right sidebar		Red, white, blue
Fresh Bananas	Lack of yellow	Two, fixed Right sidebar		Blue, white, light
Green Marinée	Versatile	Two, fixed Right sidebar		Green, white, light
Hemingway	Staggered-column theme	Two, fixed	Custom colors Theme options	Black, dark
iNove	Stylish	Two, fixed Right sidebar	Theme options Translation-ready	White, light
Jentri	Vintage	Two, fixed Right sidebar		Red
Light	Tabbed navigation	Two, fixed Right sidebar		Blue, white, light
Ocadia	Rounded edges	Two, fixed Right sidebar		White, light
P2	Inspired by Twitter	Two, fixed Right sidebar	Front page post form	Blue, white, light
Quentin	Dignified	Two, fixed Right sidebar		Brown
Simpla	Minimal	Two, fixed Right sidebar		Light, white
Solipsus	Flowers	Two, fixed Left sidebar		Dark
Sunburn	Sidebar on home page	Two, fixed Right sidebar		Dark, black, orange

Table 3.4 Continued

Name	Description	Columns/Width	Other Features	Colors
Supposedly Clean	Simple	Two, fixed L or R sidebars	Theme options	Red, blue, green
Sweet Blossoms	Pink lovers	Two, fixed Right sidebar		Pink
The Journalist v1.3	Minimal	Two, fixed Right sidebar		White, light
The Journalist v1.9	Minimal	Two, fixed Right sidebar		White, light
Thirteen	Flora	Two, fixed Left sidebar		Green
Toni	Fluid	Two, fixed Right sidebar	Custom colors	Blue, white
Treba	Easy on the eyes	Two, fixed Right sidebar		Tan, light
Unsleepable	Monochrome	Two, fixed Right sidebar		White, light
Vermilion Christmas	Vivid	Two, fixed Left sidebar		Seasonal, green, red, holiday
White as Milk	Dairy	Two, fixed Left sidebar		White, light

Choosing a Theme

Making the decision as to what theme you want is difficult. The actual mechanics of choosing and implementing a theme, once you do know what you want, are easy.

WordPress even offers help in narrowing down the themes to those that meet your requirements by offering a Feature Finder, as mentioned earlier in this chapter. There's also a Popular link so you can see what other people are using.

For useful information on available themes in WordPress.com, also see:

- Article, Choosing a WordPress-dot-com theme:

  http://ourtimes.wordpress.com/2007/04/29/choosing-a-wordpresscom-theme/

- WordPress support page on themes:

  http://support.wordpress.com/themes/

 tip

If you want to avoid having your theme look like others', avoid the most popular themes, as well as the default theme, Kubrick, and themes that look a lot like it, such as Contempt.

Follow these steps to choose a theme:

1. Go to your blog's Administration area.

2. In the Appearance menu, choose the Themes subpanel. Your current theme is highlighted, and a set of 15 randomly chosen themes with options for browsing themes appears.

3. Click the Feature Filters link. The Feature Filter appears, as shown in Figure 3.5.

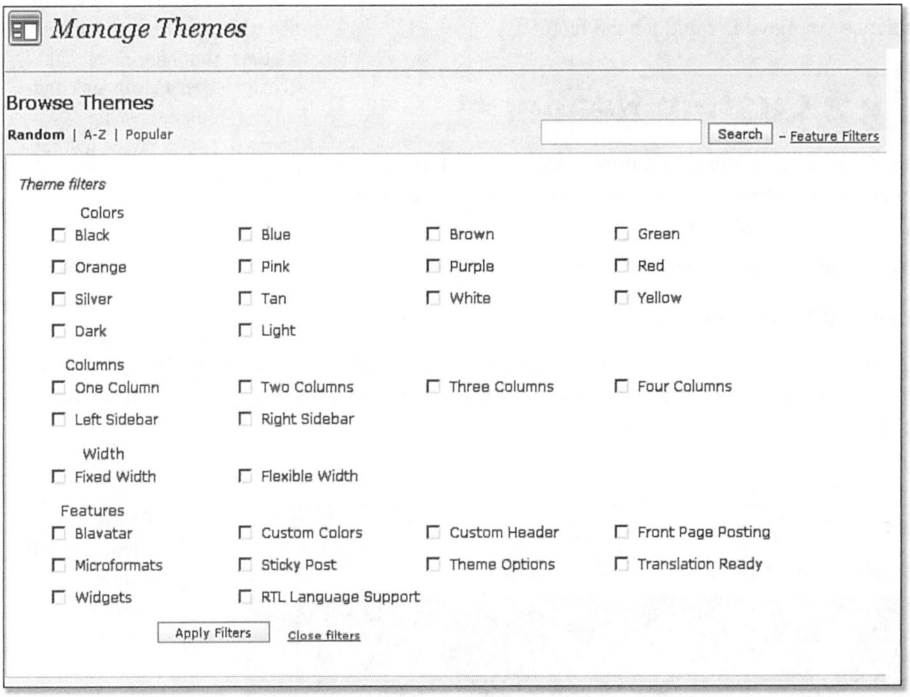

Manage Themes

Browse Themes
Random | A-Z | Popular   [Search] – Feature Filters

Theme filters

Colors
- ☐ Black   ☐ Blue   ☐ Brown   ☐ Green
- ☐ Orange   ☐ Pink   ☐ Purple   ☐ Red
- ☐ Silver   ☐ Tan   ☐ White   ☐ Yellow
- ☐ Dark   ☐ Light

Columns
- ☐ One Column   ☐ Two Columns   ☐ Three Columns   ☐ Four Columns
- ☐ Left Sidebar   ☐ Right Sidebar

Width
- ☐ Fixed Width   ☐ Flexible Width

Features
- ☐ Blavatar   ☐ Custom Colors   ☐ Custom Header   ☐ Front Page Posting
- ☐ Microformats   ☐ Sticky Post   ☐ Theme Options   ☐ Translation Ready
- ☐ Widgets   ☐ RTL Language Support

[Apply Filters]   Close filters

Figure 3.5
Filter features for finding fine themes.

4. Click the check box for each feature you want included in your set of themes. Each box you tick narrows the selection. If you check too many boxes, you might not get any themes on your list.

   The Left Sidebar and Right Sidebar check boxes specify whether, when a thin sidebar column for widgets is included, it is on the left or right of the main column that holds the blog post.

5. Click the Apply Filters button. A list of themes that fit your selected options appears.

> **caution**
> Don't click on the Back button in your browser while using the Feature Filters dialog box, or you'll return to the Administration area and have to start again.

6. Scan the results for interesting themes. To preview a theme, click the thumbnail of the theme or the Preview link.

7. To activate a theme—even if it's just an experiment—click the Activate link. The theme will be applied to your blog.

8. To change to a different theme, repeat steps 1–6.

Study your selected theme carefully to ensure that you like it, that it fits your blog's current and anticipated content, and that it fits the audience you have in mind for the blog.

tip

It's okay to cycle through a few themes in a few days while you're experimenting, and you can get blog visitors involved by asking them to comment on different looks. Once you make a choice, though, try to keep your theme stable for many months at a time. Your blog visitors get accustomed to a given look and feel and won't appreciate change if it seems to be just for the sake of change.

Changing a Custom Header

Short of modifying CSS, as described previously and in Chapter 12, the main customization option is to modify a custom header, if your theme makes this available.

Follow these steps to modify a custom header:

1. Go to your blog's Administration area.

2. In the Appearance menu, choose the Custom Header subpanel. The Your Header Image screen appears, showing your current header image, as shown in Figure 3.6. Note that you also have the option to reset your header image.

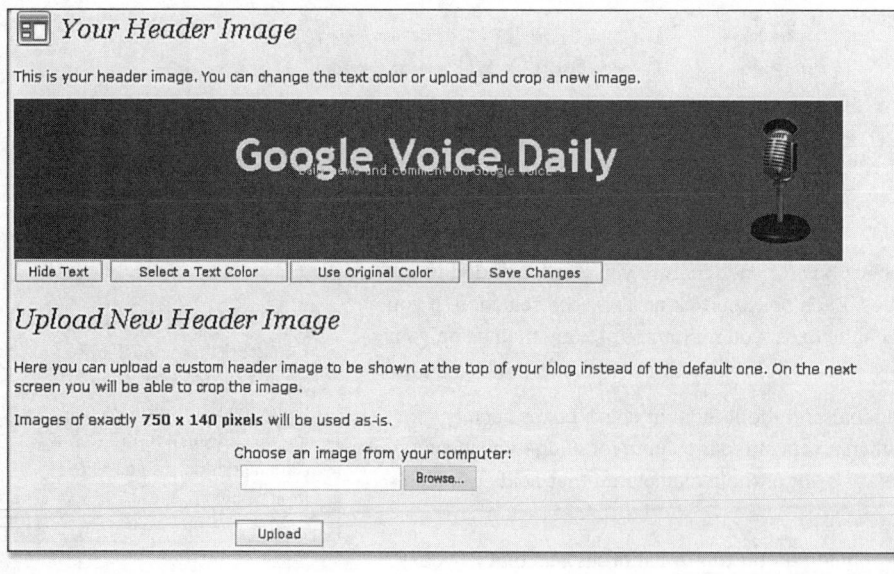

Figure 3.6
Give yourself a new (header) image.

3. Create a new header image and save it to disk. Note the image size given in the Upload New Header Image page and consider creating an image of exactly that size to avoid distortion (see the sidebar, "Creating a New Image for Yourself").

   Use a graphics program to create the new header image. One of us (Smith) uses Microsoft Paint for this kind of quick-and-dirty graphics work; the other (McCallister) uses Inkscape, an open source graphics editor. WordPress accepts a variety of graphics formats, but PNG is a good choice for any image that isn't a fairly large photograph. JPEG tends to distort text. If the image is a photograph, experiment with PNG and JPEG to see which gives you the best look in a reasonable file size.

4. Click the Choose File button. Navigate to the image you've created and upload it.

5. Change the text color using the Change Color button; this causes a color wheel to appear. Use the Original Color button to change the text color back to your theme's default. Use the Hide Text button to hide the text generated by WordPress so you can use text you've already placed in the image, or no text at all.

6. When you're happy with the result, click Save Changes.

Creating a New Image for Yourself

Creating a new header image is fun. Consider creating an image of exactly the size specified for this header. That way, you avoid distortion if an image is stretched or squeezed to fit the header area. (Distortion is worse if the image you create has to be stretched or squeezed more in either the horizontal or vertical dimension, rather than equally in both.)

To make your header image match the rest of your blog's appearance, consider using an eyedropper tool or similar tool to select one or more colors from your blog's theme. Use the captured color(s) in your header image.

Simple headers work best, as the header is overlaid by text that the user has to be able to read. A solid color or simple fade from one shade to another might be the best choice for most of the background. Our favorite trick is to find an image that fits the blog and add it to an otherwise simple header image. The image can be your picture or any other image relevant to the blog, and that you have the rights to use. This provides a visual signpost that the site visitor has come to the right place when they visit.

Save the overall image and its elements as you proceed so you can experiment further with them, or restore the header if you need to later.

Once you get the color and image right, experiment with different text colors. The color wheel in WordPress is awful and doesn't allow you to enter a specific color value. You'll want to experiment with colors in your graphics program, and then use the color wheel to re-create the color you've already chosen. Alternatively, hide the text that WordPress puts on the image and use text you've added in your graphics program instead.

Our experience is that time as we know it ceases to have any meaning when we start experimenting with graphics; hours just disappear. Keep your image simple and try not to spend too long on it; you might well find an early effort to be your best.

Changing mShots and Related Links

There are two extra features that WordPress has begun to include in every blog that have created a fair amount of controversy in the user community. This is largely because WordPress introduced these features without telling people, and with the default value set to On. Overnight, many people's blogs changed, and they weren't too happy about it.

The two features are mShots and Related Links:

- An mShot is a large thumbnail of the sites at the other end of a link. The thumbnail is too small to read, which is what would be necessary for it to be useful, but too large to easily ignore, blocking your view of the blog you're visiting.

- Related Links is a widget that automatically generates links to other WordPress blogs that are related. The algorithms that determine what other blogs are related don't work very well, so what this really is for most bloggers is a semirandom selection of other WordPress blogs.

If these features are turned on in your blog and you don't like them, you might want to turn them off. If they're turned off in your blog, you should turn them on long enough to experiment with them and see if they add value.

In their current form, we tend to side with those who find these features more intrusive than helpful. They also are both quite distinctive and mark your blog unmistakably, for better or worse, as a WordPress blog.

In the case of our main blogs, Notes from the Metaverse (open source code—McCallister) and Google Voice Daily (Google Voice news and views—Smith), we're trying to reach audiences that aren't necessarily WordPress-oriented, so we aren't seeking to have our blogs stand out in this way. However, given that these features are available, you should experiment with them and see if you want to use them yourself.

Follow these steps to turn Extras on or off:

1. Go to your blog's Administration area.

2. In the Appearance menu, choose the Extras subpanel. The Extras screen appears, as shown in Figure 3.7.

3. To enable mShots, check the Enable mShots Site Previews on This Blog check box. To disable mShots, clear the check box.

4. To disable Related Links, check the Hide Related Links on This Blog, Which Means This Blog Won't Show Up on Other Blogs Or Get Traffic That Way check box. (Yes, that's right, what you do to change the setting is the opposite of what you do for mShots.) To enable Related Links, clear the check box.

5. Click Update Extras to put the settings into effect.

caution

The check box for turning off the Related Links Extra uses confusing and somewhat ominous language: Hide Related Links on This Blog, Which Means This Blog Won't Show Up on Other Blogs Or Get Traffic That Way. The wording even suggests that normal links in your blog will be hidden.

All the wording really means is that, if you don't show the Related Links Extra in your blog, your blog won't show up in other people's Related Links Extra either. (It's hard to see how this exclusion benefits site visitors or bloggers, which should be the point of the whole exercise.)

However, the association between related blogs is usually weak enough that you aren't likely to get much traffic from Related Links anyway; both the Related Links on your site, and the link to your blog when it shows up as a Related Link on another site, are as likely to be a distraction as a help to blog visitors, so the warning shouldn't worry you much.

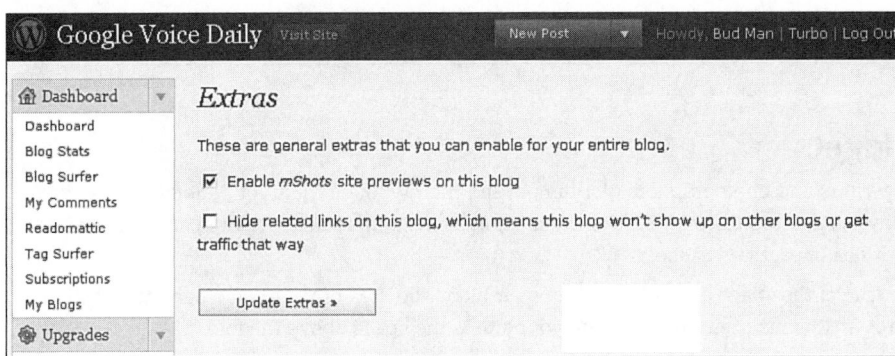

Figure 3.7
Decide if you want Extras.

Adding Available Widgets

As described earlier, a widget is a small piece of code that drives the content of a small boxed area in a sidebar of your blog. A widget has been described as a mini plug-in; plug-ins are potentially larger and more powerful pieces of code that cannot be used with WordPress.com blogs, only with the WordPress.org software.

As a WordPress.com user, nearly all of the themes you can choose are able to accommodate widgets, and most come with one or more already installed. For instance, the Contempt theme, shown with the blog Google Voice Daily in Figure 3.3 earlier in this chapter, includes the Archives, Categories, Links, and Meta widgets, making up part of the theme's personality.

As a WordPress.com user, you can easily add more widgets from the 25 or so that are available to WordPress.com users. WordPress.org software users have a choice of many more

 tip

As with themes, Automattic occasionally adds a new widget to those available for WordPress.com users. To see new additions, visit http://blog.wordpress.com and search the blog for "widget."

plug-ins, and can create their own. The way widgets are handled in WordPress.com versus the software available from WordPress.org is similar to the way themes are handled. Table 3.5 sums up the similarities and differences.

Table 3.5   Themes, Widgets, and Plug-ins in WordPress.com Versus WordPress.org

	WordPress.com	WordPress.org
Themes Available	About 70	About 1,000 free via Automattic, many more free and paid for
Modifying Themes	Modify available themes using CSS with CSS Extra (about $15/year)	Modify any theme or create a new one
Widgets Available	About 25	—
Modifying Widgets	Modify a few of the available widgets using HTML (free)	Modify any widget or create a new one
Plug-ins Available	—	Hundreds
Modifying Plug-ins	—	Modify any plug-in or create a new one

Placing Widgets

Newspaper writers and photographers glory in getting their work on the front page of the newspaper, especially if it's above the fold. This is the most eye-catching and important space in the entire newspaper. It has impact and cachet.

The same is true of the space above the fold in your blog. The area of your home page that's visible when a visitor first opens their browser onto your site is the space above the fold.

One of the primary attractions of blogs is that the latest and greatest new information always, automatically, goes in this prime spot. For your widgets, though, only a few can be above the fold, and only one can be in the most visible position at the very top.

Give some thought to the ordering of your widgets so the most important to users go highest. Don't order the widgets to please yourself—as your own most frequent site visitor, you'll always know where to find things. Think instead about your regular site visitors and what they're likely to need.

Preserving Existing Widgets

When you first choose a theme, it includes widgets. For instance, the initial theme for the Google Voice Daily blog, Contempt, includes four widgets:

- Archives, with links to each month's blog posts
- Categories, with links to the site's categories, in alphabetical order
- Links, the blogroll of blogs you would like your site visitors to check out
- Meta, links to administrative functions

The creator of the theme specifies the values for any data that goes with each widget. For instance, in Contempt, for the Links widget (titled "Blogroll"), the link name is shown, but not the link description or rating.

caution

When you visit the Widgets page for your blog, the widgets included in your blog do not show up in the sidebar area to which you drag widgets you want to add. If you add a widget to the sidebar, all the existing widgets are removed. You have to re-add them to the sidebar.

As soon as you add widgets to the sidebar, the widgets that were already there are removed from your blog. You have to re-add them if you want to keep them.

If you want to change the settings for a widget in your blog, you need to re-add it, and then set the values as you desire.

Adding New Widgets

From the perspective of a WordPress.com user using a theme that can accommodate widgets, there are three types of widgets:

- Widgets already built in to your theme and, therefore, already part of your blog.

- Additional widgets available to WordPress.com users (about 25 total). You can add any of these additional widgets to your blog. A few can be modified by using HTML and text. We describe these widgets in this section and tell you how to modify them in Chapter 9.

- Plug-ins, which are super-widgets, only available to WordPress.org users. WordPress.org users can choose from a much larger set of plug-ins available to WordPress.com users, modify any of them, and create their own as well.

Even though there are only about 25 widgets available to WordPress.com users—far less than the 70-odd themes to choose from—each one presents a separate "Nero" decision for you to make—yea or nay?

We've provided Table 3.6 (located in the next section) to help you decide. The table has a lot of information about each widget. However, although the table will help you eliminate many widgets from consideration, there will still be several that you won't be sure of. We suggest that you try adding the widgets you're not sure about to your blog (yes, all of them). Only then can you decide which ones you really want and delete the rest.

Having used trial and error, we further recommend that you consider as many additional rounds of trial and error as needed to settle on the right order for the widgets.

Here's how to add additional widgets to your WordPress.com blog, assuming your theme permits it (as nearly all do):

1. Begin by visiting your blog (from a user's point of view) and writing down the names and content of any widgets that are already part of your blog. You might want to capture a screenshot so you have a record of the status quo ante and to help you preserve the aspects you like as you make changes to your widgets. (See the following sidebar, "Capturing the Screen," for details.)

2. Go to your blog's Administration area.

3. In the Appearance menu, click Widgets. The available widgets are listed; see Table 3.6.

4. Drag a widget you might want to use into the Sidebar area to the right. If the widget can only be placed in your blog's sidebar(s) once, it disappears from the Available Widgets list and appears only in the Sidebar area. If the widget is able to be placed in the sidebar(s) multiple times— possibly with different option settings for each instance—it remains available in the Available Widgets list.

5. Enter any fields that need to be filled in for the widget, such as the Archives Title and Categories Title in the example shown in Figure 3.8. If the fields' contents make you reconsider, click the Remove link to remove the widget.

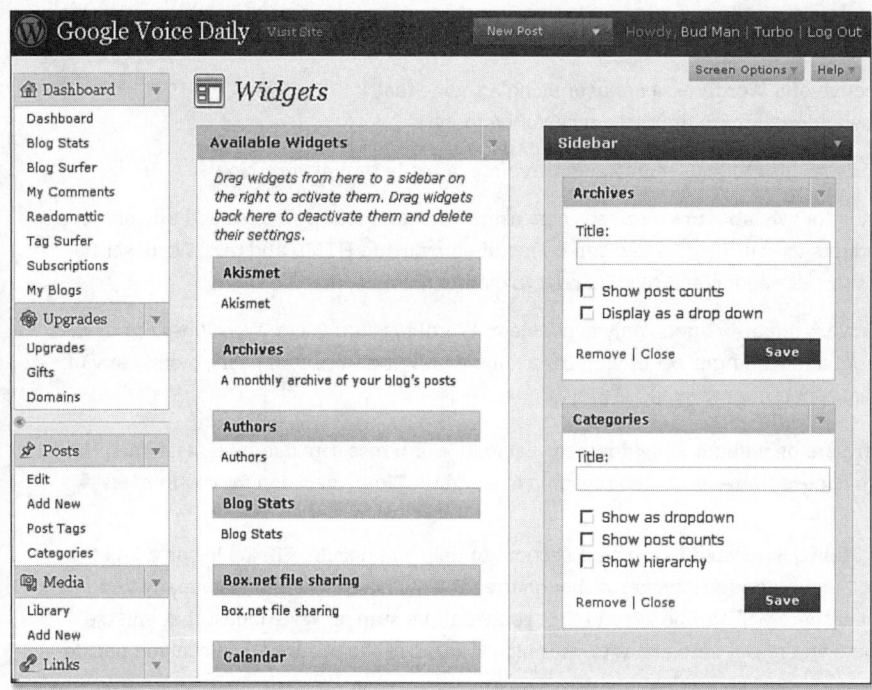

Figure 3.8
Specify how many posts per author.

6. Click the Save button to save any information you've entered.

7. Click the Close link to close the widget's entry fields.

8. Repeat steps 3 through 7 for as many additional widgets as you want to add.

9. To reorder the widgets, drag and drop them in the sidebar.

10. Click the Visit Site button to see how the widgets look on your site. Don't be surprised if you want to change some of the settings after viewing the widget in place. You might even want to change pre-existing data such as the name assigned to a category or contributor.

 **tip**

To place a widget last in the list, you have to drag it to a higher position first, until a spot opens up, marked by a dotted line. Then drag it down to the location you want.

> **⚜ caution**
> While adding widgets, don't use the Back and Forward buttons, and don't have multiple windows open at once with the Administration area in one and the current view of your blog in the other. If you do this, screen and even database updates might not keep up with you, and you might not get a true picture of what's going on.

11. To return to your Dashboard and continue making changes, choose the appropriate Dashboard (assuming you have more than one) from the My Dashboards menu. Repeat the preceding steps until you have the widgets you want, in the order you want them.

> **Capturing the Screen**
>
> To capture the screen in Windows, press the PrtSc key for the whole screen or Alt+PrtSc for the currently active window. (On many keyboards, in particular laptop keyboards, you might need to hold down the Function or Fn key to access the PrtSc capability, and Fn+Alt+PrtSc to capture the currently active window.)
>
> Capturing the screen copies the screen or window to the Windows Clipboard. You can then paste the Clipboard contents (Ctrl+V) into any program that can handle a Windows BMP file, such as Microsoft Paint, Microsoft Word, Adobe Photoshop, and so on, and then save the resulting image to a file.

A Brief Catalog of Widgets

The widget descriptions available for WordPress.com blogs, shown in the Widgets page in the Administration area, are quite limited. To properly design your blog, it's helpful to know in advance what the widgets are and what they do.

Tables 3.6 through 3.8 group the widgets into three categories:

- **Blog-specific links** (Table 3.6)—Most of the widgets take information from within your blog and make it available to your blog visitors.

- **Social media links** (Table 3.7)—Several widgets help you tie other social media where you have an account into your blog. For instance, Facebook seems prominent in the list of social media links by its absence; perhaps a widget for Facebook is on the way.

- **Power tools** (Table 3.8)—A few widgets bring in enhanced capabilities from other sites; the RSS and Text widgets are highly customizable.

The number of widgets available is a bit deceptive. You don't want to add too many to your blog; they'll distract from it and confuse your users. Also, there are only a few prominent positions near the top; widgets farther down are likely to be little-used. So be selective.

However, you can do a lot with widgets, and it's worth thinking carefully about which ones you want to use and experimenting with different ones, and with their positions.

Table 3.6   Blog-Specific Links Enhance Your Site

Widget	Functionality	Settings	Copies
Akismet	Spam statistics	N/A	No
Archives	Links to your posts, one link per month	Title, Show post counts, Displays a drop-down	Yes
Authors	Links to your posts, one link per author	Title, Show x posts per author, Avatar size	No
Blog Stats	Total site visits	Title, Label: "hits" or your entry	No
Calendar	Links to your posts, one link per calendar day	Title	Yes
Categories	Links to your posts, one link per category	Title, y/n for dropdown, post counts, hierarchy	Yes
Category Cloud	Links to your posts per category in a cloud	Title, # categories, font sizes	No
Gravatar	Show your Gravatar image	Title, user, Size, alignment, URL, description	Yes
Links	Your blogroll of sites you recommend	Y/N to show all links, image, name, description, rating	Yes
Meta	Log in/out, admin, feed and WordPress links	Title	Yes
Pages	Your blog's WordPress Pages	Title, sort order, exclude specific pages	Yes
Recent Comments	Links to recent comments	Title, # comments, avatar size or none, colors	No
Recent Posts	Links to recent posts	Title, # posts	No
Search	Search your blog	Title	Yes
Tag Cloud	Links to your posts per tag in a cloud	Title	No
Top Clicks	Links to popular clicks on your blog	Title, display length, # URLs to show	No
Top Posts	Links to popular posts on your blog	Title, # posts to show	No

Table 3.7   Social Media Links Bring Your Online Life Together

Widget	Functionality	Settings	Copies
del.icio.us	Tie your blog to your del.icio.us account	Title, your login, # links, bookmarks	No
Flickr	Photos from your Flickr account	Title, Flickr RSS URL, # photos	No
Meebo	Allow IM chats among you and your users	Find and paste HTML code	No
Twitter	Display your tweets from Twitter	Title, username, # tweets, show replies, default text	Yes

Table 3.8 Additional Functionality Is Always Welcome

Widget	Functionality	Settings	Copies
Box.net file share	Link to downloadable files for site visitors	Width, Height of box	No
Platial MapKit	Mapping tool for your blog users	Paste MapCode	No
RSS	Entries from any RSS or Atom feed	Feed URL, title, # items, y/n to show content, author, date	Yes
SocialVibe	Tie your blog to one of dozens of charities	Choose charity	No
Text	Flexible "canvas" for text, links, and/or other HTML	Title, text/HTML block, paragraphs y/n	Yes
Vodpod Videos	Your users can watch web videos on your blog	Paste HTML code, enable widescreen player	No

Getting the Most Out of Widgets

Widgets were only introduced to WordPress.com in 2007 and many blogs underuse them. They just let the space taken up by the sidebar sit there, not doing anything.

Widgets are a great addition to WordPress.com, and the concept has been a spur to development using the software available from WordPress.org as well. There are at least a few widgets that can be considered must-haves, especially as your blog grows:

- **Archives** or **Calendar**—Archives lumps your posts together, one month's entries per link; Calendar shows the posts per day. In a typical blog, with postings every day or two, Archives is great for helping track your posts over time and to get a quick feel for the blog's progress; as the month-by-month links accumulate, your blog develops a visible history. Calendar is a great alternative for a busy blog with more than one post a day.

- **Categories**, **Category Cloud**, **Tag Cloud**, **Search**—These are all connections into your posts by concept or keyword, using the orderly structure of categories, the more will-o'-the-wisp flavor of tags, or the raw power of search. (Tag clouds are trendy and a fun addition to your blog.)

- **Links/Blogroll**—These are almost a must-have for blogs that depend greatly on other blogs for content and commentary—that is, for most blogs.

- **Meta**—Meta is great for managing your blog. It allows you (and any collaborators) to log in to your Dashboard from the blog front page.

- **Pages**—Pages acts as a navigation bar you can edit, a must if you have more than a few pages.

- **Recent Comments**—We hate to tell you this, but many blog visitors will find the comments on your site more interesting than your posts. This widget is great if you get a reasonable number of comments, and is likely to encourage more.

- **Top Posts**—It might seem vain to put up your own Hall of Fame, but this is a great entry for new visitors to use—especially if your site is gaining in popularity and bringing in lots of them. (You can do something similar with the Text widget instead; it's more work, but you can choose, order, and even describe the links.)

Note that these widgets are all from the Blog-Specific Links category; that's because the key to a blog is always your posts (plus visitors' comments, if you're lucky enough to have them). Tools that organize your posts, help people get to the best ones, and see which ones are related to each other are all powerful additions to your blog.

Widgets that tie your blog to social media are great for any kind of social media that you're active in, and where your blog and your social media use are related. If they're unrelated, you might help your blog users more by leaving the widget out.

The widgets we describe as power tools are good if they fit the spirit of your blog. As with social media widgets, you can overdo them if they don't fit what you're trying to do in your blog—to the extent that you never figure this out precisely!

There are two widgets, though, that are special:

- **RSS**—This widget takes RSS feeds from anywhere on the Web and brings them into your blog. A good set of RSS feeds can be even more valuable than your postings! For instance, the climate change blog Climate Ark has an RSS feed of headlines, shown in Figure 3.9, that's among the best around for its topic and is widely used.

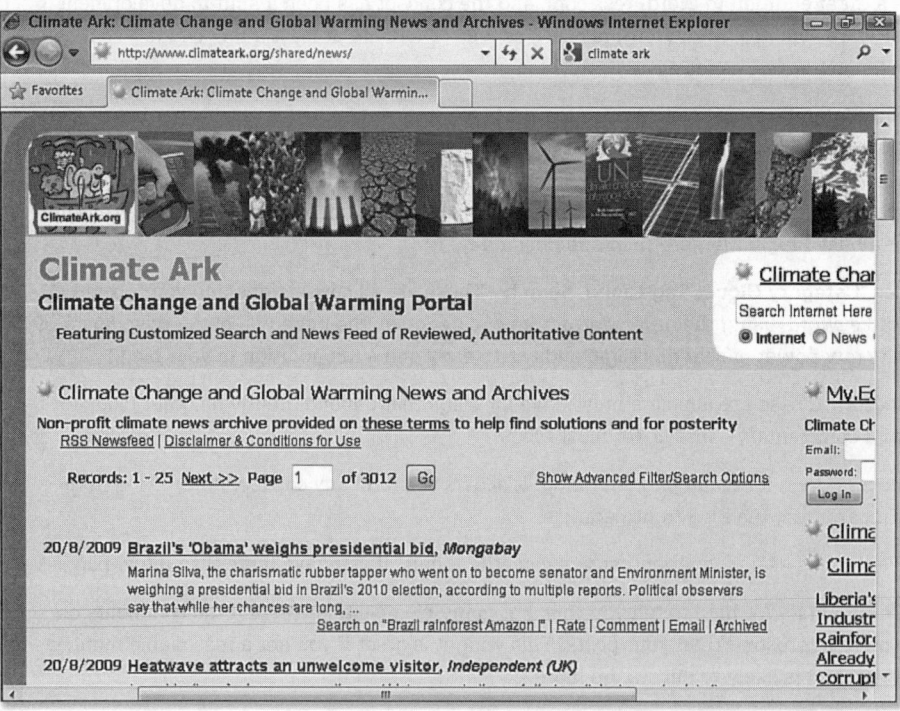

Figure 3.9
Climate Ark has a famous RSS feed.

- **Text**—This is the ultimate power tool among widgets, as it's highly customizable indeed. You can even use it as a form of very short blog posting, updating it every day.

Both of these widgets support multiple copies, so you can take them as far as your imagination will go. If you start making extensive use of one or both of these widgets, some of those two-sidebar themes start to look pretty good!

RUNNING YOUR BLOG

IN THIS PART

CREATING YOUR FIRST POST

What Is a Blog Entry?

A blog entry is a separate posting to your blog. Blog entries, also known as posts, are the core of blogging. They can be composed sitting at your computer, sent in by email (see Chapter 2, "Starting Your Blog Right"), or even, using third-party tools, sent in via text message or transcribed from a voice message.

Functionally, a blog entry can be as short or as long as you want. Your blog visitors will expect a complete thought of at least a few sentences, though a "coming soon" announcement or a quick update can be briefer.

If there's any such thing as a typical blog post, it's about the length of a newspaper editorial, six to eight paragraphs of a few sentences each. Much longer posts are all too common, but are often a misuse of the medium and unlikely to be read by some of your visitors.

We recommend that you include images in your posts as often as possible. Using images in your posts is described in Chapter 6, "Using HTML in Your Widgets and Blog." Some large blogs require contributors to include at least one image per post. The result is that the blog is much more interesting and evocative to visitors than a blog with few or no images. If the image is for general, illustrative purposes, you don't even need to reference it explicitly in the text.

Including audio and video in your posts is quite different and there's a lot to consider. There's a difference between linking to audio or video in your post because it's relevant to your theme versus focusing your posts on audio and video, creating and being responsible for the content yourself. We delve into the details of using audio and video in Chapter 10, "Adding Upgrades, Audio, and Video."

Just as no man is an island, at least according to the poet John Donne, no blog posting stands alone. It holds a place in a series of posts, and you tag and categorize it as well. (Tagging and categorizing your posts in a clear and useful way is key to making them searchable and usable.)

WordPress also supports a powerful commenting capability for posts. You can turn comments off, but this misses half the point of blogging. There is even commentary in the blogosphere holding that a blog without comments isn't really a blog. Tagging and categorization, along with comments, is described in Chapter 5, "Taking Posts Further."

The steady accumulation of postings and comments is the entire point of blogging. We encourage you to become an expert at posting, which is described in this chapter. You should use WordPress's many capabilities, and all your own skills, to make your posts interesting and useful to your blog visitors. The ability of your posts to attract interesting and useful comments, in turn, is a hallmark of a successful blog.

We will say about posting what was famously once said about voting: Post often and early. Improve your posts, even after they're published. Then improve tagging and categorization continually. Respond to comments that need a response and make an effort to encourage comments as well.

Why Keep Posts Short?

There can hardly be a more controversial question in blogging than the ideal or acceptable length for a post. However, we can begin with several known facts.

Reading from the screen is much harder than reading from a printed page, so people tend to scan or skim instead. Also, research shows that the average person spends about two minutes looking at a story, article, or video clip before moving on, unless they're very interested and not very busy. Also, the average person reads from the screen at about 200 words per minute. (This sidebar is about 200 words long.)

These facts indicate that you can expect someone who's interested in, but not completely enthralled by, your topic to read about 400 words onscreen before moving on. Graphics help attract attention initially, and "chunkifying" your text—using headers, bullets, and so on—might refresh the reader's willingness to continue on farther into your post.

Two more facts: Twitter, the popular new tool for micro-blogging, has a limit of 140 characters, about 20 words, per tweet; text messages on mobile phones, even more popular, are limited to 160 characters, about 25 words. Whatever people's tolerance for long blog posts has been in the past, it's probably decreasing rather than increasing—especially among younger people who tweet and text a lot.

Using the QuickPress Tool

QuickPress is the quick-and-dirty posting tool for WordPress. It occupies a small corner of the Dashboard and is best used for posts with few HTML features and very little in the way of images or multimedia. (You can use these items in QuickPress, but you won't be able to see what you're doing very well. As a result, the quality of the post might suffer.)

Use QuickPress, as shown in Figure 4.1, for jotting down a quick thought or bringing in a media item for later editing before you publish. You can even use it to post a "coming soon" note for your blog that you then delete when you post a full entry. (You can edit the "coming soon" note into a complete entry.)

Figure 4.1
Use QuickPress to get a draft into your queue of work or to quickly add a brief post to your blog.

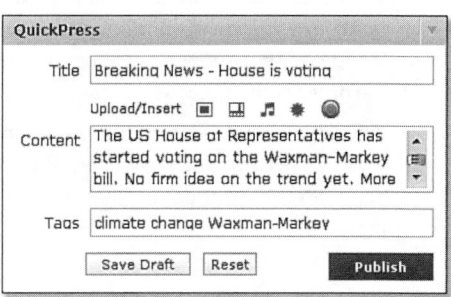

Posting with QuickPress from the Dashboard is easy:

1. Enter the title. Entering an interesting and entertaining title is always worth a bit of thought, even if you're in a hurry.

2. Enter the text.

3. Add any images or multimedia. For any but the simplest media nugget, you should probably be working in the full Add New Post/Edit Post editing area.

4. Enter tags. Always tag posts carefully; they give your post legs for future reuse and help with search engines. See Chapter 5.

5. Click Save Draft to capture your entry for later rework or Publish to put it straight on the Web.

As you will have seen if you've used WordPress before, QuickPress not only gives you very little room to work, it also lacks several elements of the full Add New Post/Edit Post area. Its most important deficits include the following:

- **Spell checking**—If you commonly misspell, this alone might be a stopper for you.

- **HTML tools**—You can't easily access HTML features, such as bulleted text, bolding, or linking, and there is no mode for viewing HTML-tagged text.

- **Access to categorization**—Although there is a strip for tagging, there's no list of categories to assign your post to.

- **Direct switching into a larger-screen mode**—You have to Save Draft or Publish before you can access your post in regular editing mode or Full-Screen mode.

 **note**

Using QuickPress is like writing the short, highly formatted poems called haiku: You use the constraints involved to create something that's better because it's appropriate to the tool. Learn to use QuickPress when you need to get a short, punchy post entered and saved as a draft or published; that's its purpose.

The QuickPress tool has a more subtle deficit with regard to screen space. It's positioned on the Dashboard page in such a way that you need to have the Dashboard almost filling the width of your screen to use the QuickPress area, small though it is. Blogs are very connected to other web content, though, and you might want to have a web page or a document, even the currently live version of your blog, open next to the Dashboard. Using two or more windows together is easier when using one of the other editing modes.

tip

If you don't use QuickPress often, you can hide it. In the Dashboard page, just click on the title bar that says QuickPress to contract or expand the QuickPress area.

You can switch between QuickPress and the larger editing areas by saving a draft, then opening it. If you have to do this right away, it just means you wasted time going into QuickPress in the first place. So only start out in QuickPress if you mean to finish your thought, save or publish it, and move on.

Adding a New Post

The main tool for creating and posting a blog entry is the Add New Post page, which is the same as the Edit Post page except for the title. We'll refer to both as the Add New Post page for simplicity's sake, but be aware you'll be using the same page for editing posts too.

The Add New Post page gives you access to all the powerful tools of the WordPress.com site, including spell checking, HTML-based text formatting, linking, and more.

Entering, formatting, and revising text in the main Add New Post page is the core activity in most WordPress blogging. We assume that you've entered text before and formatted it in a word processor. However, we don't assume that you have web publishing experience. WordPress is a web publishing tool that works in a closely managed environment, so learning about it means learning about web publishing.

The Add New Post page comes in two versions. The version that you get to first is the version shown in Figure 4.2, with the post integrated into a WordPress page with the Dashboard and other capabilities available. These additional features make the page like a workbench crowded with tools: There's plenty of stuff handy, but not much actual room to work.

The image and text in the figure are a good example. The image takes up about half the space, so only 25 words of the text show. Even if you scroll down in the post so the image is offscreen, only about 60 words show at a time.

Thankfully, the Add New Page screen also comes in a full-screen version. To reach it, you simply click the Full-Screen Mode button, called out in Figure 4.2.

note

The layout of the main WordPress web page is a bit frustrating. If you make the browser window narrow, the work area in the middle is squeezed to a narrow column, preserving the less-used functionality on the sides. Other web pages preserve the width of the central viewing or working area and allow extra stuff in the rail, as it's called, on the right, to disappear first. The way WordPress does it means you need to use WordPress in a wide browser window, hopefully on a wide screen as well. You can never have too much screen space when working on your blog in WordPress.

Figure 4.2
Using Add
New Post in
a crowded
WordPress
page is
tricky.

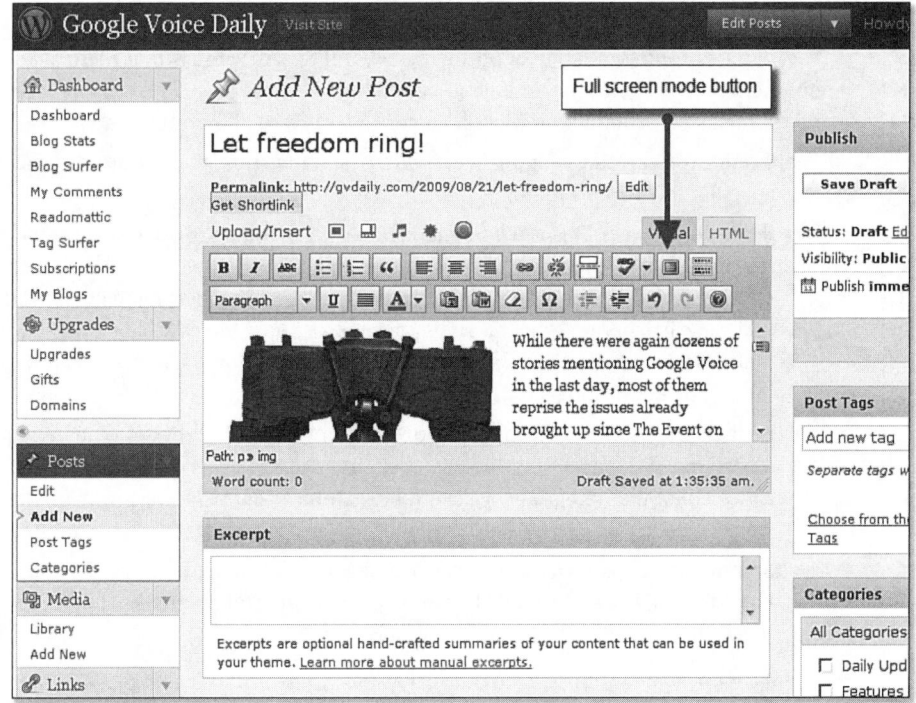

We describe how to create or edit a post next, and we assume you'll be doing most of your work in Full-Screen mode. This not only allows us to focus on the screen where you're likely to do most of your work, but it also allows us to focus only on the functions directly related to getting your post written and edited. The other capabilities, such as tagging and categorizing your post, are only available in the Add New Post area that shares the screen with the Dashboard and other WordPress functionality.

 tip

We recommend that you avoid doing anything except light work on the Add New Post/Edit Post page when the Dashboard and so forth is showing. The constrained space limits your imagination as well as your ability to get things done and can contribute to errors in your posts, accidentally deleting text, or other disasters.

Tools for Posting

Part of the joy and frustration of becoming a WordPress devotee is that there are so many tools out there that can help you—the good news—that it's hard to find just the right one—the bad news. This is particularly true when it comes to tools for editing your posts.

That's right: You can edit your posts elsewhere, and then post them to WordPress. A few of the most-popular tools are as follows:

- **Press This**—Press This is a bookmarklet, a small addition to your browser. When you're surfing the Web and find something of interest, highlight it, then open Press This. It opens up a small WordPress post window with the selected text already copied in and with tags and categories available. Apply any finishing touches and post the new blog entry—or save it as a draft for later rework. You can find information about Press This in the WordPress Codex at http://codex.wordpress.org/Press_It.

- **ScribeFire**—ScribeFire is an extension only for the Firefox browser. One of us (McCallister) is a big Firefox aficionado—it's open source, don'tcha know—and a big ScribeFire user as well. It's a nice editor that integrates well with blogs from either WordPress.com or WordPress.org and makes creating links easy. For more information, visit www.scribefire.com.

- **Smartphone apps**—WordPress has useful apps for posting from the iPhone and BlackBerrys, possibly with more to come. Check the applications store or market for your smartphone for these and possibly other WordPress tools.

There are many other tools, some of which work with WordPress.com blogs, others that work only for blogs based on WordPress.org. If you search online for one or more of the preceding tools, you'll find references to many more as well.

Working on Posts in Full-Screen Mode

Once you click the Full-Screen Mode button, your post appears in a window that, as the name implies, fills the screen area almost entirely with the editing window. A post in the full-screen area is shown in Figure 4.3.

Note that, even with a large image included, a great deal of text shows. In Full-Screen mode on a medium-resolution screen, before adding any images, about 400 words can be shown—enough for many typical blog posts. This is more than six times as many words as you see in the normal Add New Post window described in the previous section.

In Full-Screen mode, you can also more easily narrow the Add New Post window, while still maintaining context, and align another window—perhaps a document window for copying and pasting your own work, or a browser window for reference—beside it. Even in the narrowed Full-Screen mode editing window, you can see perhaps 200 words, enough to give you valuable context.

Figure 4.3
Using Add New
Post in Full-Screen
mode is easier.

While there were again dozens of stories mentioning Google Voice in the last day, most of them reprise the issues already brought up since The Event on Friday. There were just a few interesting and new comments on Google Voice itself, net neutrality and the role of the computing industry.

Orlando Sentinel: Review: Let freedom ring with Google Voice

Blogger and newspaper writer Etan Horowitz gives a detailed review of Google Voice, which he's used since GrandCentral days. He describes the service as allowing you to put a "virtual wall around yourself", including screening your calls and blocking some people completely. He identifies convincing people to contact you on a new number as the biggest hurdle to using Google Voice, along with making your Google Voice number show up in the Caller ID of people you're talking to. He concludes that "Google Voice is worth it for most people, especially the self-employed, business travelers and students".

My take: A good description, except for leaving out cheap international calls from a landline or, particularly, a cell phone.

PC World: Inevitable: Apple Should Accept Google Voice

Well-known tech journalist David Coursey calls on Apple and AT&T to let customers have Google Voice. He cites their "user-hostile" policies and how AT&T could begin to repair its image. He also describes how the companies have "already lost big in the court of public opinion" and have much more to lose as the FCC proceeds. This follows an useful earlier summary of where the Obama FCC is going.

Coursey cites the App Store problems and the iPhone's lack of multitasking as key weaknesses. He also points out that, at this point, there aren't many good alternatives. Palm Pre is only just emerging, still with a weak selection of apps. Android is

Working in HTML

The Full-Screen mode for adding and editing posts, which we recommend in this chapter as your primary tool, does not include access to the underlying HTML code of your page. You can only use the HTML tab in the more restricted view available in the Shared-Screen mode. This is particularly restrictive for working in HTML, which requires lots of screen space for you to see enough code and text to figure out what's going on. For HTML editing, you might want to work in a separate HTML editor and then cut and paste the result into WordPress—a clumsy process, but possibly the best choice.

The WordPress.com site that you use for blogs hosted by WordPress has many advantages, but support for working directly in HTML is not one of them. In fact, WordPress.com is intended to make life easier for those who *don't* want to work in HTML. Chapters 7 and 8, "Adding Features to Your Blog," and "Tracking Statistics and Bringing In Visitors," respectively, describe how to use HTML in WordPress.com when needed, but if you are skilled in HTML and want to use your knowledge, you might be better off using the WordPress software directly.

See Chapter 1, "Getting Started with WordPress," for more on the difference between WordPress.com and WordPress software. See Chapter 11, "Installing and Upgrading WordPress Software," and subsequent chapters for information on downloading and using the WordPress software.

Using Basic Formatting Commands

WordPress makes it easy for you to use core HTML formatting commands. It only allows you to use a small subset of the formatting commands that are available in a full-featured word processor such as Microsoft Word. It doesn't allow you to do page layout at all. (You can try, but your page layouts will look ugly in the highly formatted WordPress themes, and the specific "look" you tried so hard to achieve will break down in different browsers and on various devices.)

The point, though, is not to think about what WordPress *can't* do, but about what it *can* do. The following list describes the core formatting capabilities, all HTML-based, that WordPress makes available to you:

- **B** **I** **ABC** **Bold, italic, and strikethrough**—Use these simple text formatting commands judiciously, but use them.

- **Bulleted lists and numbered lists**—These are usually displayed in a somewhat ugly way in a web browser, but are still very important for breaking up long blocks of text, as we've done in this book.

- **Blockquotes**—Blockquotes are usually displayed in an ugly way in web browsers as well, but they're an accepted way to call out quoted text.

- **Left-, center-, and right-justification**—Most text in web pages is left-justified, also called "ragged right," as is the text in this book. Centered text is good for captions. Right-justified text is often used to set out a comment or for attempts at complicated page layouts.

That's it: nine options, the entire set of commonly used HTML formatting commands that WordPress makes available in its main formatting menu.

Even among this limited set of commands, blogs traditionally don't use all of them. The name *Word*Press is no accident—bloggers tend to take their cues from traditional newspaper and magazine journalists, who use words, not formatting or images, as their tool for communicating.

Traditional journalists often submit their stories in text form and don't see how the story will look when laid out until after the story is published. Just think: Highly paid, famous journalists have less control than you do in WordPress!

Why do bloggers use even the limited formatting available in HTML so little? The reasons vary. Using **bold**, along with using ALL CAPS, is often considered to be shouting by bloggers. *Italic* looks better in print than on computer screens, due to screens' low resolution. ~~Strikethrough~~, however, is sometimes seen in blogs, where it has developed an ironic use (see the Tip describing strikethroughs in the section "Using Hyperlinks as Formatting," later in this chapter).

In blogs, bulleted lists are used rarely—too rarely, we would say—and numbered lists are often reserved for numbered steps, which are rare in blogging. Blockquotes are common, though they could be used more, given how much blogs refer to other texts.

As for the three types of justification (left-, center-, and right-justification), most blogs are left-justified (ragged right), unlike a lot of print journalism, which is usually fully justified, with both left and right margins flush.

Using ragged right for blogs and full justification for print makes sense from the respective perspectives, if you'll excuse the unintentional rhyme. A blog is displayed on a computer screen, and fully justified text on a low-resolution screen tends to have gaps that are too large and clump into ugly runs down through a block of text.

In print, where higher resolution is the norm and where the reader has often paid for the newspaper or magazine in question, a high-quality appearance is achieved by using the more formal full justification. (However, you can also see large gaps between words and runs of whitespace in newspapers, which have narrow columns and relatively low resolution—the least friendly form of print for full justification.)

The limited width of the page available in a WordPress blog, the limited length that your blog posts should assume, and the wide variety of ways that web pages are read are all arguments for simplicity. Content is king; formatting is secondary and supportive. It should never be the point.

However, to say that formatting is secondary and supportive is not to say that you shouldn't use it at all. Many bloggers complain about the limited formatting options available to them on the Web in general, and in WordPress in particular—and then underuse the ones that are indeed available and handy. Try to use the formatting that is available to make your blog posts easier to scan, for readers who are so inclined, and more interesting and rewarding when read carefully.

Why HTML Matters in Posts

We discuss Hypertext Markup Language (HTML) extensively in Chapter 8, but we also need to briefly mention its role in WordPress.com-based sites here. This is so you understand the capabilities as well as the limitations of WordPress.com better.

WordPress.com is one of the most powerful and effective sites around for creating and publishing web pages. It achieves this power in part by limiting you to existing themes, which are adapted to blog posts as the main content. The capabilities and limitations of HTML, the underlying language of web pages, are very much in evidence within WordPress.

The reason you can easily do certain kinds of text formatting—headings, bolding, and bullets, for example—is that these are the ones that are supported right in the core of HTML. The reason you can't do many other kinds of formatting, and the reason you can't achieve precise positional control of text and graphics in your blog entries and blog pages, is because HTML doesn't support it.

By using core HTML, your blog entries can be viewed on a very wide range of devices, from cell phones to screen readers for the blind. You can surpass these limitations using HTML code that you add in yourself (see Chapter 9, "Adding Graphics to Your Posts"), WordPress software rather than a WordPress.com blog, and more advanced formatting capabilities such as CSS (Cascading Style Sheets), but your pages then won't be as easy to create, nor able to be viewed usefully on as many devices, as WordPress.com blog pages.

The purpose of using the WordPress.com site is to allow you to concentrate on your blog's content plus some rough formatting, and then let the finer points of formatting take care of themselves.

An Example of Text Formatting

This book uses many formatting elements that are the same as, or similar to, the core HTML set mentioned here. In particular, we use a combination of bolding and bullets to present some ideas in easy-to-identify chunks that draw your eye to topics of interest.

One difference between print and the Web is who decides how things look. For a book like this one, a book designer and others will have thought long and hard about exactly how a bulleted list, for instance, should look, and adjusted the layout down to the point—a printer's measurement that's been standardized at 1/72nd of an inch.

On the Web, HTML only specifies what formatting to put in; each specific web browser has its own rules for how the formatting looks. It seems to us that some initial decisions got made in a hurry for the first browsers that were created, and then copied in other browsers over time for the sake of backward compatibility. The result is not very pretty.

How do these elements look in a WordPress blog? Figure 4.4 shows one example, from the news roundup, a regular feature in the gvDaily.com blog maintained by one of the authors (Smith).

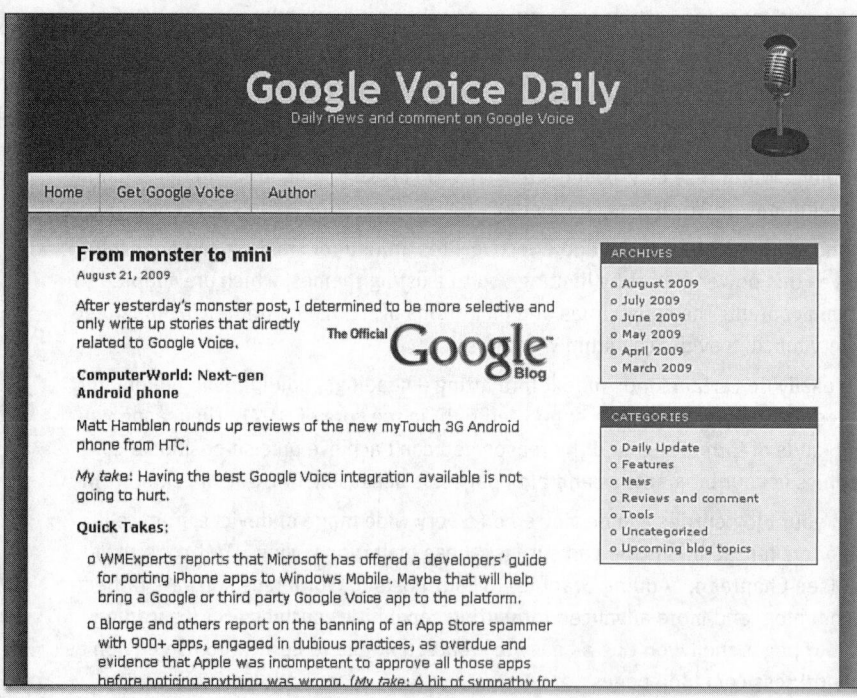

Figure 4.4
Real blogs use (simple) formatting.

The blog's header comes from the WordPress theme, and is about the right size relative to the text. (Some HTML headers are way too large relative to the normal text size.) To highlight different stories, the blog uses a formatted combination of text and links, both in bold. Although the links offer the ability to click away, the formatting and content seek to give the reader the gist so as to keep them onsite most of the time.

In gvDaily's news roundup postings, links are used to support key points and to support key reader goals, such as a link for military people to get a special invitation to join Google Voice. Although those readers might well follow the link, it pops up in a new window. The blog, remaining onscreen in its own window, invites readers to continue reading after they've signed up. (Some web users hate this kind of nannying, though; "I know where the Back button is," they might say if asked.)

At the point in the post where the reader might be expected to get tired of reading, the posting concludes with Quick Takes, an area of brief bulleted highlights with less formatting. This is a way of telling the reader, "just bear with us a little longer." Again, the links are meant to be supportive of the content rather than distracting from it.

If you lack experience in using HTML-style formatting such as that used in the example, it can be very useful to try using it yourself, even in a made-up example, and keep the result handy for reuse.

Using Hyperlinks as Formatting

Hyperlinks, or links for short, are familiar to you from your own use of the Web. As a blog author, though, it's worth considering the link options that WordPress gives you.

You can:

- Link any text you want to any web page by entering its URL in WordPress.

- Have the link take the user to a new location in the same window or open up a new window, which leaves the current blog post onscreen.

- Add text that's shown when the user hovers their mouse over the link, giving an additional clue about the destination.

WordPress takes a tremendous amount of hassle and worry out of the process of creating and maintaining links. Creating links and keeping them up to date is much harder in many web page creation packages, or when working directly in HTML, than it is in WordPress.

We discuss the use of links in detail later in this chapter. However, because of the way people's visual systems work, and because of their experience in using the Web, links serve as a kind of formatting as well.

Links are displayed in underlining and in a different color than other text—usually blue for unvisited links and purple for recently visited ones. (The most common definition of *recently visited* is within the last 30 days.) Underlining is traditionally used for emphasis in other forms of publishing, as is color (when the budget allows for it); the way in which links combine underlining with colored text ensures that links jump to the reader's attention.

Evidence has also been gathered by testing people as they surf the Web. Web surfers are always on the lookout for answers and for novelty. It's said that the most powerful words in marketing are

 tip

Use strikethough to carry off an Internet-friendly form of ironic humor. Simply write something very direct or pointed, apply strikethrough to the strongest word or words, and then add some words that are gentler or more politically correct. This makes it look as if you'd edited yourself, or been edited by someone higher-up, and forgotten to take out the original wording. An example: "The reasoning behind my boss's decision was, as usual, ~~incomprehensible~~ sophisticated."

"new" and "free;" web surfers are always looking for new information and free answers to their questions and concerns.

Links catch the eye and offer the reader (*your* reader) escape to something that might be better—more interesting factually, more attractive to look at, more authoritative—than your blog. Many readers initially scan a web page by looking at headings, figures, captions, bullets, and links. If nothing grabs them, they don't bother to read further; instead, they surf on to another page.

So links are a two-edged sword. Pages with no links look boring and might quickly be left behind. Pages with lots of links to different destinations encourage the kind of restless prowling that makes up much of web surfing.

So use links to help maintain your readers' interest, visually and in terms of substance, and to support the points you're making in your blog. Link to supporting evidence. Don't think of it as linking away; think of it as linking in support, in a way that's more likely to bring readers back to your blog.

Using Secondary Formatting Commands

WordPress offers a second row of formatting commands beneath the first row of buttons. The commands in the second row are either less useful in most WordPress blogs, less well-supported in HTML, or both.

This second row of options opens up if you click the last button in the first row of formatting commands. WordPress calls this the Kitchen Sink button. Click it once to make the second row of formatting commands appear; click it again to make them disappear.

Here are the Kitchen Sink formatting commands, along with the reasons why they're not in the first set of options:

- **Format**—These special formats, which apply to a whole line of text at a time, specify paragraphs, addresses, preformatted text, and six levels of headings. The only ones commonly used on web pages are headings, but most blog posts should be too short to need headings within them. However, for long posts, of say 10 paragraphs or more, adding a couple of low-level headings is a good idea. (Editing rules say you should never have just one heading of a given level.)

  As for the other choices, it's good to use preformatted text for quoted instructions and other special uses.

- **Underline**—Underlining is great in print, but when used online, people think it means a hyperlink. Avoid using it in your blog for anything except hyperlinks.

- **Full justification** (flush left and flush right)—Computer screens are low resolution, so the spacing added to achieve fully justified margins tends to show up as ugly gaps or even distracting "rivers" of white space coursing downward through a block of text. Full justification also has a formal or professional connotation that's contradictory to the friendly feel of blogging. So, full justification is not a very useful format for blogs.

- **Text color**—Using color for your text might sound like a good idea at the time, but it tends to make text harder to read and reduces the multiplatform accessibility of web text. Also, web users are used to having text color as an indicator of linked text, so using text color for other purposes will confuse them.

- **Custom characters**—HTML has specific support for special characters such as the registered trademark symbol and ampersands. Use these, but each for its intended purpose, not as a kind of do-it-yourself formatting. Please.

In addition to the first group of commands, there is another pair of buttons you can use:

-  **Outdent**—Outdent reverses indenting, which is made available by the next button after the Outdent button. It's not clear why WordPress places the Outdent button before the Indent button (as do many other word processing tools). The Outdent button is disabled unless you've selected indented text.

- **Indent**—You can indent almost any text. Indenting sets the text apart from text around it. However, in the narrow columns available for your main text in most WordPress themes, there's limited scope to use indenting very much.

> ⚠ **caution**
>
> The Kitchen Sink button in the Add New Page area, which opens up the secondary formatting commands—the area WordPress jokingly refers to as the Kitchen Sink—is very easy to miss if you don't already know what it does. Try clicking the Kitchen Sink button a couple of times to open up and hide the secondary formatting commands so you know how to get to them when you need to.

The one thing you might be surprised to find lacking in WordPress formatting is the ability to directly specify fonts. Methods for specifying fonts were a late addition to HTML and are best managed through a newer, separate standard, CSS (Cascading Style Sheets). The use of various fonts in web pages is a big success, but WordPress's creators prefer, with some justification, to have fonts be specified behind the scenes, within a theme, rather than let you specify them explicitly in blog posts.

Adding Links

Links and graphics are the two most important elements that distinguish the Web from two predecessors:

- Text-based media, which lack links (footnotes and cross-references are ways to try to accomplish the same thing)

- Previous hypertext systems, which had limited or no graphics support

So adding links to your posts is really important for taking advantage of the Web as a medium.

The acronym HTML stands for the phrase Hypertext Markup Language. The "Hypertext" part, which means hyperlinks (links for short), is right up there at the front of the name.

Added to this is the nature of blogs themselves. Blogging is a kind of conversation, a way to share opinions and resources and respond to others' opinions and the resources they refer to. This should encourage a lot of linking as part of the back-and-forth; and, on the better blogs, it does.

If you survey a range of blogs, though, you'll find that many of them are severely or entirely lacking in links. Why?

One reason is that blogging is a somewhat egotistical act—or at least it is when we do it! Perhaps the problem is that many of us bloggers find it difficult to imagine anyone wanting to click away from our pearls of wisdom.

Another reason is that blogging developed with many fairly tight-knit groups of bloggers who visited one anothers' blogs regularly. Links weren't needed; it was just assumed people in a core group had each seen what the others had posted.

However, the way people use blogs is changing. There are many more blogs and people are busier. Many people arrive at blogs via search engines. They won't have read any of the previous posts to the blog they've arrived at, let alone other blogs that the blogger might assume are common knowledge for his or her audience. So links are needed now more than they were before.

The third and final reason for lack of linking is probably lack of technical savvy. The HTML for hyperlinks can be complicated, and it's certainly easy to make mistakes with.

Offsetting this, one of the best things about WordPress is its standardized, easy-to-use support for creating links. WordPress cuts out some of the options, hides the remaining complexity, and makes creating and removing links quite easy indeed.

A final reason many web publishers, not just bloggers, might reduce their use of links is that links tend to break over time, due to someone moving the page or piece of content you're linking to. This is less of a problem for blog entries, which are often assumed to have a limited shelf life, and which users won't necessarily assume you're going to be maintaining. (A corporate website, on the other hand, is expected to be perfect throughout, and attracts derision if it falls short.)

 **caution**

Only the most advanced web page tools even try to help protect you from the knotty problem of links breaking because content on the other end gets moved, changed, or deleted. In WordPress, this maintenance work is entirely up to you. Maintenance is less of a problem for normal blog entries, with their limited shelf life. However, if you create content that's meant to live a long time, such as a blogroll or page of resources—or if some of your posts get traffic long after they were first put up—you'll need to regularly check the links in them to make sure the links are still valid.

So we recommend you set your ego aside, take advantage of WordPress's capabilities, and use links freely in your posts. You will distinguish your blog in a very positive way if you use links, especially if you use them in a savvy way. In the next section are our recommendations for doing just that, and step-by-step instructions for adding links to your blog post.

Linking Strategy

The value of links as formatting elements in posts, and existing studies of web usability, imply a few rules for using links effectively:

- **DO: Use links in your posts**—Links are one of the most valued elements on any web page and people tend to avoid pages that lack them.

- **DO: Use links to highlight key points**—Linked text gets extra attention, so use links to highlight key points, but only where this makes sense.

- **DO: Make link text short and meaningful**—The evolving style online is to only highlight a few key words as link text. This improves the impact of the key words and enhances scannability.

- **DO: Use "click here" occasionally**—Underlining the words "click here," or even just the word "here" in the phrase "click here," doesn't communicate much detail to the reader who is scanning your blog post looking at headers, graphics, captions, bullets, and links. It does work, though; people tend to click such links.

- **DO: Specify what's at the end of a link**—Readers should understand from the surrounding text what they'll find at the end of a link.

- **DO: Consider opening links in a new window**—People tend not to like links that open a new window instead of replacing what's in the current window, but it keeps you from losing site visitors who might have not wanted to lose your page. Some sites warn users by adding a phrase such as "opens a new browser window" next to such links, but this extra step is a bit clunky for a typical blog.

For each of the preceding Do's, doing the opposite is, of course, a Don't. You might wonder, though, if there are any other Don'ts to consider.

We can think of a few:

- **DON'T: Produce screenfuls of text with no links**—You should be writing short, punchy text full of interesting points, and such text tends to be link-friendly. Text that has no natural place for a link might not be the most suitable text for a blog.

- **DON'T: Use obvious links**—Don't link to the home page of the New York Times, or even to less-obvious home pages, unless you're specifically discussing the page itself. Trust your site visitors to use search engines for the easiest stuff.

- **DON'T: Use links for word definitions**—Assume that your readers know how to find and use a dictionary, either online or in print. You should define new terms, but a link is not the way to do it. However, linking to a clever or humorous definition or use of a term can be a plus. (Ambrose Bierce's famous *The Devil's Dictionary* is a good resource, and it's available online to be linked to freely. Sample definition: "ACQUAINTANCE, n. A person whom we know well enough to borrow from, but not well enough to lend to.")

- **DON'T: Overpromote links**—Don't promise more in the link text than the destination of a link is going to deliver. It's usually better to describe a site as "interesting" rather than "fantastic." When in doubt, give your own opinion: "one of the best sites" might be overpromotion, but "one of my favorite sites" isn't, unless you use the same phrase to describe hundreds and hundreds of sites.

Creating a Link

Actually creating a link in the Add a New Post page is easy, whether you're in Mixed-Screen or Full-Screen mode. The process is the same:

1. Prepare by getting the URL. In a web browser, navigate to the page you'll be linking to, select the URL in the top of the browser window, and copy it to the Clipboard.

2. In the Add a New Post page of WordPress, highlight the text that you want to make into a link. Highlight the text carefully with the mouse, not by double-clicking on a word, to avoid including spaces in the link. (If you create a link that includes a space at the end, the link will look awful and you'll have to redo it.)

3. Click the Insert/Edit Link button . The shortcut is Alt+Shift+A.

4. In the Insert/Edit Link dialog box, shown in Figure 4.5, paste in the link URL—the web address of the web page you're linking to. Be sure to include the web page prefix, http://, at the beginning of the URL, but only once, not twice, which is an easy mistake to make.

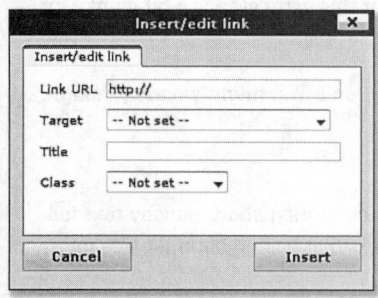

Figure 4.5
WordPress makes linking easy.

5. Enter the Target choice: either Open Link in the Same Window or Open Link in a New Window. For speed, click the down arrow, and then press the letter O once for the first option and twice for the second.

6. Enter the Title, which is text that appears when the user hovers the mouse over a link. The Title is also likely to be read aloud by screen readers used by the blind. Search engines sometimes use title text as well.

7. In most cases, ignore the Class. The Class specifies how the link text is aligned, but you generally don't want to set that here.

8. Click Insert to insert the hyperlink onto the selected text.

Honestly, it's a bit of a mystery why the Unlink button 🔗 is made available (and enabled), along with the Link button, when you highlight text that isn't link text. (The Outdent button, described previously, doesn't become enabled unless you select text that's *in*dented.) Perhaps the Unlink button will work the way we expect it to in a future revision of WordPress.com.

> 🎙 **tip**
>
> As shown in the steps, get in the habit of copying the hyperlink you want to use as the Link URL into the Clipboard before selecting the text you're going to link. That way, the process is much smoother and easier, as you begin by simply pasting the URL into the dialog box.

Saving, Checking Your Spelling, and Publishing Posts

Saving your work while you're creating a post is something most people are too *slow* to do. Publishing posts is something people are generally too *quick* to do, making mistakes that they regret later.

It's only natural that you're in a hurry to publish. You should check the spelling and review your post carefully first, though.

It's also only natural that you'll sometimes spot mistakes only after you publish. So we recommend that you check the post again after you publish.

Here are the specific steps we recommend for publishing a blog entry:

1. While working in Full-Screen mode, return to Mixed-Screen mode every 10 minutes or so. Click the Save Draft button to save a draft. Although WordPress autosaves regularly, it can be easy to get confused among autosaved versions, some of which might not have changes in them, and lose work.

2. When you believe you're ready to publish, return to Mixed-Screen mode to save a draft.

3. Return to Full-Screen mode to check the spelling in your work. (The spelling checker needs room to display alternatives.) Click the Toggle Spellchecker button to have the spelling in the document checked. Words that the WordPress spelling checker is not familiar with will be marked by a squiggly red underline. (How can it not recognize "Google"? We're just asking.)

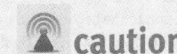

caution

We recommend that you do most of your work in Full-Screen mode, but sadly, there's no easy way to save your work while in Full-Screen mode. To avoid possibly losing your work, toggle out of Full-Screen mode every 10 minutes or so and save a draft of your work.

4. To check WordPress's suggestions for a marked word, click the word. A pull-down menu with options appears, as shown in Figure 4.6.

5. To replace the marked word with the suggestion, click the suggested word. WordPress replaces the selected word. To ignore the specific word, choose Ignore Word; to ignore all occurrences of the same spelling, click Ignore All.

6. Return to Mixed-Screen mode.

7. Save changes.

8. Right-click the Preview Changes button. From the context-sensitive menu that appears, choose Open Link in New Window.

9. Now you'll work in each of the two windows in turn. Review the preview in the new window. When you find things you want to change, return to the Add a New Post window and make the changes.

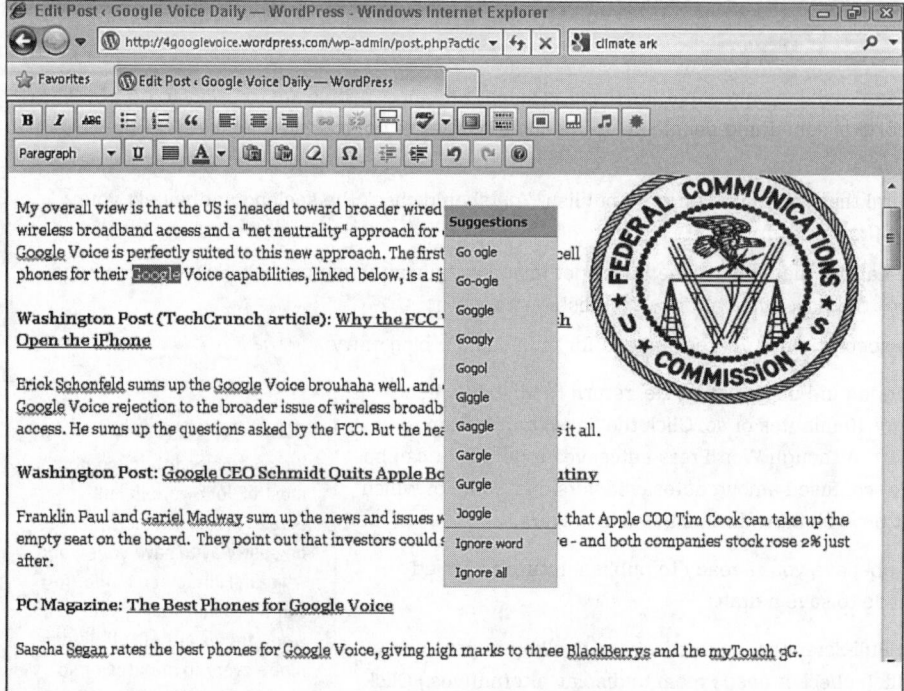

Figure 4.6
The spelling checker squiggles unrecognized words.

10. In the Preview window, check all the links in the post to make sure they work.

11. Repeat steps 6–10 until you find no more problems.

12. Click Publish to publish the post. The window will change from Add a New Post to Edit Post, if it hadn't done so previously.

13. Right-click the View Post link or the Visit Site button. From the context-sensitive menu that appears, choose Open Link in New Window.

14. Review the site in the new window. When you find things you want to change, return to the Edit Post window to make the changes.

15. Repeat steps 12–14 until you find no more problems.

16. Consider checking the site in additional ways: Walk away from the site, then come back and review it. Get a good night's sleep, then come back and review it. Print the posting out and review the printout. Print the posting out and have someone else review the printout.

 tip

Many of us find that the best checking method is to print out a copy of the blog posting, then hand it to someone else to review. This is effective partly because we read better in print than onscreen, so it's easier to catch mistakes. It's also effective because knowing that someone else might find an error in your work makes you check it that much more closely yourself.

Keep trying different checking methods until you develop a process that results in posts that are nearly error free.

Blog visitors are strange about mistakes. Some are quite forgiving, taking them in a "just among friends" spirit. Others, though, can be very harsh. Some people just assume you're an idiot if you make more than the most infrequent and occasional spelling or wording error. And there are some specific mistakes, such as mixing up "its" and "it's," that invite universal derision.

Even a careful process of repeated checking won't guarantee that you'll never make a missteak. (We did that one on purpose, we swear.) If you check several times, though, your blog will probably have fewer errors than an awful lot of blogs out there, including some that are part of major newspaper sites. This should help you get your message across better to all your site visitors.

Tags and Categories

Very few bloggers use tags and categories to anything like their full potential. According to Lorelle VanFossen, editor of the famous blog, *Lorelle on WordPress*, categories are like a table of contents for your blog; tags are like an index. We've deferred the discussion of tags and categories to Chapter 5, but be aware from the get-go that tags and categories are just as important—perhaps more important in some cases—than the contents of most of the individual posts that you write.

TAKING POSTS FURTHER

Doing More with Posts

Many WordPress blogs get about as far as we've described in previous chapters: A user signs on, sets up their blog, and starts posting. Some visitors come and occasional comments are made, but the blog doesn't develop much further.

Such blogs continue for as long as the blog owner maintains interest, which often isn't all that long. This low level of engagement is true for many WordPress.com blogs and even sometimes for WordPress.org users, despite the fact that they invest more effort in setting up their blog.

This book exists for those who want to go further, to understand more about how a blog works, and to do more with their blog. This chapter is the beginning of taking your blog to the next level.

In this chapter, we describe categorizing and tagging your blog posts and updating links and your blogroll, a list of links to your blog.

Nothing we describe here is strictly necessary to the core blogging activities of writing posts, posting them, and having people who already know about the blog visit and read your posts. What all these efforts are good for is making your blog easier to find for casual visitors and web search users, more interesting, and more useful. This should increase visits, get more comments, and help you write better posts. Which should increase visits, get more comments, and help you....

Trees and Forests

Blogging brings to life that ancient philosophical question: If a tree falls in the forest, and there's no one there to hear it, does it make a sound?

People blog for different reasons, but most bloggers at least want to make their blogs available to people who are likely to be interested in the content. Others have overtly commercial motives and want to capture as many eyeballs as possible to monetize them—the sort of language that grates on the ears of those with more purely creative concerns.

The great thing about blogging is that we can all learn from each other; we can even pursue different goals at different times. The nonprofit WordPress community, made up of thousands of enthusiasts, supports and manages the open source WordPress code base, all while sporting a profit-making head, Automattic.

So it doesn't matter what your motives are; you can blog for any reason you want, and you can work to bring in more users for any reason you want as well. Whatever your motives for blogging, though, it's likely that building up your audience will help you achieve them.

Putting Your Posts in Categories

The Web has unleashed a creative explosion from people—and a corresponding mania to find what's valuable among the outpouring. Putting your posts in categories is a great contribution to helping your blog visitors find the posts that are likely to be interesting and useful to them.

Remember that in the previous chapter, we described categories as resembling a table of contents for posts and tags as being like an index. A topic rarely shows up in two places in the table of contents and, similarly, categories should be brutally simple, whereas the same keyword or topic can show up many places as shown by the index, which is a lighter and more flexible tool.

Categorizing is a fair amount of work, and doing it badly might be worse than not bothering to do it at all. It's worth putting in the effort to learn how to categorize your posts and to manage the categories so they're useful from the beginning of your blog and continue to be useful over time.

 tip

The average person can remember 4 to 7 things in short-term memory—so if someone is looking through a list of your categories to find what's interesting, having only that many will make it easy for them. People also are used to dealing with lists of 10 and groups of a dozen.

Beyond that number, a list—such as a list of categories—might look too long for someone to bother with; the Web being what it is, they might then surf away somewhere else. (You might be hard pressed to make constructive use of a longer list as well.)

If you have more than 10 or 12 ways to describe your posts, the simple solution is to use tags, described later in this chapter. The extreme solution is to start another blog or two to accommodate what is clearly your very broad range of interests!

How People Think About Categories

People like to put things into firm, fixed categories. The Dewey Decimal System, used by libraries, and the taxonomies used to classify plants and animals were both great intellectual achievements in classification.

Unlike either of these two systems, WordPress categories are quite flexible. You can change them at any time and you can even, horror of horrors, put one post into multiple categories. Not a very purist thing to allow—but a very useful one.

Categories also tell you something about the things that are being categorized. When you expose your categories to visitors, for example with the Categories or Category Cloud widgets, people will size up your categories (and, with Category Cloud, their popularity) to decide how interesting your blog is likely to be to them.

Your categories also might directly inspire new posts. Once you create a Vegetarian Meals category on your cooking blog to host your vegetarian lasagna recipe, the temptation to fill out the category might then pull you in a direction you hadn't planned on.

So enjoy the categorization effort; it's an important part of your ongoing interaction with your blog visitors and with the topics that emerge as you add new posts to your blog.

Where Do Categories Appear?

The categories you assign a post to are listed at the bottom of the post when it appears in your blog. The categories also appear in the Category and Category Cloud widgets; we recommend you use one or the other. You can also choose to have the categories appear in feeds of your blog posting, as described in Chapter 2, "Starting Your Blog Right."

Using and Creating Categories

Putting posts into categories is easy—so is creating categories as you go along. This kind of bottom-up categorization is at the heart of using categories.

Follow these steps to categorize a post—in an existing category or one you create on the spot:

1. In the main Add/Edit Post screen, click the down arrow on the Categories header, if needed, to expand it.

2. Click the Most Used tab to see if any of the Most Used categories are the best home(s) for your post, as shown in Figure 5.1. Click the check box(es) next to the category or categories that fit.

caution

As your list builds, try hard to fit your posts into existing categories; few categorizations are exact, but it's better to have 10 slightly fuzzy categories than 30 precise ones.

Figure 5.1
Start with the Most Used categories.

3. Click the All Categories tab and review the categories shown to see if you need to modify which category or categories to assign your post to. Click to clear or select check boxes as needed to properly classify your post.

   If you're sure that the post, or some important aspect of it, doesn't fit in the existing categories, consider whether a tag is the appropriate way to help your site visitors find the post before creating a new category.

4. To add a category, click the Add New Category link. The Add New Category fields appear, as shown in Figure 5.2.

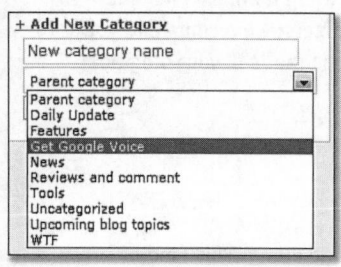

Figure 5.2
Adding a new category is easy.

5. Enter the new category name. Consider the name carefully to make sure it's broadly recognizable.

6. Consider assigning the category to a parent category. Yes, you can put categories within categories. However, we recommend against this in most cases. Even if you end up doing this, it's better done when you're explicitly revising your categories list, as described later in the chapter.

7. Click Add to add the category. The category is added immediately. It will appear in the All Categories list, not the Most Used list. WordPress will thoughtfully put a check next to the new category to assign the currently active post to it, so clear the check mark if it's not appropriate for this one.

8. Continue editing the checked and unchecked categories to assign your post appropriately.

9. When you're done categorizing your post, click the arrow next to the Categories header to hide the categories and open up more room for editing.

Managing Categories

WordPress not only allows you to assign and create categories on the fly, but it also includes a whole interface just for managing them. This kind of thoroughness is part of the reason WordPress has surged to its current leading position among blogging tools, so you might as well take advantage.

Don't let the availability of powerful tools tempt you into overdoing it, though. As mentioned earlier, we recommend that you use as few as four categories, and try hard to keep the total at a dozen or fewer. More than that is hard for your blog visitors to parse and for you to manage successfully.

WordPress also allows you to create subcategories. We recommend that you resist. Categories should be deeper than they are broad; that is, there should be more entries in a typical category than there are categories. This suggests that a reasonable number of top-level categories should be able to handle at least a couple of hundred posts.

What's more, web users are extremely impatient. The typical visitor to your blog will consider himself or herself to have done very well indeed to have looked through your category list and chosen a category to click on. If another level of categories then appears, then one frustrating reality, and two nearly intolerable possibilities, will occur to your visitor:

- **Reality**—The user has to make another choice.

- **Possibility 1**—The user might have to make *yet another* choice after that one.

- **Possibility 2**—The user might have gone down the wrong branch of a tree that's suddenly revealing itself to be rather complicated, and might have to make *many more* choices up and down the hierarchy to find what he or she is looking for, if it exists at all.

There are, of course, exceptions—for instance, if the subcategories are both obvious and well defined. If you've divided a list of classic pop songs into vinyl, tape, and CD, it might be logical to have 33s, 45s, and 78s for the vinyl category and 8-track and cassette for the tapes. These subcategories are so obvious that they won't cause your blog visitors undue confusion or anxiety. In such a case, consider first making them all top-level categories, but you might in this instance choose to use subcategories.

Most blog posts, though, don't lend themselves to such rigid categorization. Most blog categories are naturally fuzzy—so all the better if they're both simple and few.

 caution

Yahoo! lost its one-time leadership in the web search market partly because it relied on complex categorization schemes to organize web content. Don't repeat their mistake on your blog; keep your categorization scheme simple and, preferably, single-level.

> ## Capital Categories
>
> When you name categories, it's worth giving capitalization a bit of thought. We recommend that you take the easy way out and only capitalize the initial letter and any proper nouns, such as people's names and place names. It can seem cool and official to use title-case capitalization, in which most words receive initial capitals (used in most of the headings in this book and in newspaper headlines).
>
> However, this style is tricky; it can be very difficult to remember exactly which words *don't* get capitalized, especially late at night when you should be in bed instead of blogging. Using initial capitals for most words in titles is also gradually going out of style anyway. Strong use of initial capitals is largely outmoded in British English, which is surprisingly (to an American) influential internationally: in the UK itself, which is a huge technology market, in the British Commonwealth (which includes India, for one example), across other former British imperial holdings (Hong Kong, anyone?), and among readers of *The Economist*, just for starters.

Follow these steps to manage your blog's categories directly:

1. In the Administration area for your blog, in the left column, choose the Posts header, then Categories.

2. The Categories management page appears, as shown in Figure 5.3.

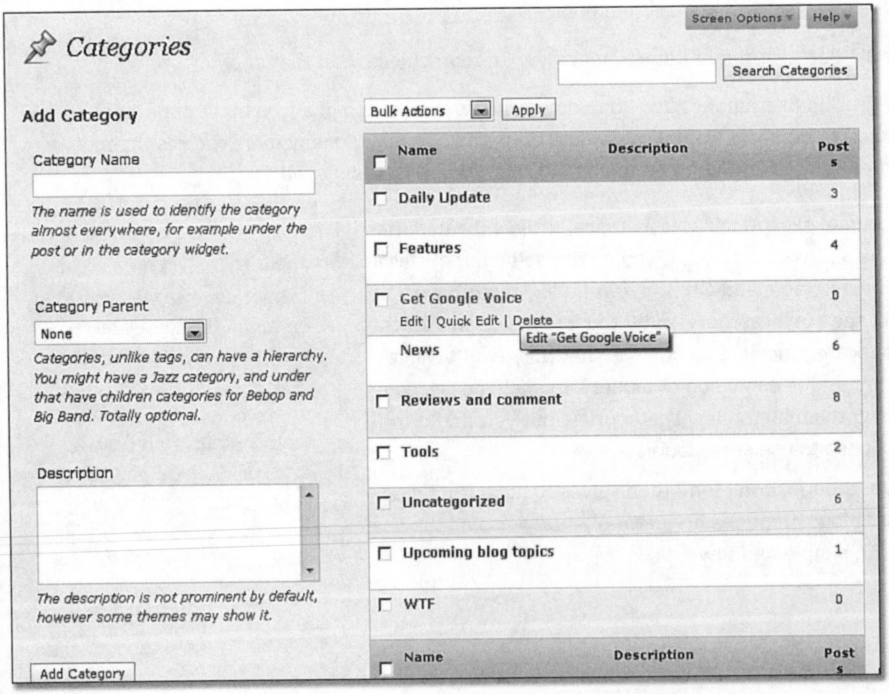

Figure 5.3
Manage categories from the top down.

3. To add a category, enter the Category Name, assign a Category Parent from the pull-down menu, and enter a Description if descriptions are displayed by your blog's theme. Click the Add Category button to add the category.

4. To modify a category, hover the mouse cursor over its name to make editing options appear, as shown in the figure. The options for modifying the category are Edit (step 5), Quick Edit (step 6), and Delete (steps 7 and 8).

5. To Edit the category, click Edit underneath its name. The Edit Category page appears, as shown in Figure 5.4. Change the Category Name, Category Parent, and/or Description. Click the Update Category button to make the change. Then jump ahead to step 9.

    The category is modified. Check your theme to see if the Description shows before making the effort to modify descriptions.

6. To change just the name of the category, click Quick Edit under its name. The name appears in an editable box. Make any changes and click the Update Category button to put the change into effect. Then jump ahead to step 9.

 **tip**

If category descriptions don't appear in your theme, the only place you'll see them is on the Categories page described here. In that case, it's probably only worth entering and managing the descriptions if there are multiple authors on your blog and you want to support consistency in the way all authors use categories, or if you want to remind yourself as to the purpose of a category over time.

Figure 5.4
Change the Category Name, Category Parent, and if supported in your theme, the Description.

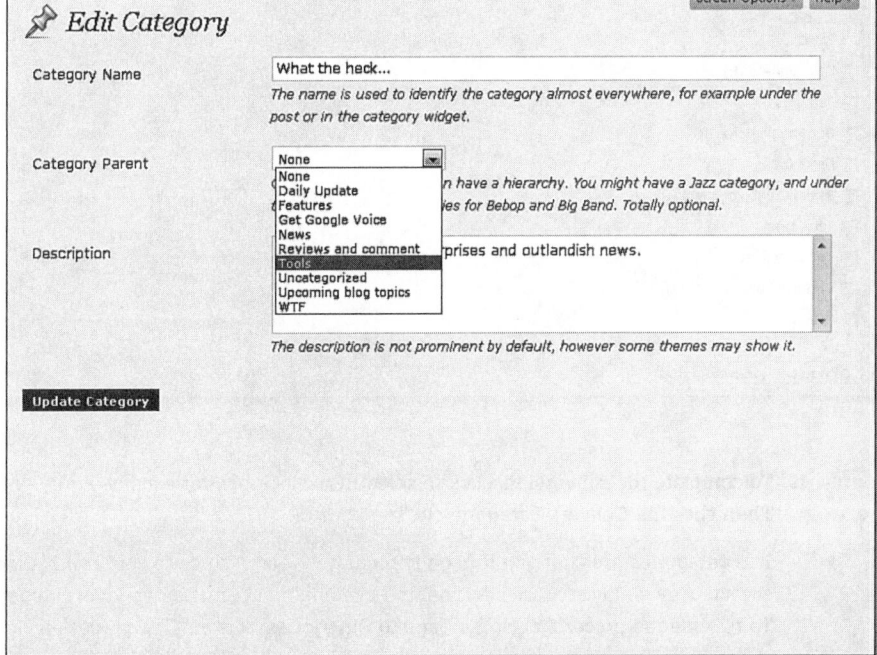

7. To delete one category at a time, click Delete under its name. A dialog box to confirm the deletion appears. Click OK to delete or Cancel to change your mind and keep it.

8. To delete several categories at a time, click the check box(es) next to each of the names of the categories to be deleted to select the check box(es). Then click the Bulk Actions menu at the top or bottom of the list of categories. Choose Delete and then click the Apply button; a dialog box appears to confirm. Click OK to delete or Cancel to change your mind and keep the categories.

 **tip**

To select all the categories at once (that is, to put a check in all the check boxes), click the check box next to the Name column header at the top or bottom of the list. To clear the selection, click the check box next to the Name column header again.

9. To change a category to a tag, click the Category to Tag Converter link at the bottom of the screen. The Convert Categories to Tags screen appears, as shown in Figure 5.5.

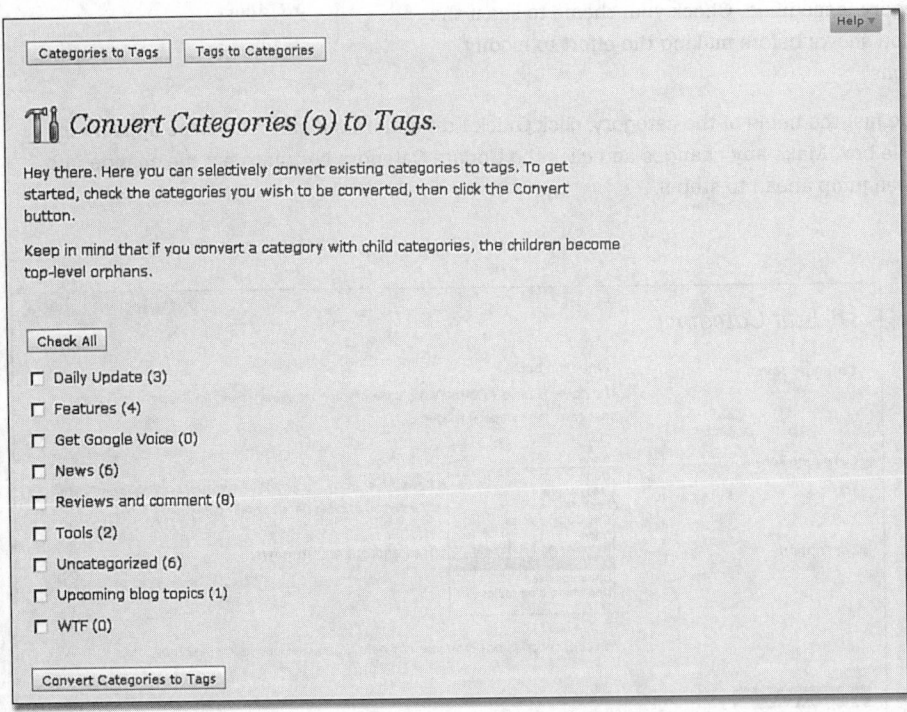

Figure 5.5
Convert categories to tags easily.

10. To complete the conversion, click to select the check box for each category you want to convert. Then click the Convert Categories to Tags button.

The categories are changed to tags immediately—no chance to confirm! A confirmation page is shown. Any child categories left behind become independent top-level categories of their own. To reverse the process, click the Tags to Categories button. This process is described later in the chapter.

tip

To go straight to the Categories to Tags screen, go to this URL (inserting your blog's username in place of *blog-name*):

http://*blogname*.wordpress.com/wp-admin/admin.php?import=wp-cat2tag

To go straight to the Tags to Categories screen, go to this URL (inserting your blog's username in place of *blogname*):

http://*blogname*.wordpress.com/wp-admin/admin.php?import=wp-cat2tag&step=3

Moving Posts Among Categories

You can always change the categories a post is in as part of editing the post, as described in the previous chapter. Sometimes, it's helpful to begin with a list of all the posts in a given category, which helps you decide if all of them belong there, or if some of them should be assigned to other categories, instead of, or in addition to, their current category assignments.

 tip

Any time you click on a category name, all the posts in that category appear in a list. If you're in your blog's Administration area at the time, the list of posts will be editable, including the categories of each post.

Follow these steps to work on posts by category:

1. From the Posts menu in the Administration area, choose Categories. The Categories page appears, as previously shown in Figure 5.3.

2. To see the specific posts that belong to a category, click the number of posts next to the category name, under the Posts column header. An editable list of posts in that category appears in the Edit Posts screen, as shown in Figure 5.6. It's similar to other Edit Posts lists, but all the posts shown are in the category that you chose by clicking its number of posts. (The posts might be in additional categories as well.)

3. Within the Edit Posts list, you can change the category of a post. Click Edit to review the post, change its category, or create a category, as described in Chapter 4, "Creating Your First Post." Click Quick Edit to change the categories and some other aspects without being able to review the post or add a new category, as shown in Figure 5.6.

Should a Post Be in Two Categories?

We recommend that you try to make your categories mutually exclusive, meaning that each post only goes in one category. This is easier on you and on your blog visitors. It might mean, though, that a post sometimes doesn't show up in a category where you or a user expects it because it belongs more strongly in a different category. Still, having each post in one or, at the most, two categories simplifies things for all involved in the same way that having fewer categories does. Once you have a simple set of categories, use tags to provide additional ways to find your posts, not more categories.

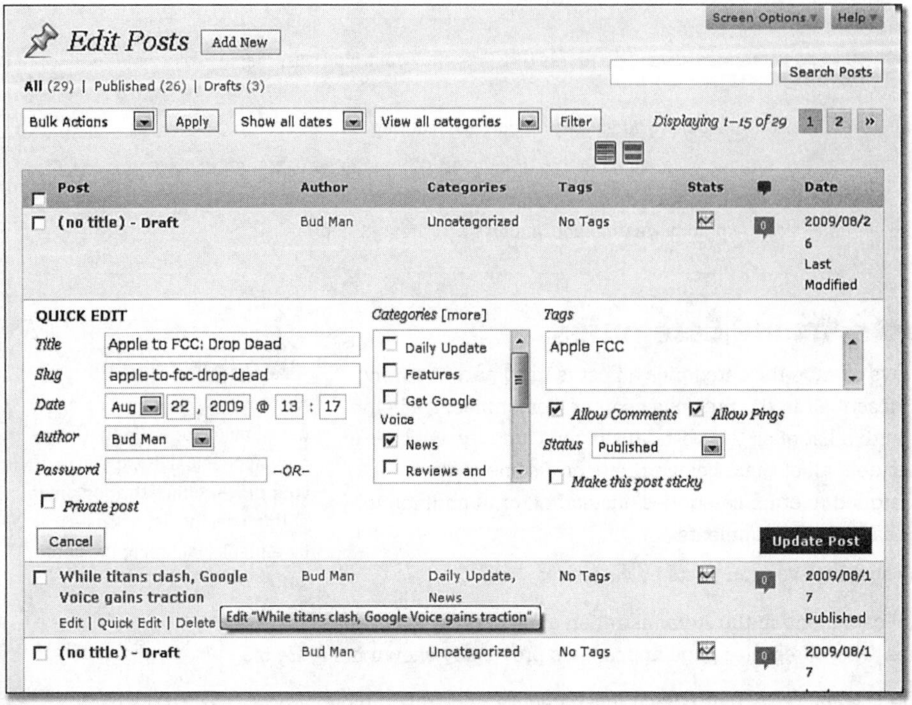

Figure 5.6 Review and change which categories a post is in.

You can change categories and also tags in Quick Edit. However, in Quick Edit, you can't see the content while you're doing it, which removes a major source of information needed for assigning categories and tags. You also can't add a category from within Quick Edit. So it's best to get in the habit of clicking Edit instead, unless you have a simple and specific change of categories already in mind.

To return to the Categories page, click the Back button in your browser, or click Categories under the Posts header in the leftmost column again.

If you really want to get your categories right, you need to be able to see a lot of information at once: basically, all your posts and all your categories. The most effective way to do this is to print out all your posts and physically sort them into piles by category. This engages your senses in a way that working onscreen doesn't, and is likely to lead to the best results—*best*, that is, until some new idea occurs to you for how to categorize your posts....

Tagging Your Posts

Tagging your posts should be simple and fun. At the same time, it's really important.

You should seek to do it well—not *right* because there's no one right way to tag your posts.

What determines whether you've done well in tagging your posts? Tags exist for people using a search engine and for your blog visitors to find your posts. So tags are done well if people searching for a topic find your posts when they should; that is, when the posts are relevant to their search topic.

Relevance, like beauty, is in the eye of the beholder. Most of us putting things up on the Web want more: more visitors, more pageviews, more time spent by people on our site.

Visitors to sites, especially blogs, want either of two things. The first, and main goal, is quick answers or quick help. People using the Web are often very task-oriented and search in a quick, twitchy way for specific results. This still leaves room, though, for serendipity—finding a blog post that's interesting, funny, or enlightening, but that doesn't necessarily help complete a specific task.

If you write your posts well, they'll be both useful and interesting. If you achieve this balance, you'll help task-oriented people complete their tasks, while at the same time brightening the day of those who are more open to serendipity.

Tags should help with both. Tags should answer two main questions:

- **What would this post help someone do?** Answering this question helps generate tags for people who are researching a given topic, such as financial scams or the feeding habits of killer whales. Tags of this sort tend to be nouns mentioned in your post, such as proper names of people and specific things mentioned in the post.

- **What makes this post interesting?** Answering this question helps you identify what's special about your post, what makes it different from other resources out there, such as company websites, Wikipedia pages, and so on. Tags of this sort tend to be adjectives that describe your post but might not appear in it, such as *funny* or *comprehensive*. Tags of this sort might also be nouns that don't appear in your post, such as larger categories that the things mentioned in your posts belong in: *mass delusions* for financial scams or *mammals* for a post about killer whales.

 note

Managing tags for your posts is both very similar to managing categories and, arguably, less important. Therefore, this section is somewhat abbreviated compared with the previous section, "Putting Your Posts in Categories." Please review the section on categories as well as this section to understand in detail the relationship between categories and tags and how best to manage both.

Tags are the wave of the future. Google became the leading search engine, and a major corporation by any measure, through its unmatched support for free-form searching. Tags are your bid to make your posting accessible to exactly this kind of free-form search.

 tip

You can learn quite a bit about your own blog by looking at its tag cloud, a list of the tags used in your blog, with the most used appearing largest and most centrally. You might be surprised by what's important and what's missing.

I Can't Find My Tags

The tags you assign to a post are listed at the bottom of your posting in your blog. They also appear in the Tag Cloud widget, described in Chapter 4, which we recommend you use. You can also choose to have tags appear in feeds of your blog posting, as described in Chapter 2.

Using and Creating Tags

When you add tags to a post, it doesn't matter if you've used them before or not. WordPress adds the tag if it's new or counts it as a repeated use of the tag if not.

Follow these steps to add tags to a post:

1. In the main Add/Edit Post screen, click the down arrow on the Post Tags header, if needed, to expand it.

2. Click the Choose from the Most Used Tags in Post Tags link to bring up an updated tag cloud for your blog, as shown in Figure 5.7.

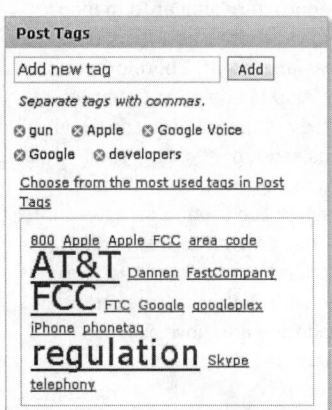

Figure 5.7
Use the built-in tag cloud
to remind you of tags.

caution

You should review the entire content of each blog posting for potential tags, including reviewing any images and considering what tags might apply to them as well. Unfortunately, the full-screen view of your post doesn't have a place to add tags. The most flexible and effective way to tag your post is to look at it in full-screen view and write down tags on a piece of paper, then enter them as described here. Alternatively, copy your posting into a word processor or text editor window, and delete phrases and sentences while copying and pasting, or typing, words into a list of tags. At the end, you'll have deleted the entire posting and created a complete list of applicable tags. Then enter the tags as described here.

3. Enter tags that apply to your post. Scroll down through the post in the edit window and enter tags as you go. Separate tags with commas; this allows you to enter multiword tags.

Consider all versions of a name or term that someone might enter. For instance, someone searching for Ford might be looking for Ford cars, ex-President Ford, or the Ford of Firth in Scotland. So enter general terms such as "ford" as well as more specific terms such as "gerald ford," "president ford," or "ford of firth." Also consider synonyms and related terms, such as "Richard Nixon," who appointed him as vice president, for Gerald Ford; or "Scotland," where it's located, for the Ford of Firth.

4. As you enter tags, click the Add button every few terms to clear the entry line. Click the X next to a previously added tag to clear it.

The tags you've already added will appear beneath the Add New Tag area with X's next to them.

5. Continue reviewing your posting and adding appropriate tags.

6. When you're done adding tags to your post, click the arrow next to the Post Tags header to hide the Post Tags area and open up more room for editing.

As with categories, to really get tags right, you need to be able to see all your posts and all your tags. The most effective way to do this is to print out all your posts and a list of your tags and mark up each post with tags already in the post and related terms that should serve as tags. As with categorization, this engages your senses in a way that working onscreen doesn't, and is likely to lead to the best results.

 **caution**

Be sure to separate tag names with commas; otherwise, WordPress will treat two or more terms as one, which undermines the usefulness of your tags.

 tip

News cycles on the Web can peak in just a few hours—news appears, people write articles about the news, people blog on it, and then everyone is on to the next thing. If you blog about news, write and post quickly, and include tags from the beginning to help searchers; otherwise, you'll miss out on the majority of potential visitors, who will be searching during the peak of interest.

Managing Tags

WordPress allows top-down management of tags just as it does of categories. The usefulness of top-down management of tags is not as clear-cut, as tags work a lot better if they're right from the beginning. However, cleaning up your tags might help you better understand what your blog is really about and inspire new posts that take you and your site visitors further into topics of interest.

One temptation in managing tags is to amalgamate tags into fewer terms. This is good if it eliminates obscure terms that no one uses and strengthens links to more popular terms. However, part of the joy of the Web is its support for even the narrowest interests. Don't eliminate pathways that might serve a small number of people very well, even if most people in the public at large wouldn't know what a given tag means (or what you and your "insider" site visitors mean by the way you use it) in a million years.

Follow these steps to manage your blog's tags directly:

1. In the Administration area for your blog, in the left column, choose the Posts header, then Post Tags.

2. The Tags management page appears, as shown in Figure 5.8.

3. To add a tag, enter the Tag Name, and enter a Description if it's supported by your blog's theme. Click the Add Tag button to add the tag.

   It doesn't really make a lot of sense to add a tag separately from adding a post, unless your theme shows tag descriptions—in which case, the opportunity to edit the tag description is the reason to enter the tag here.

4. To modify a tag, hover the mouse cursor over its name to make editing options appear, as shown in the figure. The options are Edit (step 5), Quick Edit (step 6), and Delete (step 7).

note

You should capitalize tags appropriately to the way you mean them. Capital letters are ignored in searches, but when people see a list of tags associated with your post, they'll recognize the tag much better if you've capitalized it as you mean to use it. This is where the difference between a President "Ford" and to "ford" a river can be quite important.

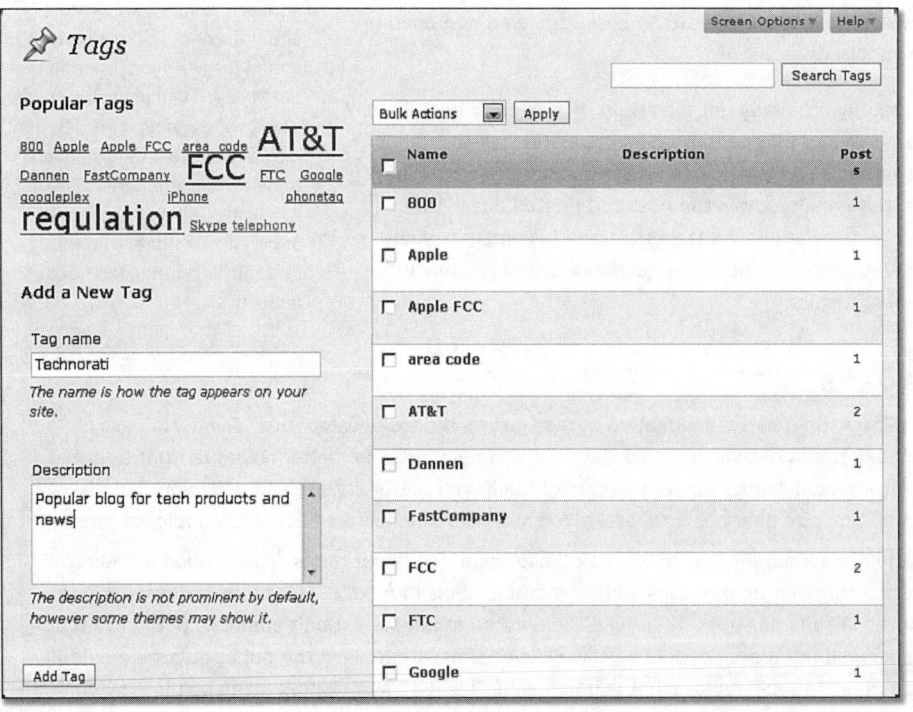

Figure 5.8
Manage tags from the top down.

5. To Edit the tag, click Edit underneath its name. The Edit Tag page appears. Change the Tag Name and/or Description. Click the Update Tag button to make the change. You've completed these steps.

   The tag is modified. Check your theme to see if the Tag Description shows before making the effort to modify descriptions.

6. To change just the name of the tag, click Quick Edit under its name. The name appears in an editable box. Make any changes and click the Update Tag button to put the change into effect. You've completed these steps.

7. To delete one tag at a time, click Delete under its name. A dialog box to confirm the deletion appears. Click OK to delete or Cancel to change your mind.

8. To delete several tags at a time, click the check box next to each of the names of the tags to be deleted to select them. Then click the Bulk Actions menu at the top or bottom of the list of categories. Choose Delete and then click the Apply button; a dialog box appears to confirm. Click OK to delete or Cancel to change your mind.

> **tip**
>
> If tag descriptions don't appear in your theme, the only place you'll see them is on the Tags page described here. In that case, it's probably only worth entering and managing the descriptions if there are multiple authors on your blog and you want to support consistency in the way they use tags.

If a tag is getting a lot of use, and if it would fit in your categorization scheme, it might make sense to change the tag into a category. To make this change, use the Convert Tags to Categories page, as shown in Figure 5.9. Unfortunately, you can't reach this screen directly through the Tags page; you have to go in through the Convert Categories to Tags page, as described previously and shown in Figure 5.6. Alternatively, enter the URL directly (inserting your blog's username in place of *blogname*):

http://*blogname*.wordpress.com/wp-admin/admin.php?import=wp-cat2tag&step=3

> **tip**
>
> To select all the tags at once (that is, to put a check in all the check boxes), click the check box next to the Name column header at the top or bottom of the list. To clear the selection, click the check box next to the Name column header again.

The process is similar to the process for converting categories to tags, as described previously. Tags become independent top-level categories, and the new category is added to relevant posts alongside any other categories associated with each post.

Changing Tags Associated with Posts

You can always change the tags assigned to a post as part of editing the post, as described in the previous chapter. Sometimes it's helpful to begin with a list of all the posts associated with a tag.

Follow these steps to work on posts by tag:

1. From the Posts menu in the Administration area, choose Tags. The Tags page appears, as shown previously, in Figure 5.8.

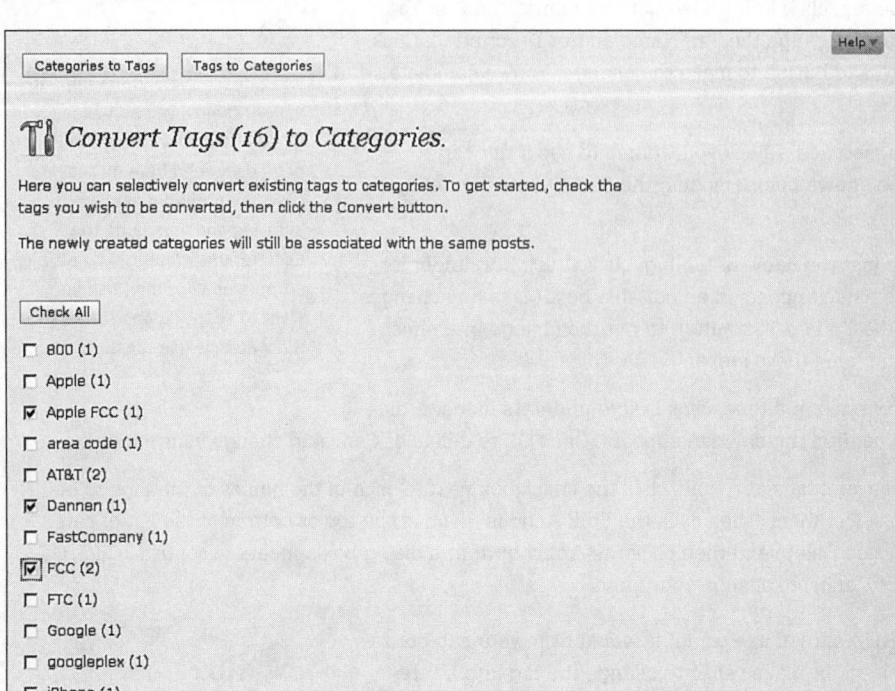

Figure 5.9
Convert tags
to categories
easily.

2. To see the specific posts that belong to a tag, click the number of posts next to the tag name, under the Posts column header. An editable list of posts with that tag will appear in the Edit Posts screen, as shown in Figure 5.6. It's similar to other Edit Posts lists, but all the posts shown are associated with the tag you chose by clicking its number of posts.

3. Within the Edit Posts list, you can change the tags associated with a post. Click Edit to review the post, change its tag, or create a tag, as described in Chapter 4. Click Quick Edit to change the tags and some other aspects without being able to review the post or add new tags, as shown in Figure 5.7.

You can change tags and also categories in Quick Edit. However, in Quick Edit, you can't see the content while you're doing it, which removes a major source of information needed for assigning tags. You are able to add tags from within Quick Edit. Because you can't review content at the same time, it's best in most cases to choose Edit instead.

4. To return to the Tags page, click the Back button in your browser, or click Post Tags under the Posts header in the leftmost column again.

 tip

Any time you click on a tag name, all the posts with that tag appear in a list. If you're in your blog's Administration area at the time, the list of posts will be editable, including the tags associated with each post.

Updating Links and Your Blogroll

A blogroll originally started out as the list of blogs that your blog commented on—and of blogs whose blogger and users might be expected to read your blog in return.

You only need to worry about this area if you use the Links widget, which exposes your blogroll to the world. However, the Links widget is so valuable to you and your blog visitors that you should consider adding it, as described in Chapter 3, "Creating Your Blog's Look," if you haven't already.

As the world of blogs has become more hierarchical and less communitarian, with some blogs reaping hundreds of thousands of page visits and others just a few, blogrolls are less a list of members of a community and more often a list of resources that you and your blog visitors can draw on.

Many of the big blogs don't keep a blogroll or equivalent, for fear of losing traffic to what have become their competitors. Those of us who run smaller blogs still use our blogs to comment on what happens on the bigger ones.

Think of your blogroll as a set of reference points for you and your site visitors. This frees you to comment in a focused way on your own blog, not necessarily having to reproduce information or even commentary that's appeared elsewhere. You can focus on adding value by additional commentary and by your own news.

Managing your blogroll is very similar, functionally, to managing categories and tags. Unlike categories and tags, there's less of an explicit link—your blog posts aren't assigned to links in your blogroll, as they are to categories, nor do links belong to one or more specific posts, as tags do.

Most of the blogs you link to should be in your blogroll, and most of the links in your blogroll should be linked to in your posts. By keeping a loose but lively and up-to-date correspondence between your posts and your blogroll, you'll better serve yourself, your blog visitors, and the blogging community at large.

 tip

WordPress assigns a numeric identifier, called a Link ID, to each entry in your links. You can sort your links by Link ID but, oddly, it's not displayed. This is something you will only encounter in programming using the WordPress API and not something you need to concern yourself with in managing specific blogs.

 **note**

The way in which you manage your blogroll is very similar to—and, arguably, less important than—managing your categories and tags, as described previously. We recommend that you become familiar with the general functionality of WordPress in managing such lists as it relates to categories and tags, and then use your knowledge to manage your blogroll as well. The steps given here are somewhat abbreviated, due to their similarity to the steps for categories and tags described previously.

Adding New Links

Some of the ideas we've introduced previously for other lists in your WordPress blog, such as categories, apply to your blogroll as well:

- People can easily remember about 4 to 7 things in short-term memory; a list of 10 is quite long and a dozen is about as much as anyone will bother to deal with.

Taking Posts Further

- Having categories for your blogroll can make people anxious, frustrated, and confused. (Including you, trying to manage them!) Try to keep your blogroll to one top-level list. If you have so many entries that you have to categorize them, use short, sharp, and simple category descriptions.

When adding new links, don't create a new blogroll link for every blog or other site that you do, in fact, link to. Specific links are already present in your blog postings.

Just include links to your most frequently used sites, the ones that you feel are necessary background for your own blog or important references in carrying out the kinds of tasks your blog visitors are out to perform. Sacrifice whimsy and serendipity to information and utility. (Unless part of the point of your blog is whimsy and serendipity, in which case links that support them are informative and useful!)

With that in mind, follow these steps to add links to your blogroll:

1. From the Links menu in the Administration area, choose Add New. The Add New Link area appears, as shown in Figure 5.10.

2. For the link, enter the Name, Web Address, Description, and, if you're using them, Categories.

   The best name is the name the website itself uses, which enhances memorability and recognizability for your blog visitors. The web address must include the prefix, http://, as well as www. if that's part of the address. The description will be shown when your blog visitor hovers the mouse over the link, or you can optionally expose it directly in the blogroll.

   The Categories area includes links to either All Categories or Most Used categories. This is probably overkill, as neither you nor your blog visitors will enjoy dealing with categories of blogroll links in most cases, and if you do use them, they should be simple and few. See the "Link Categories" section, later in this chapter, for more on categories.

3. Select the target. The target controls the behavior of links to your blogroll when the user clicks on them—whether they open in a new window or tab with no frame (_blank), completely replace the current window or tab with no frames (_top), or show in a window or tab that's framed or not as with the current window (_none). The difference between the latter two options only matters if your blog uses frames, which it probably doesn't. The _top option is the default and probably the best fit to user expectations; "I know where to find the Back button" is what users often say if you "nanny" them by opening a new window or tab or opening the link in a framed window or tab.

4. Check or clear the Keep This Link Private check box to specify whether the link will be visible. Why would you add a link, only to keep it invisible, you might ask? The only reason we can think of is that you might hide it with the intent of exposing it later, for instance if you haven't been using a link much lately, but think you might in the future.

 tip

One of the authors (McCallister) added categories for his blogroll—and, in doing so, ended up with several near-duplicate categories (one called Linux and one called Linux/Open Source, for instance). If you create categories for your blogroll, they're managed by WordPress right along with categories for posts; make sure the overall list of categories works well for both purposes.

Figure 5.10
Manage the
links in your
blogroll.

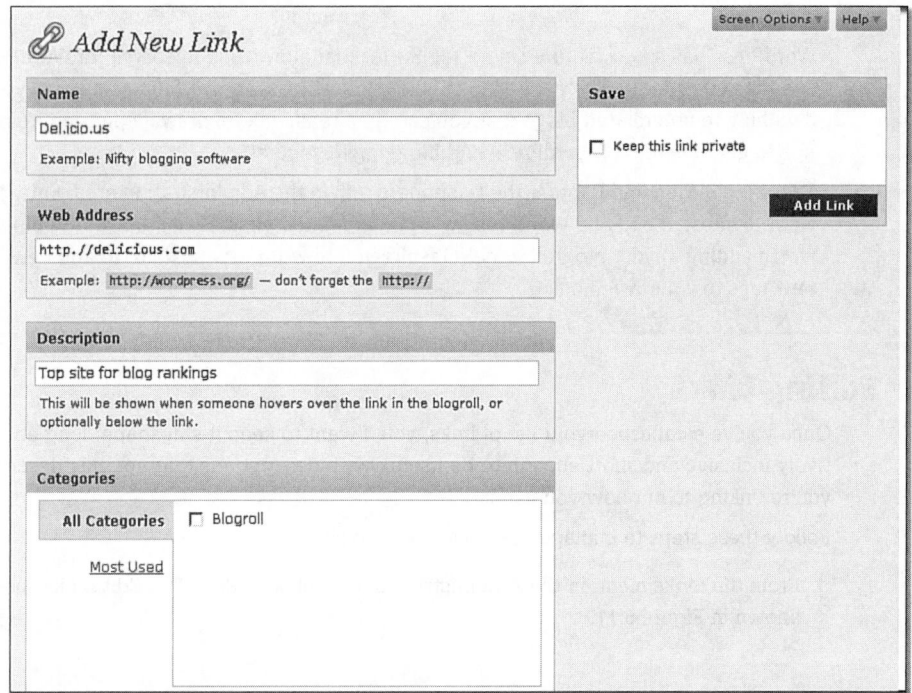

5. Specify the Link Relationship (XFN). Most of us can ignore this. Only use it if you know something about these kinds of relationships and/or are part of a network of blogs and sites that uses them. This is a bit like the dating status on Facebook—the one that causes so many arguments when one person in a couple describes themselves as single and the other person describes themselves as dating someone. For more information, visit the XHTML Friends Network at http://gmpg.org/xfn.

6. Specify Advanced fields. Most of us can ignore this as well. You can specify an image to go with the link (which you can optionally choose to expose in the Links widget), notes to yourself about it, and a rating. (The fact that you link to the site at all seems to us to be enough of a rating.) You can also enter the RSS URL for RSS feeds, but this is only useful if your theme exposes these URLs or as a note to yourself.

7. Click Add Link to add the link.

 note

Yes, we do recommend you use Descriptions for links in your blogroll because these Descriptions always appear to the user (when the user hovers the mouse over a blogroll link). Given the way the description is displayed, keep it short and sweet.

Tag Surfing

WordPress has a new feature called Tag Surfer that allows you to search for WordPress blogs that use tags you specify. The general idea is to enter at least some of the same tags you use on your own blog to find related blogs that you can then read, link to, draw inspiration from, or otherwise use to get more out of WordPress and blogging in general.

To try Tag Surfer, find it under the Dashboard link in the Administration area. Enter the tags you want to subscribe to and WordPress will pull in related posts. See if any of the blogs involved are worth adding to your blogroll or help inspire you to write new posts or to add new categories or new tags to your own blog.

Editing Links

Once you've established your list of links, you'll want to keep it shipshape: long enough to be relatively inclusive and short enough to be useful, with descriptions that not only describe the site you're linking to but how you use it.

Follow these steps to manage the links in your blogroll:

1. From the Links menu in the Administration area, choose Edit. The Edit Links screen appears, as shown in Figure 5.11.

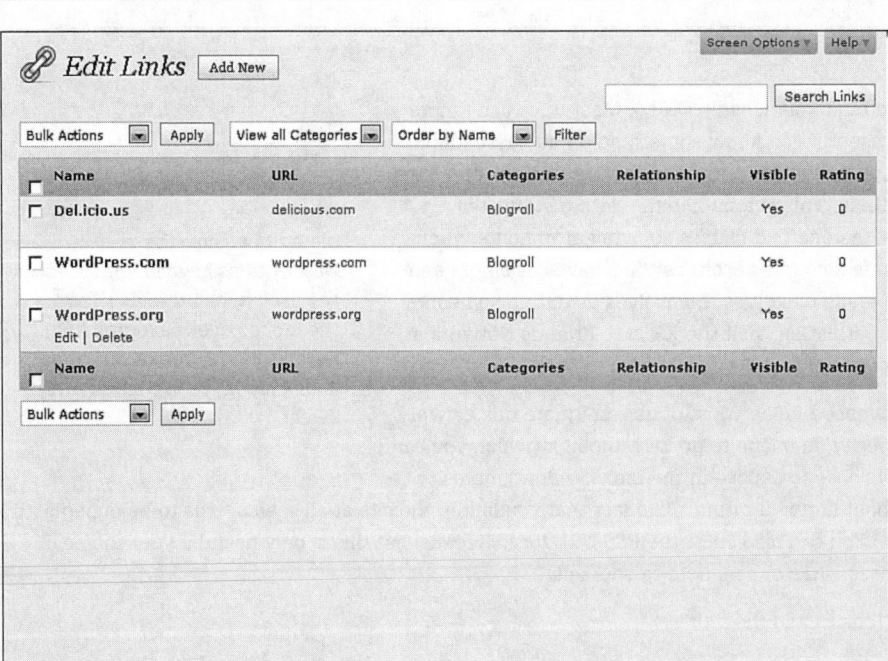

Figure 5.11
Manage the links in your blogroll.

2. Within the Edit Links screen, hover the mouse over a link name to edit or delete it. Use the check boxes and the Bulk Actions pull-down menus at the top and bottom of the list of links to delete several links at once. Use the pull-downs to view all categories of links or specific categories (if you've categorized them), and to order the list by name, Link ID (not displayed), address (that is, URL), or rating.

3. To edit a link, mouse over the link name, then choose Edit from the options that appear. Fill in the fields as described in the "Adding New Links" section, and click Delete to remove the link or Update Link to save your changes.

Link Categories

We generally don't recommend putting blogroll links into categories, as it makes both managing and using your blogroll overly complex. However, there are some cases where this makes sense. For instance, if your blog concerns two disparate topics, such as your professional role as a project manager, and information about your specific industry, such as cucumber harvesting, you could have separate categories for links relating to project management and links relating to the growing and harvesting of cucumbers.

If you do put your blogroll links into categories, follow these steps to manage the categories:

1. From the Links menu in the Administration area, choose Link Categories. The Link Categories screen appears.

2. Within the Link Categories screen, you can add a category, edit categories and descriptions, or delete categories.

3. To see all the links in a link category, click the number of links shown in the list of link categories. The Edit Links screen appears, as described in the previous section, with a list of links that you can edit or otherwise manage.

Be sure to maintain your link categories carefully, as users could become frustrated if they click through link categories and still don't find what they're looking for.

USING HTML IN YOUR WIDGETS AND BLOG

How HTML Can Take You Further

Much of the effectiveness of WordPress comes down to how much it lets you do without any kind of coding. Millions of wonderful blogs have been launched and are living full and productive lives because WordPress, and other tools, hide any kind of machine talk from the user.

However, at some point you might want to put down the handsaw and sandpaper and pick up some power tools. WordPress is carefully designed to let you go as far as you can without power tools, then gracefully add just as much or as little coding as you need to get the results you're looking for.

The first and simplest power tool that you can use with WordPress is HTML. HTML is an acronym for Hypertext Markup Language, which is the underlying language of web pages. It controls what appears on a web page and affects how things are laid out. HTML was all people had for writing and maintaining web pages for the first several years after the Web was invented in 1989.

HTML also provides a front end for the protocol that determines how web links and domain names work, called HTTP, or Hypertext Transfer Protocol. HTML code that sets up hyperlinks—the links you click to move from one web page to another—serves as a front end for HTTP.

You can use HTML in WordPress.com—in fact, it's always just a click away. The HTML code underlying your blog entries is available on the HTML tab whenever you are writing or editing a blog entry.

There are some fairly routine tasks in WordPress that you can only do using HTML. For instance, if you want to add a YouTube video to your blog, YouTube provides you with HTML code. You have to find the right spot in the HTML for your blog entry and paste in the HTML code that YouTube provides.

One of the most useful widgets, and the most customizable one, is the Text widget. The Text widget allows you to use HTML for formatting text, creating links, and so on.

In this chapter, we introduce the use of HTML as it can be used in the WordPress.com environment. This is useful whether you just want to do a few simple things with your blog postings and the Text widget, or if you want to go much further. To go further, you'll need additional tools, which are described throughout this book.

Power Tools for Better Blogging

You can use several major types of tools to improve your blog. The way you use them varies across WordPress.com and WordPress software–based blogs, with more power made available as you take on more responsibility for your blog.

Our intent in this book is to always provide a salmon ladder so that you can learn a moderate amount, improve your blog, and repeat—all the way from beginner to power user.

You can use HTML in any WordPress blog, including WordPress.com blogs, as described in this chapter. What you're actually using in WordPress, and what we show in this book, is XHTML, a newer and somewhat stricter version of HTML.

The people behind WordPress, users, and the entire web-oriented community are caught up in a shift between standards at present. XHTML was meant to be the replacement for standard HTML, but it now appears that HTML will be replaced by a new version, HTML 5, instead. XHTML is, therefore, looking to be something of a placeholder.

Everything we show works as either HTML or XHTML, unless noted otherwise. So if you want to go writing a lot of (X)HTML code of your own for use in WordPress blogs, start by looking at the differences between them as described in the WordPress Codex:

http://codex.wordpress.org/HTML_to_XHTML

CSS, or Cascading Style Sheets, is a further addition to HTML that allows you to take a more thoughtful and managed approach to editing web pages. WordPress themes are written in CSS. CSS had a rocky beginning because of competing standards and varying implementations, but its future looks secure.

As a WordPress.com user, you can change the CSS in your theme and preview the result at any time. You will need to buy a $15 per year CSS upgrade to actually change the CSS in your WordPress.com theme, all described in Chapter 10, "Adding Upgrades, Audio, and Video."

As a WordPress software user, you can use many more themes, modify them freely, and create your own, all using CSS. This is described beginning in Chapter 11, "Installing and Upgrading WordPress Software."

The other major technology you can use for turbocharging your blog is PHP, which stands for PHP Hypertext Preprocessor. PHP is a scripting language. It's used to write plug-ins, which can add a great deal of capability to blogs based on WordPress software, and which are described beginning in Chapter 13, "The WordPress Toolkit: Plug-Ins." Widgets, a limited selection of which are available to your blog, are described in Chapter 3, "Creating Your Blog's Look," this chapter (the Text plug-in), and Chapter 8, "Tracking Statistics and Bringing in Visitors" (the RSS plug-in). Widgets are limited versions of plug-ins.

The major tools for modifying your blog are as follows:

- Themes, with a limited selection available in WordPress.com and a much wider selection in WordPress.org-based blogs

- Widgets, a limited selection of which are available in both WordPress.com and WordPress.org-based blogs

- HTML, which can be used in WordPress.com and WordPress.org-based blogs

- CSS, which can be used with WordPress.com blogs to modify a theme via a CSS add-in, and can be used freely in WordPress software-based blogs

- PHP, which can be used to create plug-ins, but only in WordPress software-based blogs

How's that for a salmon ladder?

HTML Basics in WordPress

There are lots of good books about HTML out there, but using HTML in the WordPress environment is unique. Many of the problems that make using HTML a hassle are handled for you, and the WordPress environment can teach you HTML as you work.

In this chapter, we use WordPress to demonstrate the basics of HTML. Once you have a feel for HTML itself and how it works in the WordPress environment, you can use other HTML and XHTML resources to go further, applying what you learn in your WordPress blog as you go.

The key tool we'll use is the Visual and HTML tabs in the WordPress Post editor. (The Post editor is the same for adding new posts, editing existing posts, and creating pages—standalone web pages you can integrate into your blog.)

The formatting that WordPress makes available to you on the Visual tab is the formatting that's made available in the most basic HTML, supported by the widest range of browsers across the widest range of systems.

The Post editor has tabs that allow you to work in *Visual* mode or HTML mode. Visual mode is what the user sees when they visit your blog. In HTML editors, Visual mode is often referred to as WYSIWYG, pronounced "whizzywig," for What You See Is What You Get.

 **note**

The HMTL basics described here are the same for WordPress.com or WordPress software-based blogs.

HTML Tags

The basics of HTML can be unraveled by looking closely at its name: Hypertext Markup Language.

A *markup language* is a set of codes inserted within a flow of text that describe how the text should be formatted, or that give other instructions. A markup instruction in HTML is called a *tag*.

A typical tag looks like this: <b>. The angle brackets indicate that the text inside them isn't to be displayed—instead, it's an instruction.

Many tags come as beginning and ending tags, like this:

`The last word in this sentence is displayed in <b>bold</b>.`

That's how the text would look on the HTML tab. On the Visual tab, or in your blog after you publish, the same sentence would appear like this:

The last word in this sentence is displayed in **bold**.

So in HTML, you format a word as bold by surrounding it with the beginning bold tag, <b>, and the ending bold tag, </b>. Similarly, you use the <i> and </i> tags around words or characters that you want to display in italic.

HTML was developed in accordance with a strong set of ideals, alongside strong practical concerns, which sometimes conflicted.

For instance, HTML is meant to convey *meaning*, not *formatting*. The bold and italic tags are formatting tags. They're tremendously popular because each "does what it says on the tin," across a wide range of devices to boot.

The meaning behind the styles might be different from their look. An HTML purist would prefer to use tags that specify the meaning rather than the formatting. So, to follow along with the theory behind HTML, you should use <em> to emphasize text and <strong> to make it appear strongly. What this means in practice is that HTML purists use <em> for italic and <strong> for bold, along with the corresponding ending tags, even though the pure tags are much harder to remember and take longer to type.

CSS is meant to be a triumph of the purist approach because it separates meaning from the specifics of how something appears. In practice, CSS just gives you the tools to spend far more time working on the details of appearance, often well beyond the importance of the underlying text.

So that's the markup language part of HTML. Figure 6.1 shows the HTML source code underlying a post on gvDaily.com. To complete our look at the words behind the acronym HTML, let's look at the HT, or Hypertext, part.

**note**

We're not just introducing these HTML specifics for fun, or your general education; they're needed for you to understand why WordPress handles HTML the way it does, which would otherwise seem confusing. We've simplified years of history and acres of onscreen and in-person exchanges among competing opinions to the bare bones that affect how you write HTML code for WordPress.

tip

You can see HTML in action on any web page. Almost any web browser has a command that displays the underlying HTML-tagged text. In Internet Explorer, the command is on the View menu, and is called Source; other browsers use the same or similar wording. The View Source command causes the HTML, CSS, and other code underlying the web page to display.

Figure 6.1
You can easily view the source code behind any web page.

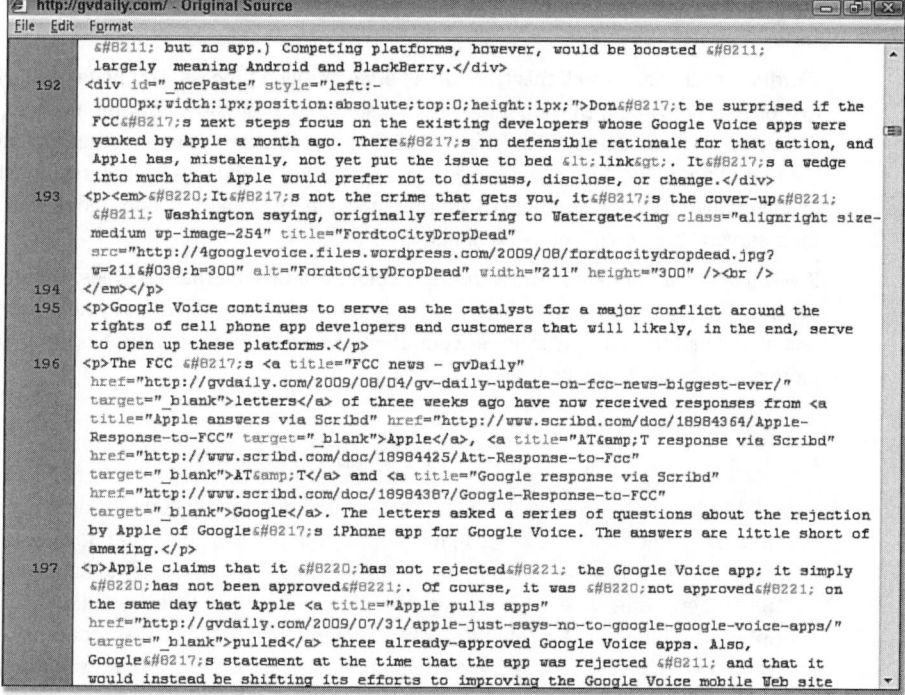

```
http://gvdaily.com/ - Original Source
File  Edit  Format
        &#8211; but no app.) Competing platforms, however, would be boosted &#8211;
        largely  meaning Android and BlackBerry.</div>
192     <div id="_mcePaste" style="left:-
        10000px;width:1px;position:absolute;top:0;height:1px;">Don&#8217;t be surprised if the
        FCC&#8217;s next steps focus on the existing developers whose Google Voice apps were
        yanked by Apple a month ago. There&#8217;s no defensible rationale for that action, and
        Apple has, mistakenly, not yet put the issue to bed &lt;link&gt;. It&#8217;s a wedge
        into much that Apple would prefer not to discuss, disclose, or change.</div>
193     <p><em>&#8220;It&#8217;s not the crime that gets you, it&#8217;s the cover-up&#8221;
        &#8211; Washington saying, originally referring to Watergate<img class="alignright size-
        medium wp-image-254" title="FordtoCityDropDead"
        src="http://4googlevoice.files.wordpress.com/2009/08/fordtocitydropdead.jpg?
        w=211&#038;h=300" alt="FordtoCityDropDead" width="211" height="300" /><br />
194     </em></p>
195     <p>Google Voice continues to serve as the catalyst for a major conflict around the
        rights of cell phone app developers and customers that will likely, in the end, serve
        to open up these platforms.</p>
196     <p>The FCC &#8217;s <a title="FCC news - gvDaily"
        href="http://gvdaily.com/2009/08/04/gv-daily-update-on-fcc-news-biggest-ever/"
        target="_blank">letters</a> of three weeks ago have now received responses from <a
        title="Apple answers via Scribd" href="http://www.scribd.com/doc/18984364/Apple-
        Response-to-FCC" target="_blank">Apple</a>, <a title="AT&amp;T response via Scribd"
        href="http://www.scribd.com/doc/18984425/Att-Response-to-Fcc"
        target="_blank">AT&amp;T</a> and <a title="Google response via Scribd"
        href="http://www.scribd.com/doc/18984387/Google-Response-to-FCC"
        target="_blank">Google</a>. The letters asked a series of questions about the rejection
        by Apple of Google&#8217;s iPhone app for Google Voice. The answers are little short of
        amazing.</p>
197     <p>Apple claims that it &#8220;has not rejected&#8221; the Google Voice app; it simply
        &#8220;has not been approved&#8221;. Of course, it was &#8220;not approved&#8221; on
        the same day that Apple <a title="Apple pulls apps"
        href="http://gvdaily.com/2009/07/31/apple-just-says-no-to-google-google-voice-apps/"
        target="_blank">pulled</a> three already-approved Google Voice apps. Also,
        Google&#8217;s statement at the time that the app was rejected &#8211; and that it
        would instead be shifting its efforts to improving the Google Voice mobile Web site
```

What distinguishes HTML as a *Hypertext* Markup Language is the use of additional tags that refer to hypertext links. For instance, here's the HTML code to link some text to the WordPress.com home page:

To go to WordPress.com, click <a href="http://www.wordpress.com">here</a>.

This code causes the word *here* to become a hypertext link. By default, the word *here* is displayed in blue and underlined. When the user clicks on it, the contents of the browser change from the page with the sentence in it to the WordPress.com home page.

The a in the tag stands for *anchor*. (Anchor management is important in complicated websites.)

The href in the tag stands for *hypertext reference*. A chunk of text that isn't a tag, but is used in a defined way within a tag (as is done here), is called an *attribute*. *Hypertext* means that text can exist in various files, on various web servers.

The great thing about learning and using HTML in the WordPress.com environment is that all sorts of hassles are handled for you. You work at the level of individual posts; WordPress handles making up the complete page by putting your post within a theme, as described in Chapter 3. WordPress also hosts your files.

This saves you from one of the biggest hassles in web publishing. Traditionally, web developers create web pages on their own machines. Once everything's right, the web developer then transfers the web page to a web server.

During this transfer, all sorts of things can go wrong because the files go to a different machine, with a different folder structure. The links between files are easily disrupted by the transfer, and all sorts of hassles ensue.

WordPress.com handles all this through a very controlled process. You never upload the title and text of your post at all; that's handled by the Add/Edit Post page. For graphics and, if you choose to use them, audio and video files, you upload files one at a time using another tool, and only then use the files in your blog. You never have to worry about creating a set of link relationships on one machine, then transferring them to another machine. (Automattic might move your blog around on their servers, but you never see this happen.)

If you move to a WordPress software-based blog, you take on these hassles. Different hosting providers might protect you from them to a greater or lesser extent, but you're never quite as protected and carefree as in WordPress.com. However, on a WordPress.org blog, you do have much more power to do things your way.

HTML Support

The late 1990s saw an explosion in Internet-related business called the "dot-com boom." Internet-related companies that had never made a dime in profit, and some that had yet to even generate any revenues at all, were valued at many millions and even billions of dollars. Those that could actually show profit were valued at far more; AOL, famous for helping millions get dial-up subscriptions to the Internet, acquired publishing and film giant Time Warner at the peak of the boom in 2000. A decade later, the merged company is seen as being worth more without AOL than with it.

HTML was at the center of this boom, and the pressure on HTML to do more and more, so websites could do more and more, was enormous. Microsoft (Internet Explorer) and Netscape (Navigator) were the two main companies competing to add new HTML tags to their respective browsers. (Navigator eventually provided the base for today's popular Firefox browser.)

CSS went through a similar boom. In its early days, it was less standardized and less well-supported than HTML. A reliable CSS core that's in widespread use today has evolved.

It's still common today for a web page to not work well on some browsers. In particular, highly functional sites such as banking sites will often work reliably only on recent versions of Microsoft Internet Explorer on Windows-based systems, leaving users of other browsers and other systems, such as Safari users on the Macintosh or Firefox users on various platforms, in the lurch.

Although many of the additions to HTML became more or less standardized, savvy providers—such as the folks behind WordPress—count on HTML only for a core set of agreed-on functions that work not only on personal computers but on all kinds of devices, from smartphones to screen readers for the blind. You can count on your WordPress blog to be accessible to a very broad audience indeed.

The Visual and HTML Tabs

Let's take a close look at the Visual and HTML tabs to get a feel for the differences. Figure 6.2 shows the editing area for both.

Figure 6.2
The Visual
and HTML
tabs do most
of the same
things in dif-
ferent ways.

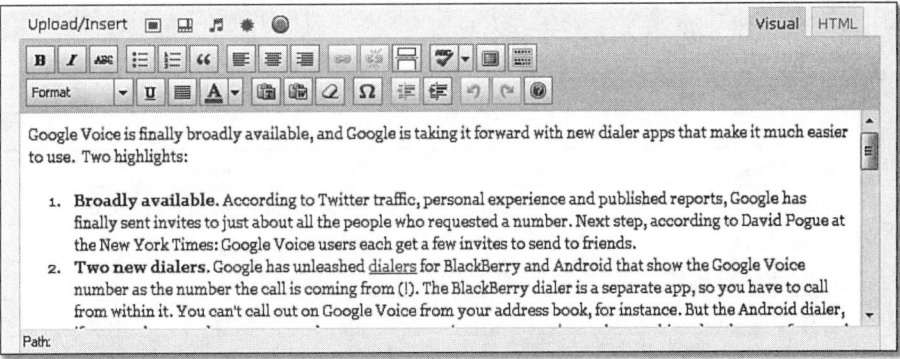

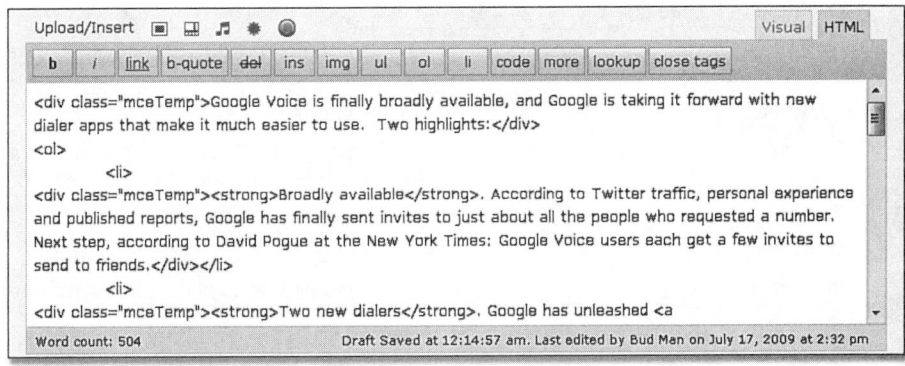

The buttons available on the Visual tab are a close match for those on the HTML tab. Table 6.1 shows the correspondence between one and the other. The first section shows the main, or top, line of editing buttons; the second section, the second line of editing buttons, only appears when you click the Kitchen Sink button on the first line.

Table 6.1   Buttons for Visual and HTML Tabs

Visual Tab	HTML Tab	Meaning
Image	img	Insert image
B	b	Bold
I	i	Italic
~~ABC~~	~~del~~	Strikethrough
Bullets	ul	Unordered list (bulleted list)
Numbers	ol	Ordered list (numbered list)
	li	List item (bulleted or numbered list)
Left-align		Text aligned left, ragged right

Table 6.1 Continued

Visual Tab	HTML Tab	Meaning
Center		Text centered
Right-align		Text aligned right, ragged left
Link	link	Hyperlink
Break link		Remove hyperlink
More tag	more	Provide special link to the complete post
Spell-check		Check spelling
Full-Screen mode		Expand to editing window only
Show/hide kitchen sink		Display/hide additional formatting options
Paragraph pull-down (includes Address, Preformatted, headings 1–6)	code	Various text formatting options
Underline	ul	Underlined text (can confuse readers by looking like a link)
Centered		Centered image
Text color		Change the display color of text (can confuse readers who think the text is a link)
Text import		Bring in text from text editor
Word import		Bring in text from Microsoft Word
Remove formatting		Change text to plain, unformatted text
Outdent		Reverse any indenting
Indent		Indent the text by shifting the left margin to the right
Undo		Reverse most recent change
Redo		Re-instate most recent change
Help		Go to Codex (note that this is not very specific help)
	ins	Inserted text, that is, to note updates
	lookup	Look up item in dictionary
	close tags	Add ending tags to open items, but check where WordPress puts them

Character Formatting

The character formatting commands that are made available in WordPress are the ones most widely supported in HTML: bold, italic, and—a bit of a latecomer to HTML—strikethrough.

Figure 6.3 shows text on the Visual tab of WordPress using the bold, italic, and strikethrough formats. The beginning words of each sentence are in *italic—How, Where, What, Why.* The word *you* is repeated in **bold** four times. The word *so* is shown in ~~strikethrough~~.

Figure 6.3
Formatting is easy to understand on the Visual tab.

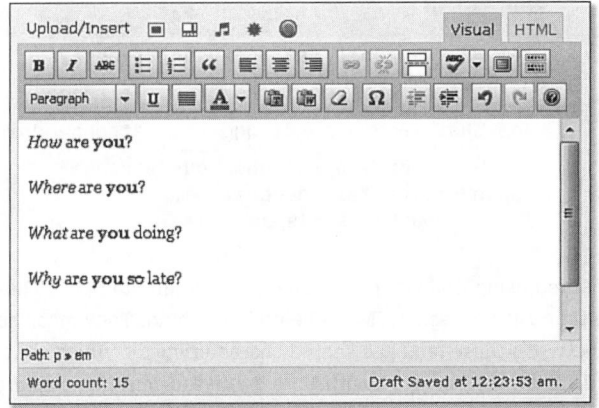

Figure 6.4 shows the same text on the HTML tab. You can see the HTML codes that cause the formatting on the Visual tab to be displayed.

Figure 6.4
Formatting is a bit trickier on the HTML tab.

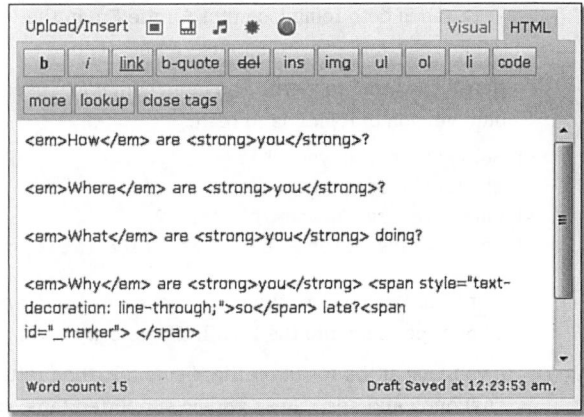

Now, what's going on? Table 6.2 shows the text in visual and HTML modes for comparison.

Even though WordPress displays the bold button as **B** on the Visual tab and **b** on the HTML tab, it actually implements bolding with the `<strong>` tag, not the `<b>` tag. This is a combination of practicality—no one would know what WordPress meant if they showed *strong* in the button—and purity in the use of HTML.

Similarly, the `<em>`, or emphasis, tag is used for italic.

Table 6.2 Visual Versus HTML Text

Visual	HTML
How are **you**?	`<em>How</em> are <strong>you</strong>?`
Where are **you**?	`<em>Where</em> are <strong>you</strong>?`
What are **you** doing?	`<em>What</em> are <strong>you</strong> doing?`

Why are **you** ~~so~~ late?	`<em>Why</em> are <strong>you</strong>`
	`<span style="text-decoration:`
	`line-through;">so</span> late?`

Strikethrough is implemented using CSS via the `<span>` and `</span>` tag pair. These tags are like a red flag to let you know that classic, basic HTML is being left behind. They mean something like this: "The span of text between these tags has shared characteristics," which are then defined within the opening tag. In this case, the `style` attribute defines formatting, called `text-decoration`, which is `line-through` to produce the strikethrough effect. It's understandable that WordPress uses CSS for this; the strikethrough effect is implemented in HTML as `<s>`, `<st>`, or `<del>` (for *delete*) in various versions of HTML.

Still, the pure version is much harder to read. If you get some experience working with HTML, you learn to ignore the HTML tags when you want to read the underlying text. It's much harder to ignore `<strong>` when you're scanning in this way (because it's actually a word) than `<b>`. The `<em>` tag is both reminiscent of Auntie Em in the *Wizard of Oz*, or an em dash if you work with typography, and easy to confuse with `<strong>`.

Here's the same text with the more commonly used tags, so you can see how much clearer a less pure version of HTML is to read:

```
<i>How</i> are <b>you</b>?
<i>Where</i> are <b>you</b>?
<i>What</i> are <b>you</b> doing?
<i>Why</i> are <b>you</b> <st>so</st> late?
```

WordPress will accept the more commonly used, and easily understood, tags, such as `<b>` and `<i>`, if you type them into the HTML tab, or copy them in from a tool that uses them.

If you look at the result on the Visual tab, then return to the HTML tab, the tags will be changed to `<strong>` and `<em>`. Less widely supported tags, such as `<st>`, are simply dropped; you'll have to notice they're missing and reenter them in a WordPress-approved form on the HTML tab, or by using the buttons on the Visual tab.

The Mysterious `<p>` Tag

The paragraph, or `<p>`, tag is one of the greatest sources of frustration in HTML editing.

The `<p>` tag was originally used to indicate formatting, not meaning; you dropped one in when you wanted to end one paragraph and start another one.

Most web browsers display some blank space at the start of the next paragraph. It's common for web page designers to often want either no extra space or a lot of extra space.

If you didn't want the extra blank space, you used the <br>, or break, tag instead, to force a line break. However, if you wanted more space, you were stuck. Most browsers are programmed so that, if you use multiple <p> tags, multiple <br> tags, or a mix of both, the "extra" tags are ignored. You can't get the extra spacing conveniently with HTML.

Over time, the paragraph tag has often been used as a container tag, with a <p> tag at the beginning of a paragraph and </p> at the end. This is a more purist approach, in that the beginning and ending tags denote, "this is a paragraph unit," whereas <p> by itself meant, "put a paragraph break here!"

In CSS, it's more common to use the <div> tag to indicate a division, the exact nature of which is defined in a style sheet. This is powerful but obscure, as you have to look in the style sheet file to understand what the <div> tag will do. And because one style sheet can override another—that's why they're called Cascading Style Sheets—you might have to look in many files to figure out what's going on.

WordPress hides tags such as <div> from you in HTML mode; it must be that it's confusing enough without them!

Now that you see how hard it is to get HTML to give you a break, you can understand the frustrations web designers have suffered for years. It's common for web designers to relate how frustrations with HTML, CSS, and various browsers have led them to break down in tears.

List Formatting

It's good to understand the list formatting in WordPress because lists are very convenient (for you and your readers), but also a frequent source of frustration with HTML. Browsers tend to display lists in ugly ways—with a wedge of blank space in front of the first list item and no spacing at all between items.

It's quite common for HTML maestros to use all sorts of tricks to make lists come out better and for CSS experts to use CSS, in an approved way, to get excellent results.

HTML implements lists by specifying the type of list up front, then surrounding each line in the list with tags to show it's a list item. This makes it easy to switch between the two types of lists that HTML supports:

- **Unordered list**—*Unordered* means "it doesn't matter what order is used," but HTML always displays the items in the order you provide them. Unordered lists always show up as bulleted lists. However, calling them *unordered* instead of *bulleted* is part of the preference in HTML for specifying meaning, not specific formatting details.

- **Ordered list**—*Ordered* means "the order is important," and browsers always display ordered lists as numbered lists.

The group of items in unordered (bulleted) lists are surrounded by the <ul>/</ul> tab pair. Each list item is preceded and followed by the <li>/</li> tag pair, with *li* standing for *list item*.

In ordered (numbered) lists, the items are surrounded by the <ol>/</ol> tag pair. Just as with unordered lists, each list item is preceded and followed by the <li>/</li> tag pair.

Table 6.3 shows two lists as they appear on the Visual tab and the HTML tab.

Table 6.3   Visual Versus HTML Lists

Visual	HTML
These are a few of my favorite Shakespeare quotes:	These are a few of my favorite Shakespeare quotes: `<ul>`
All the world's a stage, And all the men and women merely players.	`<li> All the world's a stage, And all the men and women merely players.</li>`
The evil that men do lives after them; The good is oft interred with their bones.	`<li> The evil that men do lives after them; The good is oft interred with their bones.</li>`
The course of true love never did run smooth.	`<li> The course of true love never did run smooth.</li>` `</ul>`
From first to last, my favorite Shakespeare quotes are:	From first to last, my favorite Shakespeare quotes are: `<ol>`
The little foolery that wise men have makes a great show.	<li> The little foolery that wise men have makes a great show.</li>
The web of our life is of a mingled yarn, good and ill together.	<li> The web of our life is of a mingled yarn, good and ill together .</li>
There is nothing either good or bad, but thinking makes it so.	<li> There is nothing either good or bad, but thinking makes it so.</li> </ol>

Note that the formatting for the lists looks very similar; the only difference is the use of the <ul>/</ul> tag pair for one and the <ol>/</ol> tag pair for the other. When editing HTML, it's easy to change from one type of list to the other just by changing two u's to o's or vice versa.

Also note how the list items in the column of HTML code are indented, as they are in WordPress, for both the unordered (bulleted) and ordered (numbered) lists. This indenting has nothing to do with the HTML code itself; it's called "prettyprinting," whether it's used for onscreen display or a physical printout. Prettyprinting is used with various kinds of code to make it easier to work with. Some HTML editors have very elaborate prettyprinting, including further use of indentation, colors, fonts, text styles (bold, italic, and so on), and any other ploy that helps make it clearer what's going on in all that code.

You can see that, even in this brief example, the HTML code takes up a lot of space on the page. The same is definitely

 **note**

It wouldn't be a bad idea for Automattic to include a full-screen HTML editor alongside the full-screen version of the editor for the Visual tab in future versions of WordPress. Until then, you'll have to find workarounds.

true onscreen. A big part of the reason that WordPress is a poor HTML editor is the limited screen space available for the contents of the HTML tab in the Shared-Screen mode of the Post editor.

Linking

Linking is the creation of hyperlinks in HTML code. Hyperlinks are at the very core of the Web.

Specifying a link can be quite difficult and links are easy to make a mistake in or to have break even after they've been working for a while. Luckily, links in WordPress are simplified, without taking away much from what you can do. And you can always dive into the HTML and make a link as complex as you want.

For light work with a WordPress.com or WordPress.org-based blog, though, the main reason for understanding linking is that it's one of the main reasons you'll work in HTML rather than on the Visual tab. This is for two reasons:

- Many websites give you HTML to add to your page if you want, for instance, to include a video. The Google Voice website gives you HTML to include a Call Me button for your Google Voice number. AltaVista gives you code for various Translate This buttons for your blog, and so on.

- Linking is also useful for the Text widget that we describe later in this chapter.

There are three forms of links worth being familiar with:

- **A link to a home page**—An example is as follows:

    Visit `<a href="http://www.wordpress.com">WordPress</a>`.

    HTML is doing a lot of the work for you here. When you give a domain name as the link destination, a web browser looks for a web page called any of the following:

    ```
    index.htm
    index.html
    home.htm
    home.html
    ```

    These web page names are privileged in that you don't have to enter them for a web browser to look for them. You don't even need to know which one of the four forms the website's author used; any of them will do.

- **A link to any web page**—An example is as follows:

    Visit the new Great Stuff list at `<a href="http://www.wordpress.com/greatstuff/ latest.htm">WordPress</a>`.

    This takes you to the WordPress.com site, into a folder called `greatstuff`, and to a web page called `latest.htm`. (Web page files always end in `.htm` or `.html`.)

- **A link within a web page**—An example is as follows:

    Visit the new Great Stuff list at `<a href="http://www.wordpress.com/greatstuff/ latest.htm#item20">WordPress</a>`.

As with the previous example, this takes you to the WordPress.com site, into a folder called `greatstuff`, and to a web page called `latest.htm`. It then goes one step further and scrolls down to a special type of tag called an *anchor* within the file. (If the anchor is missing, the link takes the user to the top of the page.) The anchor takes this form:

```
<a name="item20"><h4>Item 20</h4></a>
```

In this case, the anchor is around a header, as is commonly the case. For anchors of this type, the `<a>/</a>` tag pair doesn't have to surround anything, as it marks a point in the file rather than a designation. However, some of us like to surround text with the tag pair so that if things are moved around, the intended destination of the anchor is clearer.

 **caution**

Web pages and named anchors within web pages change and are moved around all the time. Blog postings are somewhat specific to the time when they're written, so you don't necessarily have to recheck them over time to make sure the links are okay. But for static pages, or your top few all-time favorite posts, you might want to periodically check links and repair any that have been broken by changes at the destination end.

These are the kinds of links that you'll need for the Text widget, described later in this chapter. For links within web pages, you can add anchor tags to your own blog posts or static pages, and you can look in the HTML code for a web page, as described previously, to find existing anchor tags to which you can link.

Anchor Management

Technically, the beginning of a link is called an anchor, as well as the destination. A named anchor within a file, such as the `item20` anchor described previously, is simply a specific type of link.

However, most people, even HTML authors—who tend to be careful with words—still use the term *link* or *href* for the beginning of a link. The term *anchor* is used for specific, named anchors within files.

So if you read or hear anchors being discussed, it usually means a named link destination in a web page. Unless you're hanging around down at the shipyards, in which case, anchors aweigh!

The More Tag

WordPress includes a WordPress-only tag called More that shows how HTML works—and how WordPress uses it to make your life as a blogger easier.

The home page of your blog shows your most recent posts. However, if a post has a More tag in it, only the part before the More tag displays. The part after the More tag only shows if the user links to it, either from your blog home page or somewhere else.

The More tag looks like this:

```
<!--more-->
```

As far as HTML is concerned, any tag that begins with the exclamation point character, !, is a comment. Web browsers ignore such tags, so you can put remarks to yourself in them. Comments are often used for notes to support project management for website creation and updating, such as a list of changes to the site.

However, WordPress.com is not just any website. It can set rules by which, for instance, comment tags can be analyzed and treated as meaningful if they meet certain rules. The More tag is a specialized comment tag.

You can insert a More tag in your post at any point you like to make your blog home page act the way you want it to.

HTML Editing in WordPress

The Post editor is quite good as a WYSIWYG editor and really, really poor as an HTML editor. Here's why:

 **tip**

Many users expect to see the whole of the most recent blog posting when they visit a blog home page. You can put up new posts with no More tag, but insert it in older posts. That way, you can include whole posts on your home page for your most recent one, two, or three posts (or however many posts pleases you), and only initial teasers for older entries.

- As a WYSIWYG editor (that is, on the Visual tab), the Post editor offers buttons for HTML features, easy integration of content from text editors or Microsoft Word, spell-checking, and a Full-Screen mode.

- As an HTML editor, the buttons are confusing and, much worse, there is no Full-Screen mode. HTML eats screen space, and being forced to work in the narrow confines of the Shared-Screen mode of the Administration area makes it almost impossible to see what you're doing. The lack of basic capabilities, such as Find and Replace, really shows in HTML editing as well.

Because the Post editor is a poor HTML editor, the ability to use WordPress for HTML work is limited. If you need to do extensive HTML work with your WordPress blog, you should work in a different editor, and cut and paste between the other editor and the Post editor.

The possibilities for becoming confused and losing time or losing work when you're switching back and forth between editors are obvious, but manageable.

There are a lot of HTML editors out there for different platforms, and there's no one universal standard. A wide range of editors appeared when the Web exploded in popularity in the 1990s; some editors that were popular then are no longer supported or receive minimal support, a picture which changes year by year. For example, the widely popular FrontPage tool from Microsoft has been *orphaned*—withdrawn from sale and left without updates. Microsoft replaced it with a much more technically oriented set of tools, called the Microsoft Expression Studio, that competes with the widely respected, but also complex, Dreamweaver suite from Adobe.

To find an HTML editor for your computer type, search online for reviews. You can find adequate basic editors as freeware or shareware, then upgrade to paid software if and when your needs dictate.

What Tags Can I Use?

If you know something about HTML, you'll be wondering just what tags you can use. If you use external resources to learn more about HTML, you'll soon be wondering the same thing.

Here are the tags you can use that we've already mentioned (though WordPress might convert them to other tags): a, b, `blockquote`, br, del, `div`, em, `li`, `ol`, p, s, `span`, `strike`, `strong`, and `ul`.

Here are some additional tags, with a word or two of description so you can follow up on the interesting ones: font (yes, you can specify fonts in your blog!), h1, h2, h3, h4, h5, h6 (headers, from biggest to smallest), hr (a horizontal rule or line), img (insert an image using similar rules as for a web link), and table (powerful and potentially dangerous, as tables often work differently on different browsers).

Just for completeness, here are the remaining tags that are supported (several of which are dependent on the table tag): address, abbr, acronym, big, caption, cite, class, code, col, dd, dl, dt, i, ins, kbd, pre, q, sub, sup, tbody, td, tfoot, tr, tt, and var.

We mentioned previously that WordPress uses XHTML. What does this mean to you as you work directly in HTML?

Not that much because most of the additional complexity of XHTML comes at the level of the overall page and its major divisions (head, body, and so forth), which WordPress handles for you.

Here are a few key rules to follow to make your code work as XHTML:

- **Use all lowercase for HTML**—This was always the "cool kids'" way to write HTML code, but in XHTML it's a rule.

- **Nest tags properly**—If you surround a word with the <b>/</b> tag pair, then make the same word the beginning of a link, the <a> and </a> tags should surround the <b> and </b> tags, not be intermixed with them.

- **Use tag pairs**—In particular, always use the <p>/</p> tag pair, not the <p> tag by itself.

- **Always put attribute values in quotes**—Before, you might have worried whether a browser was too stupid to tell the difference between an attribute and an argument. Under XHTML, the answer is officially "yes." So format a link, for instance, this way:

  Come to the <a href="www.metaverse.wordpress.com">Metaverse</a> for more.

If you follow these simple rules, your HTML code should work well in either an HTML or, as with WordPress, an XHTML environment.

As with HTML tools, there are many sites about HTML and XHTML; some are out of date, some might not be technical enough, some might be too technical, and some might be just right for you. Search for the tag name you're wondering about, along with the keywords "HTML tag" to find a variety of sites that will define the tag name for you. You'll soon find a site you like.

Here are tags you can't use, for security reasons: embed, frame, iframe, form, input, object, and textarea.

YouTube as an Example of Embedded HTML

YouTube is a good example of a service that provides you HTML to put in your web page—in the case of WordPress, in your blog posting.

YouTube is a great service to use with WordPress. When you put a YouTube video on your site, all you really put on your site is a link. The actual video stays on YouTube's servers, not on WordPress's servers.

When your blog visitor clicks the Play button on a video, the streaming all happens between YouTube's servers and your user's machine. Your blog isn't directly involved at all.

The really cool thing is that you don't pay for any of this. Before YouTube, it was common for web publishers to pay high fees to have video streamed—partly because of the very large amount of data being transferred and partly because of the extra command and control code and bandwidth required to achieve good streaming performance. If you wanted the hosts to compress your video, that would cost even more. Google, YouTube's owner, pays for all of this for you. (And, as of this writing, continues to lose a great deal of money on YouTube, but that's not your problem.)

Your visitor will know it's a YouTube video because it has the word *YouTube* stamped into the image, but a bit of branding is a small price to pay. You get to share the information, entertainment, or other benefit of the video with your blog visitor with little hassle and no expense.

You can use either HTML or a new approach called oEmbed to embed a video. With oEmbed, you simply insert a URL, not a chunk of HTML code. However, using the HTML code gives you more control, so it's good to know how to use both.

Here's how to use HTML to host a YouTube video (other services that provide HTML for you to paste in are similar):

1. If you have a post in progress that you'll be putting the video on, save it and preview it to make sure there are no problems before you insert the HTML code for the video.

2. Go to YouTube at www.youtube.com. If you have a video, upload it; you'll find instructions in Chapter 9, "Adding Graphics to Your Posts."

3. Find a video you want to share on your blog, or go to the video you just uploaded.

4. On the right edge of the YouTube web page with the video, find the area with the fields labeled URL, which has the web page address of the video, and Embed, which has the code you need to embed the video in your blog.

5. Click the Customize button next to the Embed code. Additional embedding options appear below the embedding code. The example shown in Figure 6.5 is from The Onion, a satirical website.

6. Set or clear the check boxes to include related videos, show a border, and enable delayed cookies. Click the rectangles to choose a color scheme and set a size for the video.

   As you change the settings, the embedding code is changed. Try changing the size and you'll see the change in the values assigned to the width and height attributes, which are visible onscreen next to the prompt. (Note the XHTML-friendly quote symbols surrounding the values.)

   We recommend you generally say no to related videos, yes to including a video, and yes to delayed cookies (which only sets a cookie on your user's machine if they play a video, not just when they see the preview image). Choose the color scheme and image size that best fit your blog posting.

7. Click in the code area next to the Embed prompt and copy the code.

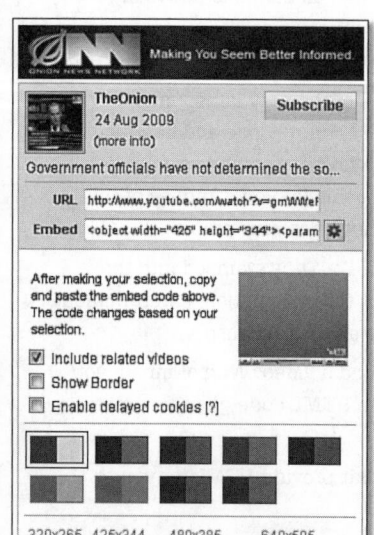

Figure 6.5
The Onion will make your blog
visitors cry—with laughter.

8. In your WordPress post, click the HTML tab.

9. Scroll up and down in the blog post's HTML code to find the spot where you want to insert the video. This can be difficult in a long post. You might need to copy the HTML code out to another program, such as a word processor, and use its larger window, Find capability, and other functions to find the right spot, and then return to WordPress to insert the video in the spot you found.

10. Paste in the HTML code, as shown in Figure 6.6.

11. Preview the post to make sure the video works and that the settings you chose in YouTube are the best choices for your blog posting.

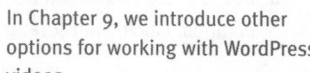

note

In Chapter 9, we introduce other options for working with WordPress videos.

12. If needed, return to YouTube and change the settings, repeating steps 6–11 until you're happy with the result.

When you're done, you'll have your blog posting where you want it, looking how you want it.

Figure 6.6
HTML isn't
usually funny,
but the result
can be.

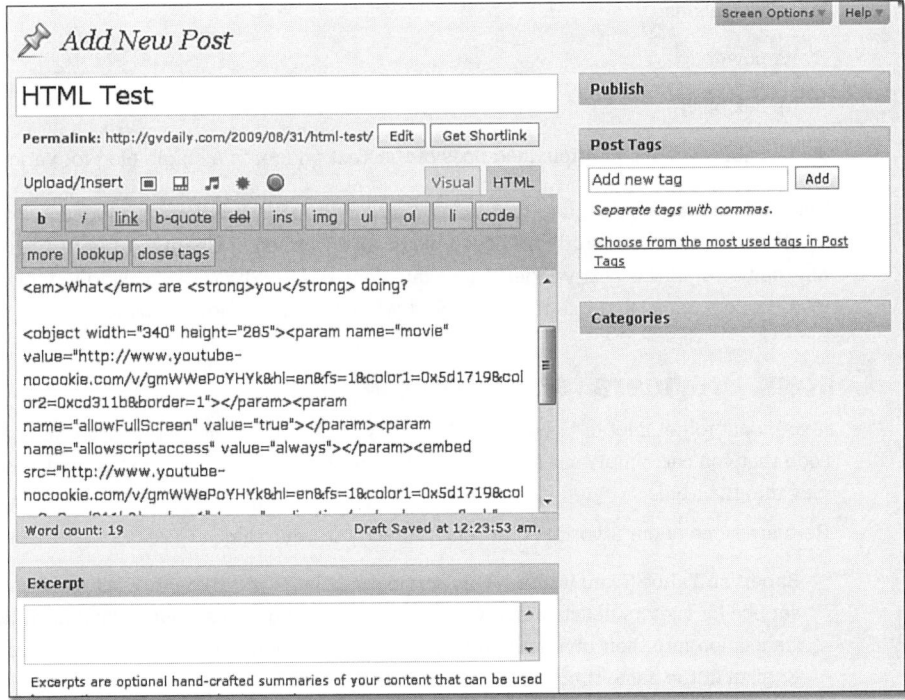

 caution

The terms of service for WordPress.com prevent commercial activity. Many online commercial activities begin with cutting and pasting HTML code into your web page or blog. Resist the temptation to engage in commerce.

You might find some borderline activities you can get away with, for a greater or lesser period of time, but the WordPress community won't like it. You're likely to find that you need the support of the WordPress community to visit your blog, link to your blog from their blog postings, show you how to improve your blog, put you on their blogroll, and so on. Also, eventually, you might get an official "cease and desist" request from Automattic, or simply find the offending feature removed from your blog.

There are no such restrictions on commercial activity for blogs based on the WordPress software supported by WordPress.org. If you want to engage in commerce on your blog, move to WordPress.org. If you aren't quite ready to do that yet, continue on WordPress.com, learning how to run a good and useful blog, and then move to WordPress.org when you're ready. Chapter 11 tells you how to upgrade.

Using the Text Widget

In Chapter 3, we described the widgets you can use with a WordPress.com blog in detail. We left out the details on two of the best widgets because they need more explanation to use properly. The Text widget is covered here; the RSS widget is described in Chapter 8.

According to the WordPress.com support pages, the Text widget is the most popular widget of all, for three reasons:

- Its power

- Its flexibility

- The ability to use multiple instances of the Text widget in a single blog for various purposes

The Text widget is so popular that many plug-ins—the big brothers of widgets, which are only available to WordPress software-based blogs, as described in Chapter 10—are available for enhancing the power of the Text widget. One example is the WYSIWYG Text widget, which makes it easy to add colors, links, and images to the Text widget without knowing code.

Content Providers for the Text Widget

If you want to get a lot of power into the Text widget quickly, several content providers provide code that you can simply cut and paste into your Text widget. Your Text widget becomes a gateway into their blog.

Here are some of our favorites that relate directly to your blog:

- **Babelfish Yahoo Translation**—This service translates your blog for visitors. This is a marvelous service for visitors because many web users have English as their second or third language; a translation into their own language helps them get more out of your blog and improve their English at the same time.

- **ClustrMaps**—This is a hit counter that tracks where your blog visitors come from. It is fun, informative, and likely to generate comments.

- **Delicious**—This site, shown in Figure 6.7, is probably the most influential social media site for bloggers to blog about blogging—and track what they like most. Getting attention on this site sends your visits skyrocketing. Check it out—then join.

Here are a few content providers that add functionality to your blog:

- **Bitty Browser**—People can surf the Web in a widget! Shown in Figure 6.8, Bitty Browser is great for helping people go someplace you recommend without really leaving your blog at all. It is highly configurable and hours of fun.

- **Flickr**—Get into your Flickr photos. This is great if you're a Flickr user, or willing to become one to easily add photos to your blog.

- **Last.fm and Pandora**—Get the latest charts from Last.fm and favorite songs on Pandora. Let people listen while they surf your blog!

- **YouTube**—You can have a permanent YouTube window in your blog. It's great fun, but perhaps a good way to lose visitors who go off to YouTube instead?

Figure 6.7
Make delicious
your friend.

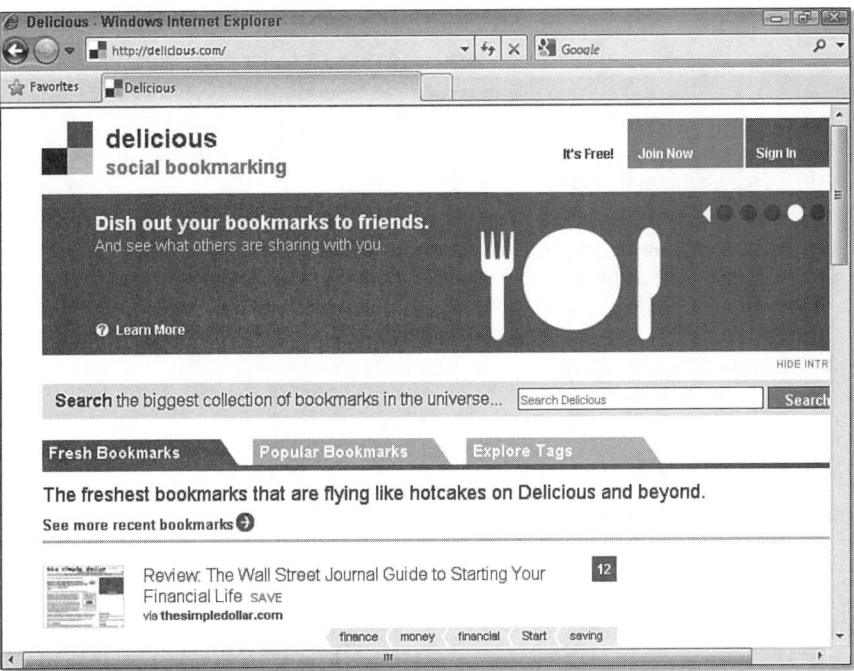

Figure 6.8
Bitty Browser
has plenty of
power.

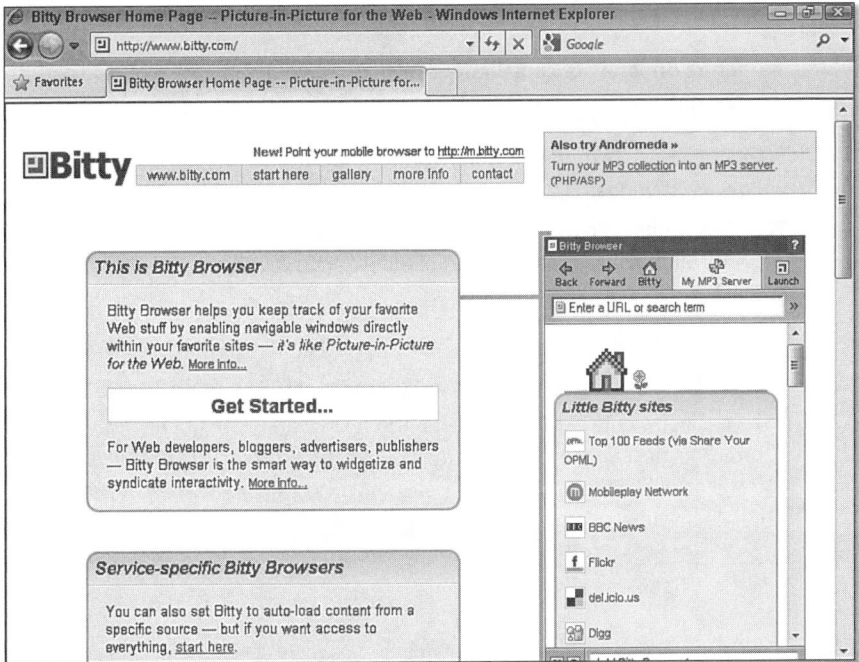

Links to these content providers and more are available on the Text Widgets page in the WordPress Codex:

http://codex.wordpress.org/WordPress_Widgets#Using_Text_Widgets

---

 caution

We'll briefly repeat the kid-in-a-candy-store warning that we gave with regard to widgets in Chapter 3; it's especially relevant when you see all the content providers for the Text widget. If you use more than a few widgets, including different versions of the Text widget, your visitors are likely to ignore most or even all of them. Be somewhat selective in deciding how many Text widgets to try on your blog; then try them, and be even more selective in deciding which ones to keep. Focus on relevance to your own blog as the deciding factor. (You can also ask your blog visitors to contribute their opinions on which widgets are best; that's part of what a blog's for, isn't it?)

Things You Can Do with the Text Widget

Now that you've seen some of the great things content providers can give you for the Text widget, what can you do with the Text widget yourself?

Here are just a few ideas to get you started:

- **Lists of key posts**—You can list your top posts of all time, or by a specific topic. You can link to the most commented posts. You can create a "getting started" list on your main topic(s) for newcomers. This can be a great way to help people get to know your blog.

- **About you/about your topic**—You can give a few words of introduction or welcome and perhaps links to a few key resources, on or off your blog.

- **Picture directory of contributors**—You can create a directory of blog contributors with their photos.

For more on the Text widget from WordPress.com support, visit http://support.wordpress.com/widgets/text-widget/.

The Text widget can contain text, HTML code, and small images. At one time, JavaScript was allowed, but it caused too many problems. The Text widget cannot contain code such as JavaScript or Flash.

Getting Images into the Text Widget

The easiest way to get an image into the Text widget is to upload it to the WordPress Media Library, as described in Chapter 9. Then use the URL from the Media Library in the Text widget. The HTML looks like this: `<img href="URL">`, where URL is the web address of the image provided by the Media Library.

A Simple Sample Text Widget

You can create Text widgets when you add the Text widget to your blog. Here's an example of creating a Text widget; the one shown here combines text, graphics, and simple HTML:

1. In the Administration area, click the Appearance header, and then click Widgets. The Widgets page appears, as shown in Chapter 3.

2. Drag the Text widget from the Available Widgets in the center of the screen to the Sidebar on the right. The Text widget opens up.

3. Enter a title for the widget. This is important; a poor or confusing choice of title might annoy people every time they see any page of your blog.

   We've titled the example widget ANDROID-RELATED POSTS, in reference to Google's Android operating system for mobile phones. (Widget titles always display in UPPERCASE.)

4. To add a graphic to the widget, upload it to the Media Library, as described in Chapter 8. Then copy the URL into the Text widget, using the img tag.

5. To add text and HTML to the widget, enter it in free-form fashion. Be sure to click the Automatically Add Paragraphs check box, unless you want to add a lot of <p> and </p> tags yourself.

   For our sample site, a typical entry contains the name of a post, surrounded by code to link it to its permalink. The result looks like this:

   ```
   <a href="http://gvdaily.com/2009/04/24/dialing-international-who-needs-mobile-
   minutes/">Dialing International: Who Needs Mobile Minutes?</a>
   ```

6. Click the Save button regularly to save your work.

7. When you're finished, click Save one last time, and then click Visit Site.

   Our sample Text widget's code along with the resulting widget are shown in Figure 6.9.

When you're done, always review your work, note what works well, and consider how to improve it.

For the Text widget described here, for instance, here are the things we like:

- A nice, distinctive image—easy to find for repeat visitors

- A good location—the main keyword, Android, is right at the front of the widget title

- A clear, simple topic

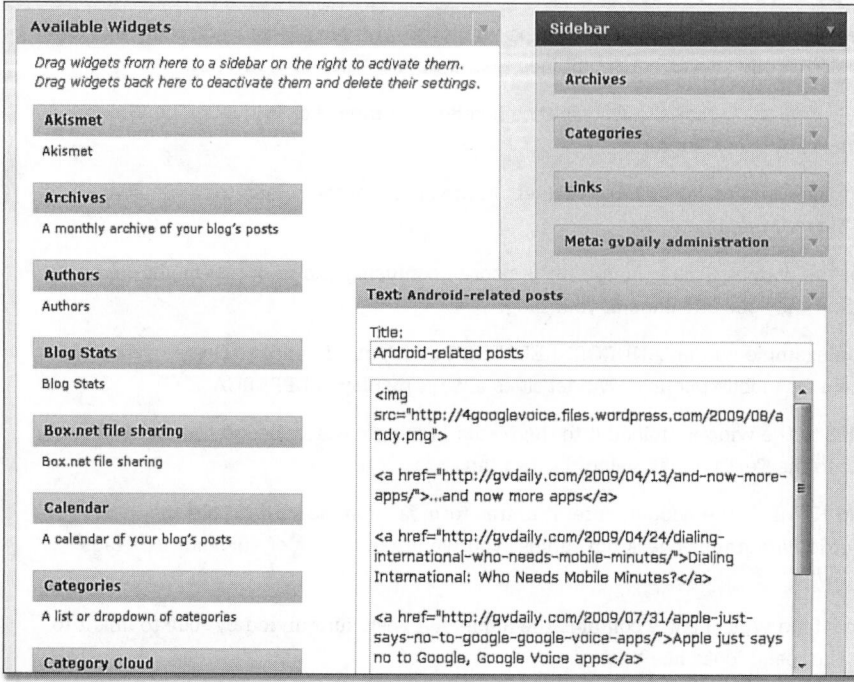

Figure 6.9
Text widget code isn't pretty...but the results can be beautiful.

Here are the ways we'd probably revise it on a second try:

- Revise the HTML code so that links move up into the space next to the figure, using vertical space better.

- Add some guiding text such as "Most recent first" at the beginning, or even dates next to the posts, so people knew what was recent and what was historical.

- Add a post to the site explaining what Android is and how it's relevant to the main topic of the site, Google Voice, then link to that in this widget.

 tip

There is another way to create Text widget contents. Just create the content like it's a blog posting, using both the Visual and HTML tabs as needed. Preview the posting to make sure it's what you want. Then cut and paste the HTML out of the Add/Edit Post page's HTML tab into the Text widget and view the result.

7

ADDING FEATURES TO YOUR BLOG

Making Your Blog Better

The core of blogging is that it's an ongoing conversation between yourself and the people who visit your blog. Some of those people are bloggers themselves, some are visitors who comment, and the vast majority are *lurkers*—people who read your posts, but rarely or never comment themselves.

You can think of your blog as being like a tree, with a core approach that reflects a certain set of interests and beliefs as the trunk. You can, in effect, make the tree bigger by adding static pages. Static pages, which visitors can refer to again and again, add to the base of your blog.

The major categories for your posts—whether you do a careful job of specifying them explicitly, or whether they're implicit—are the branches, and the posts themselves are the leaves or needles. As you add more posts, you build up the tree.

You can build up the tree faster, and in directions you wouldn't have anticipated yourself, if you add other users and administrators to your blog.

Many WordPress features are like ornaments on the tree. They draw attention to the tree as a whole, and perhaps to certain parts of it.

Comments are the best ornaments of all. They increase the value of your posts by adding new perspective and new information. They show comeone cares.

Pings are like comments, but hosted on another blog, and can expose your blog to people who would never see it otherwise. WordPress notifies you of comments and pings.

Polls and ratings are a light form of comment. People can express their opinion with just a few clicks, while demonstrating that they're interested in being part of the conversation.

All of these elements work together. Better posts, better categorization and tagging, more comments, poll results, and ratings each contribute to the other.

Many bloggers reach a kind of moment of truth after blogging for awhile. After perhaps a few months, a number of posts have accumulated and the basic direction of the blog has been established. Pageviews might settle into a certain range, depending on the news or other kinds of events on a given day.

If the blog is left alone at that point—which is easy to do—your interest and visitors' interest might fade. The alternative, which WordPress does more to enable than most competing approaches, is to use what you've learned to improve and reinvigorate your blog.

You can do this gradually or in a quick burst of energy; both approaches have their fans and their good and bad points. If you go through this book gradually, and use the suggestions in it to improve your blog, you'll see results over time. Or you can take a quick-burst approach and do a lot of work in a week or two.

The features described in this chapter all represent things you can do to make your blog more interesting and more fun for visitors.

Support Is Temporarily Closed?

We doubt we are the only ones to have been shocked the first time we clicked the Help link from a WordPress administrative page and got the error message shown later in this chapter, in Figure 7.1: "Support is Temporarily Closed."

This seemed really strange. It's not like we tried to access some kind of live help feature that might or might not be staffed at certain times. This is just normal searching the support area for information.

If Google or another major automated service goes down for a couple of hours, it's big news. And WordPress, to its credit, seems to do an excellent job of keeping its millions of blogs up and running For some reason, however, Automattic seems to think it's acceptable to take its Help database offline on an all-too-regular basis—and WordPress bloggers, if their lack of protest is any indication, seem to be used to it.

We suppose this is good for WordPress book authors because you can't turn a book on or off. It's definitely not the best thing for WordPress bloggers! (And yes, we'd rather see the right thing happen for bloggers, which we also are, rather than just for authors.)

You can work around much of the obstruction by using a search engine to find answers. Start with the word *wordpress* and then the search terms relating to your question. For official answers, include both *wordpress* and *codex* in the search. One way or the other, the odds are good that you'll find an answer.

Adding Users to Your Blog

WordPress has an odd way of describing people who can contribute to your blog, manage comments, and so on. In addition to you, the blog owner, the roles WordPress recognizes are Administrators, Editors, Authors, Contributors, and Subscribers. WordPress calls all those with administrative capability *users*.

As with some other WordPress capabilities, the bias here is toward power and control rather than simplicity. Six roles (blog owner, plus five roles the blog owner can assign) is a lot. The U.S. Army commands a force of more than a million with just seven ranks: private, corporal, sergeant, lieutenant, major, colonel, and general. Then again, WordPress.com hosts millions of blogs, so perhaps six roles is not overkill after all!

 **note**

The WordPress practice of calling people with administrative capability users seems strange because for most of us, when not in a WordPress context, user means end user; someone who comes along, reads your blog, comments if they feel like it, and leaves, but can't alter any of the blog's structure. In WordPress-speak, a user is everyone but an end user!

Understanding WordPress User Roles

The best way to describe such closely spaced roles is to list what they can do. From the bottom up:

- **Subscriber**—Reads comments, comments, and so on.

- **Contributor**—Writes posts, and manages them, but someone else must publish.

- **Author**—Publishes his or her own posts, in addition to having all the capabilities of a Contributor.

- **Editor**—Manages and publishes other people's posts, in addition to having all the capabilities of an Author.

- **Administrator**—Uses all administration features without limits.

- **Blog owner**—Holds the Administrator role, possibly along with others. For WordPress.org blogs, the blog owner also maintains and backs up the database and manages the WordPress file repository (see Chapter 11, "Installing and Upgrading WordPress Software").

As blog owner, you can create new users (that is, what anyone else would call by one of the role names), assign a role to each new user, and assign a default role for new users (see the following list).

For most smaller blogs, you can get by with a smaller array of roles. We recommend two or three:

- **User** or **Subscriber**—Reads comments, comments, and so on. You only need to make this role explicit—make people subscribers who have to have a WordPress login—if you're having trouble with some users and have to require a subscription for someone to comment.

- **Contributor** or **Author**—Decides whether to let people who write posts publish their own posts, which makes them Authors (which is what we recommend), or just a Contributor who has to wait for someone to publish posts for them (which, if you're going to be controlling, should be you, we suggest).

- **Editor/Administrator/Blog owner**—Usually the blog owner is the sole superuser and is the only one with access to administration; IOHO (that's In Our Humble Opinion, not a misspelling of Ohio), this is easier for other "users" (as WordPress calls them) and for you as well.

Why do we recommend obliterating the Contributor versus Author division and just making anyone who writes posts an Author, able to publish their own posts?

There are three main reasons:

- **Simplicity**—A great attraction of blogging is simplicity. Don't add unnecessary structure.

- **Timeliness and informality**—Two big and related plusses of most blogs are timeliness and informality; timeliness is lost directly if a separate publishing step is needed, and informality tends to go due to self-editing by a self-conscious Contributor, or directly, when you yield to the temptation to edit in your opinions, approach, or wording instead of the original author's.

- **Editability**—It ain't print; if you don't like something, you can always change it postpublication. If you're quick, you can make the change before many people see the original. If you aren't quick, think of what you would have given up in timeliness by holding the piece until you could get around to it.

As for administration, it's a lot easier to have one administrator (in the broad sense of the term, not the specific WordPress role). When there's more than one, you can feel a kind of seasickness as you wonder if the ground (that is, what your blog "is" and where things are) has shifted under your feet.

The usual solution to this is to institute a change-control process with proposed changes, permissions, and approvals, but now we're talking a lot of overhead. Better to give away one important piece of power—allowing users to publish their own contributions directly—and keep the rest for yourself.

>  **note**
>
> For an impressively detailed description of the roles available for WordPress "users," visit http://codex.wordpress.org/Roles_and_Capabilities.

Inviting Users and Assigning Roles

Bringing new users—that is, of course, people with administrative capability—into your WordPress blog is easy, but only if each of the people involved already has a WordPress account. Follow these steps:

1. If you plan to add a new user, ensure they have a WordPress account and that you have their email address handy. Anyone can get a WordPress account at www.wordpress.com.

2. In the Administration area, under the Users menu in the left column, click Authors and Users. The Users page appears, as shown in Figure 7.1.

Figure 7.1
The Users
page allows
you to add
new users to
your blog.
Note also
that Help was
offline when
we initiated
this process.

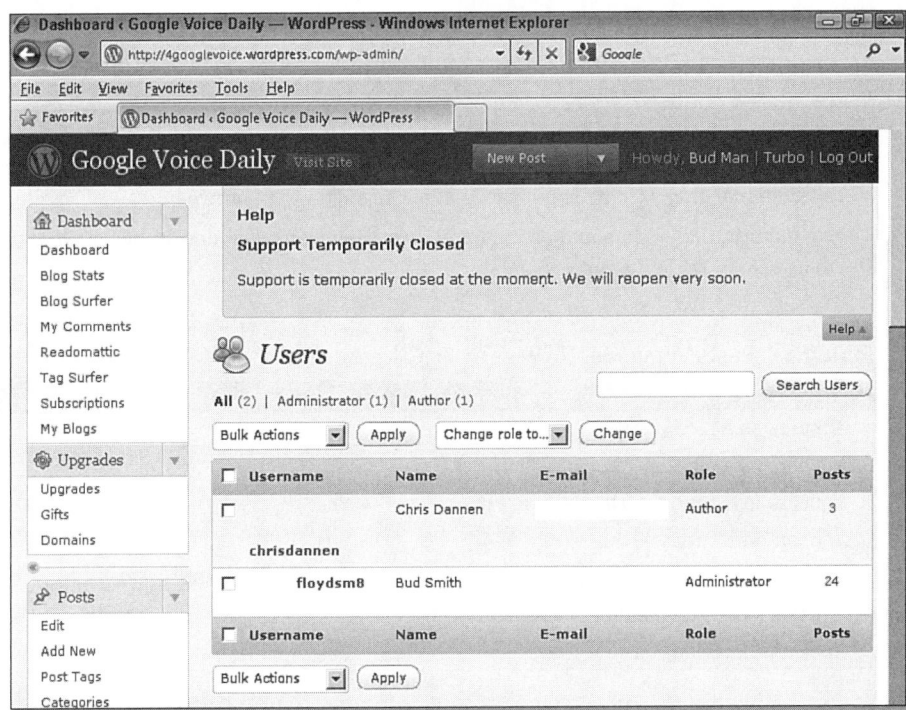

3. Enter the email address of the user.

4. From the pull-down menu, choose a role for the user. The roles are in random order, neither in order of increasing capability, decreasing capability, or alphabetical. (The order is Contributor, Administrator, Editor, Author.)

   Contributors can write posts but not publish them; Authors can write posts and publish them; Editors can manage others' posts; Administrators can use all the capabilities in the Administration area.

5. Click the Add User button.

6. The user's name (from their WordPress account) and other information is added to the Users area.

In the Users area, you can show all users, or all users of a specific type; remove users or change their roles, using check boxes and pull-down menus; or click on the number of posts for a user to see all posts by that user.

Adding a Static Page

Static pages are what the rest of the world calls web pages. It's a page on your blog in which no blogging content appears.

WordPress is notable among blog publishing tools for having a robust static page capability. It's so robust that you can use WordPress to build a traditional website with no blogging capability at all, a traditional blog with no static pages at all, or anything in between.

It's important to understand all the differences between posts and static pages so you know when to use each. Table 7.1 sums them up.

Table 7.1   Posts Versus Static Pages

	Posts	Static Pages
Appears as a blog post	Yes	No
Appears as a static page	No	Yes
Appears in category archives	Yes	No
Appears in monthly archives	Yes	No
Appears in by-author archives	Yes	No
Appears in search results	Yes	No
Appears in navigation	Yes	No

As you can see from the table, posts and pages are entirely complementary; there's almost no overlap between them.

What are the implications of this for your blog? All information in your blog, especially important information, should appear in posts. That's the only way people are going to find it if they experience your blog by reading posts—live, as they appear, or in archives—or via search. Search is becoming the default way of finding information for many people, so to be search friendly, information must appear in posts.

However, key information should also appear on static pages. Many of us still resort to using the navigation to get certain kinds of information or for context—a quick read on the content, structure, and purpose of a site. This can be before, after, or instead of searching for information.

If key information isn't available in static pages, it will never be found by at least some people. So you should build up your static pages over time to include everything important in your blog.

How do widgets fit in this? On most blogs, news sites, and similar sites, top-headlines lists and so on are additional to search and standard navigation; they're shortcuts. So you should use available widgets, and your own semicustomized versions of the

 tip

If you want to create a fully functioning website in which the blog is only one of several attractions, refer to books and other resources about creating websites, and talk to people with experience in it. Plan the website in a top-down manner, drawing on the bottom-up experience you've gained in WordPress. Then implement your site using WordPress, but in such a way that no one would guess what tool you used to create the site. (Except, perhaps, for the fact that you have a very good blog on it!)

Text widget, to highlight certain things (including, if you want to, your static pages), but not as an alternative to putting information in posts or static pages.

There are two potential guiding principles for adding static pages: on an ad hoc basis or as part of a plan. No sensible standard website is developed without a plan, but WordPress is great for supporting both casual efforts and bigger, planned projects.

WordPress allows you to easily add one-off pages for various purposes. If you keep going, at some point you'll probably create a mess. Then you can step back and reorganize the static pages—or perhaps your entire blog—into something you can really be proud of.

We'll describe how to add one-off pages here—and why you might want to do it. Over time, you might also want to take a more planned approach.

Planning Static Pages

Static pages are great for information that doesn't change often and that supports your blog entries.

Many blogs have key information about who the blogger is and what the blog is for buried in early posts. If the purpose of the blog changes over time, or the authoring team expands, this is apparent to people who follow your blog carefully, through blog entries as well.

The difficulty comes about after your blog has been around for a while. You, as the blogger, feel that all the information needed to understand your blog has been put out there—and it has. Regular visitors to your blog probably have a pretty good idea as to what it's for.

But as your posts accumulate, it's no longer easy—or even possible—for newer visitors to get a sense of what's going on, at least not unless they're willing to go back and read everything ever posted to the blog. Newer posts tend to assume the blog visitor knows information that's effectively buried in older posts.

Newer posts can also get a bit dull because older ones might have already addressed the key information or even controversies in the area of interest, leaving less to discuss. A blog can become reactive, with new posts focused on relatively small scraps of news that impact the issues or area the blog is concerned with.

This same problem can occur with traditional websites. It's why two pages that can be found on almost any website of any size are Contact Us and About Us, or similar pages.

The need for pages covering these areas is perhaps even greater on a blog than on a traditional website. Blogs tend to be very personal. If the information needed to understand what you're about is spread across a lot of previous posts, the newer entries might not make much sense to new visitors.

With that in mind, the following sections list some pages you should consider creating for your blog.

About the Author(s)/About the Blog

For a one-author site, this kind of page gives background that establishes your authority in the area(s) you blog about. It doesn't matter if you have no authority in a traditional sense—bloggers actually can become authorities through their blogs. Visitors, though, will want to know your credentials; if a healthy interest in a topic, and the blog itself, are your only credentials, just say so.

People want to know how to relate to you as an author. If you're an authority—in a sense, talking down to them, however nicely you do it—then they'll want your credentials. You can also position yourself as a partner with your blog visitors, a fellow seeker of knowledge, conversation, or other goals. You can even position yourself as the learner and ask your blog visitors to be the authorities. A new site called Aardvark, at www.vark.com, is shown in Figure 7.2. It's set up just for this purpose.

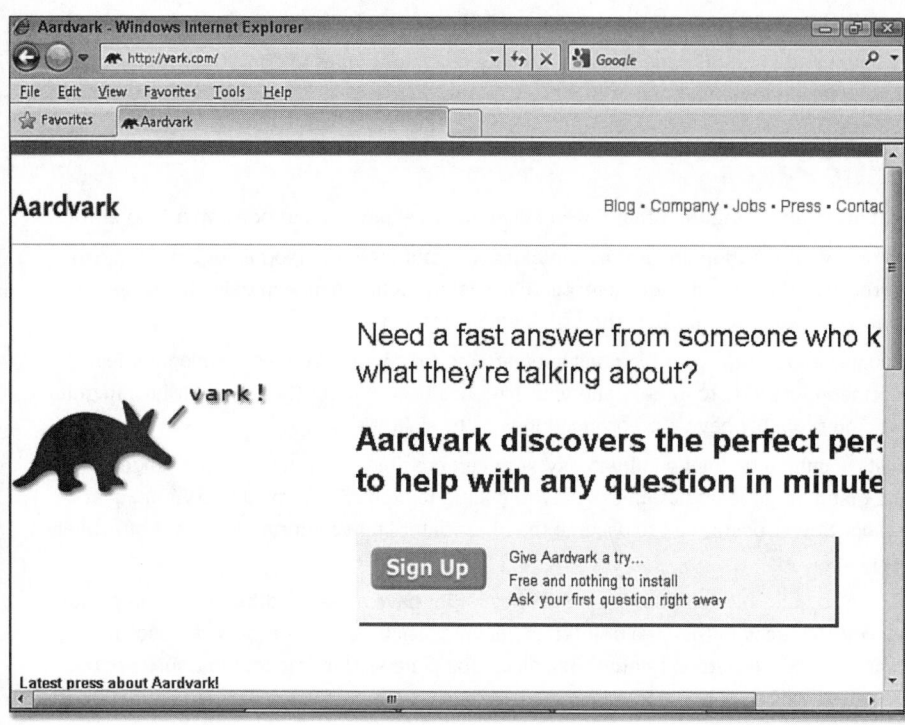

Figure 7.2
Vark.com
helps you
learn—or
share what
you know.

The thing that really annoys people is when you position yourself as an authority and overtly talk down to them when you don't have the necessary background or knowledge to do it. By providing your background information online, you help your blog visitors understand how to relate to you. This kind of information might encourage not only site visits but comments.

An "About" page is even more important on a blog with more than one regular contributor. Site visitors will want to know the overall purpose of the blog and the relationship of different authors of the blog within that. If two of the blog's authors disagree, who might the visitor want to pay more attention to? Where is each author coming from?

This kind of page can focus more on the people involved (About the Authors) or about the blog itself, with authors advancing the blog's purposes (About the Blog). If the latter, you can actually call the section "About the Blog," or use the name of the blog instead.

Contact Us

A Contact page is perhaps the most-used page on a traditional website. People get enormously frustrated when they can't find such a page or when it doesn't include desired information. When this information is present, visitors feel that they're in good hands, and use the site with confidence.

A robust example of such a page is shown in Figure 7.3: the Contact Us page for the U.S. Central Intelligence Agency. (No, it's not classified!) Consider visiting it to see how an agency like the CIA handles different kinds of contacts, from the routine (employment confirmation for credit checks) to the highly sensitive (intelligence information for the war in Iraq). It's at www.cia.gov/contact-cia.

Figure 7.3
The CIA has contact info—and a Kids' Page.

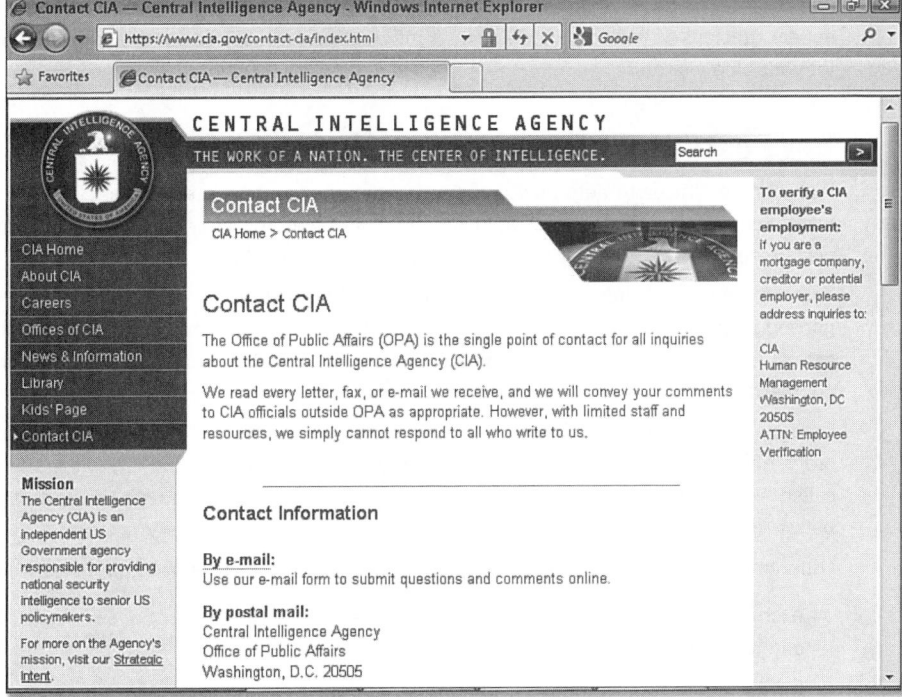

People often use websites purely to get contact information for other means of connecting with someone. Someone might want to reach you as well.

However, your blog visitors probably don't expect you to provide a phone number, but if your blog is anything except purely personal, they probably expect, or at least would like, to have the ability to contact you via email.

If the only way of contacting you is through the blog itself—by posting a comment, for instance— say so. If you're willing, you might want to say that people can leave a comment, with their email address in it, asking for you to contact them, and you'll respond to them by email.

caution

There are programs that search the Web looking for email addresses so they can be added to mailing lists. The mailing lists are used to send spam emails advertising all sorts of things—some legal, some not; a few worthwhile, most not. Most of this junk can be blocked by your email system's spam filter, but to put the robots off the track, consider not including your email address in simple, machine-readable form. Adding some indirection to your email address, such as writing "budsmith (at symbol) gmail (dot) com" is usually enough to fool machines without making things too difficult for humans.

Also be aware that people might be able to contact you by using information in your blog to search for, and find, your email address, phone number, employment, or other information online. One of us (Smith) recently found a coauthor for a book this way. If "the truth is out there" anyway, it will appear gracious of you to provide contact information (at least an email address) in a handier form for your blog visitors.

Top Posts and Widgetalia

Widgets are written to help provide information and resources that your site visitors are likely to want. Some of the top widgets feed back into your blog with information such as highest-ranked posts (see Chapter 3, "Creating Your Blog's Look," for details).

You can provide this information in more managed forms that are easier to use and with more supporting information in a static web page on your site. Widgets, for example, are mechanical; a widget can only show your top posts by number of visitors and in a machine-specified order, such as by popularity.

It might be, though, that some of your most popular posts tell a story if you put them in the right order, and that a few key posts aren't among your most popular. By creating a static web page called "Key Posts" or something similar, you can meet your user's needs—to understand your blog better and get pointers to the most important posts—better than a widget can.

Other widgets are also good indicators of possible topics for static web pages as well:

- **Archives**—Your Archives widget can get quite tall after half a year or so; a static web page might be a better approach.

- **Authors**—You can combine author information with links to top posts and all posts by a given author.

- **Key Comments**—You can highlight interesting comments, encouraging more comments from people hoping to make the list on your static web page.

- **Links/Blogroll**—With a static page, you can provide contextual information as to why a site is valuable for visitors to your blog.

This is only a beginning. Static web pages allow you to mix and match information; you can put information about a blog author, links to their key posts, and links to all of their posts together, just for one example.

tip

If you're really clever, you can "steal" cool stuff for your static web pages from the WordPress Administration area. (It's not really stealing; the information is yours, and WordPress is open source, so do as you like!)

For instance, the Users page in the WordPress Administration area, mentioned previously, includes links to all the posts by a given author. It would be nice to have that in a static web page, wouldn't it?

Well, the link to all posts by a given author is just a WordPress database query like this one:

http://mygreatblog.wordpress.com/wp-admin/edit.php?author=123456789

The query includes the underlying WordPress blog name and the unique author ID. If you use this URL in your static web page, it will return the same list as it does when used within the WordPress Administration area.

You can reuse other such URLs from the Administration area and widgets to improve your static web pages.

Designing a Static Page

When you design a static page for WordPress, you don't really have control of the whole page. Your new page appears within your blog's look and feel, and the sidebar or sidebars that are part of your theme remain as well.

The good side of this is that WordPress still takes care of a lot of the HTML/XHTML complexities for you, as they have to do with the code for the page as a whole; you only need to worry about what appears on the page itself.

Your users also are likely to have fairly low expectations for the design of your static web page. In fact, they probably expect your static web page to look like a blog entry, which is how they tend to look in WordPress unless you put a fair amount of work into designing them to look different.

You do need to think about how your static pages relate to each other. Try for a very simple model at first: Just have one level of navigation with a single page per level. This extends your blog while maintaining the simplicity that people expect from a blog.

When you start to have submenus of navigation, people have to think about your blog as a website as well as thinking of it as a blog. This can make the heads of your site visitors hurt. People tend to avoid doing things that make their heads hurt, even if the avoidance happens at a subconscious level. So don't do that or they'll avoid your site.

If you create so many static web pages that you need sublevels of navigation, that's fine, but it means you might need to redesign your site as a static website that has at least one really excellent blog in it, rather than as true blog-first blog. Develop or borrow the expertise needed to create a really good traditional website and go for it.

 tip

Use the Text widget (see Chapter 6, "Using HTML in Your Widgets and Blog") to create supplementary navigation for your site and static web pages. This might be more obvious and more convenient for blog-oriented users than the navigation that comes with the theme you're using.

Creating and Editing Static Pages

The steps for creating or editing a static page are similar to each other, and are also very similar to the steps for creating or editing a blog posting.

To create a static page, follow these steps:

1. In the Administration area, under the Pages menu in the left column, click Add New. The Add New Page page appears, as shown in Figure 7.4.

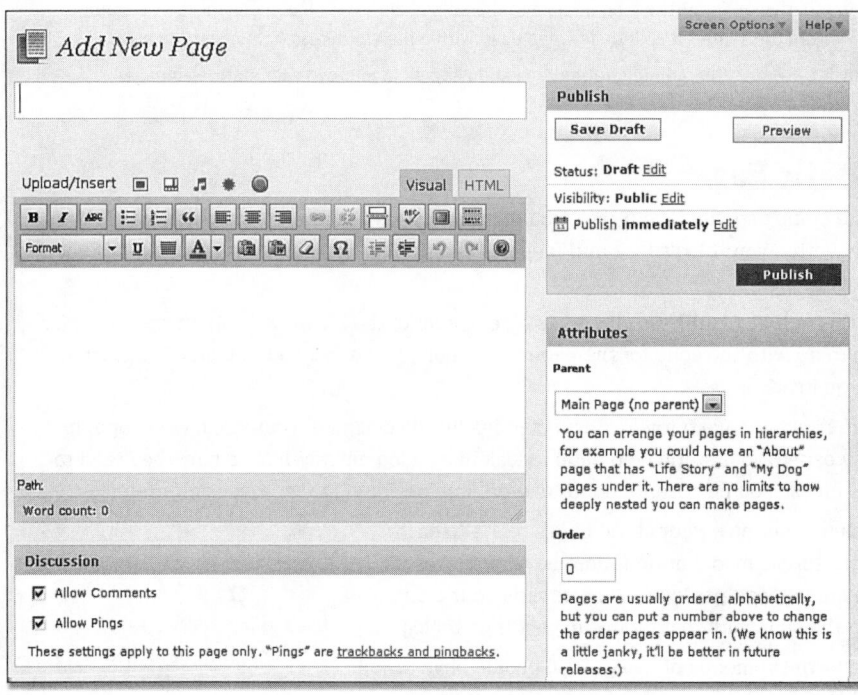

Figure 7.4
Adding new pages builds up your site.

2. Use the Visual and HTML tabs, as described in Chapter 4, "Creating Your First Post," and Chapter 6, respectively, to create your static web page.

   Whereas blog posts are typically read more like a magazine or newspaper story, web pages are more often skimmed by people looking for key pieces of information. Keep text brief. Use bulleted lists, headings, and graphics to break things up. Help your blog visitor get back to reading your wonderful blog postings!

3. Use the check boxes to allow or not allow comments and pings.

   We recommend that you consider not allowing comments; a static page is structural rather than conversational. An exception would be if you were giving a page a trial and asking for comments during the initial period.

As for pings, it might make more sense to allow them. That way other blogs can link to valuable reference information that you provide in your static pages. However, both choices are up to you; there's no right answer.

4. Use the pull-down menu to choose an author for the page.

For static web pages, the actual authorship—who wrote the content—is less important than the ownership, that is, who's responsible for the page going forward. Use the pull-down menu to specify the owner of the page rather than the actual author.

5. Choose a parent for your page from the pull-down menu.

We recommend avoiding the use of parent pages as much as possible to keep the navigation for your blog simple. If you do need parent and child pages, take the time to design your blog as a website to keep it easy to use.

6. Use a number to specify the order of your pages.

This is admittedly a clumsy way to do it: Use the Order box to specify the order of your pages, from 0 on up. The default order is alphabetical, but you should take charge and use the Order box to specify the order for pages to display in. A typical location for a Contact Us page is last or rightmost in the navigation.

7. Click the Publish button to publish your page.

Publish your page, but check it carefully before and after. Check static web pages even more carefully than blog postings; whereas people might excuse the occasional hasty mistake in a blog posting, they'll see static web pages as more permanent, structural parts of your site. Mistakes here will be taken as evidence, especially by people who disagree with some of the viewpoints in your blog postings, that you are really, truly, and irredeemably an idiot.

---

 caution

One of the authors (Smith) helped with the editing of a book in which a Table of Contents entry was dropped in the transfer from proof to printing. This left the book with a serious error, but one only noticeable to careful readers.

Yet even people who like the book often comment first on the missing entry, and it's been the starting point for some negative comments about the book on Amazon, which almost certainly affects its sales. Everyone involved in what is otherwise a fine book is eagerly waiting for the current printing to sell out so the error can be fixed!

Although your blog isn't a printed book that people pay for, it's still true that everyone's a critic. In many cases, even minor errors will get more attention than otherwise wonderful information or opinion. The bigger your blog becomes, the harder you should work to reduce errors to a minimum, especially in static pages.

Adding Polls

In the beginning of this chapter, we compared a blog to a tree with a trunk, branches, and ornaments. Ratings and polls are among the brightest and shiniest ornaments around. They're also among the most controversial.

Why? The underlying question, which also comes up when you're writing, titling, and publicizing your blog posts, is: How far should you go to get attention for your blog?

Polls and ratings each have their problems. We're all accustomed to polls being presented along with qualifying descriptions as to their accuracy. If you pay close attention to published polls, you'll have seen that sometimes polls are misrepresented as being more, well, representative than they really are.

Political campaigns have even created push polling, in which the point is not really to gather information, but to put unsettling allegations into the heads of the people you're supposedly polling.

A typical push polling question goes something like this: "If you were to be told that (our opponent) was a lying, thieving creep—who picks out all the red M&Ms for himself every time he passes a bowlful, not even leaving us even one—would all this make you: (1) very, very, unlikely to vote for him; (2) very unlikely to vote for him; (3) not sure." The results are then reported as: "Large numbers of those polled are very unlikely to vote for our opponent (and leave us some red M&Ms, darn you)."

So polls on websites get a hard time. Let's all agree, going in, that a blog poll is not representative. It's just for fun! People want to know how other people who visited the site and bothered to vote—so, not "the average citizen"—voted on a question. And, in a more positive version of push polling, you can create fun or funny questions that are even more entertaining than the results you get.

Seen in this light, polls on your site are a lot of fun. If you can get enough visitors, and make the poll interesting enough that it gets a reasonable number of votes, it can also be a valued addition to your blog.

Creating and editing polls are very similar; creating a poll tells you just about everything you need to know about editing one. The overall process for creating and editing polls is also very similar to creating and editing blog posts, though the details are different.

Here, we only describe creating a poll in detail; for editing, we'll count on what you learn in creating a poll, plus your knowledge of editing other WordPress items such as posts, as described in Chapter 2, "Starting Your Blog Right."

Follow these steps to add a poll to your site:

1. In the Administration area, under the Polls menu in the left column, click Add New.

   The Create Poll page appears, as shown in Figure 7.5. Note that the heading also includes a link to List Polls, which is actually where you not only see a list of polls, but can edit them as well.

 note

Fully integrated polling is a relatively recent addition to WordPress, thanks to Automattic purchasing PollDaddy in October 2008. Supporting polls on a site is quite tricky; each poll requires the creation of a database to store the information in the poll and the responses, and displaying the latest poll results to users requires a query to that database. In the past, you had to create an account and even pay to have polls on your site. Since October 2008, and hopefully for many years to come, it's all integrated and free.

Figure 7.5
Help your visitors entertain them-selves with polls.

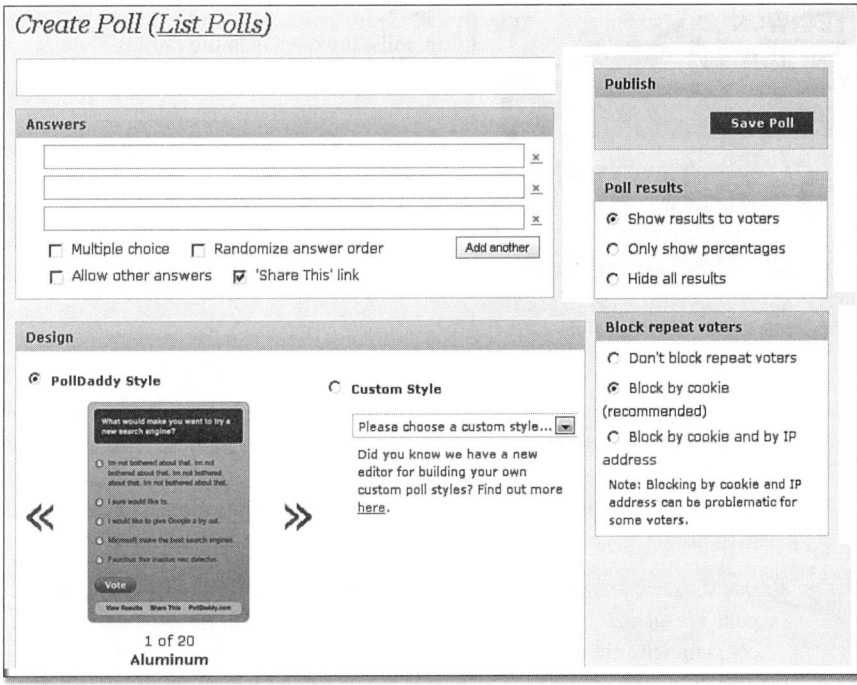

2. Enter the poll question at the top of the page. The poll question is very important indeed. You'll get very different answers to this question: "You want to help your country by running for office, don't you?"; as opposed to: "You don't want to be one of those scumbag politicians, do you?" Try for a light, neutral tone.

Figure 7.6 shows a poll result from TechWorld, a popular blog. It shows that 99% of people regard green IT—that is, the use of information technology in a way that is better for the environment—with skepticism. Yet lots of people are at least a bit skeptical of just about anything. If the question had asked, instead, "Is there interest in green IT in your organization?" a similar proportion might have answered "yes" to that as well, which would have appeared positive for green IT instead of negative. Still, if the intent was to get people going, this poll certainly did.

3. Enter the answers to the poll. If you're trying to maximize responses—always a good idea, unless your blog gets a lot of traffic—yes or no answers are best, as they're easiest to choose and often yield entertaining results. You can enter other answers than just Yes or No, but keep them short, or risk losing potential voters. It's also good to give a logical progression to answers, such as from least to most, to make it easier for the visitor to find the answer they want to give.

4. Use the check box to choose multiple choice or No. Multiple-choice questions demand a lot more thought than one-answer questions, and different people have different standards for how many answers they see fit to provide. The responses are also harder to make sense of. Avoid checking the multiple-choice option unless it's very well suited to your purpose.

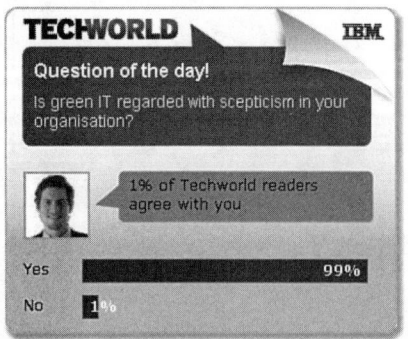

Figure 7.6
In polls, the devil is in the details.

5. Use the check box to randomize the answer order or No. Randomizing answers prevents an answer from getting picked more because of its placement in a list rather than its actual meaning. This is good for casual polling and important for serious polls. Don't use this for answers that have an inherent order, such as lowest to highest, or a customary order, such as yes, then no.

6. Use the check box to allow other answers. Allowing other answers is probably bad for your poll; polls are all about simplicity. They're great for learning from your site visitors though; they can come up with things you never thought of. (Also, perhaps, an occasional obscene suggestion you had considered anatomically impossible, but don't worry—your users won't see the actual text entered, just you.)

7. Use the check box to add a Share This link. Share This is a *viral* feature—a (frighteningly named) characteristic making it easy for a desired action, such as taking your poll, to spread from one person to another.

8. Choose the Design from among the many options. Choose from among the PollDaddy styles—20 as of this writing—and widths (three for most styles). The options are listed in Table 7.2. Most of these styles will clash with many blog themes, due to color, size, or both, so your actual usable choice in your specific blog is probably fairly limited.

   To expand your usable choices, Wordpress.org users can create Custom Styles with another visual editor that lets you edit colors, widths, borders, and the like. If you know CSS, you can even draw up your own style sheet to upload to your blog. Because there is some JavaScript involved in custom styles, WordPress.com blogs are restricted to the standard PollDaddy styles. To learn more, visit http://support.polldaddy.com/custom-poll-styles/.

9. Choose whether to show results to voters. You can show the (numeric) results, only percentages (which helps keep people from knowing if you have embarrassingly few votes), or hide the results. We favor the first if you have a reasonable number of voters and the second if the number of voters is likely to be smaller than you'd prefer. (At very low numbers, even the

percentages are a giveaway; for instance, an exact 75/25 split will look like you received exactly four votes, split three to one. The odds that larger numbers of voters would split so precisely are low.)

10. Choose whether to block repeat voters. You can not try to block repeat voters, block by cookie, or block by cookie and by IP address. The more restrictive choices are more effective but also potentially more problematic for your poll users. WordPress recommends blocking by cookie, to balance effectiveness with avoiding problems for users.

11. Save the poll. Click the Save Poll button. It now appears in the list of polls available from, among other places, the Edit option under the Polls menu in the WordPress Administration area.

12. Create or open a post to which you'd like to add the poll.

13. Navigate to the spot where you'd like the poll to appear.

14. Click the Add Poll button. This is a round button near the buttons for Add Image, Add Video, and so on. A list of currently available polls appears.

15. Under the poll you want to use, click the Send to Editor link. The poll is added to your post. You won't see any sign of it on the Visual tab, but on the HTML tab you'll see a WordPress shortcode like this: [polldaddy poll=1955058]. A shortcode is a special HTML-like code used and understood by WordPress software.

 **note**

For more information about using polls in WordPress, see http://support.wordpress.com/polls/.

16. Click the Publish button to publish the post. The poll appears in your post.

17. To edit polls, bring up a list of polls by choosing Edit in the Polls menu on the Administration page, by clicking List Polls in the Add New page described previously, or by clicking the Add Poll button while editing a post. Then click the Edit link under a poll.

18. To get the HTML code for a poll, bring up the list of polls as described in the previous step, then click the HTML Code link under the title of the poll. The shortcode and JavaScript for the poll appear, which you can then edit.

A poll within a post is shown in Figure 7.7.

 tip

To add a poll to the sidebar of your blog—which is probably a better place for it than the middle of a post—create a Text widget, as described in Chapter 6, and put the shortcode there. Only the first instance of a poll will display on a page, so if you already have it in your post, it won't display in both places.

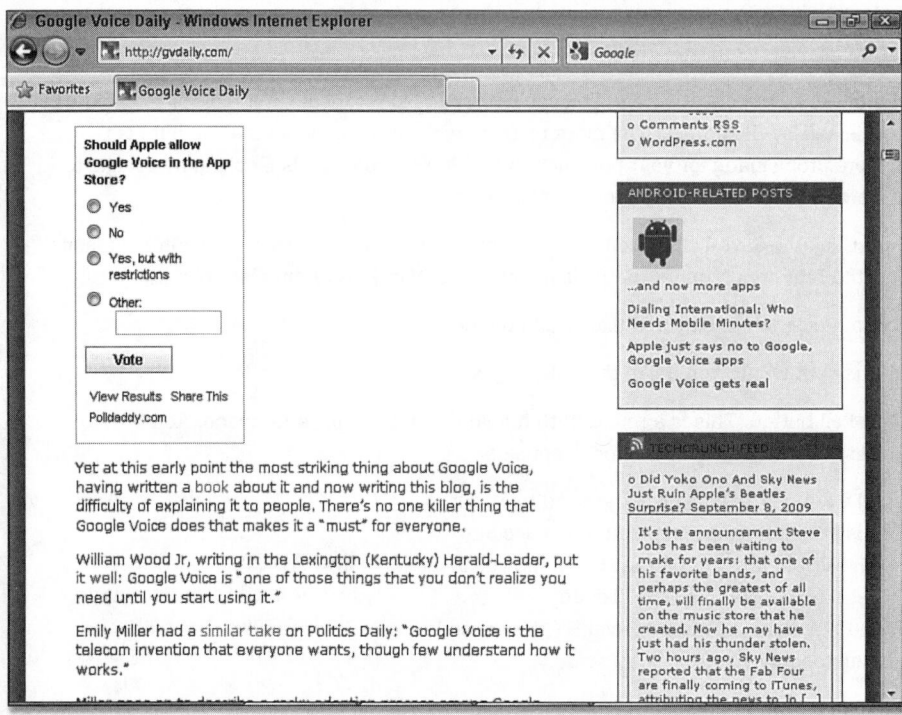

Figure 7.7
Polls don't necessarily fit well in posts.

Table 7.2 PollDaddy Poll Styles and Width Options

Name	Has Graphics?	Width Choices		
		Wide	Medium	Narrow
Aluminum	-	✓	✓	✓
White	-	✓	✓	✓
Black	-	✓	✓	✓
Paper	-	✓	✓	✓
Skull Dark	Skulls	✓	✓	✓
Skull Light	Skulls	✓	✓	✓
Micro	-	-	-	✓ (150 pixels)
Plastic White	-	✓	✓	✓
Plastic Grey	-	✓	✓	✓
Plastic Black	-	✓	✓	✓
Manga	Ink spatter	✓	✓	✓
Tech Dark	-	✓	✓	✓
Tech Grey	-	✓	✓	✓
Tech Light	-	✓	✓	✓

Table 7.2   Continued

Name	Has Graphics?	Width Choices		
		Wide	*Medium*	*Narrow*
Working Male	Man & desk	✓	✓	✓
Working Female	Woman & desk	✓	✓	✓
Thinking Male	Man w/brain	✓	✓	✓
Thinking Female	Woman w/brain	✓	✓	✓
Sunset	Palms & birds	✓	✓	✓

 tip

Ratings and polls work together on your site, along with comments, trackbacks, and pings, as means for people to interact with your blog. We covered comment and ratings settings in Chapter 2. We recommend that you try to think of all of these as different aspects of interaction with your blog and use them together.

In general, we recommend an open approach (unless your content or audience makes that unsuitable). Let people comment without moderation, unless that leads to unacceptable results; use ratings except on static web pages, where they can seem inappropriate. And finally, use polls—to encourage comments and ratings as well as trackbacks and pings.

8

TRACKING STATISTICS AND BRINGING IN VISITORS

Getting More People to Visit Your Blog

Bloggers are obsessed with visits to their WordPress blogs. One of the very best features of WordPress.com blogs is the free, detailed, up-to-date statistics that we take you through in this chapter. (The same statistics are available to WordPress.org blogs as well; just install the WordPress Stats plug-in.)

Apparently, though, the official WordPress stats aren't nearly enough. Statistics are perhaps the most popular single focus for additional plug-ins as well. See Chapter 13, "The WordPress Toolkit: Plug-Ins," for details of finding and installing the plug-ins that fit your needs for your WordPress.org blog.

Even that, though, doesn't meet everyone's needs. Google Analytics, as comprehensive a web analytical tool as most of us could imagine, can be hooked up to a WordPress.org blog as well. It takes hours to learn to use it correctly, but the results are said to be amazing. (Neither of us is that nerdy, at least with regard to blog stats.)

So rest assured that even if you're a WordPress.com user now, limited to the really rather good statistics built in to your blog's Administration area, you have a healthy growth path ahead in WordPress.org if you want to take advantage of it.

Even if you use additional plug-ins or Google Analytics, though, it's worth thoroughly understanding the official stats. That way, you can get the most out of them, and have a firm basis for understanding additional statistics offered elsewhere.

Once you know and understand your numbers, you'll want to know how to increase them. WordPress offers many tools for doing just that. Getting someone to visit your blog is half the battle; helping them get the most out of it is the other half.

One great tool for doing this is RSS feeds. The RSS feed widget brings in content from other sites and other blogs to your blog, enhancing its attractiveness. You can also make it easier for others to subscribe to your blog.

With all this in mind, we'll take you through Google Voice Daily, the blog of one of the authors (Smith). We'll show you what works and what doesn't.

WordPress Statistics

It's easy to take WordPress's statistics for granted. You should be aware, though, that they're really, really good.

The whole area of Internet statistics is a minefield of claims and counterclaims. By giving you total views in a nice chart and breaking down the source and destination of your views in several separate, easy-to-use charts, WordPress really distinguishes itself.

One reason for the value of WordPress's statistics is their focus on visits. Because WordPress.com is relentlessly noncommercial, so are the stats WordPress provides. This is actually a valuable perspective even if you have a commercial purpose for your blog. You have to get visitors before you can—here's that ugly word again—monetize them.

You might want—and you can get—many alternatives for statistics for your blog. The built-in statistics, though, are probably the best quick overview you're likely to get.

In this section, we take you through the statistics in some depth. It's worth it—everything you learn will be valuable in understanding your blog's growth (or lack thereof) as shown in WordPress statistics, and will also help you approach other statistics packages from a well-informed point of view.

Why Are You Doing This?

All of us who blog find that getting the blog postings up and edited, then encouraging and responding to comments, can seem like a full-time job.

If you also pay much attention to blog statistics, though, it really does become a full-time job. That's because increasing—let alone truly maximizing—traffic to your blog is like running a rapid-response room in politics. You need to be working on an hour-by-hour basis to see what's happening in the world, the response on blogs similar to yours, and how you can make your voice heard in the fray. And this is without even considering monetization.

Trying to make money from your blog, in addition to actually running it and tracking stats, can really put you over the edge. Most monetization efforts take a great deal of time, and many months to even begin to show results—and some efforts never do produce results.

Several prominent bloggers have quit, complaining of exhaustion from a job that's 24/7 with no natural breaks on which to take a day off, let alone a proper vacation. And trying to blog from a BlackBerry or an iPhone while sitting on a beach somewhere may just mean that you're doing a lousy job of blogging as well as a lousy job of taking a holiday.

How Great Are WordPress's Stats?

The world of web stats is, frankly, a mess. It seems obvious what one would want to know—but you might find, if you try it, that explaining exactly what you want to another person is difficult. Explaining it to a computer—or, at least, to a web stats package—can be downright impossible.

A typical web stats package is focused on pages that are largely static or regularly updated with an ongoing stream of new information. Blog posts are uncomfortably, from a statistics point of view, in-between. There's nothing static about them, but they're not just quickly disappearing tidbits either. So WordPress's ability to track and present views for each specific post is not easy to get elsewhere.

The idea of separate blogs sharing a domain and other resources is a bit beyond most web stats packages as well. Getting a typical web stats package configured to separately treat two blogs on a site is not a simple notion.

WordPress even knows enough to exclude your own visits to your blog. This is a source of noise that can bedevil other stats packages, especially on a slow day, when your own visits might be a significant part (or all of!) the total.

So enjoy your WordPress stats, and use them. Though you might go on to use other stats packages as well, you'll probably still return to WordPress's stats again and again for a quick but detailed understanding of where your blog traffic is coming from and where it's going.

So think carefully about how much time and energy you can commit to your blog—in terms of your finances, your health, and your offline relationships. The online connections you build up through blogging are fun and rewarding in their own right, but they're not usually worth risking all your offline friends and family relationships for.

If your blogging is contributing to your career or to other activities—consulting, writing, and so on—it can be very much worthwhile. And, of course, a few bloggers have hit it big with book and even movie deals.

The recent hit movie *Julie & Julia* was based on a cooking blog. The "Julie" of the title spent an otherwise boring year in a small Paris flat cooking every recipe in a Julia Child cookbook and blogging about it—as well as having various adventures.

Such big hits from blogging are few and far between. Alternatively, if you can keep your blog within the time and energy commitment that you'd otherwise commit to a hobby, it can be a very rewarding and worthwhile use of that amount of time and energy.

Also be aware that the blog can have value beyond the number of hits it gets. If it's important to you to be seen as an expert on purple aphids, having a valuable blog on purple aphids might be worthwhile just for the occasional visit you get from your aphid-loving peers, even if there aren't that many of them. (Aphid-loving peers, that is; there are plenty of aphids around.)

Do try to settle on a goal for your site. It doesn't have to be monetary: "to make more people aware of open source software" might be the goal for the Metaverse blog of one of the authors (McCallister); "to help people take better care of their cats" might be the goal of a very different type of blog. Having a goal increases the focus of your blog and makes it more enjoyable for you and, quite likely, your blog visitors.

Be aware going in that blogging statistics, like blogging itself, can consume dozens or hundreds of hours of your time with little objective return for your effort. Your statistics work will probably improve your blog traffic—but if that traffic isn't doing anything concrete for the rest of your life, you might need to downscale your statistical investigations as well as your overall effort to make it sustainable for you.

In most cases, you should look after yourself first, your blog second, and your blog statistics third (and money fourth, at least until you're ready to quit your day job); it's better all around in the long run.

Stats on Your WordPress Administration Page

Every time you log in to the Administration page of a WordPress.com blog, or a WordPress.org blog with the Stats plug-in, you see a statistics display like the one shown in Figure 8.1.

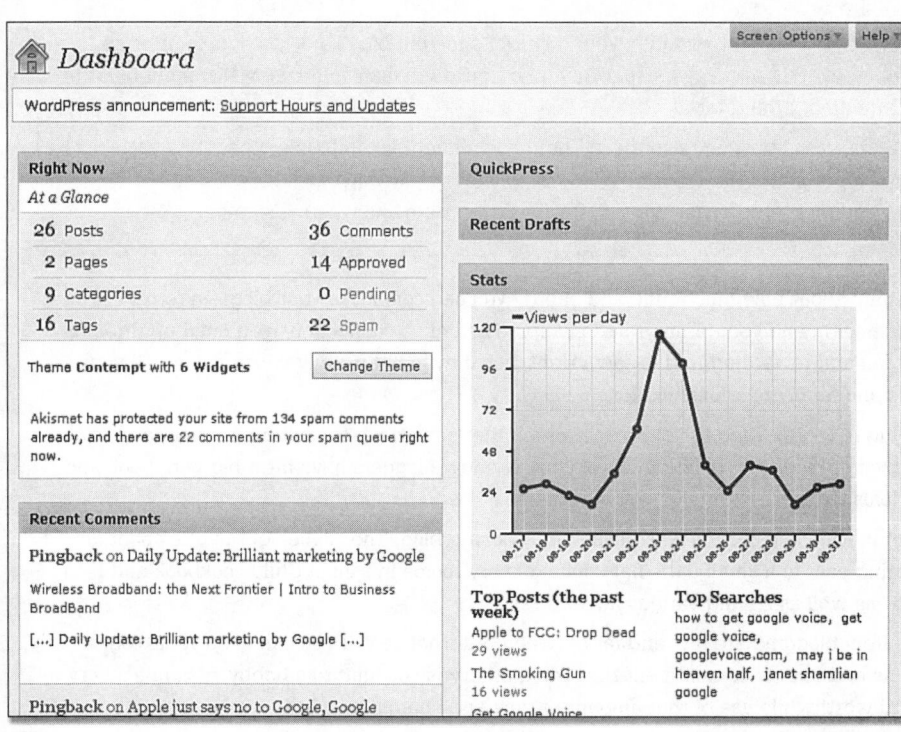

Figure 8.1 WordPress stats greet you every time you log in.

In Figure 8.1, you can see—if you look very closely—a peak in visits a few days before the day of the snap. In this case, the peak is easily explained.

The subject of the blog, Google Voice Daily, is Google's offering for telephone management, Google Voice. The most recent posting to the blog was put up the day before the highest recent peak. It was on the topic of the responses by Apple, AT&T, and Google to a U.S. Federal Communications

Commission (FCC) inquiry into the status of Google Voice on the iPhone. The posting came just a few days after the responses were received. It got a lot of search traffic, and the author of the post (Smith) also posted a comment on the TechCrunch blog in response to an article there. This drove additional traffic. Finally, among the people who've visited gvDaily in the past, some might have bookmarked or remembered it, and come to visit in time to see the new post. A few might have even alerted friends to the post.

Let's take a quick look at the stats offered in this small view before we look at the larger one:

- **Views per Day chart**—WordPress sums up your views per day for the past two weeks in one handy chart. This is really nice to have; you can see whether traffic is increasing or decreasing over time, and put daily stats in context with recent performance.

- **Top Posts (the Past Week)**—This is useful for highlighting what's hot; it would be great if the date of each post could be squeezed in here somehow for perspective.

- **Most Active (the Past Day)**—This is a nice snapshot, though a single day is a bit short as a period for analysis for most blogs. (Except perhaps on a day when something big is happening that drives traffic, especially if you post on it more than once per day.)

- **Top Searches**—This is how people get to your blog when they come in through search engines. A great pointer to what keywords have been working for you.

The Stats Page in WordPress Administration

There are two ways to see the full Stats page:

- Click the View All button in the corner of the Stats area.

- Choose Blog Stats from the Dashboard menu in the upper-left corner of the Administration area.

Either way, you soon see the full Stats page for your blog, as shown in Figure 8.2.

 note

Automattic seems well aware of how important stats are to WordPress users. It has drastically improved its stats offering within the last couple of years and places it prominently on the Administration page, as well as in pride of place as the first entry in the Dashboard menu in the upper-left corner of the Administration page—the first spot most people look at on a page. (It's a good thing for Automattic that Google invented Google Analytics for the truly obsessed, or Automattic might have had to do that as well!)

 note

The first peak of traffic for the blog occurred when Google announced that its Google Voice app was rejected from the App Store—and then, like a scene from *The Godfather*, other developers' Google Voice apps disappeared from the App Store, one by one, over the next day. Within three days, the FCC had its famous letters of inquiry out to Apple, AT&T, and Google, creating a flood of stories—and, apparently, of interest from web users. The second peak is when the companies publicized their responses to the FCC at the deadline three weeks later, as described previously.

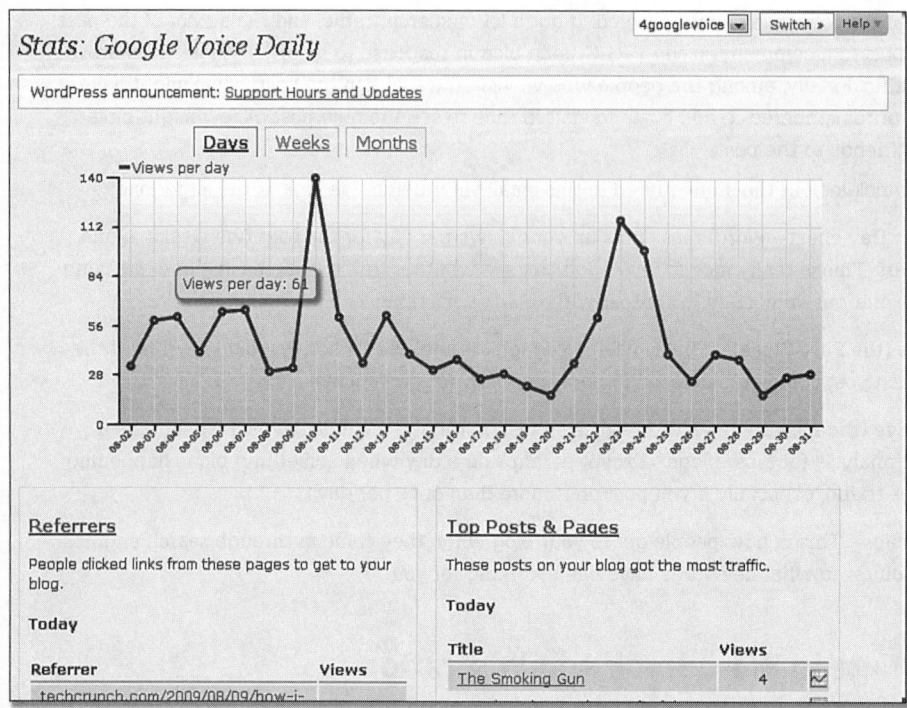

Stats: Google Voice Daily

4googlevoice ▾ Switch » Help ▾

WordPress announcement: Support Hours and Updates

Days | Weeks | Months

■ Views per day

Views per day: 61

Referrers

People clicked links from these pages to get to your blog.

Today

Referrer   Views

techcrunch.com/2009/08/09/how-i-

Top Posts & Pages

These posts on your blog got the most traffic.

Today

Title   Views

The Smoking Gun   4

Figure 8.2
The full page gives you a lot of statistical detail.

This page includes many different types of information pulled together in one useful page. Here's a quick overview of what's on offer:

- **Views per Day, Week, Month graph**—This graph can be quickly switched using the tabs Days, Weeks, and Months. This is a great way to get both detail and perspective on your blog's activity.

- **Referrers**—These are sites people linked to your blog from. If you're getting mentions in other blogs, you can see which ones are driving traffic to you (and encourage more).

- **Search Engine Terms**—These are the search terms that people are entering before they come to your blog. You need to be scoring fairly high on these terms for your blog to be getting much traffic from them.

- **Top Posts and Pages**—Here's where the traffic is going. You can examine your more popular posts to see just what makes them so much cooler than the less-popular ones.

caution

As you click on links from your WordPress Stats page for different areas—Referrers, Search Engine Terms, and so on—detailed results appear on their own page. However, the pages all have the same title, Stats: *blogname*, even though the details are different. Pay close attention to keep track of what page you're on, and which of the stats pages you've visited or not.

- **Clicks**—Where did users go from your blog? This can help you improve links you want people to click on, such as links to your other blog posts—and reconsider any links that are taking too many people away from your blog and off to other sites.

- **Incoming Links**—What are the specific links that are bringing traffic to you? Find out here.

- **Summary Tables**—This provides more good perspective in the form of high points for your blogs, as well as today's stats.

Click on each of the links to go to a detail page for that area; the detail pages are described next.

Analyzing Referrers

Referrers are other sites that send traffic to your blog. For many blogs, referrers are the single biggest source of traffic, drawing from the communitarian, sharing ethic of blogging, in which informal collections of blog authors regularly read and refer to one anothers' blogs.

The communitarian ethic is under a lot of strain as some blogs go large, with hundreds of thousands or even millions of pageviews, while others remain small indeed. You can increase traffic in this environment, though, if you're careful, smart, and not greedy about it.

When you click the Referrers link from the main Stats page, you see a list of referrers to your blog (see Figure 8.3). You can see the total page views from various referrers by day, week, month, quarter, year, and all time.

Unless you're a very active blogger indeed, the view by day is probably too fine-grained for most purposes. The view by week probably sums up the action in a typical blog best.

Getting traffic is not simple. For instance, when it comes to giving your blog post a title, the best way to get referrals from other blogs is not the best way to get search engine hits, and vice versa.

To help get referrers, give your posts a *clever* title. Clever titles for posts attract readers, and people who run other blogs are, first and foremost, blog readers.

To help get search engine hits, give your posts a *relevant* title. That means a title that includes key words from the posting. WordPress uses the title of your post for the permalink (the long-term URL) for your post. So if you use the same words in the post itself and in the post title, which then gets used by WordPress in the permalink, you're off to a running start to a good result on keyword search.

Usually, the clever title isn't very relevant, and the relevant title isn't very clever. So you generally have a choice between being clever or being relevant. Make sure to achieve at least one or the other.

 tip

To help get referrers *and* search engine hits, give your posts a title that's clever *and* relevant. One of the authors (Smith) managed this for his recent blog posting about the Google Voice app for the App Store: "Apple to FCC: Drop Dead." That's a short, punchy, clever title with the two most important keywords, Apple and FCC, right at the beginning.

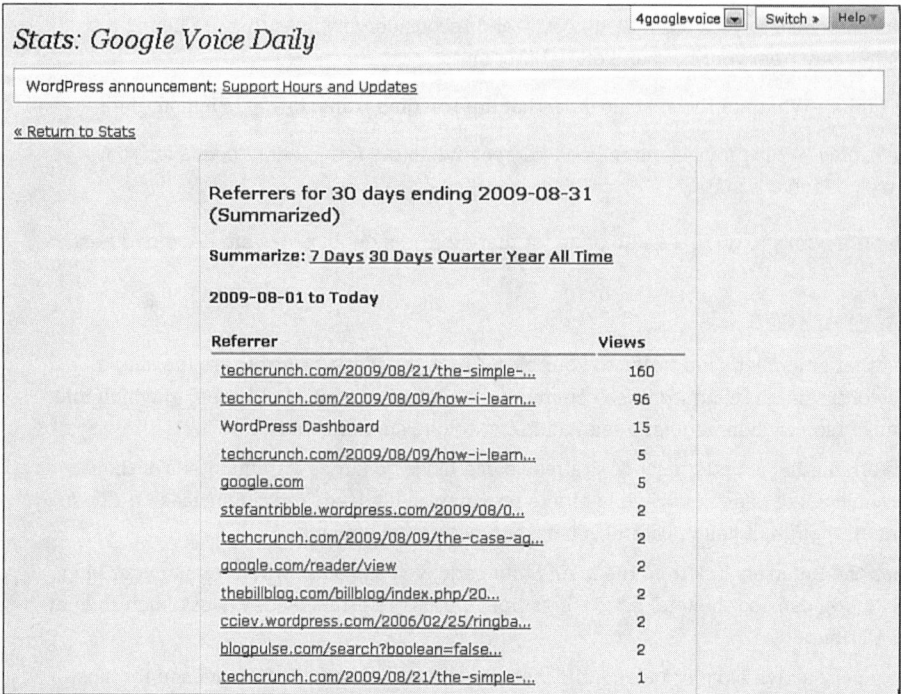

Figure 8.3
Referrers are likely to be your best source for traffic.

A "Teachable Moment" from Referrals

Note that in the example from the previous section, most of the referral traffic to Google Voice Daily came from the very popular blog, TechCrunch. This was the result of a pilot fish strategy for gaining traffic that worked. (A pilot fish follows along behind a shark, feeding on crumbs from the shark's kills.)

One pilot fish strategy for gaining traffic is to comment on others' blogs. Many sites allow you to have a link attached to your name. This link can go back to your own site.

The first time Google Voice Daily's editor (Smith) commented on TechCrunch, he included his full name and blog name at the end of the comment. This was heavy-handed and only resulted in a few blog visits. The visits were hard to track too, as was no link involved.

However, TechCrunch allows people who comment to attach a link to their name. The next time Smith commented, as shown in Figure 8.4, he didn't mention his blog directly at all—but he mentioned his own posting, and linked to his blog from his name, as part of the comment.

This was amazingly effective. Smith's comment was one of more than 500(!) that the TechCrunch article attracted. Yet Smith's one comment, somewhere in the middle of those 500 comments, was the single biggest source of traffic Google Voice Daily has ever had. (This might have been helped by Michael Arrington—Mr. TechCrunch himself—making a quick and positive comment on the posting, though not on Google Voice Daily itself.)

Figure 8.4
A single comment drove views on Smith's site.

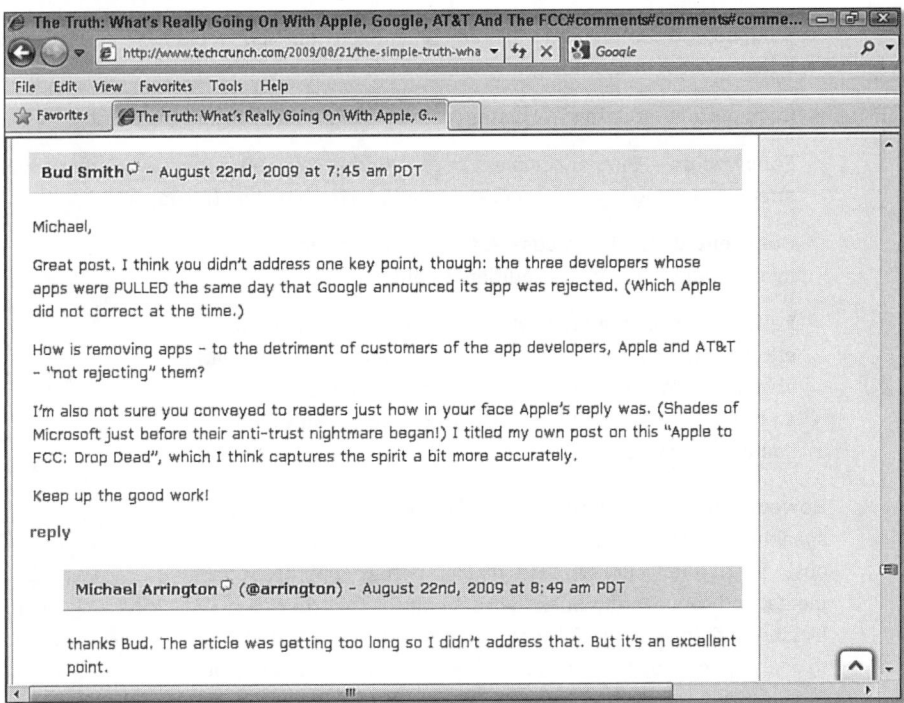

Now all this was also the result of more than a bit of luck. Smith's blog follows Google Voice, which at this writing still has relatively few users. However, it has found itself at the center of a battle among Apple, AT&T, Google, and, of all entities, the FCC, over access to Apple's App Store. This generated huge interest in the blogosphere, as the world of blogs and people who write and follow blogs is called.

Though strong results followed, Smith could have done much more. The ruling the TechCrunch article was based on occurred on Friday, August 21. The TechCrunch posting by Michael Arrington, founder of TechCrunch, went up the same day. (There's rapid response for you!)

Smith didn't get around to blogging on it until the next day, Saturday, and then went to Arrington's article and commented right after. Fortunately for Smith, people were so interested in Arrington's article that many of them read the comments—all several hundred of them—quite closely, so closely that more than a hundred of them clicked on Smith's name to go to his blog.

This was probably helped by the clever title on Smith's blog post. "Apple to FCC: Drop Dead" was a clever play on words on a famous headline many years ago, when New York City was having financial troubles. Then-President Ford's lack of interest in having the national government help was summed up by the New York Daily News in the famous headline, "Ford to City: Drop Dead." The resulting furor was so great, it is even thought to have contributed to Ford's narrow loss to Jimmy Carter in the subsequent presidential election.

All this was enough to drive traffic to Smith's blog, but he also could have:

- **Blogged and commented quicker**—A same-day posting would have caught much more of the initial interest in the ruling.

- **Been more interesting**—A better comment might have gotten more traffic.

- **Followed up**—Another comment or two, with intelligent reference to other comments in the stream following his first comment, would have increased the impact.

- **Commented on other blogs**—A few other well-placed comments might have driven additional traffic.

- **Followed up with more posts**—Smith, overly proud of his efforts, lazily left the same post up for a week, not giving later visitors or any return visitors anything new to look at. (This is a pretty big no-no for a blog, like Google Voice Daily, with "daily" in its name!)

However, the lackadaisical nature of Smith's approach (relatively speaking) did avoid some dangers. If people see you too obviously bigging up your own blog, making boring, repetitive comments, and commenting in all the same places that they're looking at themselves to follow up on a hot story, they are likely to see you as an opportunist and a pest and start tuning you out. In fact, if you overdo this a few times, your online reputation, and your traffic, might never recover.

 caution

Be very careful in commenting on other people's blogs to drive traffic to your own. Always make a real contribution—or don't comment. Be low-key in referring to your own blog. Comment rarely, building up a good reputation gradually over time. If not, you might never know how much potential traffic you've kept away from your blog by gaining, along with a brief burst of traffic, a bad reputation.

Incoming Links

Although the Incoming Links area of the WordPress Administration area's Stats page is in the lower right of the page, it's closely related to Referrers in the upper left.

The Incoming Links bears a close resemblance to the list of Referrers. If you click on the More link under the Incoming Links list, you see a Google Search result, as shown in Figure 8.5.

The Google Search term used is interesting in its own right. The term is "link:http://gvdaily.com/", which means that Google can find the sites that link to your blog. Learn to use the "link:" search term qualifier for your own blog. (If you use "site:" instead, you can find all the occurrences of a term on a site.)

The sites listed are those that include links to your blogs, either people who link to your blog, or your own comments that refer to it. Be aware that Google might only crawl your site, or referring sites, occasionally, so it will tend to leave out terms or links that are in the most recent posts.

Figure 8.5
Incoming
Links shows
exactly
where your
traffic comes
from.

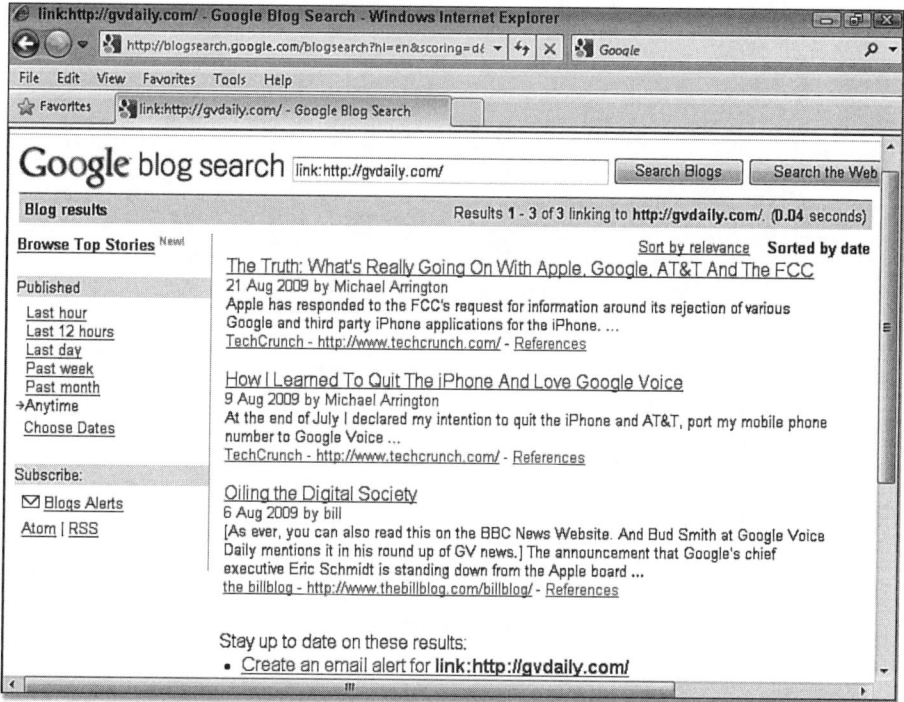

Looking at Search Terms

Search engines are a more and more important source of traffic for all kinds of websites, including blogs. Google carries about 75% of all search traffic, and other search engines seek to achieve results as close to it as possible, so Google is a good proxy for the whole world of search engines.

SEO (Search Engine Optimization) is one of the hottest buzzwords on the Web, and is likely to remain so for a long time to come. If you can get an advantage on search engine results, you'll get lots of traffic; and for many sites, that means lots of money, at least potentially.

WordPress has very good, very blog-relevant search engine reporting. It shows how many views you get and which search terms the views came from. Figure 8.6 shows top search engine terms for the Google Voice Daily blog.

For the Google Voice Daily blog, the top search phrase is "how to get Google Voice," with about one third of all the blog's search engine traffic. A quick check on Google shows that gvDaily.com shows up fifth(!) for this very specific search term. There are a lot of companies that would pay a lot of money to get in the top five for a hot search term like this one, so this is quite a good result for a blog.

Does Google Love WordPress?

People who know more about SEO than we do claim that "Google loves WordPress"; that Google seems to rank WordPress blog entries quite high on its search engine rankings. This was from a conversation at a recent WordCamp, that is, a meeting of WordPress bloggers.

This is news to us; we both feel our main blogs, on Google Voice (Smith) and open source software (McCallister) should get #1 rankings every time, but they don't. We find it reassuring to hear that Google might be giving at least some WordPress sites an even break, or even a better break than that.

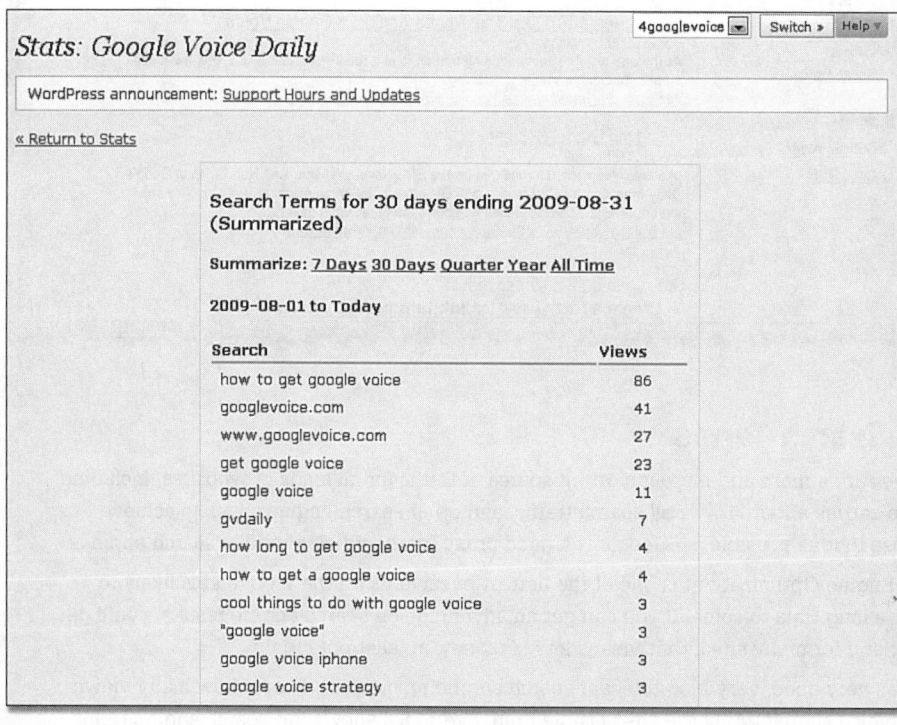

Figure 8.6
People who want to "get" Google Voice end up at gvDaily.

Unfortunately, the reason for all this search engine traffic is that a lot of people want to get Google Voice accounts, and the place to get a Google Voice account is Google. People searching for this topic probably aren't interested in the latest news about Google Voice when they haven't gotten Google Voice yet, though they might come back after they do.

Many of the visitors to Google Voice Daily who come in looking to download Google Voice might be more annoyed than pleased to find the site, though it does have instructions on how to actually get Google Voice.

You need to look closely at your search engine-based traffic. Often commentary, which is what most blogs offer, is not what people are looking for—and it's hard to search for even if you do want it. People more often want to buy products or get help with a product they already have.

Try to reverse engineer the needs people have from their search engine queries that bring them to your blog. Figure out if these are sensible needs for your blog to meet, and if so, try to improve the tie between people's search engine queries and the answers on your site.

If not, you have to somewhat discount your search engine-based traffic. People who come in on a referral from another blog probably know what they're about to get—and will be happy to read a posting or two, look around, and maybe even bookmark your blog or subscribe to an RSS feed. On the other hand, people who come to your blog as part of a search and don't find what they want aren't achieving their own purposes, nor helping you achieve yours either.

AdWords (see the sidebar) is another way to bring in traffic. The AdWords control panel is shown in Figure 8.7.

Figure 8.7
AdWords is a high-wire act that can pay off.

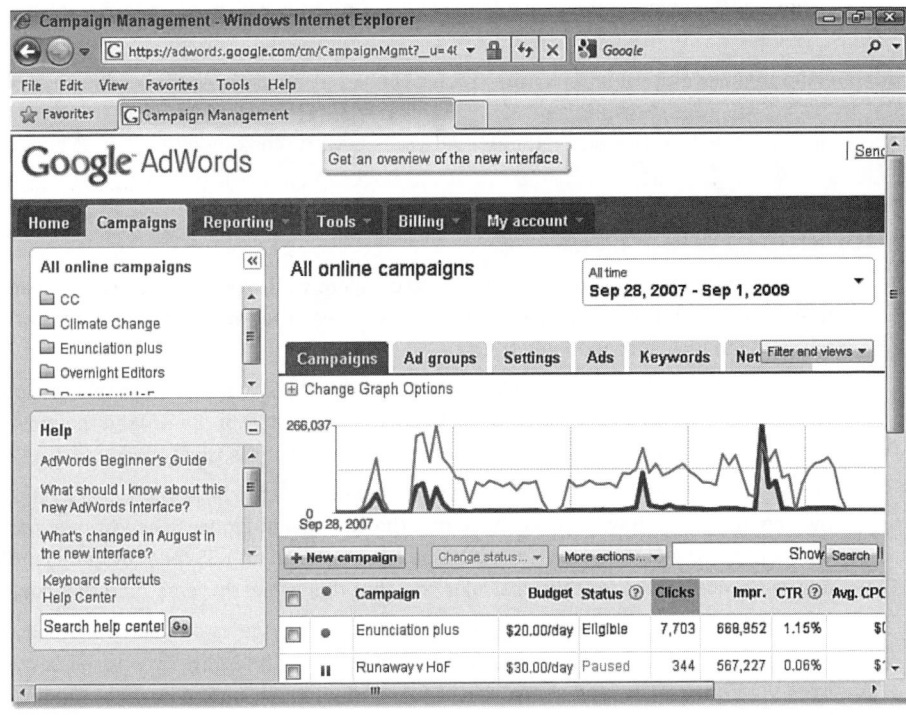

Google AdWords and Your Blog

Google has a program called AdWords that is a very effective—but also expensive—way to drive traffic. It's good for all bloggers to understand AdWords, but only good for the most commercially oriented of us to use it.

AdWords places text-based ads in the right sidebar of search results, and sometimes above them. AdWords advertisers pay for these ads, but only pay when the ad is actually clicked on. Google has done a marvelous job of making it easy to advertise using AdWords, easy to pay for your ads, and relatively easy to get traffic that you can actually monetize (that word again).

A friend of one of the authors (Smith) has a business selling books about and teaching accent reduction in London, England. She uses Google AdWords to get students for monthly classes of language learners.

She pays a few pounds a day (a pound is about $1.60 in U.S. currency at this writing) for about ten clicks on ads that appear based on search words such as *accent*, *pronunciation*, and *elocution*. These ads draw potential students to her website, from which they might call her to sign up for courses.

About half of the students for the classes come in through AdWords, making it a vital contributor to her business. Few bloggers can make as direct a connection between Google search and revenues as this. If you can, though, AdWords is worth looking into.

Top Posts and Pages

The Top Posts and Pages link allows you to compare your blog posts, as well as pages on your site, to see how much traffic they get. This is a great way to see which of your words of wit have received the most attention and traffic.

Figure 8.8 shows the Top Posts page for Google Voice Daily. You can see that one post got nearly half of all the views for the site. This is the one that the author (Smith) did the most marketing for, as described earlier, and that was related to a hot topic of the time.

To see detailed views information for a post, just click on the little chart icon next to it. A graph like the one in Figure 8.9 will appear. Note that the example in Figure 8.9 shows not only onsite views but *syndicated views* as well—views by people who read an RSS feed for the post. There were very few syndicated views for this particular post, but this is clearly something that could be built up.

If you have the time and interest, you can cross-correlate views of a particular post with search engine terms, referrals, comments, and possibly even with ratings by yourself or others of the quality of your posts. This kind of analysis is a powerful tool for improving the attractiveness of your blog to visitors, and can result in a virtuous circle of improved posts, more referrals, more search engine hits, higher ratings, and more visits, both regular and casual.

Clicks

Looking at clicks in your blog is the reverse of all your other stats. The other stats look at traffic *into* your blog; clicks looks at traffic going *out*, or from one place in your blog to another.

Figure 8.8
It's battle of the blog posts on the Top Posts page.

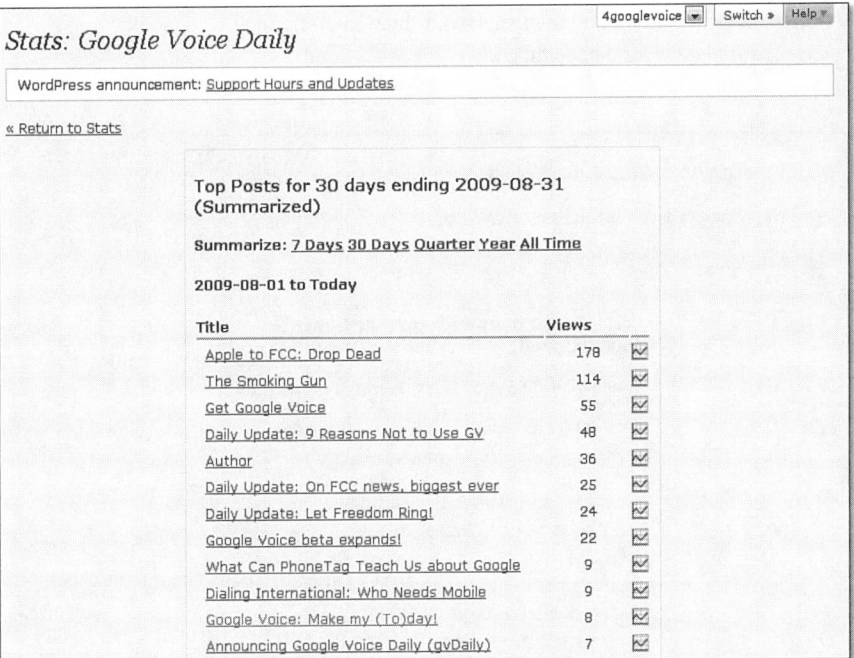

Stats: Google Voice Daily

WordPress announcement: Support Hours and Updates

« Return to Stats

Top Posts for 30 days ending 2009-08-31 (Summarized)

Summarize: 7 Days 30 Days Quarter Year All Time

2009-08-01 to Today

Title	Views	
Apple to FCC: Drop Dead	178	☑
The Smoking Gun	114	☑
Get Google Voice	55	☑
Daily Update: 9 Reasons Not to Use GV	48	☑
Author	36	☑
Daily Update: On FCC news, biggest ever	25	☑
Daily Update: Let Freedom Ring!	24	☑
Google Voice beta expands!	22	☑
What Can PhoneTag Teach Us about Google	9	☑
Dialing International: Who Needs Mobile	9	☑
Google Voice: Make my (To)day!	8	☑
Announcing Google Voice Daily (gvDaily)	7	☑

Figure 8.9
WordPress will give you amazing detail per post.

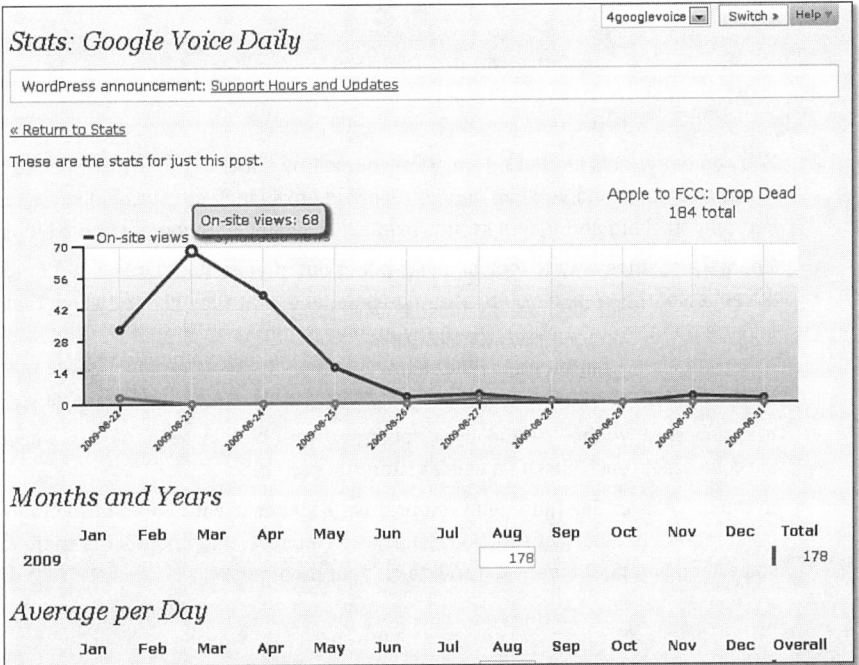

Stats: Google Voice Daily

WordPress announcement: Support Hours and Updates

« Return to Stats

These are the stats for just this post.

Apple to FCC: Drop Dead
184 total

On-site views: 68

On-site views

Months and Years

	Jan	Feb	Mar	Apr	May	Jun	Jul	Aug	Sep	Oct	Nov	Dec	Total
2009								178					178

Average per Day

	Jan	Feb	Mar	Apr	May	Jun	Jul	Aug	Sep	Oct	Nov	Dec	Overall

Figure 8.10 shows a typical clicks report. Although a valuable resource, it's missing a lot of context. Ideally, you'd like to have clicks out divided up by blog post, so you can see what's happening to users who visit a specific post.

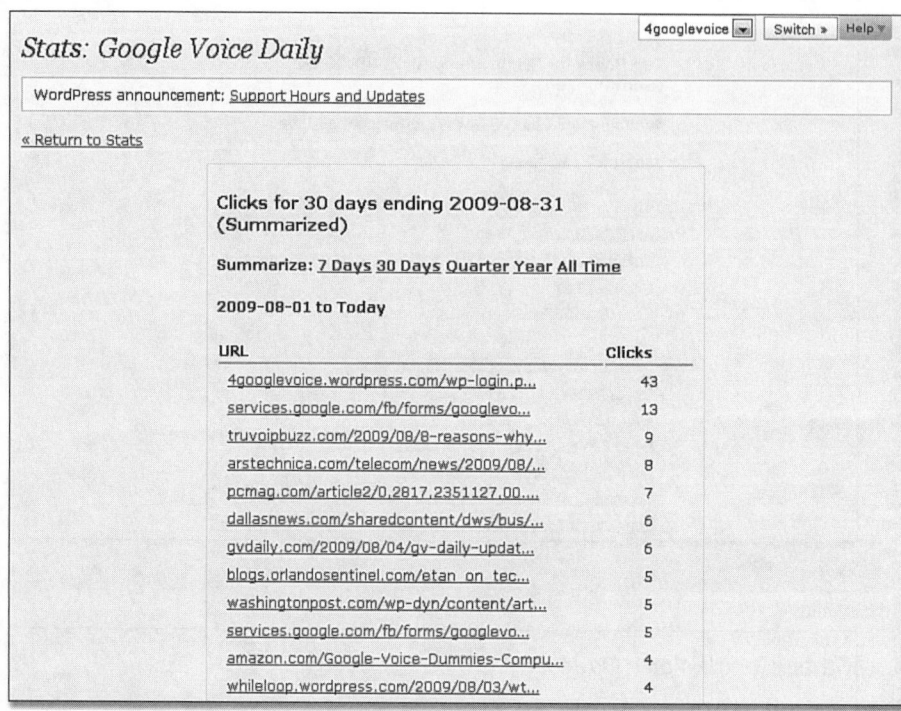

Figure 8.10
See where users get their clicks on your blog.

You can derive this kind of information yourself by matching up URLs to links out you've provided in various blogs, and you can handle repeated links (such as internal links within your blog) by carefully tracking and tallying totals over time. However, this would be a lot of work.

There's a positive way to look at clicks going out of your blog. Links are a fundamental part of the attraction of the Web. If you're offering users links that they like to follow, that shows that they're engaging with your content. (And, if you have set up links so that they open up in a new window, as described in Chapter 5, "Taking Posts Further," there's that much more reason to believe that your blog visitors might be continuing to engage with your blog even after they click.)

In some cases, you're specifically encouraging your blog visitors to go to a specific link or links, and in those cases, each click is a small victory for your blog.

In other cases, understand what might drive a visitor to click on an outbound link. If you've linked to an interesting story or function, what was so interesting about it? Is there a hint there as to something you might want to provide on your own blog?

caution

We love WordPress's stats, but the clicks display has an annoying feature. It only displays the first 40 characters of a URL, no matter how wide you make your browser window. This isn't enough for most links. And there's no easy way to get the full link to display, even by copying and pasting the text. If you're really determined, you can right-click on each link, choose Copy Link Address from the context menu that appears, and paste the (full) address wherever you want. Doing this for more than a few links gets old fast, though.

Internal clicks are great—users are getting more out of your blog than just the original post they came for, or more than just the front page. You should take the time to see what the top 7 or 10 internal links are and understand why a user might be clicking them. Then, whatever it is they're trying to do or see, make sure it's as easy as possible for them to get to it.

Blog Stats: Summary Tables

On the main Stats page, WordPress provides summary stats for your entire blog. These include total views, your busiest day, total posts, total comments, and so on.

For details, click the Summary Tables button. The tables, as shown in Figure 8.11, include totals and average by month (all months) and for recent weeks, as well as visits per day. WordPress even calculates your weekly increase or decrease as a percentage so you can quickly spot trends.

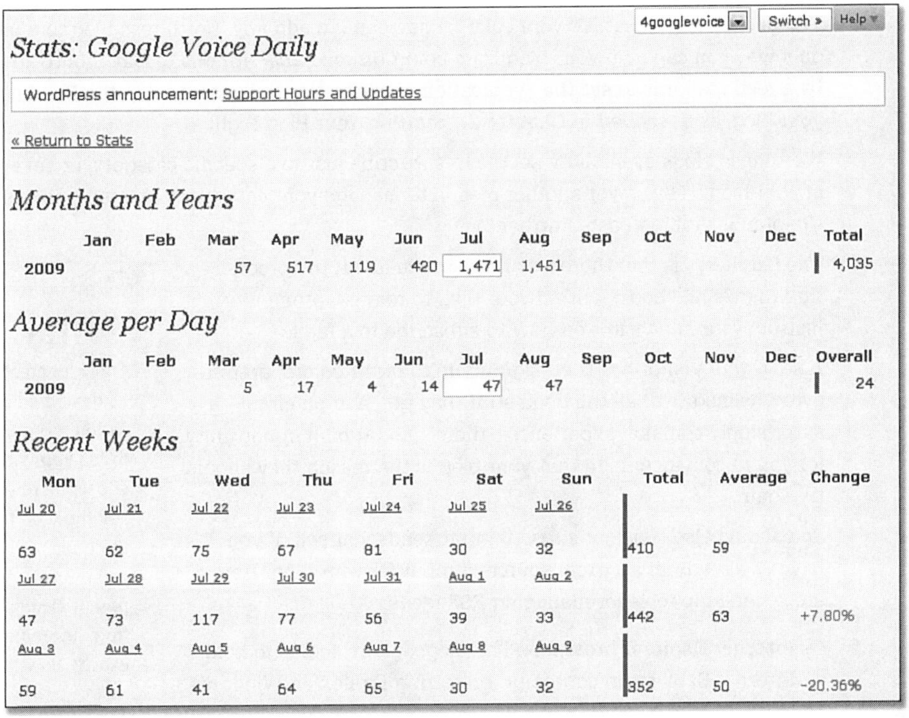

Figure 8.11
Despite the name, Summary Tables also include fall, winter, and spring (groan).

4googlevoice ▼	Switch »	Help ▼

Stats: Google Voice Daily

WordPress announcement: Support Hours and Updates

« Return to Stats

Months and Years

	Jan	Feb	Mar	Apr	May	Jun	Jul	Aug	Sep	Oct	Nov	Dec	Total
2009			57	517	119	420	1,471	1,451					4,035

Average per Day

	Jan	Feb	Mar	Apr	May	Jun	Jul	Aug	Sep	Oct	Nov	Dec	Overall
2009			5	17	4	14	47	47					24

Recent Weeks

Mon	Tue	Wed	Thu	Fri	Sat	Sun	Total	Average	Change
Jul 20	Jul 21	Jul 22	Jul 23	Jul 24	Jul 25	Jul 26			
63	62	75	67	81	30	32	410	59	
Jul 27	Jul 28	Jul 29	Jul 30	Jul 31	Aug 1	Aug 2			
47	73	117	77	56	39	33	442	63	+7.80%
Aug 3	Aug 4	Aug 5	Aug 6	Aug 7	Aug 8	Aug 9			
59	61	41	64	65	30	32	352	50	-20.36%

As you will notice here, *only* five-plus weeks of detailed data is provided. If you want to keep really careful track over time, you'll want to periodically copy and paste this information to a spreadsheet.

There's also a good argument for making daily entries in a spreadsheet, word processing document, or blog post describing that day's stats, your daily activity for the blog, and any relevant events.

---

 tip

Consider creating a page on your website with all the changes, relevant activity, and stats highlights for your blog over time. This will help you keep track of important happenings that relate to your blog, and will provide those of your website visitors who are interested a real insight into the functioning of your blog. This promotes higher interest in your blog and engagement with it by your blog visitors, which might just help the stats you're tracking to increase a bit.

How Visitors Can Subscribe to Your Blog

RSS feeds (the RSS stands for Really Simple Syndication) are an easy way to get content from a variety of blogs all assembled in one place. The one place is an RSS feed reader. RSS feed readers are an important way for blogs to get visited and read more easily, by more (human) readers.

You want your blog visitors to subscribe to your blog. That way, they constantly have the latest and greatest postings from you available to them.

There's a lot of good news and a little bit of bad news with your WordPress blog and RSS feeds. The good news is that it's very easy for someone to add any WordPress blog to a feed reader. The only way you can stop your blog from being *discoverable*—that is, easily found, added, and used— by a feed reader is to set the Syndication Feeds number of posts to 0 in the Reading Settings for your blog, as described in Chapter 2, "Starting Your Blog Right."

WordPress blogs even allow people to subscribe just to a specific category, or several categories, of your blog. (This is yet another reason to manage your categories carefully, as described in Chapter 5, "Taking Posts Further.")

The bad news is that there's so little drama about the process that there's no "hook" within your blog to remind, prompt, or instruct your site visitor on how to subscribe to a feed.

Also, if your visitor has tried signing up to feeds before, gotten overwhelmed with all the good stuff they get, and given up—a surprisingly common experience—there's no prebuilt opportunity for you to convince them that your blog is the reason they should try again.

You should also consider subscribing to feeds yourself, if you haven't already; it's a great source of input for your blog. Here are several top tools for managing RSS feeds:

- **Internet Explorer browser**—The blogosphere seems to hold Internet Explorer in contempt, preferring Firefox on Windows and Safari on the Mac, but Internet Explorer is still the most-used browser going. It also has an excellent feed tool. The user simply chooses Tools, Subscribe to This Feed; the feed shows up in the Favorites bar. Figure 8.12 shows the feed for Google Voice Daily as displayed by Internet Explorer. Note that Internet Explorer offers category feeds as well as a feed of the whole blog.

- **Google Reader**—Google Reader is a free reader with no extra software needed, just a Google account. This reader is so easy to use that it's hard not to "eat all the pies," add too many subscriptions and grow overstuffed with information.

- **Bloglines**—Also a free online service, Bloglines requires only an account. Bloglines is quite popular with old-school bloggers.

- **FeedDemon**—This service, like many of the early feed readers, requires you to download a tool to run on your computer. Once you do that, it's powerful, fast, and easy to use.

- **RSSOwl**—RSSOwl is another downloadable tool, which is open source, cross-platform (Windows, Mac, Linux), and free.

Figure 8.12
Internet
Explorer and
RSS are a
good
marriage.

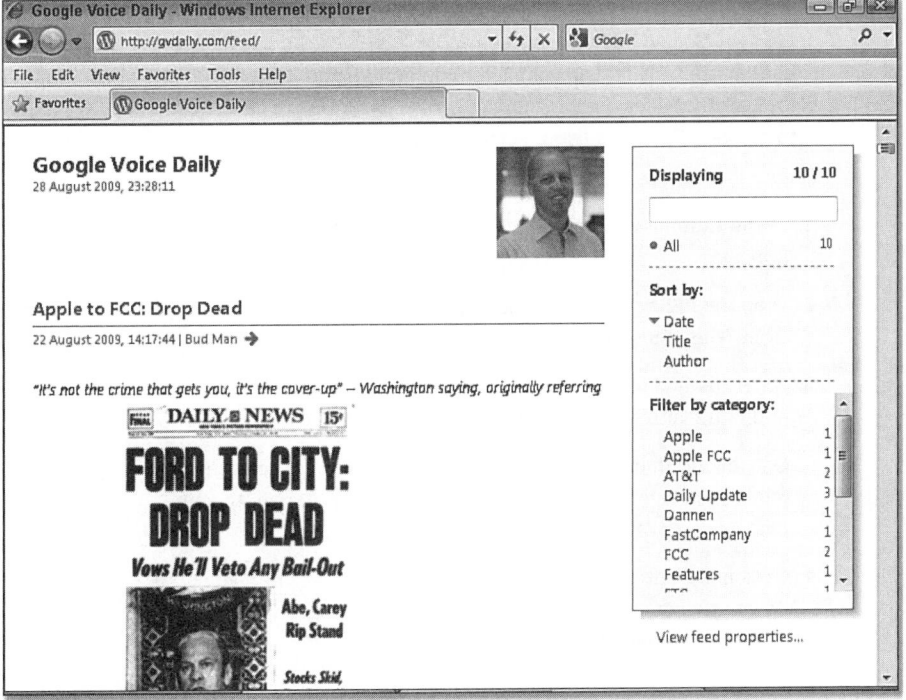

The really old-school alternative to feeds is to email either a link, an excerpt, or even (gasp) full posts to people who sign up. WordPress doesn't offer any explicit support for this, but it doesn't stop you from doing it yourself either.

Using the RSS Widget

In Chapter 3, "Creating Your Blog's Look," we described the widgets you can use with a WordPress.com blog in detail, except for the Text widget, which we described in Chapter 6, "Using HTML in Your Widgets and Blog," and the RSS widget, which we finally describe here (now that we've introduced RSS feeds).

Showing an RSS feed from certain sites on your own blog is like a statement of allegiance to groups that think certain topics are important, or that like particular styles of dealing with them as demonstrated on the blog you feed in from. You might even find yourself hoping that displaying an RSS feed from a popular site will encourage them to link back to you, quote you, or otherwise acknowledge your blog's existence.

As we always mention about widgets, it's easy to overdo it. The RSS widget is one of the widgets that you can use multiple times, each instance subscribing to a different source.

Because you can subscribe to any WordPress blog, and an awful lot of other sites, with RSS, you could literally overwhelm your visitors with RSS widgets. RSS widgets are also easy, cheap, and unoriginal. So use RSS widgets sparingly; just pick the one or two sites that are truly indispensable for you and visitors to your blog. For other sites, use a Text widget, as described in Chapter 6, to create a Favorites list or something similar.

 tip
Try an RSS feed out in an RSS feed reader yourself as a kind of trial before inflicting it on your blog visitors. Not all the blogs or other sites that are great to visit are equally great as feeds.

Follow these steps to create an RSS widget:

1. In the Administration area, click the Appearance header, then Widgets. The Widgets page appears.

2. Drag the RSS widget from the Available Widgets in the center of the screen to the Sidebar on the right. The RSS widget opens up.

3. Enter the RSS feed URL. You might have to dig around a bit to find this; adding /feed to the end of the site's URL often works.

   Get this right, or your feed won't work. Consider specialized feeds such as category feeds if that's more appropriate to your blog.

 tip
To check for an RSS feed, go to a blog or other website that you hope has a feed, then add /feed to the end of the URL in the web browser window. If a hard-to-decipher stream of text and HTML appears, you've found your feed!

4. Optionally, enter a feed title. A good title is either very simply descriptive or, additionally, indicates the importance of the feed to your own blog.

5. Indicate how many items you'd like to display in the feed, from 1 up to 20. Remember, the average person can remember 4 to 7 things, but is also accustomed to seeing Top 10 lists. Anything more than a dozen items is simple cruelty aimed at your poor blog visitor.

6. Choose whether to display the item's content (or else just the header will display); the author, if available; and the item's date. Our own opinions here are (a) the content might be overwhelming; (b) list authors if they're friends or you're a fan, not otherwise; and (c) we like dates for things—it helps us maintain our fragile grip on reality and reminds us to meet our writing deadlines, too.

7. When you're finished, click Save and then click Close. The RSS widget will appear the next time you visit your blog.

Just to convince you not to include blog content in the feed, we've done just that in the example shown in Figure 8.13.

Figure 8.13
Including content makes an RSS feed widget really big.

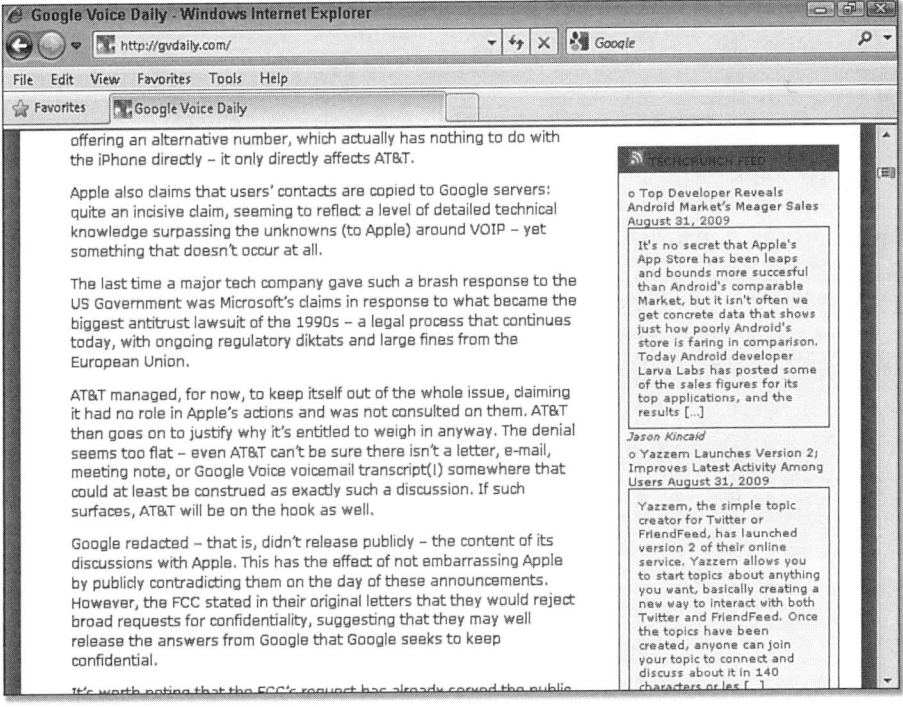

Although blog post titles sometimes don't give the user enough information to know whether to click, including content is almost always a case of TMI: Too Much Information.

TAKING YOUR BLOG FURTHER

IN THIS PART

9

ADDING GRAPHICS TO YOUR POSTS

Why Add Graphics and Other Media?

From the beginning of weblogs and the coining of the word *blog*, believed to have first occurred in 1999, blogs have gone against the trend. Graphics were always part of the very definition of the Web. Sound and audio files, even 3D interactive environments, were being used more and more. All of these trends continue today.

Yet here came blogs. This seemingly unstoppable torrent of words, words, words. Hundreds, then thousands, then millions of people—many wrestling with the technical difficulties that cursed blogs in their early days—and some even paying fairly high blogging fees, all so they could write, and write, and write.

Even more millions of people, perhaps more visitors than many might have guessed would do so, logged onto the blogs to read and comment as well.

What have we learned from this? That, yes, torrents of words are valuable on the Web—both to the writer and to the readers. Also, separately, that multimedia is very valuable indeed.

Do bloggers need media today? If this is a strict yes-or-no question, like some of the polls discussed in Chapter 7, "Adding Features to Your Blog," the answer, clearly, is: No. Many blogs are successful with boring, me-too layouts and little or no use of media.

However, it's also worth considering the story of the two hikers and the bear, which goes like this: Two hikers came onto a stream, stopped, slid their backpacks off, took off their shoes, and started splashing around.

Suddenly, downstream a few hundred yards, they saw a bear—who, unfortunately, saw them too. The bear got down on all fours and started running toward them.

One of the hikers quickly reached in his backpack and started putting on running shoes. The second hiker, despite the danger, laughed. "Even if you put on running shoes, you're not going to outrun a bear."

"I don't have to outrun a bear," the first hiker answered, tying his laces. "I just have to outrun you."

Your blog doesn't have to outrun the bear—all the big beasts of the Web, such as newspaper or television websites, which have huge budgets, design, and usability experts on staff, and the wherewithal to source or generate, get permissions for, host, and stream oodles of media.

Battle of Media Types on WordPress

WordPress is great for hosting text, as you might expect, but also for hosting images. You can always come up with some kind of complaint about almost anything, but WordPress really does a marvelous job of hosting images and making it easy to put them in your blog posting.

However, if you upload media to a WordPress.com blog, you might notice something: Most media file types aren't initially supported. You can upload the major types of graphics files and some office-document file types, such as Microsoft Word and PDF documents. (These appear in your blog as links to downloadable files, which is boring, but sometimes necessary.) However, there's no ability to upload audio or video files in free WordPress.com blogs, only images and office documents.

To upload audio files, you have to purchase some kind of space upgrade—even if you don't really need the extra space. The lowest-cost upgrade is 5GB for $20 per year. This isn't a bad price for the amount of space you get, but it's almost prohibitive if all you wanted to do was add an occasional audio file to your blog. (After you add a space upgrade, you can then upload audio file types, such as MP3 and WAV, from the media uploader.)

Video hosting is even worse for the casual media user on WordPress.com. To upload video, you need to add a whole separate video upgrade, called VideoPress (like WordPress, get it?), for $60 per year. In a world in which YouTube will upload, compress, store, and stream your video for free, VideoPress is definitely not the low-cost solution.

In this chapter, we only address images, the only media option you can pursue on WordPress.com without an upgrade. (Though linking to a YouTube video works well and is free; see Chapter 10, "Adding Upgrades, Audio, and Video.") For options that you can pursue *with* an upgrade (or with a WordPress.org-based blog), see Chapter 10. If you are a WordPress.org user, you can, of course, host your own audio and video files and stream them to your blog, assuming your hosting provider supports it.

Chapter 11, "Installing and Upgrading WordPress Software," discusses the costs involved with hosting a WordPress.org-supported blog. If you're a WordPress.com user trying to figure out what to do, when you find out what many hosting providers charge for media hosting and streaming downloads, a 5GB space upgrade or a VideoPress upgrade added to a WordPress.com account might start to look pretty good!

But there are millions and millions of blogs out there now. If you want to grow yours, you have to outrun at least some of the other bloggers, even if only by a little bit. Adding media to your blog is one of the very best ways to do it.

You might already be a media expert from other web work, or even have a blog focused largely on media. If so, this chapter will be of moderate interest to you. We're really writing this for the authors of traditional, word-led blogs—those of you who want to spice up your blog a bit, but are not quite sure how. We're here to help.

Copyright and Media Types

Copyright laws and enforcement are much tighter for graphics, audio, and video than for words. Most bloggers are, unfortunately, rather casual about copyright laws and regulations. However, the rules are confusing enough, and enforcement lax and haphazard enough, that this is understandable.

Everything put on the open Web is, thereby, made public. However, it's made public for display *within the site that displays it*. You can always link to a site to make something available to your users. (Although "deep linking" within a site, such as what Google News does with news stories, has been the subject of lawsuits, the owners of the targeted sites haven't prevailed to date.) However, there are various rules about how much you can copy from someone else's site to yours, and about how much you have to credit the source if you do.

Just to show how sensitive the topic is, we need to state, for our own protection and our publisher's, that nothing in this section is meant to be taken as legal advice. You should discuss any concerns with an appropriately qualified legal resource before making decisions with relation to copyright law.

In most cases, you're allowed to copy a few lines of text, with a reference to the source. (You don't have to include a hyperlink; it's nice, though, and helpful to your site visitors, to do so if you can.)

You can copy more text if you're doing so for educational use or for the purposes of criticizing. All the important words in that sentence have wiggle room in them, though: "more" text, "educational use," "purposes of criticizing." Satire is sometimes thought to be a particularly safe rationale for copying more than a couple of lines of text.

It's also true that enforcement often depends on the effect of your copying: A site that copies large expanses of a new book for the purpose of praising it to the skies might be less likely to get a lawyer letter than one that copies the same amount of text to condemn it! Enforcement also tends to be stricter when something is used for profit (as in a printed book that's available for sale) than not for profit, partly because nonprofit use lends itself more readily to claims that the purpose was solely educational or critical rather than for monetary gain, partly for the practical reason that it's harder to win or recover damages when there's no visible income.

Compared with "mere" words, copyright law is stricter with regard to poetry, song lyrics, music, and video, in all of which even a few words or a few seconds of content can be considered protected. (This is not exactly a compliment to we bloggers who use plain old text, is it?) People have been successfully sued for including just a few lines of lyrics in a printed book, for instance.

Be careful with regard to copyright. You can search online for guidance that's more detailed and authoritative than offered here, or consult legal counsel if needed. If you're not careful, in addition to the risk of enforcement action and penalties, you risk leaving a poor impression with your blog visitors. Some of your visitors are likely to look askance at your displaying a casual attitude to copyright, even if your approach is no worse than commonly found on the Web. If it *is* (even) worse than commonly found on the Web, many people will look askance at it!

Putting Pictures in Your Posts

You really should get in the habit of putting images in your blog postings. Doing so stretches your communications abilities and makes visiting your blog far more interesting and fun.

As well-known blogger Lorelle VanFossen, of Lorelle on WordPress fame, put it: "Photographs and graphic images are an integral part of our blogs today. We want to show people what our words often can't. Besides, pictures are fun to look at."

One of the big reasons the Web prospered is because support for graphics—initially, only the GIF file format, but you have to start somewhere—was built in to it from the very start. This was so physicists could illustrate the shared scientific papers that were the original purpose of the Web. The rest of us caught on fast enough, though.

One of the very best ways to make your blog postings better—more interesting, easier to read, and, not least, easier to find and recognize—is to follow a rule often used by journalists: at least one picture per story. (Many among the gradually dwindling band of newspaper journalists mournfully cite a new rule: "No picture, no story.")

As a blogger, and as your own boss, you aren't under that kind of pressure. You can publish without a picture, or use a picture or other image only loosely related to your topic. It's a great idea, though, to use pictures both to illustrate your postings and as a kind of icon for the story itself.

WordPress has really marvelous support for images. In release 2.9, WordPress added a built-in graphics editor, described later in this chapter. You can host up to 3GB of images on your blog site. A large, 4" by 3" image is about 100KB in size with fairly harsh JPEG compression. You can store 10 such images in a megabyte, 10,000 in a gigabyte, or 30,000 (!) in 3 gigabytes. That's enough to support one post a day, with one large image per post, every single day for 82 years. A lifetime's worth of blogging!

 **note**

WordPress used to offer only 50MB of image storage, only enough for 500 100KB images. Many bloggers were worried about running out of space. The increase to 3GB, which took place at the beginning of 2008, was a welcome and liberating move for WordPress bloggers.

Graphics Tips for Bloggers

We're going to charge through some graphics basics really quickly. Many of you will know them already; we provide a compressed introduction here in case you don't. If you want to know more, consider an introductory book about web graphics—there are several good ones out there—or search for background information online.

Here goes: Text is coded and stored extremely efficiently for the Web. It only takes about 2KB or less of storage to fill a page with text. On the other hand, photos and other complex graphics, even when harshly compressed, take up 100 times as much *storage* space per square inch of *screen* space as text. However, with WordPress's large amount of free storage and the increasingly fast bandwidth available to most web users, plus the screen space limitations imposed by a typical WordPress theme, even graphics files move over the Web to your blog visitor quite quickly, most of the time.

There are two kinds of sizes you need to concern yourself with for an image on your blog: the size of the image onscreen (its physical dimensions) and the file size of the image. The onscreen image size determines the visual impact; the file size determines how quickly the image can be transferred to the user's machine. Size matters a great deal when it comes to web images, so both kinds of size are discussed here.

Image file sizes used to be a huge concern, back when people used dial-up modems, and a really large image—for example, 1MB or so, almost a screen-filling, lightly compressed, high-quality image—might take more than a minute to download. Today, with broadband so common, even a 1MB image might take only about 8 seconds to download. However, people are finding online information so indispensable that they're viewing it over cell phones, poor wireless and cell phone connections, and so on, so that in some cases it's "back to the future" where download speeds are concerned.

Smaller files—even a file of, for example, 20KB in size, a small photograph or a larger drawn image—might take longer to download than it should because the computer and network have to do some extra work to open the image file, access the information, close the file, transmit it, and reassemble the image on the receiving end, especially if the host machine, the receiving machine, or some point along the network between them is busy. So an image in a file sometimes takes longer to display than the file size would lead you to expect.

Web graphics files are stored in three main file types, each of which has advantages:

- **JPEG (Joint Photographic Experts Group)**—JPEG is a powerful format for storing photographs and other highly detailed images. JPEG is a lossy format, that is, it removes quite a bit of information from a file, but is uniquely able to reduce files sizes of large, complex images by well over 90% with little visible degradation of the image. JPEG is the default format for photos and other detailed, shaded images.

- **PNG (Portable Networking Graphics)**—PNG is a graphics format that was designed to improve on the GIF format (see the following item). It uses lossless compression; it's the best choice for most computer-generated graphics and is competitive with JPEG in file sizes for some small photos, while not losing any data at all.

- **GIF (Graphical Interchange Format)**—GIF was the original file format for web graphics. It also uses lossless compression, like PNG, but can't handle images with a lot of shades of color very well. GIF is still widely used, but is gradually losing ground to PNG. GIF is the only graphics format supported by every web browser that supports graphics from Day 1 (which, for the Web, was February 26th, 1991, in case you need an answer to a trivia question).

Use PNG for computer-generated graphics; use JPEG for photos. For small photos (about 150 x 150 pixels or smaller), try both, compare the file sizes and appearance, then decide which to use.

The JPEG committee continues to work on the standard. There's a new version of the format, called JPEG 2000, being prepared for rollout. Figure 9.1 shows an image compressed at about 150 to 1—high, even for JPEG—in the new JPEG 2000 format, versus standard JPEG.

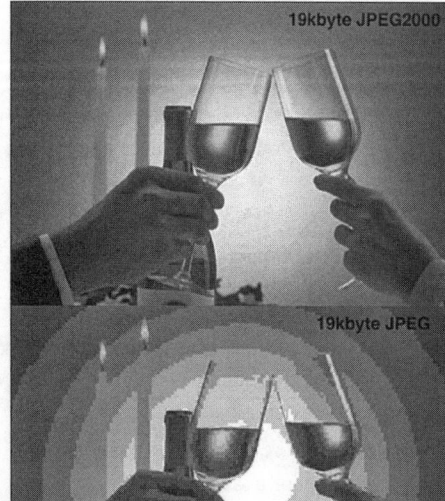
19kbyte JPEG2000

19kbyte JPEG

Figure 9.1
JPEG2000 (top) will improve on today's
JPEG (bottom).

Converting Graphics File Formats

There is a huge number of different image formats used when creating or saving images. However, almost every graphics tool available today will save images in either the GIF or JPEG format, and up-to-date versions of the better tools should also support PNG.

What if you have a graphics tool without this support? There's a simple workaround available on Windows. Get the image to appear onscreen, within the graphics tool or on a web page. Then do a screen capture (press the PrtSc or similarly named key, or Alt+PrtSc to capture only the currently active window).

Open Microsoft Paint, which is in the Accessories folder of the Windows Start menu. (Windows Vista or 7 users can just type "Paint" into the search box and select the app when it appears in the list.)

Paste (Ctrl+V) the screen capture into Paint; the entire image will be selected. Press the Esc key to remove the selection, click the Selection tool, then select only the part of the image that you want to use on the Web. Copy (Ctrl+C) the selection.

In Paint, select File, New to open a new window. (Don't bother saving the old one.) Paste in the selection and save it as a JPEG, PNG, or GIF image, as you prefer. (PNG might not be supported on all systems, including yours, in which case you're stuck with JPEG or GIF.)

Paint doesn't allow you to set important options such as gentler or harsher JPEG compression, but its limitations are also what make it so easy to use. To have more options available, use a better tool. You can find free tools, and time-limited trial versions of some quite powerful tools, on online sites such as CNET's download.com.

When creating images for use in your blog, consider three different types of images (as described in Chapter 2, "Starting Your Blog Right"): thumbnails, medium-sized images, and large images. A thumbnail should be small enough to be used for a head shot, a close-in image of a face that is typically about 70 x 100 pixels in size. (Image width is generally given before height in discussing computer graphics.)

Putting a face into such a tiny image is a harsh way to treat anyone, but a thumbnail image is still large enough to be recognizable and to liven up a post. A JPEG of this size is less than 10KB in size, and, if you really want to, you can squeeze one into the somewhat misnamed Text widget, described in Chapter 6, "Using HTML in Your Widgets and Blog."

A medium-sized image is the next size up. To most blog authors, a sensible size for a medium-sized image is about half the width of the main window in many themes, or about 200 pixels. (This is also the full width of the sidebar in many themes as well.) With a medium-sized image defined as 200 pixels, you can still have room to flow text next to an image and have a decent-looking result for both the text and the image. So a 200 x 200 size for medium-sized images makes sense. A 200 x 200 pixel JPEG image might be about 40KB in file size.

A large image should be about the width of the main blog window, or about 400 pixels. You should only take up this kind of screen space for an image that's worth showing off and, probably, devoting a fair amount of your blog posting to talking about. A JPEG of this size might be as large as 160KB in file size. This might take as long as a few seconds to transfer, even over broadband, which causes a visible pause in the loading of your blog page.

When you create graphics for your blog, WordPress resizes them to the sizes you define as the thumbnail, medium-sized, and large in the Media Settings subpanel, as described in Chapter 2. You can also use the actual size, which is our usual choice. The most valuable use for automatic resizing, to us, is to upload a larger file, and then use the medium-sized version offered by WordPress so the words can flow around the image smoothly within the blog posting.

A few tips for creating images for use in your blog:

- Use images. One of us (Smith) tries hard to use an image for each and every blog posting.

- Try to create the image size you need rather than using one of the default sizes. The effect is likely to be better. Also be aware: WordPress does not enlarge an image to one of the default sizes for you; it only shrinks it.

- Don't worry too much about compression. In particular, don't compress too harshly when using JPEG, or you and your blog visitors will suffer from an image that's visibly worse.

tip

An experienced old-school web graphics person would slide an image with a large size "below the fold," far enough down on the page that it wouldn't be visible until the user scrolled down. That way, the user doesn't notice the delay while the image downloads.

note

Graphics files are known by the three-character file types that Windows assigns to files: `.jpg` for JPEG, `.png` for PNG, and `.gif` for GIF. DOS and early versions of Windows made you deal with file extensions to do almost anything, but more modern versions of Windows hide them almost completely. Neither extreme is really the right answer.

- Use PNG for everything except photos. Even for a photo, if it's smaller than medium-sized, create JPEG and PNG versions and compare them for quality and file size. When in doubt, tilt toward the better-quality image, even if it costs you a few KB of file size.

- Crop, crop, crop. There's no need to frame photos within a background anymore, just cut to the chase (that is, the main subject). We still remember a book cover with a photo of John Dvorak, the famous "angry man" technology columnist, in which the entire front cover was a photo zoomed in to show his nose, eyes, and not much else. Such very tight cropping is overkill even for web images, but not by all that much.

- Don't spend too much time on images. Hours can disappear like minutes when you start messing with them. Give yourself some time to experiment with your first few images, then develop a routine for handling them, and work to a self-imposed time limit per image.

Uploading and Inserting Graphics

Usually, when you use graphics in your posts, static web pages, or a widget, you'll go through a few steps to do so. Conceptually, the steps are as follows:

1. Create or otherwise obtain a graphic and put it on your computer.

2. Upload the graphic to the Media Library.

3. Place the graphic in a post, on a static page, or in a widget.

When you place a graphic in a post, if the graphic is not in the Media Library already, WordPress takes you through uploading the graphic to the Media Library and placing it in the post as one overall process. This is convenient, but confuses many people. That's because combining the steps obscures the role of the Media Library as a storage location for media files, which is actually quite important.

In the following section, we present the steps for uploading a graphic and for placing the graphic into a post separately, so as to focus greater attention on the options available to you at each point.

Uploading an Image to the Media Library

Follow these steps to upload a graphic to the Media Library:

1. In the Administration area, under the Media menu in the left column, click Add New. The Upload New Media page opens, as shown in Figure 9.2.

   The WordPress uploader shown in the figure uses Adobe Flash, a multimedia technology commonly used on the Web. If you get an error message relating to Flash, and can't solve it, click the link to switch to the Browser Uploader (which just means the non-Flash uploader) instead.

2. Click the Select Files button. The Select Files dialog box opens. Only acceptable file types— JPEG, PNG, GIF, and some office document types, such as Adobe PDF, Microsoft Word, and Microsoft PowerPoint—will display.

Figure 9.2
Uploading images
is easy in
WordPress.

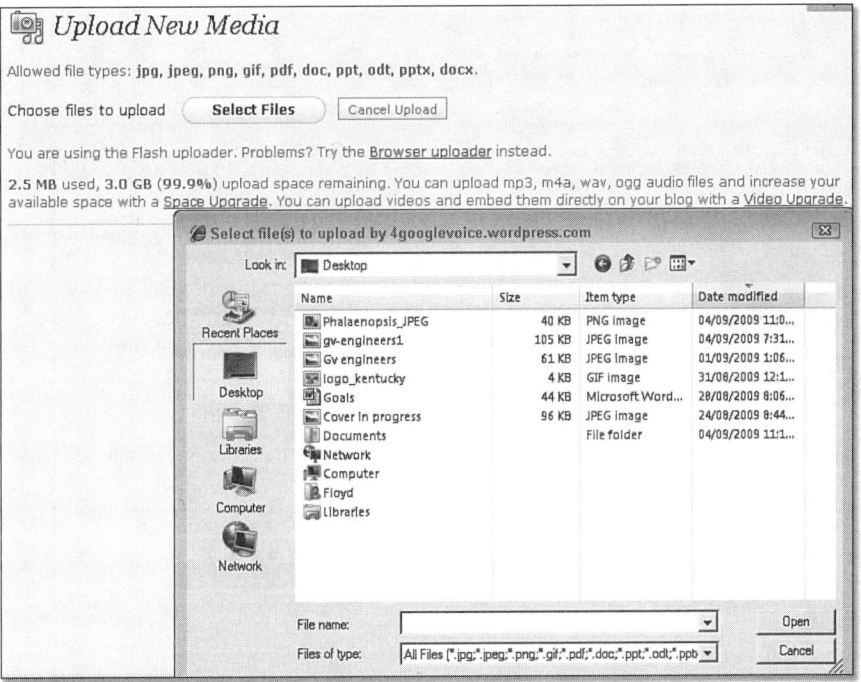

3. Navigate to the image you want. Select it and click Open. WordPress uploads the image and crunches it, which might or might not further compress the image. A thumbnail of the image appears, along with options you can set or change, as shown in Figure 9.3.

4. Change the title of your image (a title of some sort is required). This is the name of the image within WordPress. This is originally set to be the filename, but is not restricted to that. You can change it to have spaces, punctuation, and so on.

5. Provide a caption for the image. Any caption you provide is displayed centered underneath the image. Brief captions are better in most cases. The caption is also used as ALT text for the image. ALT text is displayed in text-only browsers and in specialized tools such as screen readers for the blind, so it's important to provide a caption (even if you would rather not) so as to provide ALT text as well.

6. If you want, enter a description for the image. Although a theme could display this description, in most cases it will be available only within the Media Library.

7. Inspect the file URL. This is where the file is stored. You can, for instance, use this URL to display the same image in another web page. (And so can anyone else, for that matter; see the section, "Using an Image from the Web in Your Post," later in this chapter.)

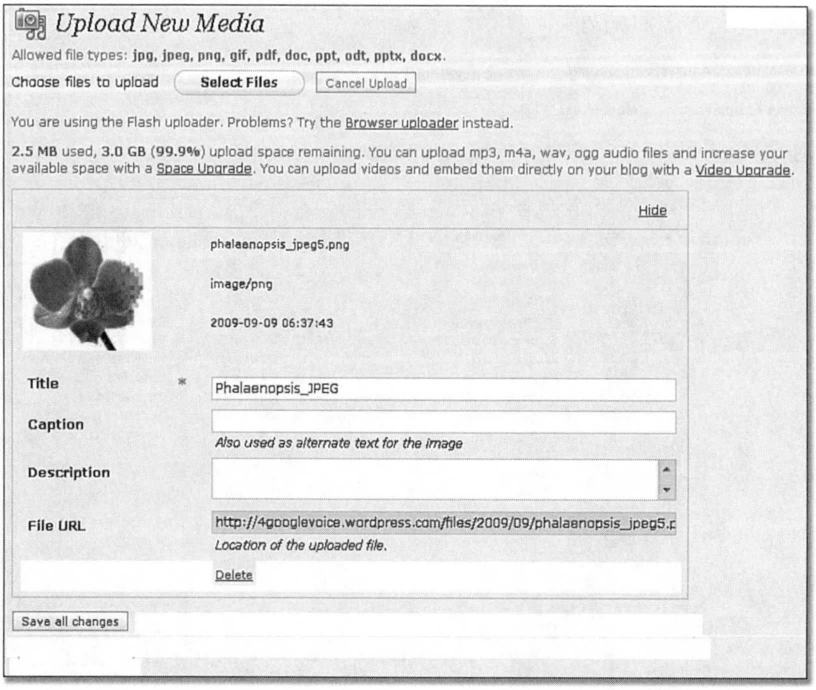

Upload New Media

Allowed file types: jpg, jpeg, png, gif, pdf, doc, ppt, odt, pptx, docx.

Choose files to upload **Select Files** [Cancel Upload]

You are using the Flash uploader. Problems? Try the <u>Browser uploader</u> instead.

2.5 MB used, **3.0 GB (99.9%)** upload space remaining. You can upload mp3, m4a, wav, ogg audio files and increase your available space with a <u>Space Upgrade</u>. You can upload videos and embed them directly on your blog with a <u>Video Upgrade</u>.

Hide

phalaenopsis_jpeg5.png

image/png

2009-09-09 06:37:43

Title *	Phalaenopsis_JPEG
Caption	
	Also used as alternate text for the image
Description	
File URL	http://4googlevoice.wordpress.com/files/2009/09/phalaenopsis_jpeg5.p
	Location of the uploaded file.
	<u>Delete</u>

[Save all changes]

Figure 9.3
Hopefully, you never meta data you didn't like when describing your image.

8. Click Update Media to save the information, with any changes you've made, to the Media Library. The file and the accompanying information—called *metadata*, in case you hear anyone use that term with regard to images—will be added to the Media Library.

⚠ caution

WordPress users often get confused, when in the Media Library, about how to get an image into a post. When you're looking at an image in the Media Library, WordPress would not easily know *which* post to put the image into. Instead, you have to leave the Media Library, choose Add Post or Edit Post, navigate to the spot in the post where you want to insert the image, click the Add Image button, and then get the image from the Media Library.

Similarly, WordPress users who are adding an image to a post often miss the Add an Image button partway through the process and end up clicking the Save All Changes button, which saves the image into a gallery without inserting it into the post. Then, confused, they go directly to the Media Library and find the image, but can't insert it from there. Follow the steps in the "Using an Image from Your Computer in Your Post" section to successfully get the image into your post.

Editing an Image After Uploading

WordPress now gives you the option of editing an image after you upload it, as shown in Figure 9.4. However, you have to get the image into an acceptable format (meaning GIF, JPEG, or PNG) before uploading it. While you're doing that, you might as well resize it. Doing it this way also saves space in your WordPress image storage area.

Figure 9.4
WordPress
has a new
image editor.

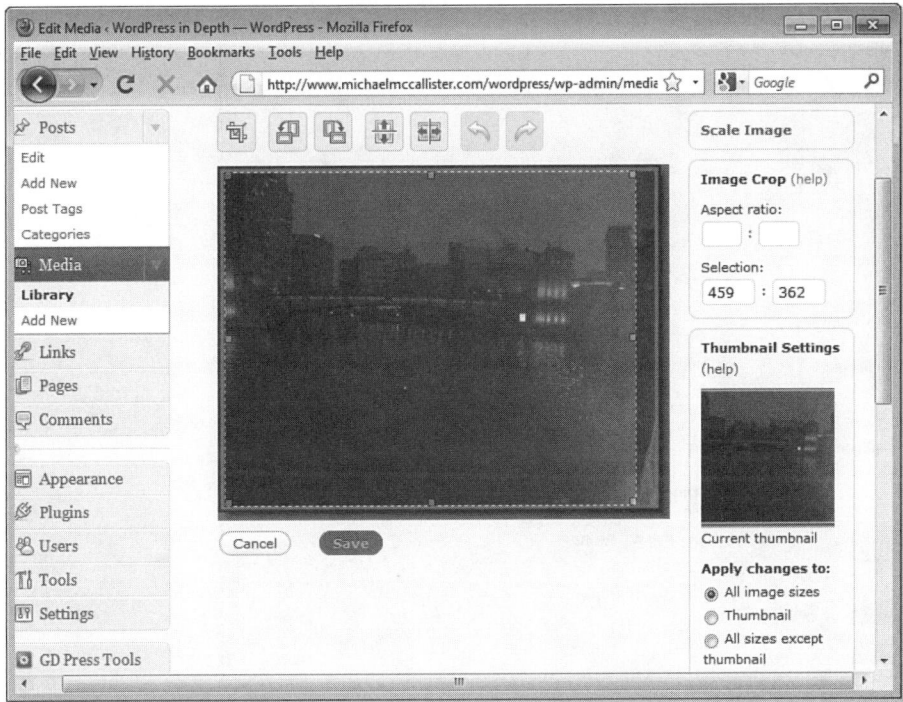

However, if you need to work on your image after uploading it, the new image editor is a good option.

Using an Image from Your Computer in Your Post

If you are creating or editing a post and click the Add an Image button, you have several options. The first option you are presented with is to upload an image from your computer. You can also insert an image from a URL (that is, stored elsewhere on the Web) or an image that's already in the Media Library. Those options are described in the next couple of sections.

Follow these steps to insert an image from your computer, by first uploading it to the Media Library, then inserting it:

1. While creating or editing a post, click the Add an Image button. The Add an Image dialog box opens. It has three tabs: From Computer, From URL, and Media Library. The first tab, From Computer, is selected by default.

2. Click the Select Files button. Select the file from your hard disk, as described in step 2 of the previous section. Once you select the file, additional fields appear in the dialog box—the same fields

as described in the previous section (Title, Caption, and Description), plus additional fields specific to placement of the image in your post. The dialog box is shown in Figure 9.5.

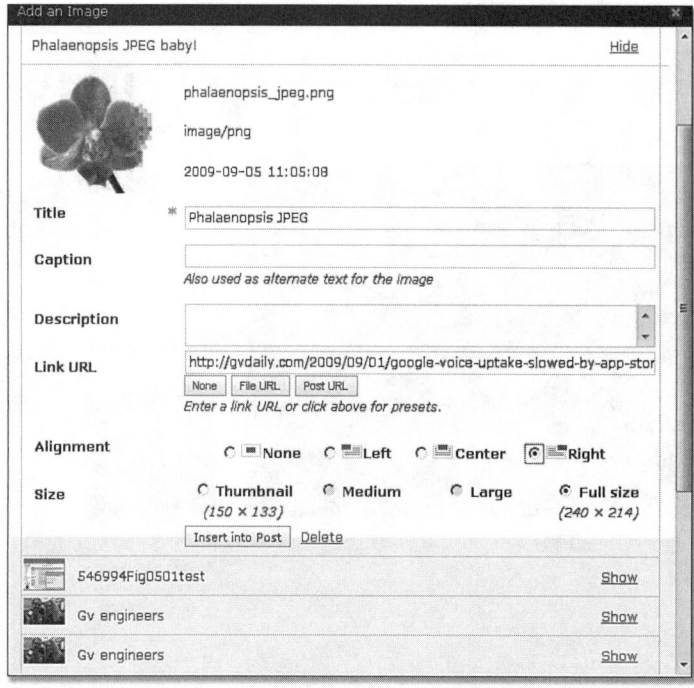

Figure 9.5
Get your image into your posting.

3. Enter the Title, Caption, and Description, as described in steps 4–6 from the previous section. These three fields go with the image into the Media Library. The remaining fields, described next, are specific to the placement of the image in the post you're creating or editing.

4. Enter the link URL by clicking one of the buttons: None, File URL, or Post URL. This URL gives your blog visitors access to the image. In most cases, you'll want to choose Post URL, as this will make sense to your visitors and provide a permanent link to the graphic. The file URL option is used if you don't enter anything.

5. Choose an alignment option: None, Left, Center, or Right. The alignment options are confusing because they don't explain key information. If you don't want text flowing next to your image, choose None. You can then left-align, center, or right-align the image using buttons in the Add/Edit Post page. If you want text flowing next to your image (space allowing),

 tip

You should only have text flowing next to your image if there's room. A good rule of thumb is to only flow text next to an image if it takes up half the main text area or less; otherwise, text can look odd in the narrow remaining area. Centering an image, while flowing text around it on both sides, is rarely a good idea; the text around a centered image is incredibly hard to read.

use the left-align, center, or right-align options. Try different options to see which looks best. (Center is only good for small images, if ever.)

6. Choose a size for the image—one of the predetermined sizes, Thumbnail, Medium, or Large; or Full Size, which really means "original size."

Among the predetermined sizes, only sizes smaller than the original are available to be selected; WordPress does not enlarge an image for you (which, in most cases, is a good thing, as artificially stretched images can look bad). If you choose a predetermined size, WordPress shrinks the larger dimension of the image to the predetermined measurement and then shrinks the smaller dimension of the image in proportion.

Do consider using a Large image if one is available, especially if you took our advice in Chapter 2 to set the dimensions for a Large image to the same width as the main posting area for your theme. If you've done this, and a Large image is made available to you by WordPress, that means the image's original size is too large for your theme. If you include an image in your post that's wider than your theme allows, and choose the Full Size option, WordPress either resizes it to fit in the theme, or it busts out of the theme, with an ugly result.

(It's not impossible that your theme's designer intended to force such images to resize, and that some do, but others bust out of the theme anyway. There's no point in pushing your—and your theme designer's—luck.)

7. Click the Insert into Post button, which is tucked into the Setting area and is easy to miss, *not* (in most cases) the Save All Changes button, which is isolated and, thus, visually more prominent.

If you click Save All Changes, the image is saved into a gallery, which you can then use in your post. However, in most cases, you'll want to insert the image directly into your post, which is only accomplished if you click the (harder-to-find) Insert into Post button.

8. Check the result in your post. If it's not want you want, click the image. Two buttons appear, as shown in Figure 9.6: Edit Image and Delete Image. Click the first to make changes to the settings described in the previous steps; click the second to remove the image from the post entirely. (It will remain available in the Media Library.)

9. In your post, if the image is small, move text around to get it to flow around the image; otherwise, leave the image by itself, with no text flowing next to it. Click the HTML button to inspect and change the HTML if you want; for instance, to resize the image to different dimensions than the options that WordPress offers.

 caution

Keep your eyes open for the Insert into Post button and be sure to click that instead of the Save All Changes button, unless you want to create an image gallery rather than actually inserting one and only one image into your post.

 tip

You can easily make an image into a link by selecting an image in your post, then clicking the Insert/Edit Link button. You'll get the same choices that you do when making text into a link, as described in Chapter 5, "Taking Posts Further." You do need to tip your blog visitors off that the image is a link though, perhaps by adding a caption that reads, "Click image to see larger picture," "Click image to visit www.greatsite.com," or something similar.

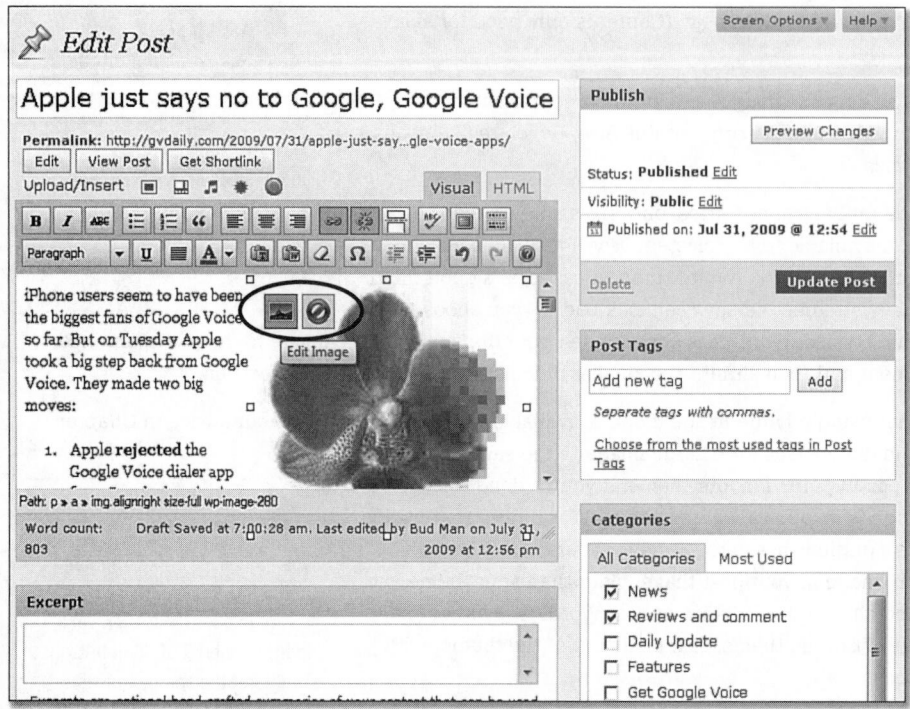

Figure 9.6
You can edit or delete images within your post.

Inserting an Office Document into Your Post

You can include an office document in your post instead of an image. To do this, simply upload a file with one of the office document types: `.pdf` for a PDF file, `.doc` or `.docx` for Microsoft Word, `.ppt` or `.pptx` for Microsoft PowerPoint, `.odt` for Open Office, and similar documents.

WordPress uploads the document to the Media Library and inserts a text link—not a graphical preview—into your post. When the user clicks the link, the file is downloaded to the user's hard disk from where it's stored in the Media Library. (For the link text, word it in such a way that the user understands what's going to happen; perhaps something like "click here to download the list of participants in a Word document.")

Be careful, though, for your site visitors' sake. The way some recent browser versions download files makes it a bit tough for users to find the files. It's also easy for the user to download a document, open it, change it, save it, and then not be able to find the document.

Consider various use cases—who might be downloading the document, why, and their level of computer knowledge—then provide appropriate support for helping them succeed.

Using an Image from the Media Library in Your Post

If the image you want to use in your post is already in the Media Library, inserting it is simpler. Follow these steps:

1. While creating or editing a post, click the Add an Image button. The Add an Image dialog box opens. It has three tabs: From Computer, From URL, and Media Library. The first tab, From Computer, is selected by default.

2. Click the Media Library tab. A list of images appears, including every image you've previously inserted into a post, as shown in Figure 9.7.

3. Scroll to the image you want and click Show. The image and options for inserting it in the post appear, nearly identical to the options in the previous section.

4. Update the image-specific options (Title, Caption, and Description) and the post-specific options (Link URL, Alignment, and Size), as described in previous sections.

5. Click Insert into Post to insert the image in your post.

6. Check the result in your post; if needed, click the image to make the Edit Image and Delete Image buttons appear. Use them as needed.

7. Move the image around in your post to get text flow right.

Figure 9.7
The Media Library gives you a choice.

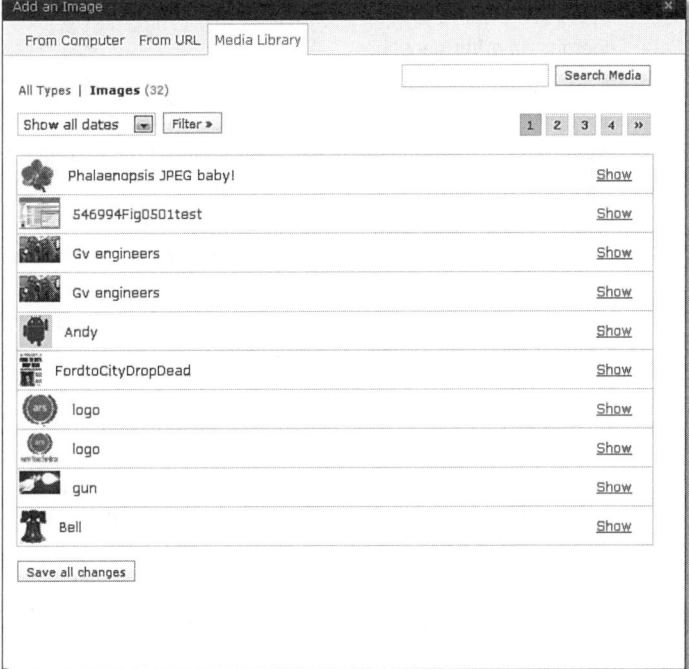

Using an Image from the Web in Your Post

Many bloggers don't know that you can use any image, from anywhere in the Web, in your blog, *without* downloading it to your computer and uploading it to the Media Library first. WordPress makes this easy, as we describe here.

When your blog—or any other web page—displays an image, the image doesn't have to be on the same server as the text and layout information in the actual HTML file that makes up the web page. In fact, it very often isn't.

The HTML file contains only text. The image is brought into the displayed web page (or blog posting) by a pointer to the location of the image file, which can be anywhere on the Web.

The pointer looks like this:

```
<IMG HREF= "www.mygreatsite.com/bigfatimage.jpg"></IMG>
```

The file is stored at a web URL, just like a web address except that it ends in the name of the specific image file that's desired. The `</IMG>` end tag is needed for XHTML, as used by WordPress.

However, the fact that you *can* do this doesn't necessarily mean you *should* do it. The first problem is copyright, as described earlier in this chapter in the "Copyright and Media Types" section.

The second problem has to do with bandwidth. If you include a picture hosted on another site in your blog, *the other site* has to pay for the bandwidth used to download it.

Frankly, these days, the charges to the other side are unlikely to be very high, or even noticeable, unless they have a little-used site and you have a very frequently visited one. However, there is still a cost involved, as well as common courtesy in not foisting charges on other people.

So you actually save other people money if you take an image from their site, download it to your computer, and upload it to WordPress, rather than if you use their image directly from their site.

However, it can also be nice to go ahead and link to the image on the other site, and include an acknowledgement of the loan in the form of a link to the original site that might generate traffic to the host. If, like most sites, they want traffic, this is a good thing.

On balance, though, it's probably best to include an image from the Web in your site only if you control the source (meaning you're paying for the hosting anyway), or if you're sure you have permission. This is the case on sites such as Flickr, which encourages you to link to their images, and includes code for hosting their images on your site. (You don't need the code, but it's a sign that Flickr is interested in having their images used on other sites.)

Follow these steps to include an image from a website in your post:

 caution

Images hosted on other people's sites can be moved or removed. To be sure that the image will never leave the spot you've linked to, bring it into WordPress.

 tip

Flickr uses something called Creative Commons Licensing to allow people who post images to explicitly grant rights to use them to a wide variety of people. For more information, check out www.flickr.com/ creativecommons/.

1. Find an image on the Web that you want to use. You might want to leave the page with the image open in one web page while you use a different web page to go to the Administration area of your blog and insert the image into your post.

2. While creating or editing a post, click the Add an Image button. The Add an Image dialog box opens. It has three tabs: From Computer, From URL, and Media Library. The first tab, From Computer, is selected by default.

3. Click the From URL tab. The contents of the dialog box change to show the title, Add Media File from URL, as shown in Figure 9.8.

Figure 9.8
Get in URLy to source images from around the Web.

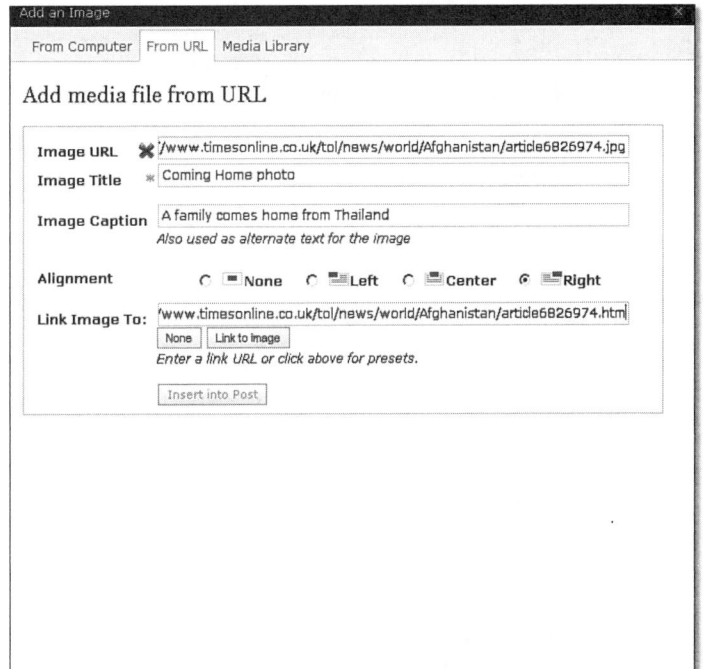

4. Enter the URL (web address) of the image. You can copy and paste this by right-clicking on the image in the web page where it lives. (On a Mac, that's Control-click.) When you right-click, a context-sensitive menu appears. Choose the Copy Image URL option from the context-sensitive menu.

   When you enter the URL, WordPress verifies it for you and alerts you if there are problems.

5. Enter a title, caption, and URL for the image, as described previously in the section, "Uploading an Image to the Media Library."

6. To link the image to an address on the Web, enter a URL or click the Link to Image button. If you link the image, it should not generally be to the image file's home on the Web (which is what the Link to Image button does), but instead to the web page in which the image originally appears. You might also want to enter a caption that lets your users know the image is linked.

7. Click the Insert into Post button.

8. After you publish the post, test the image and the link, if any, to make sure they work properly.

 tip

If you link to an image on the Web as described here, WordPress doesn't let you resize it. You can resize it yourself by clicking the HTML tab for your post and changing the width and height attributes for the image. To avoid odd-looking results, make sure to change them by the same proportion by, for instance, reducing each dimension by half. Also be aware that you're now downloading a larger image just so your visitors can see a small one, which is a bit of a waste of (the host's) bandwidth and users' time. You might want, instead, to copy the image, create a smaller version, upload that to the Media Library, and link it to the larger version, either at the URL of the file location or at the web page in which the image appears.

Creating an Image-Based or Multimedia Blog

You can create a blog that primarily uses images or multimedia to communicate, or that is primarily a discussion of information that's in one or more other media types.

Your media might be stored on a photo site like Flickr, mentioned previously, or a video site such as YouTube, as described in Chapter 10. In these cases, you might wonder, why do you need a WordPress blog at all?

WordPress is actually great for this kind of blog. WordPress provides a framework for posts that introduce, give context on, or discuss other media types. You might not host all, or even any, of the media on WordPress's servers, but WordPress can still be the first port of call.

Your WordPress blog can also be a great place to give people a gentle introduction to your work, instead of throwing them headfirst into a thousand photos you've uploaded to Flickr or a hundred videos populating your own private channel on YouTube.

We won't go into the specifics of creating a multimedia blog here as they're too variable, depending on the type(s) of media involved and where you choose to host it. Follow the steps and suggestions in this book that apply to all kinds of blogs. Then use the information in this chapter and Chapter 10, as well as information provided by the site(s) where your media files are hosted, to get started on your multimedia blog.

10

ADDING UPGRADES, AUDIO, AND VIDEO

Upgrading Your Blog

There's a smooth upgrade path from a WordPress.com blog to a hosted blog using software available from WordPress.org. In this chapter, we describe the upgrades you can get for a WordPress.com blog: Custom CSS, unlimited private users, hosting space upgrades (including audio hosting), removal of all ads, and VideoPress. These upgrades cost from about $15 to about $90 per year each.

All of these upgrades are steps toward a hosted blog using WordPress.org software, which is described in Chapter 11, "Installing and Upgrading WordPress Software." Our hope is that this book makes the process of adding WordPress.com upgrades to your blog a smooth one.

Having all these options is part of the strength of the WordPress offering. This smooth path also allows the entire WordPress effort to operate in hybrid form. Automattic, the company that owns the WordPress brand, has several products, including WordPress.com, which are supported largely by sales of these upgrades. Yet the WordPress community, largely made up of volunteers who provide most of the support for WordPress software, is far larger than just Automattic and its staff.

From an evolutionary point of view, it might be interesting to you to know that WordPress was initially only available as software from WordPress.org, beginning in 2003. Many, many people found that they could arrange hosting or set up their own computer as a web host, download and install the software, and run it successfully.

Not all of the people who were successful with WordPress software would have wanted to take on these additional challenges. But most who tried were successful and would never give up the capability and flexibility that they now have with their blogs.

Unlike most software solutions, which develop from less capable to more capable, WordPress actually developed its more professional solution first and an entry-level solution, in the form of WordPress.com, more recently; it opened to the public in late 2005.

This evolutionary perspective is valuable in understanding not only the strengths of WordPress but some challenges it has. One is that the orientation of the WordPress community is almost overwhelmingly toward the software available from WordPress.org. If you search for help on WordPress, you'll largely find material applicable to the software available from WordPress.org, and much of that information is for older versions.

Finding help specifically for WordPress.com is difficult. For instance, much of the information available for WordPress mentions various plug-ins. Imagine the disappointment of a WordPress.com user when they find out that they can't get plug-ins at all.

Part of the problem is in the naming of parts; the WordPress name stretches awkwardly over the versions. If only the good folks at Automattic had given them clear names! (WordPress and WordPress Pro, anyone?) Even books about the topic intermix the two. We hope we've produced a clear separation that allows users of both of the main types of the WordPress offering to find information that will help them in this book.

A Quick Description of Upgrades

If most of your needs are met by WordPress.com and, perhaps, a single upgrade, that might be the best option for you. If you are adding more upgrades, though, it's increasingly likely that you should consider upgrading to WordPress.org.

Here's a brief description of the upgrades available for WordPress.com and how the functionality made available by each is handled for WordPress.org. You can find all the available upgrades on the Administration page for your blog; follow the Upgrades link in the Upgrades menu.

Paying for Upgrades

You pay for upgrades to WordPress.com by buying credits, at a cost of $1 per credit. You can also buy credits for other people as gifts, though we don't know just how many of these gifts have made it under people's Christmas trees.

Payments are made using PayPal, which allows you to use a credit card as well as PayPal credit.

Custom CSS

Custom CSS is simply the ability to customize the Cascading Style Sheets code in your chosen theme. At about $15 per year, this is relatively expensive if all you've done is change a couple of colors, and relatively cheap if you make big changes to a theme, such as changing column widths and fonts.

The Custom CSS page, which describes just how to use CSS in WordPress.com with the Custom CSS upgrade, is shown in Figure 10.1. The Custom CSS page and a FAQ are linked to from the Upgrades page, and additional resources are linked to from the Custom CSS page.

Figure 10.1
Custom CSS gives you lots of power.

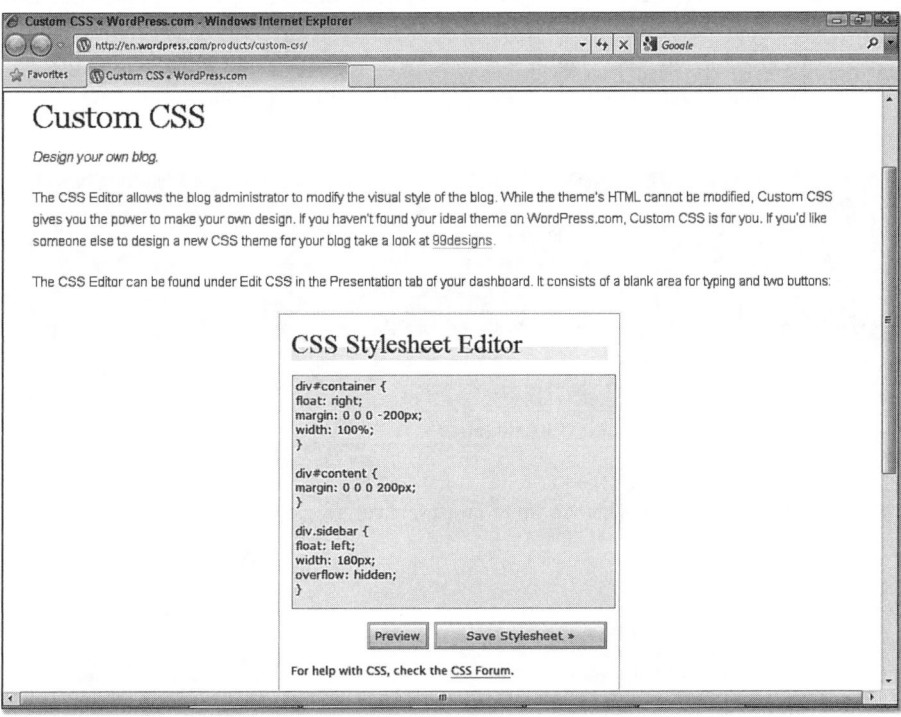

WordPress.org contrast: On WordPress.org, you have access to many more themes than the 70 or so available to WordPress.com users. You can also tweak themes to your heart's content, and create your own as well. There's really no choice here for serious bloggers.

Unlimited Private Users

If you have a private blog, it's limited to 35 users. For smaller organizations and groups, this is fine, but for larger ones, it might only be enough to run a test site. It costs about $30 per year to upgrade to unlimited private users. As with Custom CSS, this is frustrating if you only need 40 users, but fine if you have 4,000 or some other large number.

WordPress.org contrast: On WordPress.org, there's no limit on the number of users for a private blog. Also, many larger organizations that might want a private blog have the internal technical resources to easily manage a WordPress.org blog, and might even prefer the increased control offered with Wordpress.org.

No-ads Upgrade

WordPress.com blogs include ads, unless you pay for a No-ads upgrade for about $30 per year.

WordPress bloggers never see ads because they don't show up for people with a WordPress account. The frequency of ads varies depending on the topic of your blog and the eagerness of advertisers, generally and on particular topics. We've seen descriptions of the number of ads that run, which range from "hardly any" to "a lot," but there's no definitive information available.

The ads can be quite intrusive. See Figure 10.2 for an example.

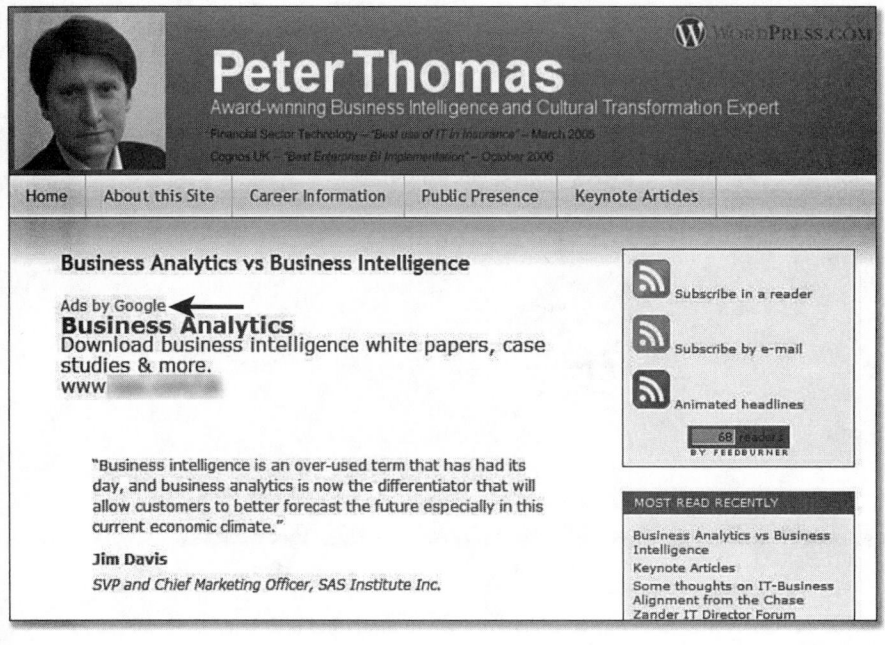

Figure 10.2
Ads can be a pain to your users.

If you get too many complaints from your blog visitors that your blog is hosting ads, you might want to consider the No-ads upgrade. Also, many blogs, even quite small ones, can't tolerate ads—either because of being strictly noncommercial or because ads that show might be competitive or objectionable. (For example, a cancer charity is not going to want to take even a small risk that a tobacco company ad might run on their site.)

This is not an unreasonably high cost to opt out of ads, but many of those who must purchase this upgrade are small organizations with limited budgets. It's also a bit frustrating to have to pay for No-ads when what you really want is the ability to run *your own* ads on your blog, and are frustrated by the complete ban on any kind of commercial activity on WordPress.com blogs.

WordPress.org contrast: WordPress.org has no ads from Automattic, and as many or as few ads, or other commercial activity (such as product sales) as you'd like.

Space/Audio Upgrades—5GB, 15GB, and 25GB

A WordPress.com blog includes 3GB of free storage, which is a very strong offering. The price for space upgrades is about $20 for 5GB ($4 per GB), $50 for 15GB ($3.33 per GB), and $90 for 25GB ($3.60 per GB—hey, the cost per GB just went up, not down, with size!). Given how hard your blog(s) will be working WordPress's servers if you have this kind of storage, these seem like reasonable costs.

The frustrating part is that WordPress requires you to buy at least one space upgrade to support audio. Without it, you can't upload any audio file type to your blog.

For smaller blogs, you could almost certainly fit the actual audio file(s), along with your text and image files, in your 3GB free allocation. You're really paying for the capability to upload audio files and streaming support for delivering them.

Of course, many people aren't going to do this just to experiment with audio; you'll host the audio files somewhere else instead. This, though, is getting you into the same hosting concerns that you're trying to avoid by staying on WordPress.com instead of moving to WordPress.org, which can be an awkward problem if you want to experiment with audio.

WordPress.org contrast: You negotiate disk space costs with your hosting provider, as well as support for streaming audio. Often this works in your favor, but these costs might be high, or the quality of service might be low, in some cases.

VideoPress Upgrade

You can't upload video to your WordPress.com blog at all without purchasing a VideoPress upgrade for roughly $60 per year.

VideoPress is an impressive service that seems designed and priced for moderately large-scale operators. If you want to experiment, or host just a few videos, you're much better off hosting them on YouTube or your own server, then linking to the video from within your WordPress blog, as described in this chapter.

WordPress.org contrast: As with audio, you negotiate disk space costs with your hosting provider, as well as support for streaming video.

Domain Names

You can add a domain name to your blog for roughly $15 per year. (See the section "Getting a Good Domain Name," later in this chapter.) You can get domain names much more cheaply elsewhere, but not as easily, nor as well integrated with your WordPress blog.

WordPress does not provide help in finding a suitable domain name. Some domain name search sites play tricks on you, such as reserving a domain name for several days just after you search for it. This has the effect of making you think it's been taken by someone else if you try to buy it elsewhere and see it gone. Even if you understand the trick, you have to buy the domain from the place that reserved the domain name.

Many domain name sellers refuse to play such games. One such seller is one of the Web's largest, 123reg.com. This site suggests alternate domain names and otherwise makes the search easier. A domain name search on 123reg.com is shown in Figure 10.3.

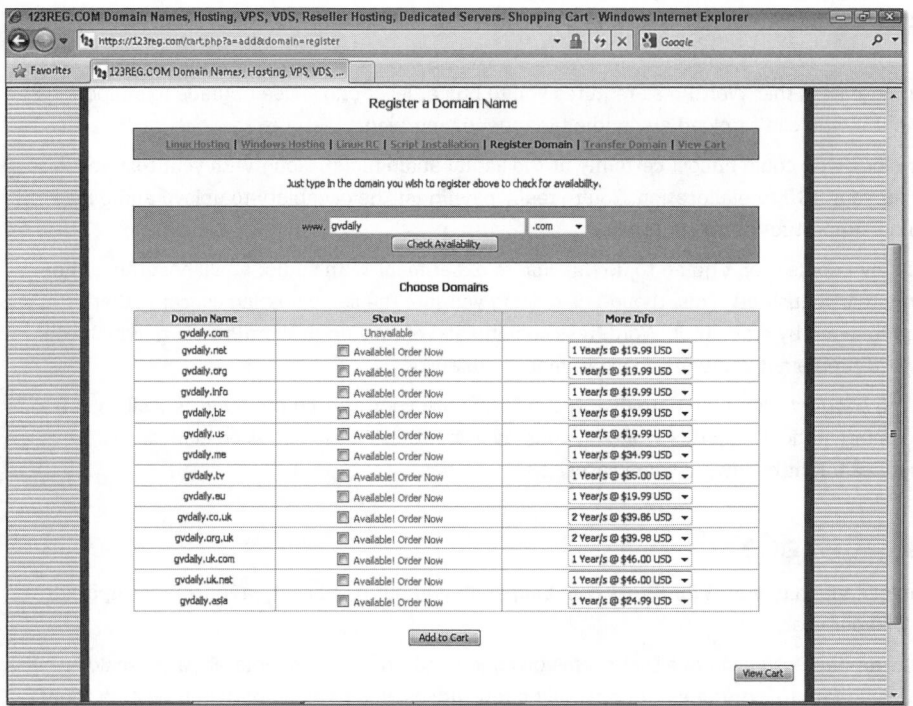

Figure 10.3
The domain name search can be exciting.

If you are ever going to get a custom domain name, then you should, in fact, do it as soon as possible. That's because you want to build up bookmarks, branding, and search engine rankings for whatever the long-term name of your site is going to be, not building them up for one name and then changing to another.

WordPress.org contrast: Domain names are cheaper elsewhere, as mentioned. The main advantage of buying a domain name for a WordPress.org blog, though, is that you don't face the prospect of later transferring your blog, and all its hard-won traffic, to a new host—a transfer that could confuse things in such a way that you lose some or most of your hard-won search engine ranking.

Global Differences

We've touched on the overall differences between WordPress.com and WordPress.org in this chapter and throughout this book. Here is a summary of the overall differences:

- **Hassle**—Finding, dealing with, and maintaining a relationship with your hosting provider is the biggest potential hassle factor in using WordPress.org, and might be the single biggest issue that drives many bloggers to WordPress.com instead.

Not all hosting providers smoothly support all of WordPress's features. One host might be good on blogging support and CSS, whereas another might be a streaming media expert. The more you will be asking of your host, the more time you should take to find a good provider, and the more you should expect to pay.

- **Cost**—Costs are likely to be higher on WordPress.org than on WordPress.com, even if staying on WordPress.com means paying for a lot of upgrades. That's because every upgrade on WordPress.com represents something you have to find and get support for from a hosting provider, so a complex, busy blog is going to be on the more expensive end for either approach.

- **Branding and commerce**—If your blog is going to be a big deal—if search engine optimization or the ability to engage in advertising and e-commerce are likely to be important to you—then you should start out how you're going to end up. That is, you should move to WordPress.org as soon as possible.

- **Flexibility**—A WordPress.com blog is sharply limited as to themes and plug-ins. A WordPress.org blog is unlimited, which does mean a time investment to keep up with new offerings and maintenance, but potentially great rewards for your blog as well.

- **Support**—Support is actually better for WordPress.org than for WordPress.com, partly because of the strong community around WordPress.org and partly because WordPress.org is the original WordPress, with lots of books and online resources largely focused on WordPress.org rather than WordPress.com.

WordPress.com is a tremendous tool, and we show you how to get the most out of it in this book. If you're serious about blogging, though, you'll probably end up moving to WordPress.org, as described in the next chapter—and once you do, you'll never look back.

Getting a Good Domain Name

One of the best ways to move up to the big leagues with your blog is to purchase a custom domain name. WordPress makes this very easy using WordPress upgrades, as described previously. WordPress also points new domain names to your blog seamlessly; it preserves the original URL, which you're issued when you get the blog, and supports access to both the original domain name and the new, custom domain name.

When you first get a WordPress blog, WordPress asks you for a name for the blog. It then gives you a web address, or *URL*, for the blog.

The blog URL is made up of the name that you provide, *prepended to*—stuck in front of—wordpress.com. So if you choose the name mygreatblog, the URL for your blog will be mygreatblog.wordpress.com.

This domain name has three parts:

- mygreatblog is the *third-level domain name.*

- wordpress is the *second-level domain name.*

- `.com` is the *top-level domain*. There are only a limited number of top-level domains, or *TLD*s as they're known; some are worldwide, such as `.com` and `.org`, and some are country-specific, such as `.co.uk`.

WordPress-based domain names such as mygreatblog.wordpress.com are quite acceptable, and can be branded fairly strongly, though not so much as a custom domain name. It's more widely respected, and easier for people to remember, for you to have a domain name all your own, such as www.mygreatblog.com. (People who hear that you're running "My Great Blog" are very likely to try visiting www.mygreatblog.com, but are far less likely to try mygreatblog.wordpress.com.)

This section tells you how domain names are made up and how to get a good one for yourself.

WordPress.com Domain Names Versus Custom Domain Names

One of the biggest issues that faces bloggers starting a new WordPress blog is whether to have a custom domain name or to just use the free domain name WordPress assigned to your blog.

The authors of this book have used both approaches for their own main blogs. One of us (Smith) has a custom domain name for Google Voice Daily, at www.gvDaily.com; the other (McCallister) has a free domain name, metaverse.wordpress.com.

It's worth noting that the Metaverse domain name is a bit of reverse snobbery—achieving status by *not* spending money. The Metaverse blog is about open source software, and WordPress is famous for being an example of a uniquely successful open source project. By keeping a WordPress.com domain name, the Metaverse blog actually stands out more in the open source community than if it had the custom domain name www.metaverse.com.

You have three choices when setting up your blog initially:

- **Plan to stick with a WordPress.com domain name forever**—In this case, your blog name, which becomes the third-level domain for your domain name, needs to be unique within WordPress. If it's not, WordPress forces you to choose another name.

- **Start with a WordPress.com domain name, but keep your options open for upgrading later**— In this case, not only does your blog name need to be unique within WordPress, but you also need to check that it's available as a second-level domain, along with the TLD `.com`, and then hope the second-level domain and `.com` combination remains available until you choose to upgrade.

- **Go to a custom domain name straightaway**—In this case, you need to do things a bit backward. First make sure that the second-level domain is available, using a site such as 123reg.com; because you won't be letting people get used to a `.com` TLD, you can use a different one instead, such as `.org` or `.edu`. You can then use the second-level domain you've identified as your blog name as well, but if that isn't available in WordPress, you can use a variant or any name at all. Again, no one will be getting used to it; you'll always publicize your blog using its own custom domain name.

A WordPress.com domain name is great for fooling around, for experimenting with blogging, and for sites that are strongly affiliated with the WordPress or open source communities. For most other sites, though—even, for instance, a site that's a fairly serious hobby or the online representation of one—we recommend a custom domain name.

In either case, we recommend that you pursue either the first or third option, not the second (deferring a decision). If you choose to wait, the domain name you want could be taken by someone else. Also, you build up brand equity in, and search engine pathways to, the WordPress.com domain name, only to lose some or even most of that when you upgrade; an upgrade that will, at least temporarily, downgrade traffic to your blog.

How Domain Names Work

The domain name is, confusingly, either two or three parts: possibly the third-level domain (such as mygreatblog in mygreatblog.wordpress.com) and always the second-level and top-level domains (such as wordpress.com itself).

Usually, people just think of the last two parts, as in wordpress.com, as the domain name. This isn't so, but it won't stop people from believing it.

People also call names such as mygreatblog.wordpress.com or wordpress.com URLs. They're correct, but many don't realize that longer names that identify specific files, such as mygreatblog.wordpress.com/images/mynosehair.jpg, are URLs as well.

URL is short for uniform resource locator. Most of the resources in question are files. If the URL was called the uniform file locator instead, a lot of confusion might be avoided.

The Web uses a bit of trickery to make things easier for the user, but it contributes to confusion as well. For instance, when you go to a big company website at www.bigcompany.com, you don't have to remember a filename; you just have to remember the name of "Big Company" and add .com to it to find the website. How does a web browser know exactly which file to get when only the domain name is given?

What's really going on is that, if you just type a domain name into a web browser, it looks for any of four different HTML files:

- www.bigcompany.com/index.htm

- www.bigcompany.com/index.html

- www.bigcompany.com/home.htm

- www.bigcompany.com/home.html

If it finds any of these four files, it displays the first one it finds. If it doesn't find any of them, it displays a "file not found" or similar error. (Big Company, of course, spends a lot of money each year to make sure this doesn't happen often.)

So now you know how domain names work—and why they can be shared without a specific filename on the end. This is valuable for understanding what's really going on as you store different files on your blog.

Choosing a Good Third-Level or Second-Level Domain Name

What makes a good domain name?

This is not an idle question. A company one of the authors (Smith) worked for paid $3 million for the website Shopping.com during the dot-com boom of the late 1990s. The main asset of Shopping.com was the domain name it owned. Needless to say, the generically named Shopping.com never rivaled the quirkily named Amazon.com as an online shopping destination.

Generic names such as Shopping.com or Pets.com rarely became successful businesses, and even more rarely became as successful as the owners of the name dreamed. Instead, a few other characteristics characterize a successful domain name:

- **Guessable**—If the site represents some real-world entity online, such as a person, a school, or a company, the web user should be able to guess the domain name from the name of the real-world entity.

- **Memorable**—The domain name should be easy to remember.

- **Spellable**—The domain name should be easy to spell once you've heard it spoken aloud.

- **Unique**—If not representing a real-world entity, the domain name should be unique, easily distinguished from similar names.

- **Suggestive**—The name should be suggestive of what the site does.

It might be impossible to meet all of these rules at once. Sites like Flickr achieve their goals by using a slight misspelling of a suggestive name, meaning that people who hear the name won't spell it right. WordPress itself is a valuable domain name as it meets all these rules.

For companies, it's critically important to have the guessable domain name for their business name. If your business is named Jobey and Mobey, you really, really want to have the domain name jobeyandmobey.com. It might be, though, that some other Jobey and Mobey that you never heard of got it first. It might even be that some domain name speculator knew of your business, bought the domain name first, and will now only sell it to you for thousands of dollars.

For the Metaverse blog, the name literally means "beyond the universe." The word originally appeared in the 1992 science-fiction novel *Snow Crash*, but has since been used to describe a variety of virtual environments. It's a great name for a blog about open source code, which can be thought of as contributing to the creation of virtual worlds. (The blogosphere itself—the collection of all blogs on the Web, along with all the people who create, comment on, and read them—can be thought of as a virtual world as well.)

For gvDaily, there's some attempted cleverness going on. The blog is about Google Voice, and its proper name is Google Voice Daily, but using that as a URL would have seemed clunky. Magazines about personal computers and the Macintosh were given names like *PC World* and *MacWeek*, not *Personal Computer World* and *Macintosh Week*.

gvDaily.com seemed like a cool and catchy name. It's also short to type. Very few domain names start with the letters g and v, so someone typing the name for a second or subsequent visit will often have the rest of the name filled in for them after typing just two letters. If the name was googlevoicedaily.com, typing the first part of the name would have to compete with the might of Google itself for uniqueness.

The intercap in gvDaily—a capital letter in the middle of a word—tries to emphasize this, emphasizing the use of a lowercase gv as an abbreviation rather than the uppercase GV. (It's all the same to the browser, which would go to the site no matter which letters someone did or didn't capitalize.)

We spell all this out (no pun intended) to illustrate some of the issues that go into choosing a domain name.

Another issue is that you don't always get it right the first time. Figure 10.4 shows the contents of the Domains area for the Upgrades menu in the Administration area for gvDaily.com. Note that the blog was briefly named GetGoogleVoice.com. This name worked well for gaining traffic—lots of people want to get, or obtain, Google Voice—but it was the wrong kind of traffic, as people who reached the site really wanted to be on the Google site where they could get a Google Voice phone number.

Figure 10.4
The domain name search can be expensive.

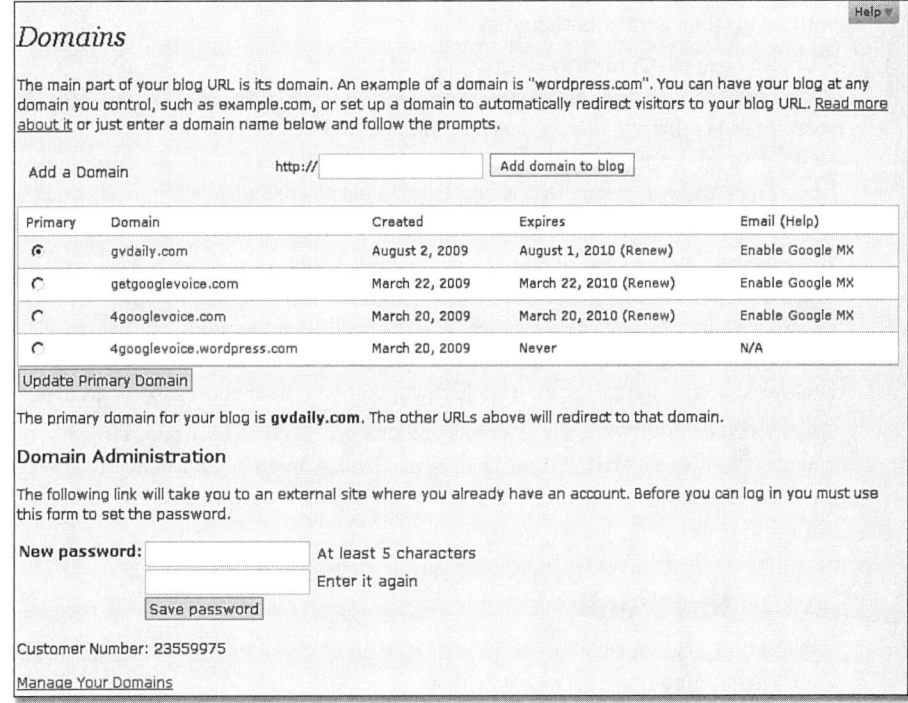

The gvDaily name seems to have worked better in terms of getting the right kind of traffic and being catchy and interesting for publicity; however, it was still a shock to lose the traffic that had been coming for the wrong reason.

Using Audio in Your Blog

Audio is a very powerful means of communication. It can be used for primarily musical purposes (with or without words) or primarily for speech (with or without background music).

Music is very powerful and evocative. However, when people hear music when they don't expect to, especially from a computer, it can also be annoying and/or embarrassing.

Given what blogs are for, there's absolutely no need for background music and other sound effects on most blogs. If you're expert with sound or really love it, sure, make it part of your blog. But don't think you need to add background music to your blog if it's not your thing.

Blogs are good for talking about music and introducing people to music that you know and love. The tremendous popularity of iTunes and many other musically oriented services and sites demonstrates a need for context, criticism, and discussion.

Using a blog to introduce music is a more natural use of music with a blog than adding background music.

When audio is used primarily for speech, it can be a very good complement to your blog. One possibility is to simply record your posts as little talks and offer them as playable or downloadable audio. This adds a new dimension to how people experience your blog. (You'll need to modify things as you go along to adjust for the fact that there are no hyperlinks or images in audio!)

You can also create a blog primarily about spoken podcasts, books on tape, and so on. As with music—perhaps even more so—a blog can add a lot of context, color, and camaraderie around spoken pieces. With downloaded audio, it's easier to successfully integrate background music with spoken words than it is to add background music to your blog.

Having said so much good about words and images, it might be a good stretch for you and your blog visitors if you make an effort to occasionally use audio in your blog. That way you—and your regulars—are ready when something comes up that you want to discuss, and that can't be shared any other way.

 caution

Part of the reason that blogs became so popular is that many people love words (plus perhaps a few images to break up the flow). Words are scannable and accessible. You can read them slowly to get the full meaning, you can stop reading to look up a word (or to answer the phone), and on and on. And from a technical point of view, words (and images) cause very little trouble on PCs compared with multimedia.

Be ready to enter a whole new world when you add audio or video to your blog. You might find yourself doing tech support or otherwise helping your blog visitors. You might well find that it's more than worth the effort—just be ready for some extra work.

Where to Host Audio

You can go a long way with audio in your blog using audio hosted elsewhere—that's already on the Web. We describe how in the next section.

This is a great way to get started with using audio in your blog with no expense and minimal hassle. Yes, the file might get moved, so links no longer work; yes, the host server might get busy and be slow to start playback, or have skips and pauses. For experimenting, though, this is acceptable.

You might want to host audio files yourself right from the start, or start hosting files yourself after you've experimented for a while. There are three main alternatives for hosting audio files on a WordPress.com blog:

- Purchase a WordPress.com space upgrade; any size will do. The Media Library uploader will suddenly start allowing you to upload audio files of four types (as of this writing): .mp3, .m4a, .wav, and .ogg audio files.

- Host your audio file on a web page creation or file hosting site of some sort; Google Sites, Dropbox, and BlogTalkRadio are alternatives we've seen mentioned favorably.

- Move up to a WordPress.org account, as described in Chapter 11. Then you can host and stream audio files for free, within any limits set by your hosting provider.

Using a separate hosting site is fine if you already have an account there and know how to use it. However, if not, you have to learn at least something about the other site to make a decision, then learn even more to use it. This is a lot of trouble. Using a WordPress.com space upgrade or moving to a WordPress.org account can start to look pretty good.

The steps in the next section can be used with a variety of file hosting options. We recommend that you seriously consider either of the WordPress-oriented options—a space upgrade or moving to a WordPress.org-supported blog.

The size of the upgrade is usually not that important. A 3-minute song in a compressed format, such as the MP3 format, takes up about 1MB. That's 1,000 songs per gigabyte. However, WAV files, which are not compressed, are much larger, about 10MB per minute of sound. (That's 30MB for a 3-minute song, or 33 songs per gigabyte.) If you use WAV files for lengthy recordings of speeches, for instance, you might need to consider the upgrade size more carefully.

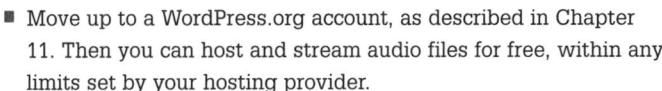

caution

The same "bandwidth stealing" concerns apply to audio as to graphics, as mentioned in Chapter 9, "Adding Graphics to Your Posts," only much more so. If you aren't sure how the owner of a site would feel about you linking to their audio file, give the other site some publicity by naming and linking to it as the source of your audio. If you think linking to someone's audio file would be unwelcome or a burden on the other site, even with publicity, send your users to the other site to listen.

Support for Audio File Playback

Amazingly, audio playback is not uniform across Windows-based or Linux-based PCs. (It is uniform on Macs.) There are still some PCs out there with no sound card support, and it's also common for the sound output or microphone support on a PC to stop working and not get fixed.

The built-in WordPress player works for MP3 files only. Almost all of your blog visitors will also be able to play back most other kinds of audio files, but even an occasional exception can be a big hassle for all concerned. Try to use MP3 files in your WordPress blog whenever possible.

Putting an Audio File in Your Blog

There are three ways to put an audio file in your blog:

- Create a download link to a file located elsewhere.

- Upload a file (MP3 only) to a host and link to it.

- Upload a file to the Media Library and insert it into your post.

We describe how to complete each of these approaches in the following sections.

Creating a Download Link

Audio files are not handled by web browsers as HTML, JPEG, PNG, and GIF files are. Instead, the web browser downloads the file to your computer. If there's an application installed in your computer that can play it, that application then fires up and offers to play the file for you or let you save it. If there's no application, the file simply downloads, waiting for you to find some use for it.

You need to understand this because some small percentage of your users will have trouble playing back audio files. Now, armed with this explanation, you can tell them what's going on.

Follow these steps to create a download link to a file stored on the Web:

1. Find the URL of the media file you want to use and copy it. You can test the link by pasting it into the address area of a browser window. The file should download.

2. In the Add/Edit Post page, click the Add Media button. This brings up the Add Media dialog box.

3. In the dialog box, click the From URL tab. The Add Media File from URL area appears, as shown in Figure 10.5.

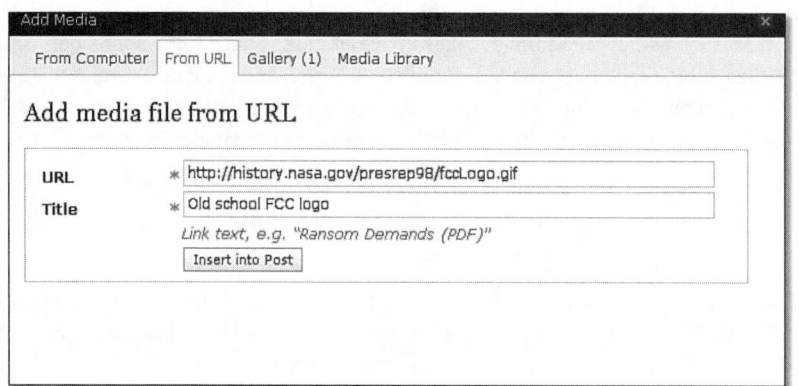

Figure 10.5
Use the Add Media dialog box to create a download link.

4. Paste the URL to the file.

5. In the Title area, enter the link text you want to use. The link text, and the text surrounding it, should indicate what will happen when the user clicks on the link.

Creating a Playback Link

A playback link is a link to a file that will play within WordPress. The WordPress audio player only works with MP3 files. (It's pretty cool that WordPress has an audio player at all.)

Follow these steps to create a playback link to an MP3 file on the Web:

1. Upload an MP3 file to a site on the Web.

2. Find the URL of the MP3 file and copy it.

3. In the Add/Edit Post page, click the HTML tab. The HTML code for your post appears.

4. Add an audio shortcode and the URL of the file as follows: [audio http://*domain*/*path*]. The player appears in your post at the location indicated by where in the HTML code you place the audio shortcode.

5. Test your page and modify it, if needed.

Uploading and Inserting an Audio File

Once you purchase a space upgrade, or on a WordPress.org-supported blog, uploading and inserting an audio file is much like uploading and inserting an image. Follow these steps:

1. In the Administration area of your blog, under the Media Library menu, click Add New. The Media Library uploader appears.

2. Select the audio file and upload it.

3. Enter the Title, Caption, and Description. As with image files, the Title is the name of the audio clip within the Media Library. The Caption, if any, displays below the audio icon. The Description is only used within the Media Library.

4. For the Link URL, leave it blank; click the None button, if needed. The player appears in your post at the location indicated by where in the HTML code you place the audio shortcode.

>  **note**
>
> For additional details on using audio, including how to customize the appearance of the audio player, visit http://support.wordpress.com/audio or http://support.wordpress.com/links/download-links/.

5. Test your page and modify it, if needed. This causes the Audio Player to appear.

6. Click the Insert into Post button. The Audio Player appears in the post.

Using Video in Your Blog

Whereas audio is very powerful, video (and its cousin, film) are the most involving media available. In fact, it once seemed that the amount of time people spend watching television would only ever increase—until the Internet came along to steal back big chunks of people's time.

Now video is an integral part of the Web. Realize, though, that video and film are experienced on a continuum. The tiny, highly compressed images, with low-quality audio, that we use in blogs and other web pages are at the lowest end. (Well, maybe just above a flip book.) Then, you move up to cell phones, then portable video players, then normal TVs, then big-screen TVs, all the way up to a movie theater, iMax cinema, or 3D screen.

Creating high-quality video or film is enormously expensive and involving. It takes experts and artists to do it right.

The video we use in blogs is interesting and helpful, but it's not high-quality enough for people to watch it for long. So we recommend that you use video as a supporting element in your blog, unless the main topic of your blog is video.

The low quality of online video gets you off the hook somewhat. Despite video's power, you don't have to use it. Or you can use it in a limited way, with an occasional clip supporting a point you're making.

The same low quality of playback gets you off the hook, to a large extent, in terms of production values as well. High-production values are largely wasted online. You can turn on a webcam, speak into it, and create a video that's considered worthwhile, if the content is good enough.

Where to Host Video

YouTube is an incredible resource for web video. There are other sites with some similarities, but YouTube is what's called a category killer, a leader that defines the market, sets standards, and holds most of the market share.

Of course, a "market" usually involves money, and money has been hard for YouTube to find. Even with the deep pockets of Google, which acquired YouTube a few years ago, behind it, there's still a lot of concern about whether YouTube can make enough money to be viable.

Until things change, YouTube will do a lot for you, all for free. You can use YouTube to upload video to the YouTube site. YouTube will compress the video—quite harshly, but, as the saying goes, whaddya want for nothing? YouTube will then host it and provide you with the HTML code to paste into your web page. All you need to do is paste the code in and be thankful you can get so much done for you for free.

If YouTube isn't good enough, WordPress offers a great alternative: VideoPress. For about $60 per year, you get free hosting for your own videos and as much bandwidth for downloads as you need. You control the degree of compression and much more.

In between YouTube and VideoPress is the option of using a WordPress.org-supported blog. With such a blog, you have complete flexibility. You determine—along with your hosting provider—what video you make available and how much bandwidth you use.

Between YouTube, WordPress.org-supported blogs, and VideoPress, you have a solid continuum of alternatives for hosting and streaming video.

Support for Video File Playback

Ironically, support for video file playback is less problematic on the Web than support for audio file playback. Most video playback requires Flash—and that's about it. Because WordPress uses Flash for its uploader, you and every other WordPress blogger are just about certain to have Flash already (along with many millions of other people).

Putting a Video File in Your Blog

There are two commonly used ways to put a video clip in your blog:

- Insert a link to a YouTube video.

- Upload a file to the Media Library and insert it into your post.

We describe how to use each of these approaches in the following sections.

Is This Book an Ad for YouTube?

You might think that we're emphasizing YouTube, a specific service, too much, but we're not. YouTube has become the generic provider of lower-end video to websites. Even the WordPress documentation prominently features YouTube, by name.

Linking to a YouTube Video

Like audio files, video files are not handled by web browsers as HTML, JPEG, PNG, and GIF files are. However, support for Flash is so widespread that it's the next best thing. You can usually count on a YouTube video to play in your browser as if YouTube were a file type supported in the HTML specification.

Follow these steps to insert a YouTube video into a blog post:

1. Go to YouTube, find the URL of the video file you want to use, and copy it. You can get the URL from the top of the browser window or from within a box that YouTube provides with videos giving the HTML code. For WordPress, you only need the URL, not the HTML code.

2. In the Add/Edit Post page, click the Add Video button. This brings up the Add Media dialog box.

3. In the dialog box, click the From URL tab. The Add Media File from URL area appears, as shown in Figure 10.6.

4. Paste the URL to the file.

5. In the Title area, enter the title you want to use. The title appears as part of the still image that's displayed in your post and also as part of the video when it's played.

Note that even visitors to your blog who don't play the video get to see a cool image that hopefully livens up your blog posting.

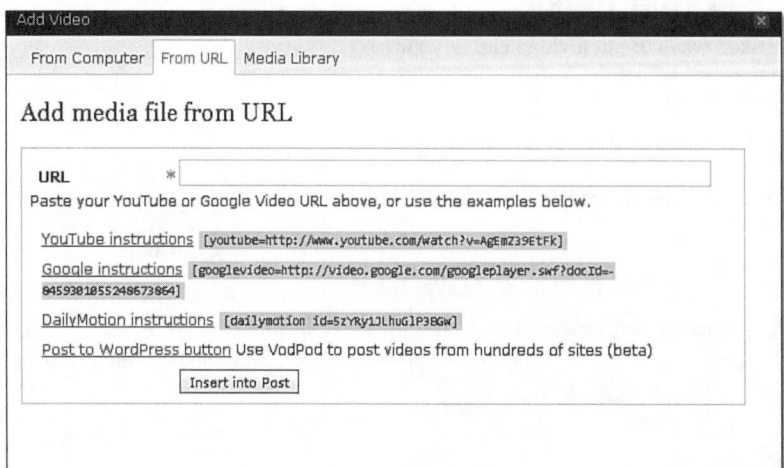

Figure 10.6
Use the Add Media dialog box to insert a YouTube video.

Uploading and Inserting a Video File (with Space Upgrade)

For a WordPress.org-supported blog, or a WordPress.com blog with a VideoPress upgrade, uploading and inserting a video file is much like uploading and inserting an image. Follow these steps:

1. In the Administration area of your blog, under the Media Library menu, click Add New. The Media Library uploader appears.

2. Select the video file and upload it.

3. Enter the Title and Description. As with image and audio files, the Title is the name of the audio clip within the Media Library. The Description is only used within the Media Library.

4. Check the check box if you want the embed code to be displayed. In most cases you will.

5. If appropriate, select a rating for your video clip. This is a voluntary step to help ensure that younger web users view age-appropriate content. If you aren't familiar with American movie ratings, G is for General audiences; PG-13 is Parental Guidance suggested, only those 13 and up should see the video; R-17 means only those who can prove they're 17 or older are admitted; X-18 means that anyone younger than 18 is expressly forbidden from being admitted. Enforcement of these standards is not very far along on the Web, though.

6. Click the Insert into Post button. The video and player appear in the post.

> **note**
>
> For additional details on using video, including statistics and how to customize the size of the video player, visit http://support.wordpress.com/videos/youtube or http://support.wordpress.com/videopress/.

IV

BUILDING YOUR OWN
WORDPRESS INSTALLATION

IN THIS PART

11

INSTALLING AND UPGRADING WORDPRESS SOFTWARE

Getting It Done For You: Hosted WordPress

You've made the decision to get WordPress running on your own website. You want access to the full power of the software and its attendant community to help you communicate with the world, or at least your little corner of it.

Previous chapters covered functionality that's common between WordPress.com and WordPress software. Starting with this chapter, we're going to help you make the most of WordPress entirely outside of the cozy environment of WordPress.com. This chapter covers the two ways of setting up WordPress on your own: through your Internet service provider (ISP) or a web hosting company (the choice for most people), and on your own computer.

Chances are pretty good that you don't want, or need, to have the headache of operating your own web server, connected to the Internet and available 24 hours a day, seven days a week. You just want some space on the web to blog when the spirit moves you. Despite the shorthand term "self-hosted WordPress," the vast majority of WordPress.org software users run their blogs on someone else's server.

 tip

Although this book is not about being your own web host, the upcoming section, "Hosting WordPress Yourself," is about running WordPress on your own computer. With a 24/7 broadband connection to the Internet and appropriate security, you could be your own host.

In this section, we want to help you find a good host for your site, and get WordPress up and running.

Finding a Blog-Friendly Host

When looking at possible hosts for your blog, you'll need to make several decisions ahead of time. Some of these options are covered in Chapter 2, "Starting Your Blog Right":

- Do you want to have your own domain name, and how do you plan to register that name?

- How much time are you willing to commit to installing, updating, and administering your blog?

- Are you planning to include a lot of images or stream audio or video from your blog?

- What are you willing to pay for blog hosting?

As with most things WordPress, you've got options when considering where to host your blog:

- ISPs offer free or low-cost websites to their users.

- WordPress.org recommends a few select WordPress-friendly hosts at http://wordpress.org/hosting. (These hosts pay Automattic a small fee for the listing.) These hosts offer one-click WordPress installations, access to multiple databases (good for running several blogs simultaneously), and financial support to WordPress to keep the WordPress websites and support forums up and functional. Some of these hosts come pretty cheap, too.

- Some hosting companies offer a range of support options for your WordPress blog. Look for the support you need.

Shopping for a web host generally involves obtaining enough disk space, bandwidth, and support for third-party software like MySQL databases and WordPress.

Disk space at a web host is the same thing as disk space on your own computer. If a web host offers 10 gigabytes (GB) of space on its hard drives with your account, when you bump up against that limit you can't save any more there.

Fortunately, simple text-based blogs have files measured in kilobytes (KB), and you could have many hundreds of posts before you even come close to hitting a 1GB space limit. Add a small image to each post, or the occasional video clip, and a minimum of 3GB should last you through your first hosting contract.

Bandwidth is the size of the pipe that brings data to and from your site. Your bandwidth use depends on two things: the size of your files and the popularity of your site. If you use your blog to keep 10 invited guests current on your daily life, bandwidth limitations are essentially meaningless to you. If you are a pop music star hosting a daily hour-long video blog designed to keep your millions of fans current on your daily life, you should get the biggest pipe available.

 note

Choose your domain name before shopping for a web host. See "Playing the Domain Name Game" in Chapter 2 and "Getting a Good Domain Name" in Chapter 10, "Adding Upgrades, Audio, and Video," for tips on finding and registering your domain.

 tip

Before you sign a hosting contract, make sure you understand what your host does when you begin to get close to your space limit. You should hear from them when you hit 80% of your allotted space. The good news is that should you underestimate your space needs, your host should be able to upgrade your space for an additional, but reasonable, fee. Be sure to shop around, as some hosts are better known for honoring their promises than others.

Web hosting companies generally give you a monthly bandwidth limit in the 10GB–50GB range. This is plenty for a standard website with a WordPress blog. Some hosts offer unlimited bandwidth, but ask them how they handle major traffic spikes, and search the Web for customer complaints.

While shopping, make sure the host supports the minimum requirements to install WordPress (more about why you need this in the next section):

- PHP version 4.3 (or later)

- MySQL version 4.0 (or later)

You'd be hard pressed to find a host that doesn't support these minimums. Run away quickly if they don't! This means they probably don't keep other software tools updated either.

Some hosts make it one-click easy to install and run WordPress on their systems, and others let you get as hands-on and customized with your installation as you want. At the very least, your host should have a Frequently Asked Questions (FAQ) page and basic information on how to install WordPress on your site. Better hosts allow you to use more than one MySQL database for multiple blogs, provide help installing plug-ins, and provide help with WordPress software updates (or handle updates themselves).

Ask as many questions of a would-be host as you need to make a good decision. Answers should be on their site or a prompt email response away. If you send an email to a potential web host and don't hear from them within 24 hours, you shouldn't do business with them.

When you have selected your web host and gotten your space on the Web, you can install WordPress on your site.

Why PHP and MySQL?

In this chapter, you will see quite a few references to PHP and MySQL, and you may wonder what they are here for. MySQL is a free relational database management system that stores and manages all the content of your blog. It is an essential prerequisite for installing WordPress. PHP is a programming language for the web. Once you've installed WordPress, a look into the installation directory will uncover a lot of files with the .php extension, as this is the language WordPress is written in.

PHP is the result of another lazy programmer's effort to simplify his life. Back in 1994, Rasmus Lerdorf wanted to eliminate some of the drudgery associated with updating his personal web page. Lerdorf wrote some Perl scripts to generate HTML tags based on some C code. In June 1995, he announced the existence of the Personal Home Page (PHP) tools, version 1.0, in a Usenet CGI newsgroup. Those tools have since evolved into a full-fledged scripting language (now officially called PHP: Hypertext Processor) with a powerful engine, Zend, and a large community of developers hacking the code. You can read more about the history of PHP at http://php.net/history.

The PHP Home Page at www.php.net defines PHP as "a widely used general-purpose scripting language that is especially suited for Web development and can be embedded into HTML. Much of its syntax is borrowed from C, Java, and Perl with a couple of unique PHP-specific features thrown in." It is open source, so anyone can contribute to its development, and works from the web server to deliver pages. As you'll see later in the chapter, PHP often pulls data out of relational database management systems such as MySQL and PostgreSQL to display web pages that look no different from pages coded in standard HTML.

The core WordPress software is written in PHP. Themes consist of PHP templates and CSS styles. Plug-ins can be written in PHP exclusively, or can include code from other languages (such as JavaScript), but need to be able to hook into WordPress to provide the necessary functionality. That is done using PHP as well.

note

There is no shortage of books to help you learn PHP and MySQL together. Julie C. Meloni's *PHP, MySQL and Apache All in One* will get you off to a great start.

Every bit of content in your blog—posts, sidebars, stylesheets, comments, graphics, dashboard, and all the rest—is stored in the MySQL database you set up during your installation (or that WordPress.com set up for you when you launched your hosted blog). What happens when your site has a visitor? In a matter of seconds, all this goes on, as in Figure 11.1:

1. A visitor's web browser calls on a page from your site.

2. The web server sees a PHP script on the requested page and fires up its PHP interpreter (mod_php5 in Apache) to execute the code.

3. Some of those PHP commands allow the script to connect to the MySQL database as the WordPress user and ask the database for the content that belongs on the page.

4. The MySQL database retrieves the requested content and sends it back to the PHP script (more precisely, to the page it's on).

5. The script, in turn, pours all of this content into a few variables.

6. The script then echoes the content from the variables for display on the page.

7. The script combines the database content with any plain HTML included on the requested page and hands it back to the web server.

8. The web server sends the HTML page back to the browser.

9. The visitor (ideally) becomes enlightened, entertained, enthralled, or some combination thereof. She tells you so on the comments page, beginning the process over again.

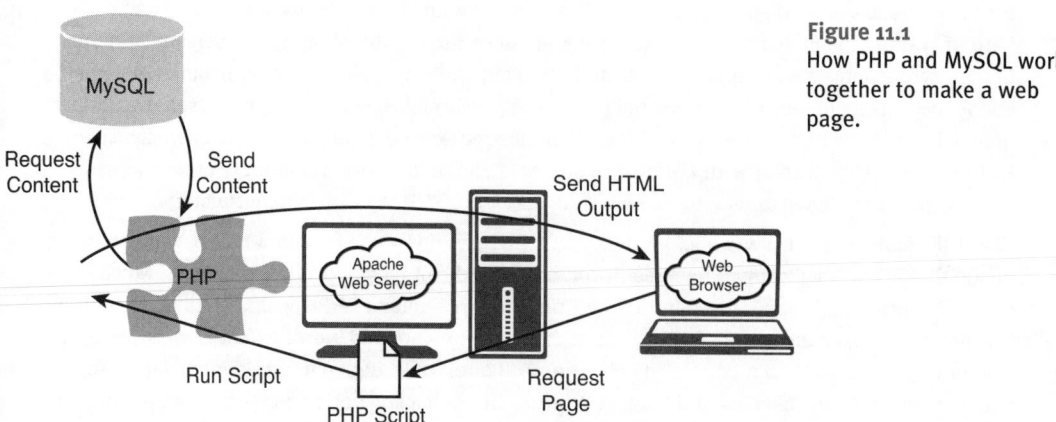

Figure 11.1
How PHP and MySQL work together to make a web page.

Why store your content in a database when it's just text? Isn't it just easier to have this material surrounded with some variant of HTML or XML tags? When you think about a blog as a moving target, a combination of static and dynamic elements, the answer becomes apparent rather quickly. Maintaining a blog full of static posts quickly becomes a logistical nightmare.

Coming up with enough blog content to keep people visiting can be hard enough without having to continually think about how many posts should be on the front page, making individual permalinked pages for each of your posts, and all the comments people make on them. This is a job ripe for automation, and the best way to automate content delivery is by keeping your data in one easily accessed place.

Using FTP to Upload Files

The last piece of the preinstallation puzzle is a means to upload files from your computer to your host. Do this with a program that uses the Internet standard File Transfer Protocol (FTP). Some of the best FTP clients are available free of charge:

- **FileZilla**—Runs on Windows, Linux, and Macintosh; http://filezilla-project.org

- **CyberDuck**—Macintosh-only; http://cyberduck.ch

- **CoreFTP**—Windows-only; www.coreftp.com

For the purposes of this section, we focus on FileZilla, which is a simple FTP client application that connects to your web host and uploads your WordPress files with just a few setup steps. When

note

You can even run a basic FTP client from your Windows or Linux command line.

you signed up with your host, most likely they gave you information about uploading files to their FTP server. Given its cross-platform character and its lack of cost, you might even find that your host has step-by-step instructions for setting up FTP with FileZilla—one of the authors' (McCallister's) host did!

After downloading and installing FileZilla, follow these steps to set up file transfer between your computer and your web host:

1. Launch FileZilla.

2. Go to File, Site Manager (or click the first icon on the left in the toolbar). A dialog box appears.

3. Click New Site to enter your information, as in Figure 11.2.

4. Here is where you insert the connection information you received from your host. This includes the following:

   - **Host**—This is usually the same as your domain name, with ftp in front, for example, ftp.myWPblog.com.

   - **Servertype**—This should always be FTP.

   - **Logontype**—For your website, this should usually be set to Normal. Anonymous FTP is for when you visit a software download site, where the keepers don't really care who you are. The Normal setting requires a password to get to.

- **Password**—This is where you supply your password. It is usually identical to your site password.

Your host might have you fill in the Account line, and you can add information in the Comments section.

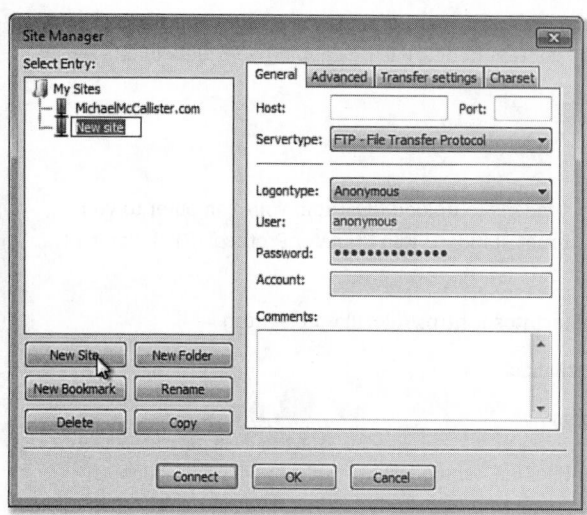

Figure 11.2
Use the General tab on the Site Manager dialog to set up an FTP connection to a web host.

5. Click the Transfer Settings tab. Select the Passive button. In Passive Mode, the client sets up all the data flow. This is more secure, especially if your firewall stops any data trying to pass through it from outside the network.

6. Click the Advanced tab (see Figure 11.3). Your host might want you to set a Default Remote Directory. This is the directory at the host server that appears when you log in. If you don't set this option, you will likely enter a directory with your username. You could set up a WordPress directory as the default too. Similarly, you might want to set your local WordPress directory as the default local directory.

7. Click Connect at the bottom of the screen. If your settings are entered correctly, you should now be connected to your host server, and you can upload files. (When you're ready to disconnect from the server, press Ctrl+D.)

When you have downloaded the latest WordPress files (see the next section), all you need to do is point the Local Site section of FileZilla to the location of the WordPress files on your own computer. Connect to your host (Remote Site) on the right side, and navigate to the directory where you want to store WordPress. Figure 11.4 shows how FileZilla looks with both sides set up. If you're ready to transfer all the WordPress files, press Ctrl+A to select them and then drag them over to the right side to begin the transfer.

Figure 11.3
The Advanced tab in the FileZilla Site Manager dialog lets you define default directories for both your local computer and your blog's host.

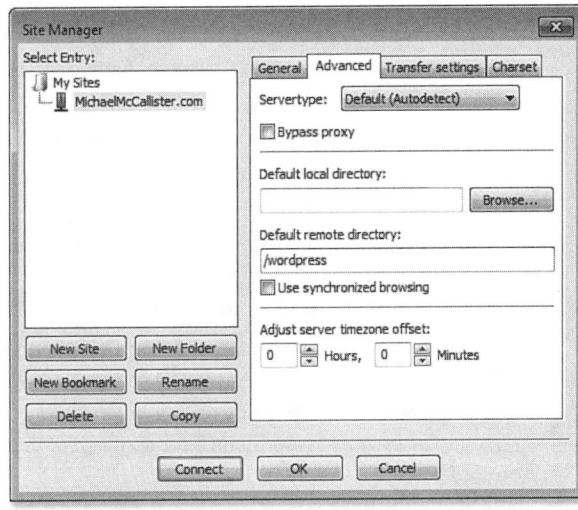

Figure 11.4
FileZilla makes transferring files to your web host a matter of drag and drop.

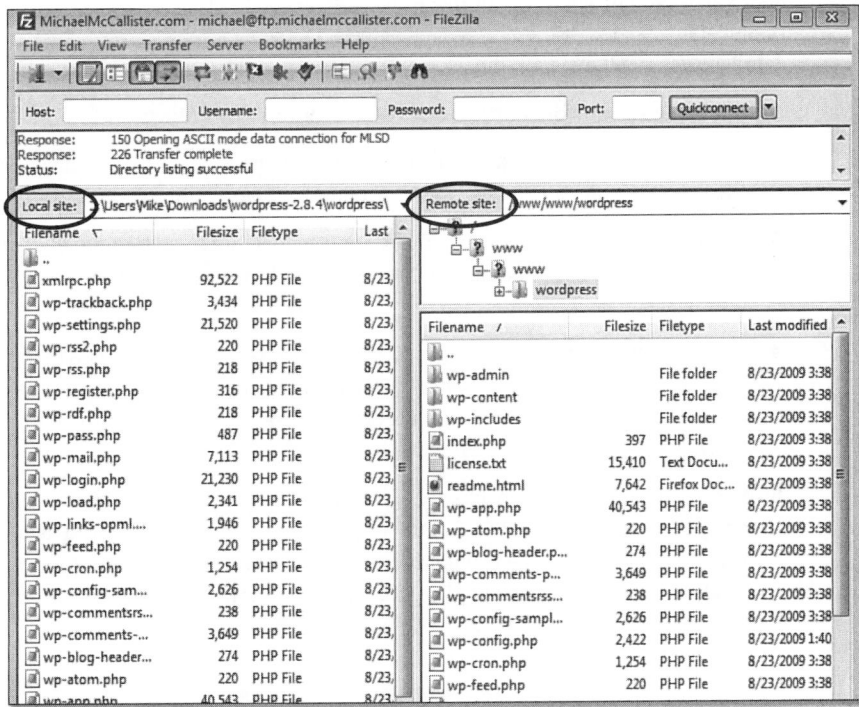

Preparing for the Five-Minute Hosted WordPress Installation

You are standing at the precipice of installing WordPress. You have your domain name registered, a host selected and paid for, and a way to download and upload files.

There's one more decision to be made before you set up your host for running WordPress: whether to have WordPress manage your entire website, or just the blogging part. Your decision affects where WordPress should be installed.

If you just plan to use your domain for your blog, WordPress can obviously do that, and you should install WordPress into the root directory of your hosting space. If your WordPress blog is only going to be part of your website, you should install WordPress into a subdirectory.

WordPress can act as a complete web content management system (CMS), handling all elements of your website, but setting that up is outside the scope of this book. See Appendix C, "Examples of WordPress Blogs," for some sites that take WordPress beyond simply managing blogs.

Depending on your host, you might have to manually install WordPress and configure MySQL and WordPress. Your host might allow you to skip some of these steps, so check with them before starting. We describe this process in excruciating detail, so you don't miss a thing.

 **note**

Your administrative interface might look different from the one shown in these figures, but your web host should have a way to connect to and configure a MySQL database using commands similar to the ones listed here. Consult with your web host if you have trouble setting this up.

1. Get the latest copy of WordPress at http://wordpress.org/download.

2. Open a browser and log in to the administrative interface for your website. When you set up your account, you should receive a username and password to access this page.

3. Locate the MySQL Database Administration section of the control panel. You will create the database in your host's administration area, as it's likely your account limits the number of databases you can have.

4. Name your database in the Database Name field. Technically, you can give this database any name you want, and your host may have some rules on prefixes for your databases. See the tip following Figure 11.5 for some advice on database naming. Click Create to confirm the name of the database (see Figure 11.5).

5. WordPress needs a way to access this database, and this is done by creating a user. Scroll down to the MySQL Users section and add a user for this database. Give the user a name and password. The Privileges area should have everything selected. Click Add to confirm. This page should look something like Figure 11.5. Write down this essential information. You'll need it for the installation:

   - Database Name

   - Database username (MySQL User in Figure 11.5)

   - The database user's password

   - The database host

Figure 11.5
Set up your database in your web hosting account administration manager.

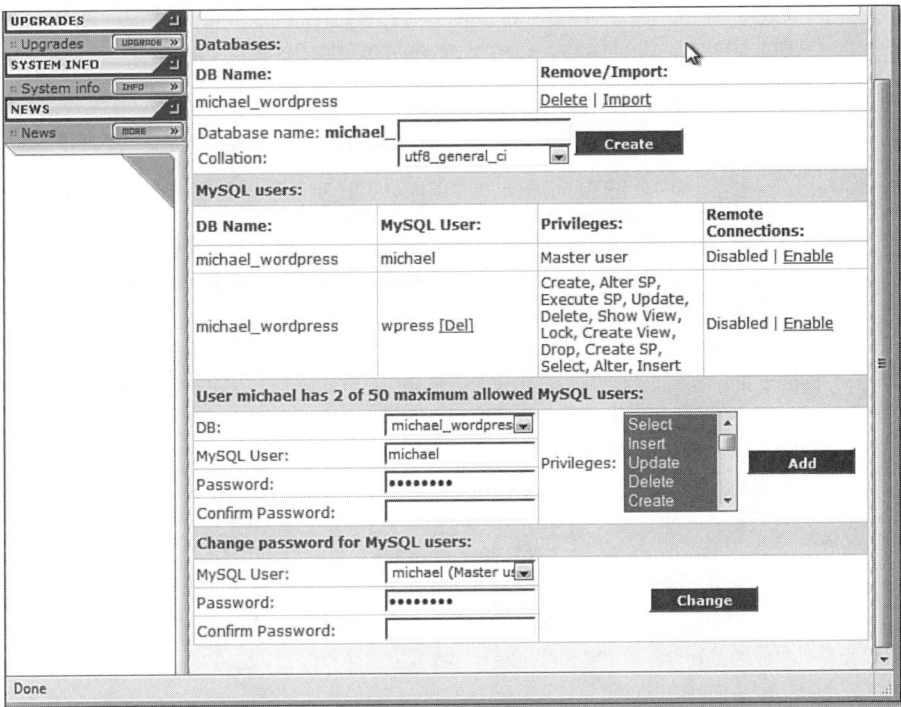

6. Here is where your decision on how much of your website you want WordPress to manage is finalized. If you plan to have WordPress manage your entire website (or your website just consists of your blog), in the root directory of your remote site, locate and rename your existing index.html file to index.old or index.backup so you don't lose either your existing home page or the default (in case you someday decide to return to a more static presentation).

7. Check the navigation in your host's administrative area and return to your main control panel (sometimes called Home). Locate the File Manager. Decide where you want to keep the WordPress files. If you want WordPress to manage your entire website, upload WordPress into the default folder, also called the root directory. If you prefer that WordPress just manage the blog portion of your site, create a subdirectory called /blog or /WordPress or some other place. Then, you can direct your blog readers to visit the subdirectory http://<yourdomainname>/blog (or whatever). For the purposes of this example, we'll use the /blog directory.

 tip

There are two ways to approach database and user naming. The most secure method is to give your databases names, usernames, and passwords that won't simplify some evil hacker's task of vandalizing your blog. The downside of that is that maybe you can't remember which database is which on those rare occasions when you want to change a configuration setting in the database. In any case, be sure to select a secure password for your database user. Meanwhile, if you're looking to vandalize this blog, don't bother. The user has been changed.

8. Open your FTP client and upload the WordPress files. You can either upload the Zip archive and extract it into your preferred folder, or extract the archive into a folder on your hard drive and upload the entire structure. What works best depends on your host.

Get Permission First!

Many, if not most, host companies employ Linux or UNIX as the operating system for their servers. As a measure of security, these systems employ a set of permissions allowing groups of users to access files. Each file has an owner and is assigned a group when it is created. Read, Write, and eXecute permissions are set for three types of users: Owner, Group, and Others (that is, the rest of the world).

Your FTP client should display the permissions on the remote system either as a string of permissions like this: rwxrwxrw- or as octal (base 8) numbers like this: 776. In the case of this example, the Owner and Users have full Read, Write, and eXecute permissions to a file. Others can read and write, but cannot execute.

Be sure that your FTP client got the permissions correct when it uploaded your files. These tell WordPress who gets access to its files. Generally speaking, your content and theme files should be listed as rwxrwxrw- (or 776), your plug-ins folder should be listed as rwxrw-rw- (766), and the admin and includes folders should be set as rwxr--r-- (744).

Your FTP client should allow you to change permissions for any file or group of files. Select the file(s), right-click in the highlighted area, select Properties, and then make the changes.

Your website's host is now prepared to receive data from WordPress. You have a database to hold your blog's content, along with all the design elements of your blog pages. It's time to begin the Famous Five-Minute Install.

The Five-Minute Hosted WordPress Installation

Now you're almost there. You have the files uploaded to the correct directory, and you have your database set up. Let's do the famous five-minute WordPress installation!

1. Go to http://<*yourdomainname*>/blog. If you did everything correctly in the last set of steps, you should see a mostly empty screen with a Create a Configuration File button (see Figure 11.6). Click it.

2. Some more introductory language appears, with a Let's Go! button. Click that button.

Figure 11.6
Begin the
Five-Minute
Install here.

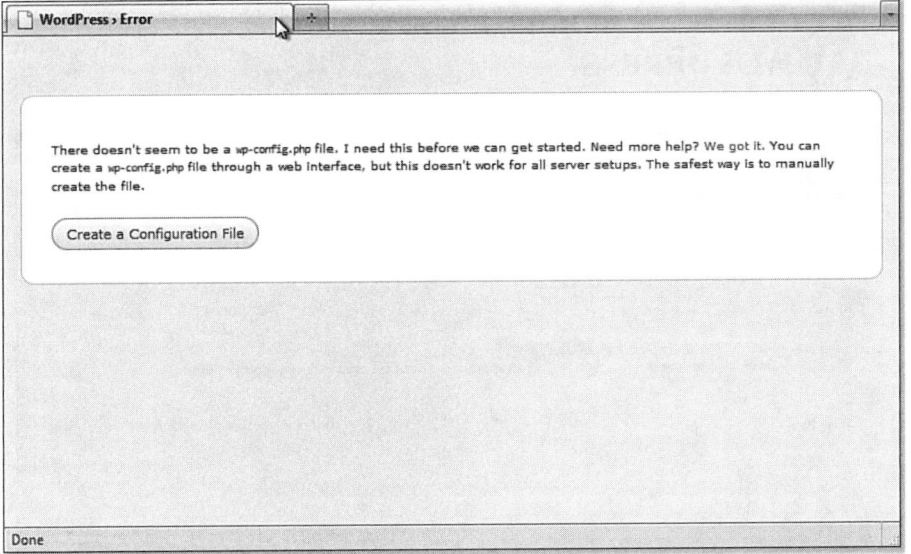

There doesn't seem to be a wp-config.php file. I need this before we can get started. Need more help? We got it. You can create a wp-config.php file through a web interface, but this doesn't work for all server setups. The safest way is to manually create the file.

Create a Configuration File

Done

3. Enter the information we advised you to write down in step 6 of the previous section (see Figure 11.7):

   ■ Database Name

   ■ Database username

   ■ The database user's password

   ■ The database host (Usually, you don't have to change this from localhost, but your hosting company might ask you to change this.)

   ■ Table Prefix (Your hosting company might ask you to change the Table Prefix from the default wp_. Otherwise, you should leave this as is.)

4. Click the Submit button. If all has gone well, you'll see a screen that looks like Figure 11.8.

tip

When you are filling out this form on the Web, you are actually editing the WordPress configuration file, wp-config.php. If you prefer to do this directly, or just want more information about setting up WordPress, see "Editing the WordPress Configuration File" later in this chapter.

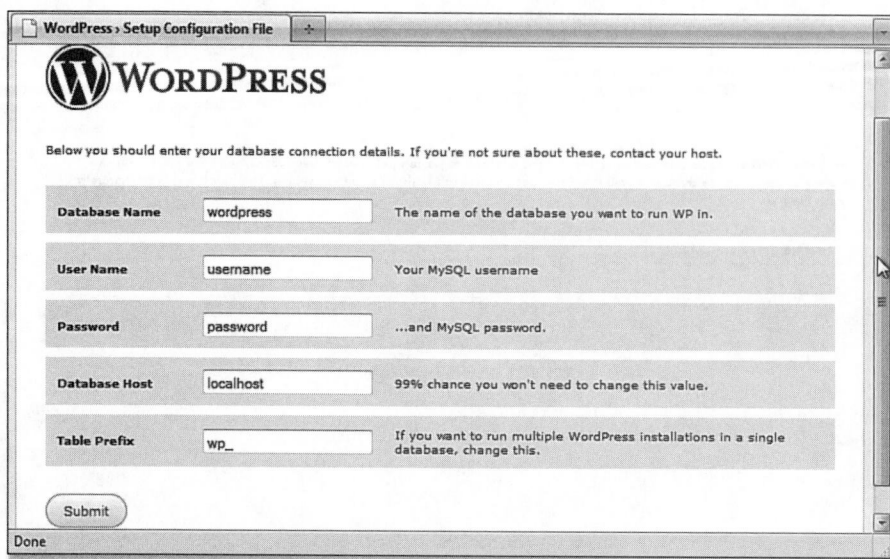

Figure 11.7
Enter your
database
connection
information
on this
screen.

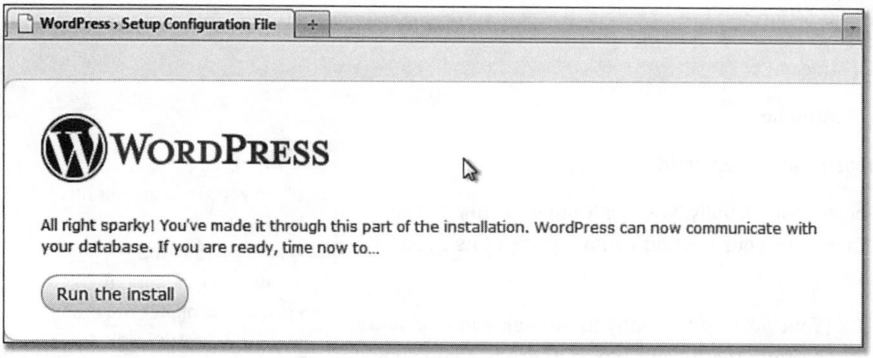

Figure 11.8
All right Sparky!
You configured
the database
properly!

5. Click the Run the Install button.

6. Fill in the three items on this screen (see Figure 11.9). We covered the relevant points related to this in Chapter 2:

   ▪ Name your blog

   ▪ Give WordPress an email address for communication purposes.

   ▪ If you're ready to greet the world, check the Allow My Blog to Appear in Search Engines Like Google and Technorati check box.

Figure 11.9
Enter your
blog's name
and an email
address on
this screen.

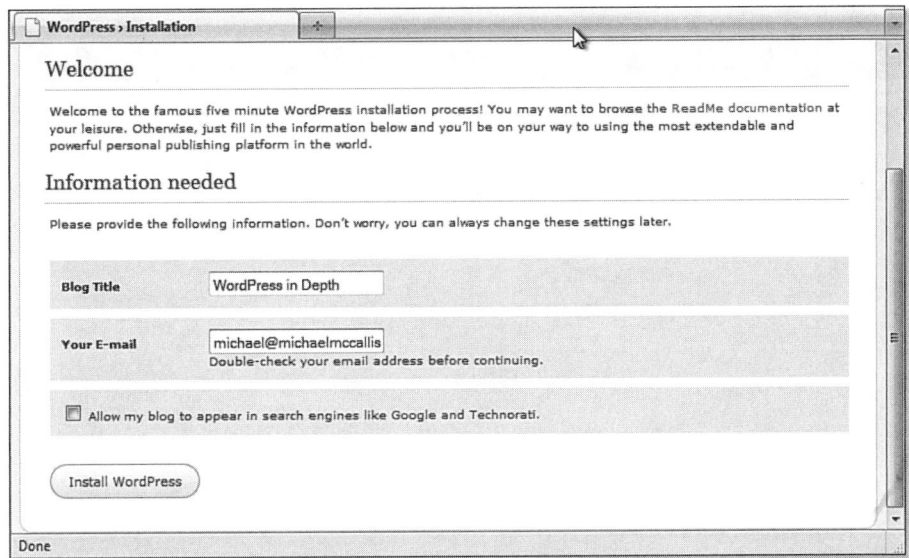

7. Click the Install WordPress button. WordPress creates the admin user and generates an initial login password for that user. This user differs from the WordPress database user you created in the previous section in that you will be logging in to this account on a regular basis to administer your WordPress settings. Write this default password down, or copy it to the Clipboard or a text file. You will need it to log in the first time. This information is also emailed to the address you listed on the Install screen.

8. Click the Login button. The standard WordPress login screen appears (see Figure 11.10).

9. Type in admin for the username and the generated password from step 7. Leave the Remember Me box unchecked. The admin account should only be used when you have specific administrative changes to make to your blog. You'll create a separate user account for your everyday blogging needs in a few minutes. Click the Login button.

10. Your administrative Dashboard appears (see Figure 11.11). The first time you log in, WordPress reminds you that you used the autogenerated password, and asks if you want to change it. The advantage of keeping the autogenerated password is that it is more secure, and using it makes it less likely that someone will steal your admin password and wreak havoc on your site. The disadvantage is that it's usually harder to remember.

The installation is complete. Congratulations!

Figure 11.10
Login for the first time as Admin with a password generated in the previous step.

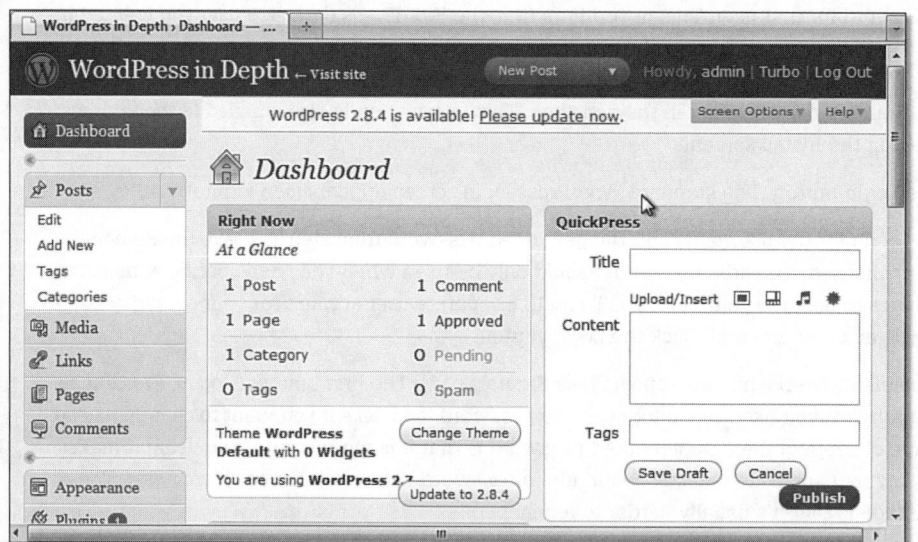

Figure 11.11
When your installation is complete, your Dashboard appears. Your first task: Decide whether to change the admin password.

Upgrading WordPress

Take a closer look at Figure 11.11, and at the top of the window you'll see one of the niftier recent additions to the WordPress core installation: Instant Updates. Prior to version 2.7, keeping your

WordPress software up to date and as secure as possible involved deleting some program files, downloading the new version, uploading the entire new version to your host, and running the installation program again. Today, it's a bit easier.

Before clicking that Update button, though, it's still a good idea to follow all these steps:

1. Back up your database. This is usually done in your host control panel, or in your database manager. Instructions for this should be provided by your hosting company. You can also install the WordPress Database Backup plug-in to simplify this process. You'll learn more about this plugin in Chapter 13, "The WordPress Toolkit: Plug-Ins."

2. Back up your WordPress files. To do this, download a copy of the wp-content folder back to your computer. This folder contains all the most important material of your blog: posts, comments, themes, and plug-ins. You can also use the Export tool to make this backup. See the next section, "Transferring Your WordPress.com Blog," to learn about this tool.

3. Turn off any installed plug-ins. Sometimes plug-ins stop working after an update. Sometimes active plug-ins can break the update itself. Before starting the update, go to the Plug-ins page of your Dashboard and check for Active Plug-ins. Under Bulk Actions, choose Deactivate. Click Apply.

This is slightly less essential when you have no content in your WordPress installation (we know you're getting anxious to start!), but an excellent habit to get into. Data loss is something to prepare for at all times.

Now you can click the Update WordPress link, and select Upgrade Automatically. In next to no time, WordPress will update itself and tell you when the upgrade is complete.

After logging in again, you can reactivate any plug-ins you want.

Transferring Your WordPress.com Blog

Now that you have your own domain, perhaps you're wondering what will become of those hundreds of blog posts sitting at WordPress.com. The short answer is that those posts can follow you to your new home. This process is startlingly easy, even knowing how simple WordPress makes blogging.

We've just covered the process of updating and upgrading the WordPress software on your host. The process for migrating a WordPress.com blog (or, for that matter, a WordPress blog from one hosting company to another) is similar.

1. Start at WordPress.com. Log in to your blog, so that the Dashboard appears.

2. Under the Tools menu near the very bottom of the left side Settings options, select Export. The Export page shown in Figure 11.12 appears.

   WordPress explains a little bit about what it will do when you click the Download Export File button. Essentially, this export file turns all your existing HTML content (posts, pages, comments, custom fields, categories, and tags) into a single XML file, which the WordPress.org software uses to transform everything back into perfectly good WordPress content at the other end.

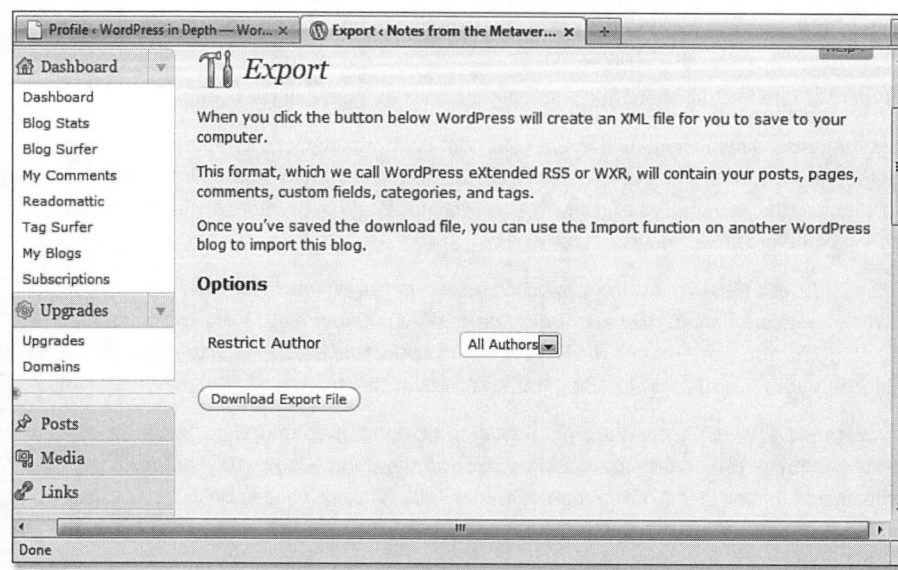

Figure 11.12
WordPress
explains
what's
included in
the export
file.

3. If you have multiple authors for your blog now, and are going solo (or some of your coauthors are not migrating with you to the new digs), use the Restrict Author drop-down menu to identify who to exclude from the export.

4. Click Download Export File. Tell your browser where to save this file. It doesn't matter where you save the file, but you may want to put it in the same folder you upload to your other site.

5. Go back to the new blog, and log in to your WordPress.org Dashboard.

6. Scroll down to the Tools menu again and click Import. The Import page shown in Figure 11.13 opens.

7. Down at the bottom of this list is WordPress. Click the link.

8. Use the Browse button to locate the Export file (with a *.wxr extension) on your system. Click to select it.

9. Click the Upload File and Import button, and WordPress does the rest.

 **tip**

As you can see from this list, you can import content from quite a few blogging platforms into WordPress. Find out more in Appendix F, "Importing Content from Other Systems."

WordPress reloads the page and confirms that all your materials have been imported. You should now see that material in your Dashboard, and in your blog.

Figure 11.13
You can
import posts
and other
files from
many other
platforms to
your
WordPress
.org blog.

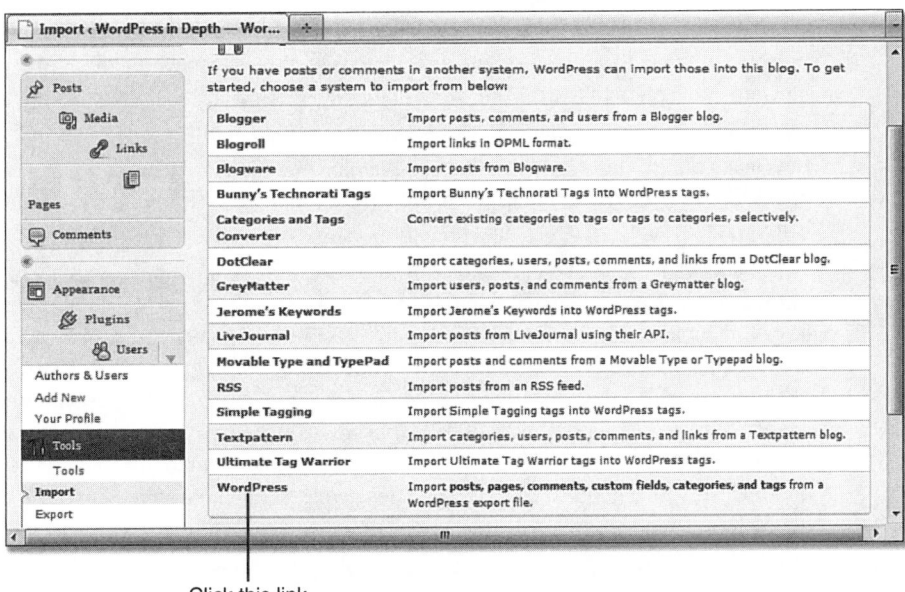

Click this link

 Note

If you run into problems uploading your file to your host, it might be a problem with your
host's PHP configuration. WXR files larger than 2MB can run afoul of a common upload limita-
tion in a standard php.ini file. Try working with your hosting company to raise this limit.

You might also try uploading your own php.ini file to your account's root directory. This configuration file should contain the following lines:

```
; Maximum allowed size for uploaded files.
upload_max_filesize = 7M
```

Now try uploading again and see if that works.

 tip

Be aware that when you export posts and comments from your WordPress.com blog, they don't go away, even
when you import them somewhere else. You should still monitor traffic on old posts to your WordPress.com
blog, as they will appear in search results.

After you have transferred your blog's data, consider adding some boilerplate "This blog has moved" language
to the front page of your old blog, and to at least some of the more popular posts.

WordPress for Mass Production: WordPress MU and BuddyPress

Do you ever think to yourself, "I know thousands of people who would love to blog. I could run a network of bloggers that size. That would be fun!"? Then WordPress MU is designed just for you.

The standard WordPress software installation can handle multiple blogs with multiple authors. How many blogs, topics, and authors you build on one WordPress installation is up to you and only limited by your host's disk space and bandwidth restrictions. WordPress MU (for Multi User) is for massive blogging operations.

Where you want to use WordPress MU (WPMU) is when you need the capability to create hundreds or thousands of essentially unrelated blogs. For example, you run a corporate intranet for a fairly large firm. In a fit of transparency fervor and the urge to generate ideas from everyone, management decides to give every employee the ability to blog. Or you're at a big, prestigious university, like Harvard, with a huge faculty and graduate student population. As the system administrator, you don't want the responsibility of having to set up every new account, and you don't need to approve every post. You want to set overall guidelines, have some rules about the overall look-and-feel, smoothly handle software upgrades across all the individual blogs, and the ability to define what's required to set up each blog. This is what WPMU provides.

The first and best-known implementation of WordPress MU is WordPress.com. As a user, you only see one form to set up your account and only the administrative pages for your blog(s). Automattic handles the rest of the overhead.

A relatively new add-on to WPMU is BuddyPress. This predefined set of plug-ins adds social networking features to a WPMU installation. Users can create profiles, update their status (as on Facebook or Twitter), link to friends inside the blog network, set up groups, and have a private messaging area.

You can try all this out now at http://mu.wordpress.org, or you can wait a bit. At WordCamp San Francisco in 2009, Matt Mullenweg announced that all of MU's features would be merged into core WordPress in some future release. As of this writing, the timing remains undefined.

To see some outstanding examples of WordPress MU, go to http://wordpress.org/showcase/flavor/wordpress-mu. For all things BuddyPress, see www.buddypress.org.

Hosting WordPress Yourself

You can install the WordPress software on any computer with web server software installed, even if that computer has no permanent connection to the Internet. That means you could even use that old computer with the dialup modem (or none at all) that has been gathering dust in your basement. Why would you want to have WordPress installed on your own computer? How would people read your blog if it wasn't connected to the Internet? We can think of at least four good reasons to install WordPress on your system—even if your "real" WordPress blog was hosted somewhere else, be it WordPress.com or at your own host:

- You are an angry person and view blog posts as a way of venting steam. You want a place to tell your boss what you really think of him/her without threatening your career. Plus, you like the WordPress visual editor, and don't need a full-blown, feature-rich web design tool to write.

- You have been on WordPress.com for awhile and want to see if you can install the Wordpress software yourself before committing to buying a domain name and a year's worth of hosting fees.

- You are considering changing themes and adding plug-ins, and want to test things out before going live on the Web.

- You want to create new WordPress themes and plug-ins, and don't want to upload your files to the Web each time you modify one character in the code.

In practical terms, you don't need a reason to give the install a try. With enough time, disk space, and bandwidth, you can do this. We're here to help.

In this section, we'll install a web server on a Windows system and get you ready for the WordPress installation. We'll also show you how to edit the WordPress configuration file manually.

Installing a Web Server and MySQL Database on Your System

If you are running the Windows operating system (no matter the version), you need to download several applications to successfully run WordPress on your computer: That includes a web server application, the MySQL database, and the WordPress software. If you want to develop plug-ins, you also need the PHP scripting language.

The good news is that the cost of all this software is $0—yes, that's right, it is free. Another piece of good news is that software developers have packaged the server app and database in a single download for Windows, so there's only one thing to install. The bad news is that you have to invest some time and effort to get it all running.

There are several packages of what is called the WAMP (Windows Apache MySQL and PHP/Perl) Stack available for download. We have had the best experience with XAMPP from the Apache Friends. The X takes the place of the underlying operating system—Windows, Linux, and Macintosh OS X. In this section, we show you how to install and configure XAMPP in Windows to prepare for your WordPress installation. The process in other operating systems should be similar, if not exactly the same.

1. Download XAMPP from http://apachefriends.org/en/xampp.html.

2. Install XAMPP by double-clicking on the downloaded file. At the end of the installation, a command-line shell will appear, and the install program will ask you some questions. Unless you know to do differently, accept the defaults.

3. When the final menu comes up, select Start XAMPP Control Panel.

4. Start the Apache and MySQL services by clicking the Svc check box next to each module (see Figure 11.14). You'll be asked to confirm each service start.

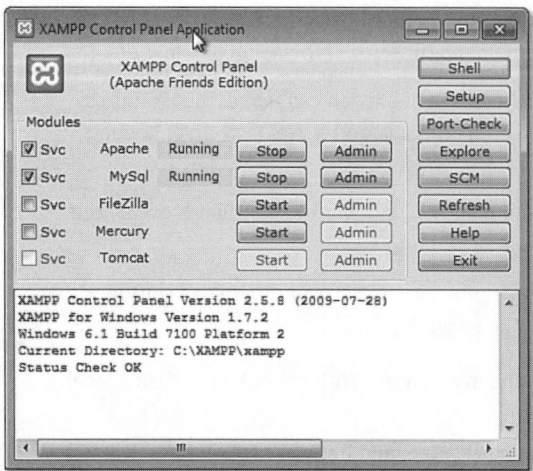

Figure 11.14
Start the Apache Web Server and MySQL database services in Windows through the XAMPP Control Panel.

5. Start the Apache server by clicking the Start button associated with it. Windows Vista and 7 users might see a User Account Control dialog box asking if you really want to install this application; click Yes. When it starts, the Control Panel will say it's running, and the Admin button will be active.

6. Start MySQL the same way. The shell-like status window at the bottom of the Control Panel will also indicate that each service started.

7. Open a browser and type http://localhost/xampp in the address bar. If Apache is running, you'll first be asked to define your language, and then (if you select English) the screen will look like Figure 11.15.

8. Open phpMyAdmin to create and configure the database. Go back to the XAMPP Control Panel. Click Admin next to MySQL to launch phpMyAdmin or click phpMyAdmin in the Tools section from the XAMPP admin page shown in Figure 11.15. This application serves as a graphical front end to the MySQL command-line administrative tool. It's written in the PHP scripting language, as is WordPress.

 **note**

You can also open this screen in your default browser by clicking Admin next to Apache from the XAMPP Control Panel.

The remaining steps should mirror the database creation steps in the earlier section "Preparing for the Five-Minute Hosted WordPress Installation."

9. Go to the Privileges tab. Click Add a New User.

10. In the User Name field, type **WordPress_**(or some other name; see the earlier tip on database user naming). Under Host, use Local. Type a password or use Generate Password (for a more secure, if less memorable, password).

Figure 11.15
A successful
configura-
tion of
Apache
through
XAMPP!

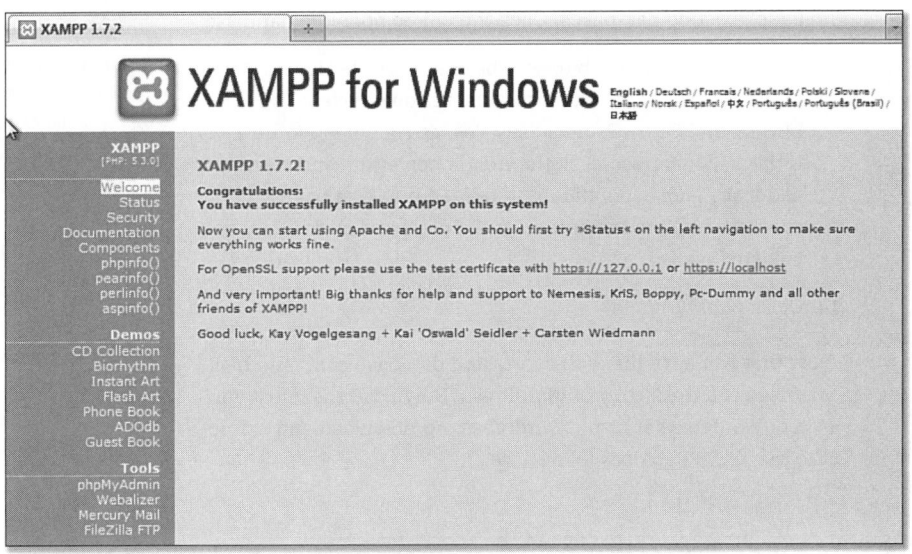

11. Under Database for User, click Create Database with Same Name and Grant All Privileges, as
shown in Figure 11.16. Scroll to the bottom and click the Go button. PhpMyAdmin generates
the appropriate MySQL commands and displays them under the phrase You Have Added a
New User.

Figure 11.16
Set up the
WordPress
database
from your
browser with
phpMyAdmin.

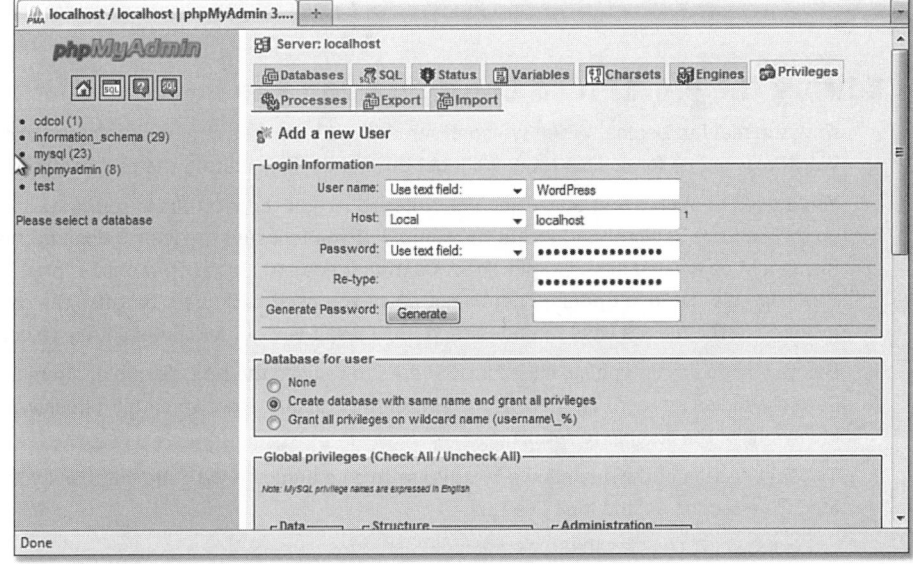

12. Click the Databases tab, and you will see WordPress on the list of existing databases. Click the link to open the database.

13. Click the Privileges tab to see the list of "Users Having Access to WordPress." Your WordPress user should have ALL PRIVILEGES, and GRANT should say Yes, as shown in Figure 11.17. If this is not correct, click the Action box at the end of the row and make sure every database-related privilege box is checked. Scroll to the bottom of the page and click Go when you are finished.

14. Close phpMyAdmin.

Now that you have the web server and database configured, all you need is a fresh copy of WordPress. Download the latest version of WordPress at http://wordpress.org/download and extract it to the XAMPP\htdocs folder.

 tip

You can name your database and user anything you want. If you're only planning to do one blog from this database, you could name the database *blogname_wp*, where *blogname* is your blog's name. For maximum flexibility, though, we recommend something more generic. WordPress doesn't constrain you when you change your mind about something.

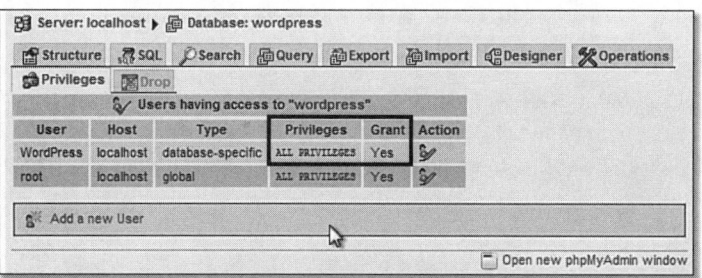

Figure 11.17
Make sure your WordPress user has all privileges, including Grant, to your database.

Editing the WordPress Configuration File

Now the real fun begins. When we configured WordPress on a separate host, we used the WordPress online form. This time, we'll get our hands dirty editing the raw configuration file.

You'll need to open a text editor such as Notepad to edit the WordPress configuration file. But first, go to Windows Explorer and locate the sample. If you followed the instructions in this chapter, this file should be located at C:\XAMPP\htdocs\WordPress\wp-config-sample.php. Yes, this is a PHP code file, but don't panic. There's not much you need to do here because the comments included in the file are easy to understand. Besides, if you do get confused, we're here to help.

Before you do anything else, click File, Save As to remove the text, "sample," from the filename. Save the file as wp-config.php. That way, in the unlikely event something goes wrong, you will always have the sample to return to.

The first section of this file allows WordPress to communicate with the database you've just created. The section should look like this:

```
/** The name of the database for WordPress */
define('DB_NAME', 'putyourdbnamehere');
```

```
/** MySQL database username */
define('DB_USER', 'usernamehere');

/** MySQL database password */
define('DB_PASSWORD', 'yourpasswordhere');

/** MySQL hostname */
define('DB_HOST', 'localhost');

/** Database Charset to use in creating database tables. */
define('DB_CHARSET', 'utf8');

/** The Database Collate type. Don't change this if in doubt. */
define('DB_COLLATE', '');
```

There are but a few lines to edit in this section:

- Where it says *putyourdbnamehere*, replace it with the name of your database (*wordpress*). Make sure the name is inside the quotation marks; otherwise, it won't work.

- Where it says *usernamehere*, replace it with the username you entered in step 10 from the last section (which should be the same as the database).

- Where it says *yourpasswordhere*, replace it with the password you entered in step 10 from the last section.

- Confirm that the DB_HOST line points to *localhost*. If it does, don't change it.

The last two items can usually be ignored. DB_CHARSET and DB_COLLATE relate to the character set used by the database. Unless you are using Cyrillic or Asian-language characters, leave these lines at the default settings.

The Authentication Unique Keys section of the configuration file is optional, but can help secure your installation. Setting these keys makes it much harder for anyone bent on cracking your blog to steal your login information, and you don't need to remember them. This section looks like this:

```
* Authentication Unique Keys.
*
* Change these to different unique phrases!
* You can generate these using the {@link https://api.wordpress.org/secret-key/1.1/
WordPress.org secret-key service}
* You can change these at any point in time to invalidate all existing cookies. This
will force all users to have to log in again.
*
* @since 2.6.0
*/
define('AUTH_KEY', 'put your unique phrase here');
define('SECURE_AUTH_KEY', 'put your unique phrase here');
define('LOGGED_IN_KEY', 'put your unique phrase here');
define('NONCE_KEY', 'put your unique phrase here');
/**#@-*/
```

At the top of the section, you'll see a link to the WordPress Secret Key service. Copy this address (http://api.wordpress.org/secret-key/1.1/) into your browser, and you'll see four highly secure keys generated for you alone. Copy all four lines and paste them back into this section of the wp-config file, replacing the default lines that ask you to *put your unique phrase here.*

The WordPress Database Table Prefix section exists for those who want to produce multiple blogs from this database. If that's you, WordPress needs to be able to differentiate this blog from your other blogs. It does this by creating separate database tables for each blog. We recommend using *wp_blogname* as the identifying table prefix. Your hosting company might also have a recommendation on how to handle the Table Prefix. The section looks like this:

```
* WordPress Database Table prefix.
 *
 * You can have multiple installations in one database if you give each a unique
 * prefix. Only numbers, letters, and underscores please!
 */
$table_prefix  = 'wp_';
```

The last section of the configuration file to worry about is the Localized Language section. This defaults to English; if you want to blog in another language, visit http://codex.wordpress.org/WordPress_in_Your_Language for information on how to set up WordPress in many (as of this writing, 64) languages.

```
* WordPress Localized Language, defaults to English.
 *
 * Change this to localize WordPress.  A corresponding MO file for the chosen
 * language must be installed to wp-content/languages. For example, install
 * de.mo to wp-content/languages and set WPLANG to 'de' to enable German
 * language support.
 */
define ('WPLANG', '');
```

As the creators of wp-config-sample tell you, "That's all, stop editing! Happy blogging!" Save the file again. The hard work is done, and it's time to run the famous five-minute installation, as described earlier in this chapter in the section, "The Five-Minute Hosted WordPress Installation."

A Quick Tour of the WordPress.org Dashboard

Whether you are installing WordPress on a remote host or on your own computer, when you finish and log in for the first time, the first thing you see is the WordPress Dashboard (see Figure 11.18). This page is where all the behind-the-scenes work required to manage your blog(s) begins. It's designed to give you everything you need to be a successful WordPress blogger, and it is configurable, so you can decide what to include and what to leave out.

Figure 11.18
You'll spend a lot of time using the WordPress Dashboard when managing your blog.

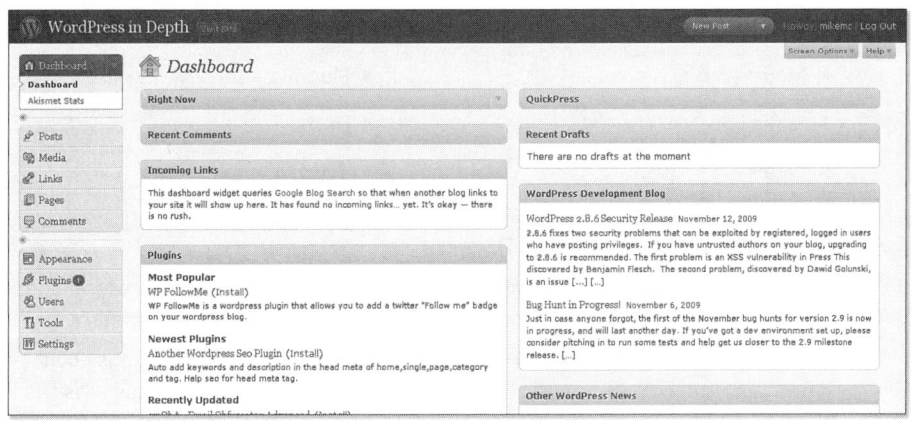

To wind up this chapter, let's take a look around the Dashboard page, and see what's available and useful. We've covered most of the important stuff included in the WordPress.com Dashboard in earlier chapters. Future chapters will cover the key tools, like themes and plug-ins. Here, we will highlight the modules that are included in WordPress software and not included in the default WordPress.com Dashboard. Table 11.1 shows some of the key differences between tools and services available in WordPress.com and WordPress.org.

Table 11.1   WordPress.com Versus WordPress.org

Service	WordPress.org	WordPress.com
Themes	Unlimited usage and creation	Limited selection, no editing except with paid upgrade
Widgets	Unlimited usage and creation	Limited availability, usage dependent on theme
Cascading Style Sheets (CSS)	Edit themes and pages	Paid upgrade required to edit themes and pages
Plug-ins	Unlimited usage and creation with PHP	Some functionality available through widgets

The Dashboard is a three-column page, with navigation on the left and various pieces of information in the two main columns. Down the left sidebar is the navigation panel, allowing you to run your blog the way you want. Though it looks a little different from the WordPress.com panel, all the menus are the same. The exception is that you can't install plug-ins on WordPress.com, but you can in WordPress.org.

There are 10 top-level menu items:

- Posts
- Media
- Links
- Pages
- Comments

- Appearance
- Plug-ins—the new one
- Users
- Tools
- Settings

Each top-level menu in the navigation panel expands when you click it, revealing more choices in that area. We'll be discussing most of these settings in the coming chapters.

Moving to the middle column, the Right Now module tells you many things about your blog at a glance. The main difference from the WordPress.com module is that it displays the version of the WordPress software you are running (and tells you if it's time to update). You also get the Change Theme button to simplify that process when you feel the time is right.

The next two modules report on people who have found your blog interesting enough to respond to it. Recent Comments lets you see who's been directly responding to your posts in the recent past, and makes it easy to reply to them on your blog. If commenters left their URL behind, you can also go visit them. Even if you haven't posted yet, the software tests itself by allowing Mr. WordPress to leave a comment explaining what a comment is.

Incoming Links tells you who has been quoting you elsewhere on the Web. This module uses Google Blog Search to find links to your blog site. It might not generate a long list to begin with, but as your sparkling, sassy prose gains buzz, this module will help document it.

The last module in the middle is a sort of news feed for plug-ins. Learn what is currently the most popular plug-in in the WordPress Plug-in Directory, and what the directory's newest and most recently updated plug-ins are. The Install link makes it easy to add one or more of these to your blog.

In the right column, the QuickPress editing module is identical to WordPress.com. We described this in Chapter 4, "Creating Your First Post." Below the QuickPress editing module is the Recent Drafts module, showing QuickPress items saved as drafts.

Below these two writing and editing tools are two RSS feeds offering news about WordPress. These feeds replace the Stats module so prominent in the WordPress.com Dashboard. Stats junkies need not panic, though. You have to install the Stats module as a plug-in before you can store it on your Dashboard, but we cover that process later, in Chapter 13.

The first feed is the WordPress Development Blog, and it is news directly from the WordPress development team, as you might expect. Find this blog at http://wordpress.org/development. Most important, this feed notifies you about new updates of the core software and occasional glimpses into what the people who work on WordPress are thinking about.

The second RSS feed is called Other WordPress News, and is an even closer look at what people in the WordPress community are thinking. The feed comes from Planet WordPress at http://planet. wordpress.org. It is a collection of about 30 blogs focused on WordPress by people actively involved in developing the core software, themes, widgets, and other material related to the platform.

Customizing Your Dashboard

Not everyone will like how things are displayed on their Dashboard. If you're one of them, know that you can make it work for you any way you want. With just a few clicks, any module outside of the navigation bar can be dragged to another part of the page, minimized, or be made to disappear. You can also change any of the existing RSS feeds to point to another blog, if you want.

To move a module somewhere else: Click the title bar of any module and drag it where you want it.

To minimize a module: Click on the downward-pointing arrow at the right edge of the module title bar. All you will see then is the title bar. Click the arrow again to expand the module.

To remove a module: Go to Screen Options at the upper-right corner of the Dashboard (next to Help). Clear the check box next to the module(s) you don't want to see anymore. (Yes, you can get them back at the same place later.)

To change either of the RSS feeds: Hover the mouse over the title bar of either the WordPress Development Blog or Other WordPress News module. Click Configure when you see it. Enter the address of the RSS feed (not the blog address!), change the title, and make any other changes you want in this dialog box. Click Submit when you're done. Unfortunately, you can't add any feeds without dismissing one of these.

Figure 11.19 shows one example of what you can do.

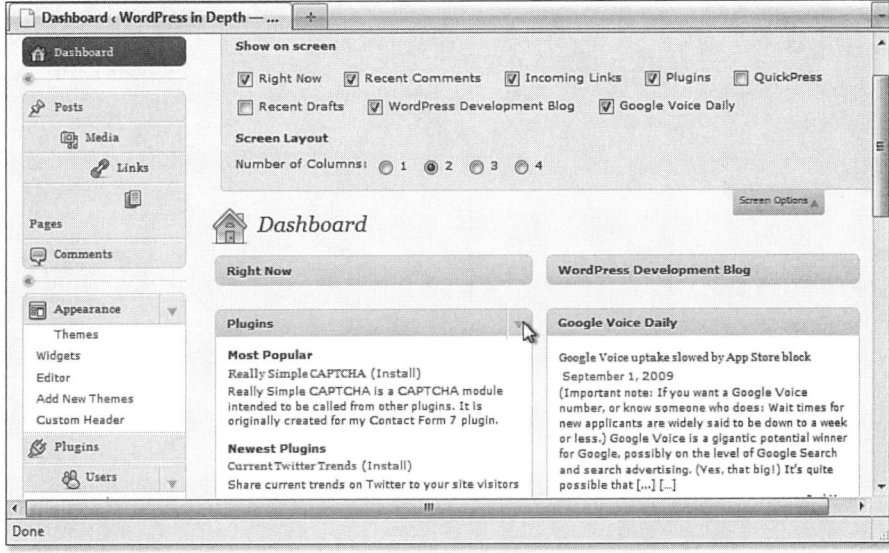

Figure 11.19
Customize your dashboard with things you want to see.

THE WORDPRESS TOOLKIT: THEMES

Shopping for Themes

As we explained in Chapter 3, "Creating Your Blog's Look," people's first impression of your blog is generated largely by the theme you select. Your theme is what your blog looks like.

In this chapter, we help you navigate the considerably expanded universe of themes available for self-hosted WordPress.org blogs. You'll learn how to find the right theme for your site. We help you evaluate whether you want to pay for a premium theme, or hire a developer to translate your exact vision. Finally, we show you how to install and activate themes on your site.

We gave you a lot of advice on selecting the right theme in Chapter 3. When you are working with a WordPress.org (self-hosted) site, your choices expand dramatically over WordPress.com, plus there's a new dimension to your selection. You are no longer restricted to the 70-plus themes available there. The universe of themes is effectively infinite, depending on your skills, available time, and the size of your bank account. Once you've decided to build a website on WordPress, you can get a theme in one of these ways:

- Choose from the hundreds of free themes in the WordPress Free Themes Directory, or search the Web for a free theme outside the directory. Once obtained, you might well be able to tweak it to your exacting specifications. Free theme developers can (and do) update their creations, which then appear in the WordPress upgrade system.

- Pay for one of the many beautiful and effective premium themes. These are usually quite tweakable as well, as are the theme frameworks that have sprung up to serve the ecosystem. These also can be updated automatically.

- Hire a web developer to create the specific, unique vision you have in mind for your theme. Updates to these themes might be harder to come by.

- Create your theme yourself. We give you some help with that in Chapter 14, "Style Sheets for Building Themes."

 **note**

What's the difference between buying a premium theme and hiring a developer? Consider the difference between buying clothes off the rack at Macy's and visiting a tailor to give you a perfect fit. Premium themes come with support (for those minor alterations) and are usually highly customizable. When you hire someone to develop your site's theme, the goal is to get something that uniquely fits your site's objectives.

As with clothes and most other things, getting that unique fit will cost you a bit more than buying off the rack. Depending on your goals, that extra expense can certainly pay off in the end.

What is best for your site depends on the aforementioned skills, time, and bank account, but also on what you intend the site to be. Do you want your site to promote a business, online or offline? Maybe you don't want your site to look like "Just Another WordPress Blog." Do you just want a home on the Web that you have control over, but don't want to obsess over the details of the web presence? A free theme will likely do the trick for you. Are you looking to learn web development, or enhance your existing skills to make yourself more marketable? Buying a theme framework might be just the investment in your career that pays dividends down the road.

How you envision your audience is another determining factor in the type of theme you use (and your choice of plug-ins, too). When your visitors are primarily friends and family checking up to see what you're up to, you probably just want something usable, with a familiar look, traditional links, and not too many bells and whistles. If you want your site to appeal to a particular niche audience, you want to make the audience comfortable and attract their interest in what you have to say. Your blog covering the latest news on mixed martial arts will probably have much bolder colors than AnntheGran's embroidery site.

Figures 12.1 and 12.2 give you a sense of the variety of themes available to you in the Free Themes Directory. Figure 12.1 is ZenLite, a single column with a white background and a natural header image. Figure 12.2 is Dark Wood, a three-column theme with a background looking like a wood-paneled office, blue headings, and white text. The nice thing is that both themes aren't too cluttered, and are readable.

Figure 12.1
Choices in the Free Themes Directory are endless. The ZenLite theme matches its name: light, airy, and slightly spiritual.

Figure 12.2
Even with a Dark Wood background, text is still readable across all three columns.

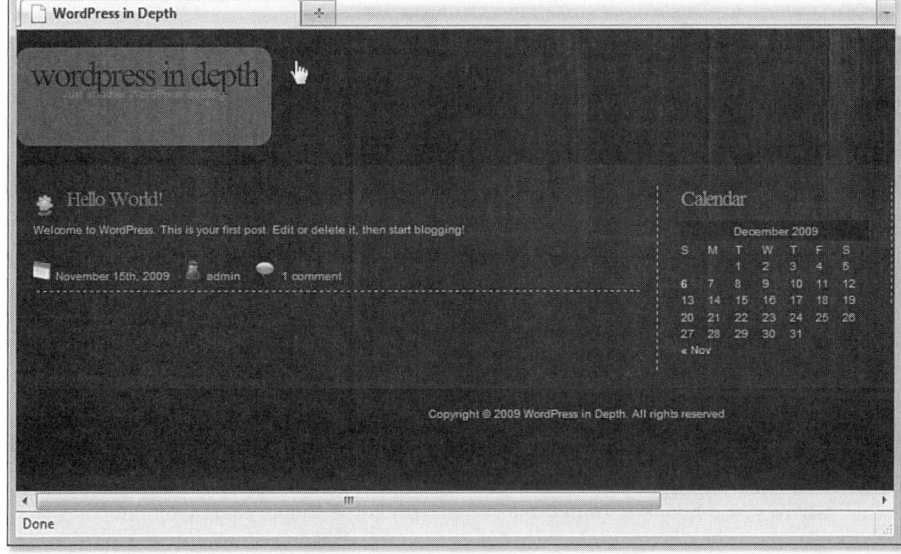

Before launching your quest for the perfect theme, it's important to do the planning up front so you choose a theme you can live with for a while. Although no theme is permanent—you can change your theme on a daily basis if you choose—chances are good your audience is more interested in your changing content, not your changing color scheme.

Now let's begin our search.

The Difference Between Designers and Developers

In this chapter, we use the terms *designer* and *developer* interchangeably to describe a person who creates WordPress themes. As you'll see in later chapters, themes are equal parts design (styles and other presentational aspects of creating a website) and development (writing and adapting PHP scripts to create page elements and bits of functionality).

One of the oddities of the Web's development is that many people who are talented graphics designers were first asked to do *graphics* design for the Web—which, actually, is hell on earth for most designers, as the Web is so limited and hard to control precisely compared with print. They then got pulled into web*site* design—a whole other skill set that requires more business knowledge, information architecture experience, and people skills. Some made the transition well; many didn't. So check a designer's skills and experience against what you need before proceeding.

Although many theme designers also develop plug-ins, and plug-ins often handle design elements, we will use the term *developer* to talk about people who work with plug-ins. Unlike designers, a developer is a developer—the skill set for different kinds of software developers isn't as different as for Web versus graphics designers.

Finding Free Themes

The easiest way to select a theme (other than the default Kubrick theme or its Classic counterpart) for your WordPress site is to take advantage of the Free Themes Directory. If you're into a more adventurous approach to finding free themes, there are more than a few ways to go about it.

Finding and Installing Themes from the Free Themes Directory

The Free Themes Directory at http://WordPress.org/extend/themes has been around since July 2008. About a year later, the themes and plug-ins directories were incorporated into the WordPress Administration page, thus making finding and selecting themes as easy as clicking the Change Theme button on the Dashboard. You are taken to the Manage Themes page shown in Figure 12.3, where you can choose from three spots to open the theme search engine:

- Click Add New Themes from the Appearance sidebar on the left.

- Click the Add New button located next to the Manage Themes title.

- Click Install Themes at the very top right of the screen, next to your username.

Figure 12.3
All three Add
New buttons
take you to
the Install
Themes
page.

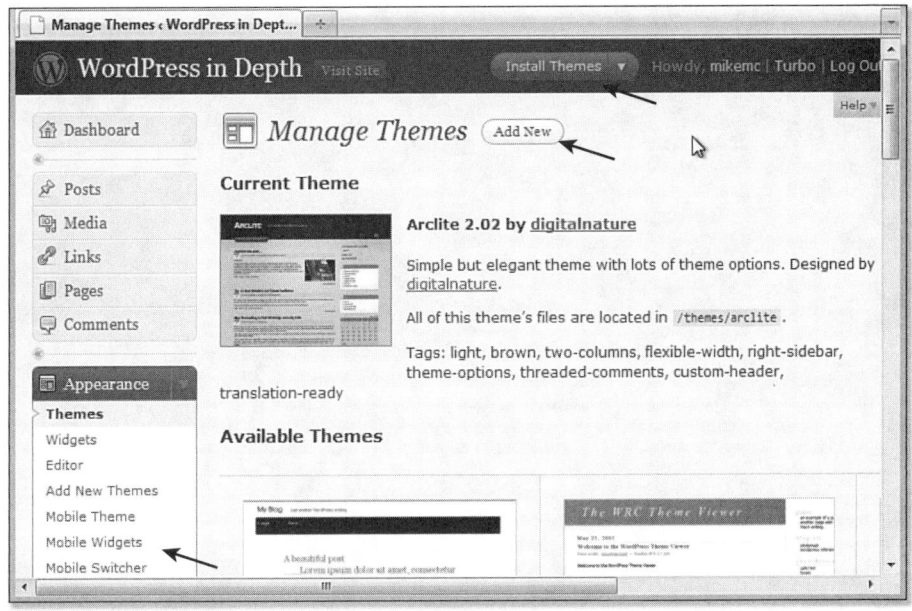

The WordPress.org theme search engine comes up, and it works largely in the same way as the WordPress.com theme search. That is, you can filter your search list based on color, columns, fixed or flexible width, and other features. The one major difference is that the availability of widgets is either a given or simply not a differentiator among the free themes. You can also define holiday, seasonal, or photoblogging-specific themes in the filters.

See Chapter 3 for more information on how to search the Free Themes Directory.

Besides the standard search, the Theme Management page lets you browse the directory in three categories: Featured, Newest, and Recently Updated. If you leave your Administrative page and go to the directory on the Web, you can also browse the currently Most Popular themes. It probably won't surprise you to learn that the themes listed in the Featured category track the Most Popular list closely. The WordPress faithful take the judgements of the folks who decide a theme is worth featuring very seriously.

 tip

Do you want a theme that includes a thumbnail image on each post? A search for "thumbnail" (no quotation marks) turned up a few options even before WordPress 2.9 built in post thumbnail support. With version 2.9 released, that number should explode.

When you find a theme you like in the directory, just click the Install link. A preview image will appear; click Install Now. The Theme Installer downloads the Zip archive containing the theme files to your hard drive. It then extracts the theme files into \wordpress\wp-content\themes\<theme-name>. That's all you really need to install a theme to your system. When the installation is complete, you can take one of three actions (see Figure 12.4):

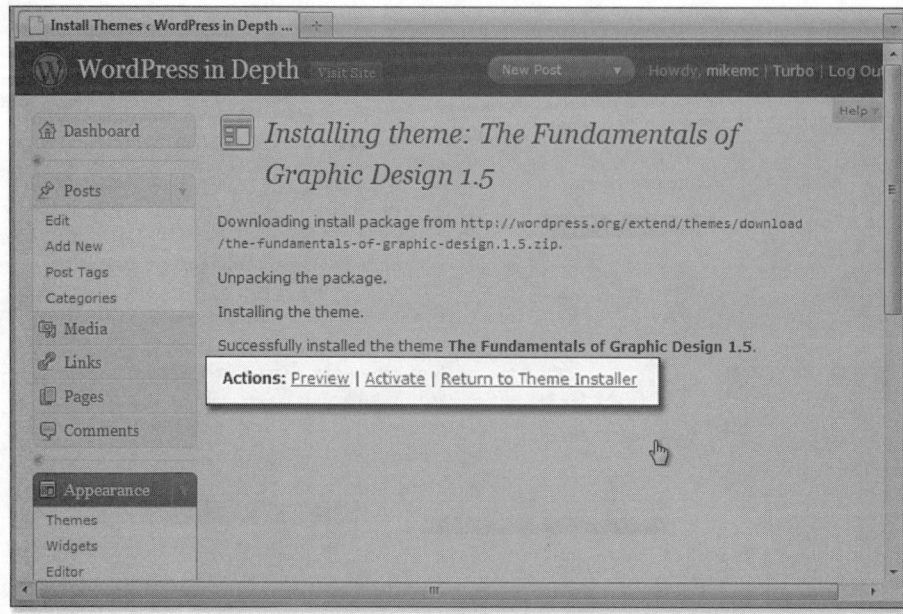

Figure 12.4
After installing a new theme, you can activate it immediately, or look for more themes.

- **Preview**—Allows you to see your existing content (including your site title and the default first post if you don't have content yet) in the new theme.

- **Activate**—Makes this theme the one that displays on your site. See more about this later in the chapter in the section "Installing and Activating a Theme."

- **Return to Theme Installer**—Allows you to search for and select another theme from the directory.

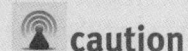 **caution**

Take a little extra care when considering themes outside the main channels. See "Security Considerations When Selecting a Theme for Your Blog" later in this chapter for some tips and caveats.

Themes obtained from anywhere beside the Free Themes Directory must be installed manually. We show you how to do that in "Installing and Activating a Theme" later in this chapter.

Some Specialized Themes

Blogs don't necessarily have to display miles of text broken up by the occasional image or bit of multimedia content. You can do many different things with your blog, and theme designers can help you create exactly what you need.

- **Microblogging**—Some pundits think the Twitter-inspired blog is the wave of the future. Posting "What are you doing?" in 140 characters or less fits many people's increasingly short attention span. Although there's no limit on how long—or short—a WordPress blog post can be, the length of the post can make a difference in how you organize your home page.

Continued...

Consider that we have recommended that you keep no more than seven full-length posts on the main page. Now think about how many column inches are taken up by a 140-character post. That would be fewer than the last two sentences. You probably want to bump up that post count so that it stretches below your blogroll.

Prologue and P2 are designed to support microblogging, which is great for simple link blogs, too.

■ **Photoblogging**—The advent of the ubiquitous digital camera has naturally given rise to using blogs to share photographs on the Web. The advantage blogs have over photo sharing sites like Flickr is that you have more complete control over how an image is presented and described. Restricted only by bandwidth cost considerations, you can caption your images, include as much descriptive information as you want, and define your own sharing and licensing rules.

Photoblogging is such a popular activity in the WordPress community that it has its own search filter in the Free Themes Directory. Checking this box returns around 20 themes tagged for photoblogging by their designers. One of these, Monotone, is also available to WordPress.com users. Many of these move the traditional sidebar items (blogroll, recent posts, and the like) into the footer so as not to distract from the impact of the images, and so as not to unduly restrict their size.

Finding Free Themes Outside the Directory

So you've gone through the Free Themes Directory, and nothing grabs you. Perhaps you've selected a theme to get started with—which we highly recommend, as it is better to blog with an imperfect look than not to blog at all—but now you want to continue the search for the theme that sings for you. What's next? A Google search for "free wordpress themes" generates millions of results (nearly 49 million as we write, and Yahoo! finds 58 million)—far more than anyone could explore in a lifetime. There must be an easier way.

The community again comes to the rescue, with many folks taking it upon themselves to review some of the better free themes out there. To our knowledge, the best of these sites is the Weblog Tools Collection (WLTC) at http://weblogtoolscollection.com. Three times a week, WLTC authors review new themes submitted by designers who participate in the WLTC Community forum.

If you find a good theme outside the Free Themes Directory, you have to install the theme manually. See "Installing and Activating a Theme" later in this chapter.

Finding Premium Themes

With hundreds of free themes to choose from, and the ability to tweak settings to get different colors, layouts, widgets, and the like, why would you buy a premium theme?

Probably the biggest reason people use premium themes is to stand out from the crowd. It's been estimated that there's one theme for every 6,000 WordPress.org users (one theme for every 3,000 WordPress.com bloggers). With millions of WordPress bloggers out there, there are going to be a lot of people with a blog that looks a lot like yours.

If you plan to build a business around your WordPress site, unless that business is designing websites, you might not want the responsibility for building and maintaining your site. You'll almost always buy a theme when your motto is "focus on the business; leave the rest to the professionals."

Searching for a Premium Developer Among Free Themes

Remember that the designer of your new premium theme could well be linked to at the bottom of your current site with the free theme. Most, if perhaps not quite all, premium theme developers started as free theme developers. It's an apprenticeship of sorts; as they learned the craft doing free themes, their skills and popularity grew, presumably to the point where the designers began to think they could possibly make a living making WordPress themes. Whether they have what it takes depends, at least in part, on the market. If you like the skills and creativity a person brings to your favorite free theme, you can encourage that developer/designer by dropping some cash in the tip jar at the theme's website. Alternatively, if you're in the market for a new look, perhaps that favorite designer has some premium themes for you to look at.

For much the same reason, even if you don't want a free theme, and want to start with a premium theme, a search in the Free Themes Directory could be fruitful. Each theme's thumbnail lists the author in the Details link. Although there's not a direct link to the author's website, you can use a people search at WordPress.org to find the designer's community member page. If that designer has any smarts, you should then be able to link directly from the member page. Conversely, if you can't find their place of business somewhere on WordPress.org, perhaps they don't do business at all.

tip

Maybe it's a little crass, but consider using an ad-friendly free theme to generate income from your blog to pay for a premium theme down the road. Searching the Free Themes Directory for "adsense" generates several themes that simplify integrating Google AdSense into your WordPress self-hosted blog.

Finding Premium Developers Using the Commercial Theme Directory

Until very recently, you had to search the Web, or click an advertisement on a WordPress-oriented website to encounter premium WordPress themes. This is changing, with the advent of the Commercial Themes Directory at WordPress.org (see Figure 12.4). Installation from this directory isn't integrated into the Administration area, but it's nice to have a single place to begin the search for the right theme to buy and the right designer to buy from.

To get a spot on this page, theme designers must use the GNU General Public License (GPL) and offer professional support options. The most-interesting requirement of all, though, is that the designer must write a haiku that serves as the caption for each developer's link. Some developers appear to be happy that their marketing slogans fit the pattern, some use humor, while still others perhaps aim to show they can be creative with words in hopes that you'll think they are just as creative with themes.

note

Haiku, in case you aren't familiar, is a Japanese three-line poem form, where the first and last lines have five syllables each and the middle line has seven syllables.

Figure 12.4
It's not exactly one-stop shopping, but the Commercial Themes Directory at WordPress .org lets you visit premium theme developers from one handy place.

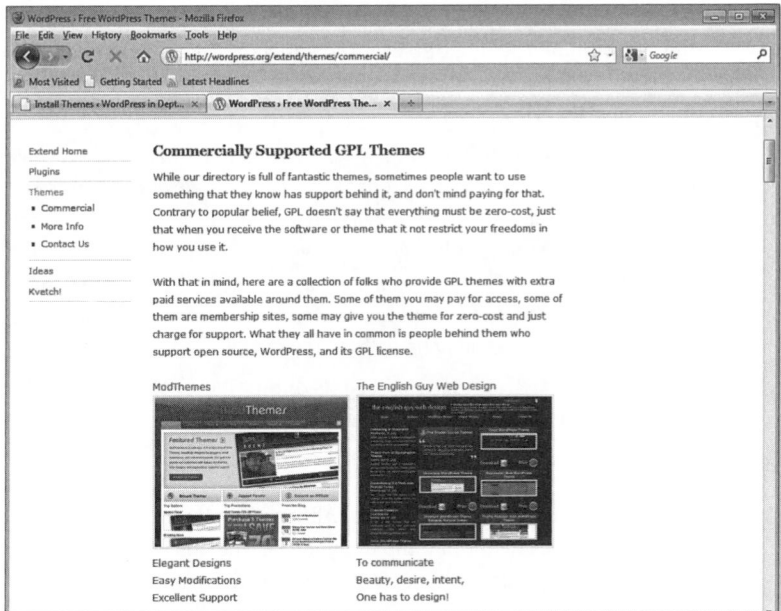

The GNU General Public License

We have occasionally mentioned the GNU General Public License (GPL). This is one of the legal engines that makes open source software go. There are many open source licenses (see http://opensource.org/licenses for a complete list), but the GNU GPL is the most common.

In many ways, the GPL codifies the principle of "share and share alike" with software. Essentially when one programmer puts code under the GPL, it tells other programmers that they can freely use the code in other software projects, but when they do, they have to grant the same rights to others.

The GPL also allows anyone to look at the code and customize it to meet a need they have. That need, or the particular solution, may not be for every other user of the software, but it has to be available to all other users. This is one reason we have plug-ins in WordPress.

Some history: Richard Stallman of the Free Software Foundation wrote the original GPL in 1989 to cover applications included in the GNU (GNU's Not UNIX) project to develop a non-proprietary version of the UNIX operating system. Version 2 of the GPL was released in 1991, and is the most widespread version of the license. WordPress, the kernel of the GNU/Linux operating system, the Mozilla Firefox browser, and many other prominent projects are covered by this version. The third version of the GPL was released in 2007 to some controversy around provisions concerning digital rights management and software patents. Bruce Byfield offers a good description of this philosophical debate at http://bit.ly/v9uHN. Some projects continue to be released under GPLv2, and others under GPLv3.

Continued...

A common misconception, even among some fans of free and open source software (FOSS), is that the GPL prohibits selling GPL-licensed software. This is commonly known in the community as the "free as in beer or free as in freedom" dispute. Wikipedia describes the terms and conditions of the license this way:

"The terms and conditions of the GPL are available to anybody receiving a copy of the work that has a GPL applied to it ("the licensee"). Any licensee who adheres to the terms and conditions is given permission to modify the work, as well as to copy and redistribute the work or any derivative version. The licensee is allowed to charge a fee for this service, or do this free of charge. This latter point distinguishes the GPL from software licenses that prohibit commercial redistribution. The FSF argues that free software should not place restrictions on commercial use, and the GPL explicitly states that GPL works may be sold at any price."

The Free Software Foundation, keepers of the GPL, explains its position at http://www.gnu.org/philosophy/selling.html.

Click a link to visit a developer's site. Although we're prepared to say that anyone who has jumped through the hoops to get into the Commercial Themes Directory passes the minimum quality test, we have also heard good things from community members about these other sites and themes (in alphabetical order):

- **iThemes (http://ithemes.com)**—Some 30 themes populate this site, in a range of prices. Click your role (blogger, businessperson, or web designer/developer) to see the range of themes suited for that role. Professional web developers can buy a one-year license to all themes here for about $500.

- **Themeforest (http://themeforest.net/category/wordpress)**—ThemeForest is "the leading open marketplace for web development," and includes theme developers for a variety of blogging platforms, including WordPress. As an open market, you can find a pretty cheap theme for your site here. A recent visit found 384 WordPress themes for sale at prices from $10 to $40. You can sort their directory using price, number of sales, user rating, and several other items. Other cool features of this site include the ability to search themes by tag, the ability to preview each theme, and even the documentation is rated! We also like the "Lost in the Woods" blog, with weekly blurbs about what's happening at the site, and some featured themes as well.

- **Thesis (http://diythemes.com/thesis)**—This site provides a very professional, highly customizable theme, designed for a noncoder's convenience. This site also provides free upgrades for life and a busy support forum.

- **WooThemes (http://www.woothemes.com)**—This global team produces at least two new themes per month. They support users through tutorials and a forum. The Showcase pages (http://showcase.woothemes.com) identify some of their themes customized for clients including Tanya Tucker, the Fox Sports Design blog, and TVScape magazine.

- **WP Remix (http://wpremix.com)**—Aimed at supporting WordPress as a full-fledged Content Management System (CMS), WP Remix gives you a WYSIWYG editor for page templates, color schemes galore, and out-of-the-box support for many popular plug-ins. The theme and site were sold by the original developer to a company called R5, Ltd in April 2009. We hope this will expand support and development for this theme.

The process of shopping for and buying premium themes are as easy, and as varied, as buying most things on the Web. Some shops use full-blown e-commerce vendors to handle the sales, others just a shopping cart application leading to a simple download. Transactions are by credit card and/or PayPal. Many developers offer subscriptions to all their themes for a monthly fee; a bargain if you're in the web design business, but overkill for just one blog.

Themeforest, serving as a middleman between designers and users, does things a little differently. You sign up for a free account that allows you to buy and sell items. To buy something, you have to first deposit at least $20 US into your Themeforest account via PayPal (either directly or through a credit card) or another firm called MoneyBookers. If you have enough money in your account, you can purchase and download the theme of your choice.

No matter where you bought your premium theme, when you have completed your purchase and downloaded your theme, you have to install the theme manually. We've come to the point where we tell you how to do that.

Installing and Activating a Theme

When you've picked a theme (or even a few finalists), installing them into WordPress is a fairly straightforward process. We've already covered the simple process for themes selected from the Free Themes Directory. For all other theme sources, including the commercial themes, it's a little harder, but it's still not rocket science.

Installing Your New Theme

All themes are mostly composed of a set of PHP scripts and Cascading Style Sheets, with occasional ancillary files. This collection of files is gathered together and compressed into a Zip archive. To install these files, follow these steps:

1. Download the `*.zip` archive to your computer. In most cases, this means clicking the Download link, then saving the archive anywhere on your computer (but most often in the Downloads folder).

2. Use a decompression program like PKZIP, StuffIt, or Ark to extract (unzip) the archive on your computer. In nearly all cases, this creates a new folder with the name of the theme.

3. Use an FTP program to connect to your web server, assuming you're not hosting your blog on your own computer, and transfer the entire *<theme-name>* folder to `/wp-content/themes` in your WordPress installation folder.

 **note**

If you're a Windows user, all versions of the OS from Windows XP on up come with a built-in file decompression utility that can access Zip archives, so you don't necessarily need one of the programs listed here.

Activating Your New Theme

You can install as many themes as your web server will hold (though you'll certainly want to leave more room for your content than your themes), but only one theme can appear on your site at a time.

To activate any installed theme on your site:

1. Log in to WordPress.

2. Click on Appearance.

3. Click Themes. The Manage Themes page opens (see Figure 12.5). Your current theme will be at the top, followed by all your other installed themes.

4. Click Activate under the theme you want to use.

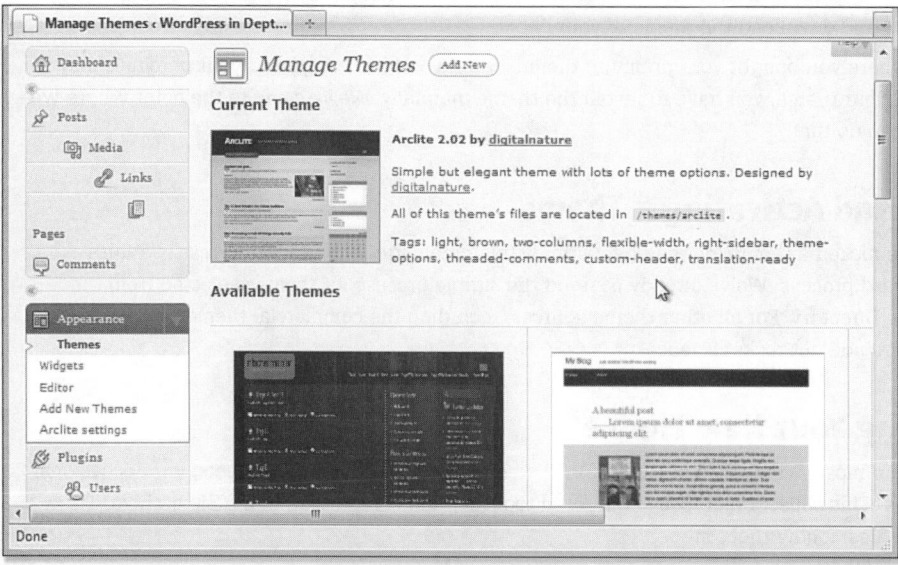

Figure 12.5
Activate a new theme on the Manage Themes page.

This theme now becomes the Current Theme in the window. If you click Visit Site at the top of the page, the new theme should appear.

Many themes have their own settings pages that allow you to add widgets and customize your themes further. We cover changing settings for one popular theme in Chapter 14.

Missing Themes

I've downloaded and extracted a new theme, but it doesn't appear on the Manage Themes page. What happened?

Most likely you extracted the theme files to the wrong place. Open the file manager for your host. Look in the `WordPress\wp-content\themes` folder. The theme should have its own sub-folder in the tree.

Another possibility is that you copied the compressed Zip archive to your host without extracting the files. If you see *‹⋯theme_name⋯›.zip* in the file manager with no corresponding sub-folder, you need to extract the files to the wp-content/themes folder.

Security Considerations When Selecting a Theme for Your Blog

When searching the Web for free themes outside the WordPress directory, be aware that not everyone on the Internet is a stand-up citizen and card-carrying member of the WordPress community. The vast majority of WordPress theme developers, no matter the experience level, are fans and friends of WordPress. You do have to watch out for that tiny minority, however.

The popularity, open code, and ease of use in making WordPress themes are attractive to those who use the Web's powers for ill. With just a small bit of obfuscated code in an otherwise innocuous and beautiful theme, your web server could become part of a zombie army of machines participating in a Distributed Denial of Service (DDoS) attack on some other website, or be used in a phishing scheme to mine passwords and other personal information from your visitors—unbeknownst to them or you.

Your safest bet is to always use themes made available through the WordPress Free Themes Directory. The folks who submit themes to the directory are members of the community, by definition, because they follow the community's rules.

Short of that, themes can be imperfect. They are collections of programming code and, thus, can have bugs. What works right on one computer doesn't necessarily work exactly the same way on another computer with a different set of applications, or a different set of WordPress plug-ins.

Whether the theme comes free of charge or is a premium theme that you're paying for, be a smart consumer. Don't be afraid to ask the developer questions before installing a theme that comes from outside the traditional channels. The speed and helpfulness of a theme developer's answers before an install will also tell you how responsive that person (or company) is likely to be in dealing with support issues later.

 **note**

Even the most upstanding members of the theming community can still have themes attacked. See how Thematic developer Ian Stewart had his birthday ruined: http://themeshaper.com/themeshapercom-hacked, and how he dealt with it: http://themeshaper.com/dont-get-hacked-wordpress-security-tips.

Ideally, you or your trusted geeky friend can look over the theme code to look for any possible issues. Once you've got your theme installed, use the WordPress Exploit Scanner plug-in that searches through your website's files and database tables and notifies you of any suspicious code. This plug-in will not clean things out for you, since that is best done yourself.

If you're skeptical at all about the safety of your suggested theme, visit the developer's site, and check on the WordPress.org forums. Get a sense of the developer's reputation, if any. Keep asking questions until the answers are satisfactory.

13

THE WORDPRESS TOOLKIT: PLUG-INS

WordPress Modular Architecture

WordPress is a modular web content management platform, meaning that when you install WordPress on a web server, you get a basic set of built-in (or "core") functionality that every other WordPress user gets, even users of the WordPress.com hosted software. Where the modular part comes in is that WordPress allows anyone to extend the software to do just about anything. A plug-in usually isn't a standalone program—it needs WordPress to do basic tasks, hence the name. Plug-in support is only included with versions of WordPress software (meaning WordPress.org and WordPress MU), as the powers that be at WordPress.com don't allow users to install plug-ins themselves.

Thousands of WordPress plug-ins have been written, with more coming every day. A scan through the Most Popular Plugins page in the WordPress Plugin Directory at http://wordpress.org/extend/plugins/browse/popular shows the variety of options you have. There are plug-ins that add functionality to your Administration page, help you generate traffic through search engine optimization, allow visitors to share your content through social bookmarking, and connect with you through your social networks. You can use plug-ins to build forums for visitors to interact with you, check your site for broken links, and back up your database. There are even plug-ins to add icons to your posts, or links, or comments, or just about any element on your blog. Which ones you include on your blog is completely up to you.

Plug-ins make your blog stand out and help to define the kinds of things you care about in your blog. Because they are completely optional bits of code and functionality, you can choose exactly which plug-ins you want on your blog, and where existing functionality is good enough.

In this chapter, we help you sort out the differences between plug-ins and widgets, find appropriate plug-ins for your site, and give you a sense of the variety of plug-ins out there.

There are plenty of "essential WordPress plug-ins" lists on the Web, but what is essential for one WordPress user might be thoroughly useless for another. The people who decide what's really essential are the WordPress development team, as many bits of plug-in code have been incorporated into the WordPress core. Meanwhile, open source software generally, and WordPress in particular, is about having choices. Have fun with your choices.

Defining a Plug-In

WordPress is not alone when it comes to allowing plug-ins to coexist with its own software. The famous iPhone App Store is nothing but a plug-in repository for the iPhone (and iPod Touch) software. When you install the Mozilla Firefox web browser, you are soon invited to install a batch of recommended *extensions* to the browser that enhance your experience or give you added functionality.

To clear up one possible area of confusion: Plug-ins and widgets have a fairly organic connection, but they are not the same thing. Widgets are usually part of a theme's sidebar or footer, and, like plug-ins, add functionality to a standard WordPress blog page. All of the following statements are true:

- Plug-ins can create widgets. Widgets cannot create plug-ins.

- Widgets are always components of themes. Plug-ins can be a theme component, but can also work directly with WordPress core.

- Widgets can be used on WordPress.com. Plug-ins cannot be used directly, but it's often easy for a developer to convert a plug-in into a widget that does the same thing.

- Widgets are always items displayed on your page; plug-ins can appear in the Administration page, on one or more pages, or work completely behind the scenes.

One final way to think of the differences between widgets and plug-ins: Widgets are always about enhancing the visitor's experience on your site; that's why they are always visible. Plug-ins can focus on user experience, but also make things easier on you as the blogger and administrator of your site.

 note

Firefox is very popular with the open source community because of its extensibility. If you go to Tools, Add-ons in Firefox, you'll see separate tabs for Extensions and Plug-ins. In Firefox, a plug-in is something that allows other applications installed on your computer desktop (including various media players, Adobe Reader, Flash, and Shockwave) to work inside the browser. Extensions add different types of functionality. Because WordPress exists on a web server, it doesn't need to work with desktop applications. So when you think about WordPress plug-ins in relation to Firefox, think extensions.

Finding Plug-Ins

The process of finding worthwhile plug-ins for your blog is very similar to finding the right theme for your blog, but the thinking that goes into your choice can be radically different. Themes are mostly about presenting a face to the world; selecting a theme is the way to define a look for your online presence.

Plug-ins are all about functionality and automation; selecting a plug-in or set of plug-ins goes a long way to defining what you want to do with your online presence. Basically, you need to decide how much time and energy you want to spend on your blog site. What blog-related tasks do you enjoy doing, and what would you rather not think about? Do you want to have control over every aspect of your site, tweaking settings every day until the system works exactly the way you want it? Do you prefer having a system that takes care of all the administrative tasks behind the scenes, making it as easy as possible for you focus on creating blog content? What is the next cool thing you can add to make visitors become readers, and readers become a community? When you have answers to these questions, you can start looking for plug-ins to help you realize that part of the vision.

In this section, we'll walk through the process of finding the plug-ins you need, once you've decided what to look for.

Finding and Installing Plug-Ins from the Directory

As with themes, the easiest way to find and install WordPress plug-ins is through the Add New page in the Administration page Plug-ins section of your WordPress blog. This page integrates the WordPress Plugin Directory into your WordPress installation.

As of this writing, the Plugin Directory hosts over 7,000 plug-ins. From the Dashboard, click Plug-ins and then click Add New. The screen offers many ways of discovering plug-ins (as shown in Figure 13.1):

**note**

Find the Plugin Directory on the web at http://wordpress.org/extend/plugins.

- Standard search, by Term (keyword), Author, or Tag

- Click an item in the tag cloud below the Search window to see plug-ins tagged with the term. As with the Tag Cloud sidebar widget, the bigger the text, the more frequent the appearance. Thus, in Figure 13.2, the Post and Widget tags have the most available plug-ins.

- Browse among the Featured, Popular, Newest, and Recently Updated plug-ins in the directory by using the links at the top of the screen.

Unlike the Free Themes Directory, the Featured and Popular plug-ins do not track each other quite so consistently. This, perhaps, reflects a possible divide between the development team and the users over which plug-ins are the most valuable, but more likely that users better know what they want. Defining a valuable theme is a much more subjective process than looking for software that can help you reach your goals.

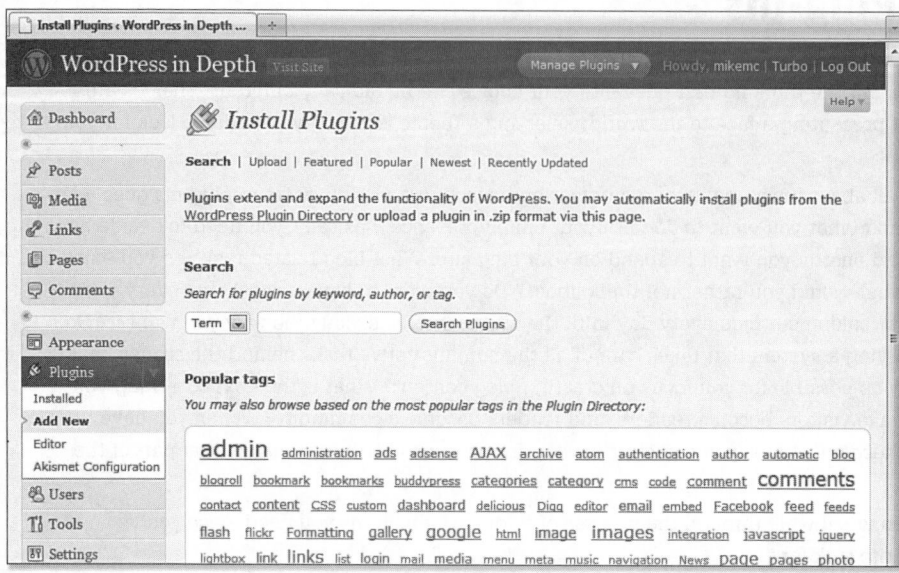

Figure 13.1
Find your plug-ins using the Add New page from the Administration page.

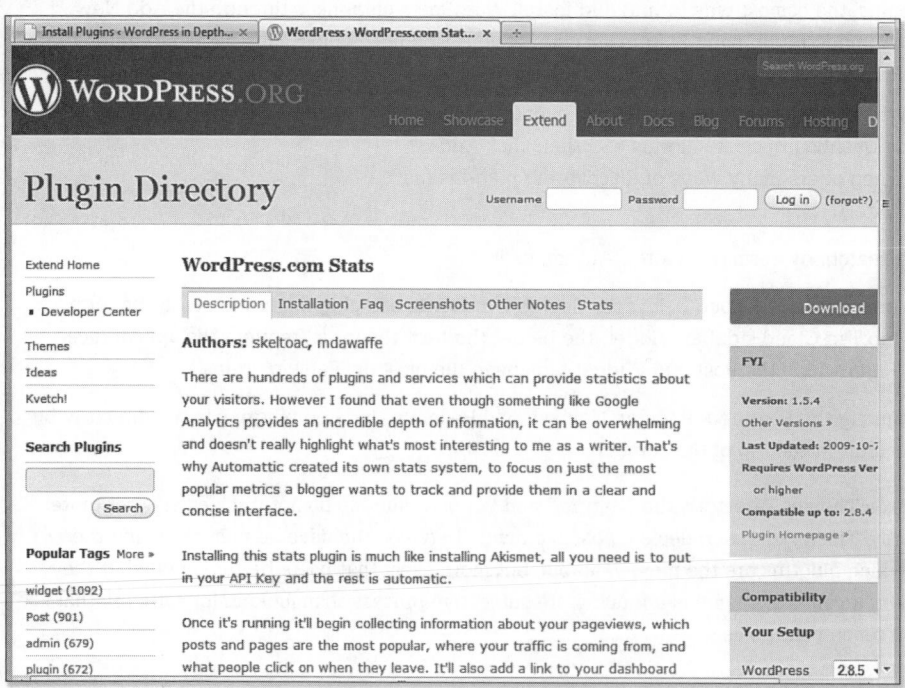

Figure 13.2
Check the compatibility rating of the plug-in you're interested in with the version of WordPress you have.

To view more information about a plug-in, click the name link in the directory. This brings you to the plug-in page, either on the developer's site or on the directory itself, as shown in Figure 13.2, with additional descriptions, user comments, and such. Click items on the link bar (Installation, FAQ, Screenshots, Other Notes, and Stats) to check out even more information.

Return to the Administration page and click Install for any plug-in you want on your site. Another Description pop-up page opens. Look this over, and click Install Now. WordPress downloads the plug-in archive and unzips it to the /wordpress/wp-content/plugins directory. Click Activate Plug-in to turn on the plug-in to complete the process.

> **🔍 note**
>
> When you browse the Plugin Directory by keyword or tag, results are displayed by most recent update. Keep an eye on the number of downloads a plug-in has before you install on the basis of an average five-star rating—unless you don't mind being the experimental guinea pig for a plug-in.

Plug-in Compatibility

One piece of information you will want to check before installing any plug-in—inside or outside of the directory—is the Requires WordPress version number (the first version of WordPress your plug-in supports) and the Compatible Up To version number (the most recent version a plug-in has been tested with; ideally this would be the current stable version, or even the beta of the next version). New versions of WordPress, which appear quite frequently, can suddenly break any plug-in.

With thousands of existing plug-ins, the WordPress team can't check every one to see which plug-ins are headed for doomsday. That testing falls to the plug-in developers. Most plug-ins work fine moving forward, but new WordPress version releases are indeed a nightmare time for plug-in developers.

Plug-ins that haven't been tested in awhile might have been abandoned as well. If the last compatible version listed is WordPress 2.0, you might want to look elsewhere.

Finding Free Plug-Ins Outside the Directory

Compared with the similar process with themes, it seems to be a little harder to find free plug-ins that are not in the WordPress Plugin Directory. Although the Google search for "free WordPress plug-ins" generates even more hits than "free WordPress themes" (87 million versus 49 million), nearly all the top 50 matches point directly to the Plugin Directory, or to developers already in the Plugin Directory.

So how do you learn about the best plug-ins? Again, look to the community for answers:

- The Weblog Tools Collection highlighted in Chapter 12, "The WordPress Toolkit: Themes," does plug-in reviews twice a week.

- Angelo Mandato does the consistently interesting WordPress Plugins Podcast, where he reviews one plug-in at a time. He also reports from conferences and interviews plug-in developers to learn more about their recent work and their craft. Listen and subscribe at www.pluginspodcast.com.

- The WordPress Plugin Database at http://wp-plugins.net is a promising idea, if somewhat neglected as a project.

Finding Premium Plug-Ins

One of the bigger controversies in the WordPress community is over premium plug-ins. Developers accuse Matt Mullenweg and the WordPress development team of drawing a philosophical/ideological line in the sand over anything other than free-of-charge and free/open source plug-ins piggybacking on the WordPress core. This seems ironic to some, as Automattic is itself for profit.

The battle heated up when the Commercial Theme repository was built and made available. Plug-in developers who sell their work for money have demanded equal treatment, but as of this writing, it hasn't happened.

Meanwhile, premium plug-ins are out there. Some are developed by the same shops that sell premium themes. Others can be found through common search engines. And some folks have put together lists of quality premium plug-ins, including Kevin Eklund's "Ultimate Review List of Best Premium WordPress Plugins" at http://tomuse.com/premium-wp-plugins-review.

In addition, the WPHacks blog occasionally reviews premium plug-ins. Find these reviews at http://wphacks.com/tag/premium-plugins.

Manually Installing and Activating Plug-Ins

When you come across a plug-in you want to try out that is not in the directory, the process of installation and activation is very similar to installing themes.

Downloading New Plug-Ins

When you find your plug-in, go to the developer's website and follow their process for downloading the plug-in. For premium plug-ins, there will likely be a financial transaction first.

1. Download the `*.zip` archive to your computer. In most cases, this means clicking the Download link, and saving the archive anywhere on your computer (but most often in the Downloads folder).

2. Use a decompression program like PKZIP, StuffIt, or Ark to extract (unzip) the archive on your computer. In nearly all cases, this creates a new folder with the name of the plug-in.

3. Use an FTP program to connect to your web server (assuming you're not hosting your blog on your own computer), and transfer the entire <plugin-*name*> folder to `/wordpress/wp-content/plugins` in your WordPress installation folder.

note

If you're a Windows user, all versions of the OS from Windows XP on up come with a built-in file decompression utility that can access Zip archives, so you won't necessarily need one of the programs listed here.

You might consider testing your new plug-in before activating it on your server.

Testing Your New Plug-In

This is the place and time where having a WordPress installation on your own computer can be very useful. Plug-ins by definition should work without hassle with the current version of WordPress core, but whether they work with every other plug-in installed on your server is another matter entirely.

Your test server does not have to be a duplicate of your production setup. Content isn't especially important; that is, you don't have to have all your posts up there, but there should be at least one post, preferably with an image attached. Your existing theme, set up identically to the production server, should also be loaded.

If you do have a test server set up, try adding your new plug-in to the setup. Run all the existing plug-ins one at a time for standard operation, and then change a setting or two to check for unwanted effects. If the plug-in passes, go ahead and upload the plug-in to the production server at your web host.

> **caution**
>
> Before installing any plug-in (including updates to WordPress core and individual plug-ins) on your web server, back up the WordPress database to another computer. You don't want to enhance the functionality of your blog only to lose your data in the process! Consider adding the WP Database Backup plug-in as one of your first installations. See the Administration part of the "Some 'Essential' Plugins" section later in the chapter.

Selection and Activation

When you have your plug-in downloaded and installed into the WordPress/wp-content/plugins directory, your Manage Plugins page should look something like Figure 13.3.

Figure 13.3 Your Manage Plugins page tells you what plug-ins are installed (ready for use) and activated (working on your blog now).

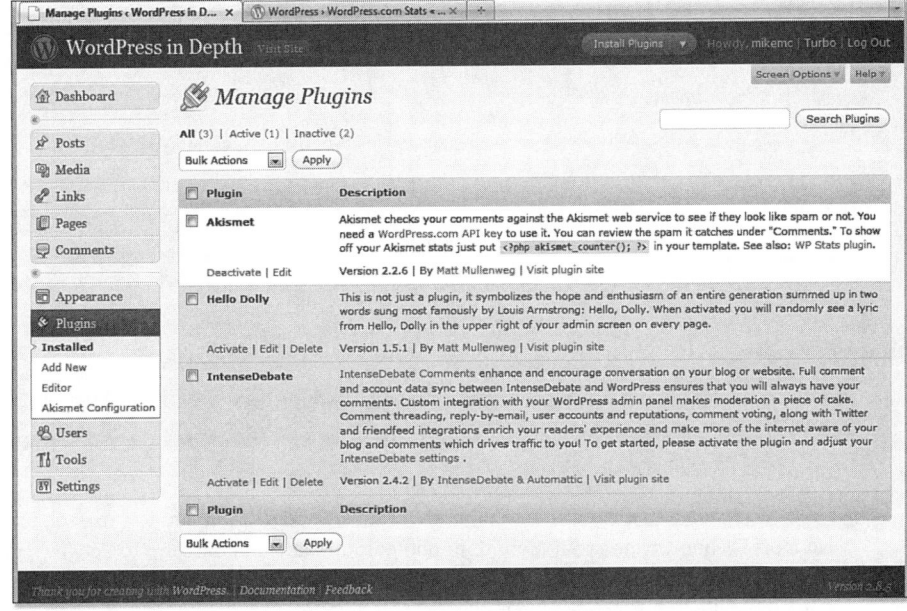

To turn on your new plug-in, click the Activate link. Some plug-ins have settings. If you don't see a Settings link on the Manage Plugins page, go to the main Settings page; click Settings from the left navigation pane. Your plug-in should have a link listed there somewhere.

When setup is complete, give your plug-in a test spin. If all is well, tell your visitors all about what you've added and how well it works. If you're so inclined, go back to the WordPress Plugin Directory and rate the plug-in, too.

Managing and Updating Plug-Ins

All software changes sooner or later, and it's true of WordPress plug-ins, too. Bugs get fixed; new functionality is added. As with WordPress core itself, the Plugin Directory tracks updates for the plug-ins stored there.

When a plug-in is updated, you should see news of the fact on your Manage Plugins page, just as when there's a WordPress update. There's also notification in the navigation pane. As always, before making any substantive change to your WordPress installation, back up your database. To install the update, just click the Upgrade link on the page. WordPress downloads the upgrade, extracts the new plugin code, and reactivates the plug-in. The upgrader then displays the results, as in Figure 13.4.

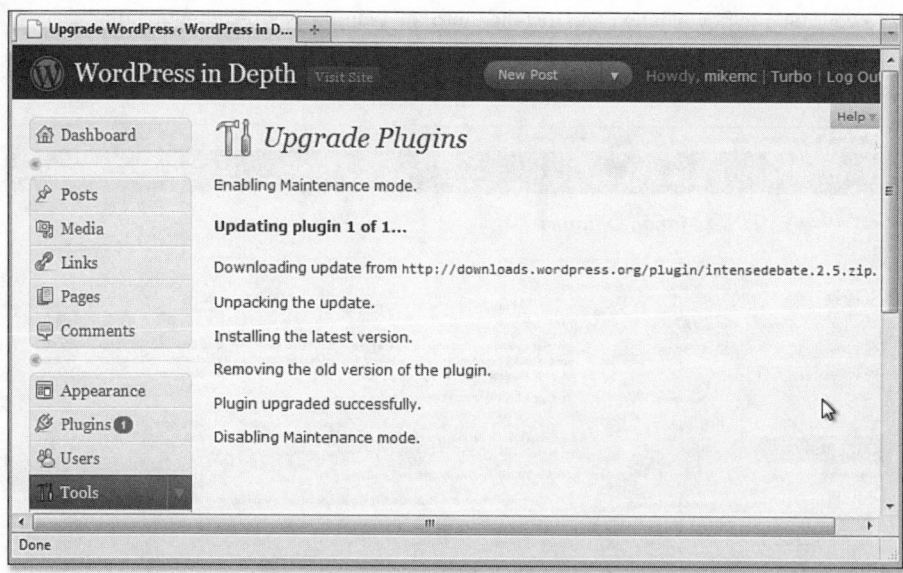

Figure 13.4
Upgrade plug-ins automatically from your Administration page.

Prior to version 2.9, if more than one plug-in had an update, you had to run each update separately. No more! When you see that more than one plug-in has an update, go to Tools, Upgrade from the navigation bar. Check the Select All box (as in Figure 13.5), then click Upgrade Plugins. You still have the option to update each plug-in separately, if you want to hear more about each update before committing.

Figure 13.5
Upgrade
multiple
plug-ins at
once through
the Upgrade
page.

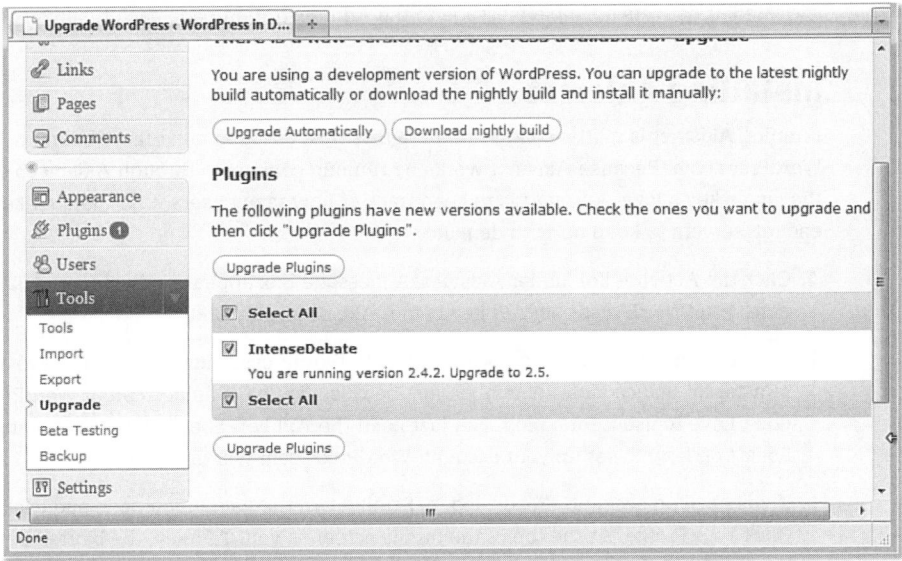

When the upgrade is complete, retest the plugin using the procedures we outlined in the earlier
section, "Testing Your New Plug-in."

Some "Essential" Plug-Ins

As noted at the beginning of the chapter, there really isn't any plug-in that is an absolute must-
have. Everyone's different. Although plug-ins that find their way into WordPress core might be
viewed by at least some as essential for everyone, you aren't even required to use every tool
WordPress offers you!

Nonetheless, there are some very useful and popular plug-ins that might serve you well. We'll use
the rest of this chapter to highlight them for you.

Basic WordPress Plug-Ins: Akismet and Hello Dolly

Two plug-ins are installed with WordPress, but are not activated. One of them, Akismet, is as near
to essential as you can get, whereas the other, Hello Dolly, is yet another signpost of the playfulness
of the WordPress project founder.

Akismet protects you and your legitimate visitors from the scourge of the blogosphere: comment
spam. Spammers use the commenting tools meant to make blogs interactive to deliver traditional
spam (that is, offers to sell assorted products of dubious origin and repute) or links to "phishing"
sites designed to steal visitors' identities (or just their money).

Simply put, if you are going to allow people to comment on your blog postings, you need to install
the Akismet plug-in. Tragically, there's no way around this as long as spammers roam the Web
looking for email addresses and other critical private information.

Hello Dolly can be thought of as the proof of concept for the WordPress plug-in ecosystem. When activated, it delivers a simple message to the Administration page each time you access it.

Installing Akismet

Running Akismet is a little complicated the first time out. You must first obtain an API key from WordPress.com. Because Akismet works by running comments through Akismet's servers, using the single key allows Automattic to keep track of how many users it has, and makes sure they have enough servers to keep up with demand.

1. Click the Activate link under Akismet. A message box appears, advising you that you have to enter your WordPress.com API key before Akismet will work.

2. Click the link in the message box to travel to WordPress.com. If you don't have an account yet, register for an account. Remember, just because you have an account at WordPress.com, you don't have to use it for a blog. You just need the API key. See Chapter 3, "Creating Your Blog's Look," on how to set up your account. WordPress.com will then email your API key.

3. If you have an account already, log in. Scroll down the navigation pane and click Users. Click Your Profile. At the top of the profile screen is your API key, the blotted out section of Figure 13.6. Select that bit of code and copy it to the Clipboard.

Your API key appears here

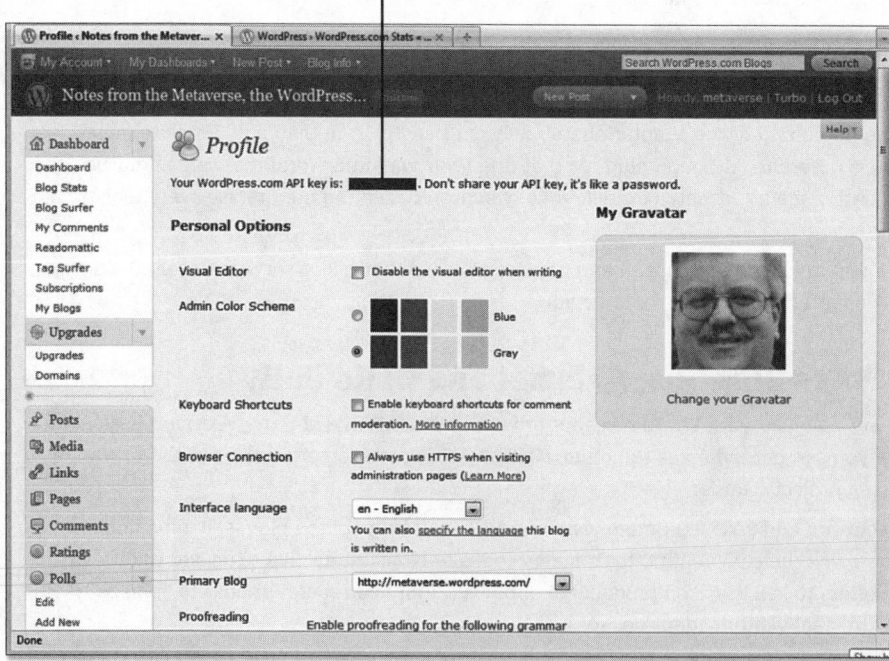

Figure 13.6
Your WordPress.com API key is located on your Profile page, along with your Gravatar.

4. Return to your WordPress.org Manage Plugins page. Click Akismet Configuration.

5. Paste your API key into the WordPress.com API Key edit box, then click Update Options to save the configuration.

Running Akismet

In Chapter 3, we described the basic operation of Akismet at WordPress.com. The application doesn't run any different in the self-hosted, WordPress.org implementation. Akismet will report on the state of the spam queue directly from your Dashboard.

Check your spam queue regularly to make sure no real comments are accidentally shuffled into spam. This does happen, though rarely enough that you are much more likely to thank your lucky stars for such an effective application, rather than curse the fools at Automattic for foisting such vile code on a trusting populace.

Installing Hello Dolly

Hello Dolly is as simple a plug-in as you can get; the Mullenweg equivalent to Hello World. It spits out a quote from the Broadway (and Hollywood) musical *Hello Dolly!* in the upper-right corner of your Administration page whenever you look at it. As Matt describes it: "This is not just a plugin, it symbolizes the hope and enthusiasm of an entire generation summed up in two words sung most famously by Louis Armstrong." So go ahead, put it on; it won't hurt anything.

These two starter plug-ins are just the tip of the iceberg for the WordPress plug-in ecosystem. The rest of this chapter will highlight just some of the variety of tools available to help you run your blog.

Administration and Security

These items help both with the drudgery of site administration and keeping your blog safe.

■ **GD Press Tools**—This is a great plug-n, especially if you tend to be obsessive about tweaking your site and database. Press Tools (the GD comes from the developer, called Golden Dragon) delivers all the information about your WordPress installation you could ever want, and helps you make some adjustments as well.

The first thing you'll notice when you install Press Tools is your Dashboard footer now has information on how much memory you're using for WordPress, along with a running total of database queries made and the page load speed. A Press Tools widget also appears on the Dashboard page with "additional options." Click the GD Press Tools tab in the left column navigation to view 10 pages of data about your installation (see Figure 13.7).

Press Tools is not just about information. Among the nicer interactive settings include: On the Posts page, you can close Comments on posts older than a specified date. Change your existing username on the Administration page. Optimize and backup your database on the Database page. A premium version supplies even more information and options.

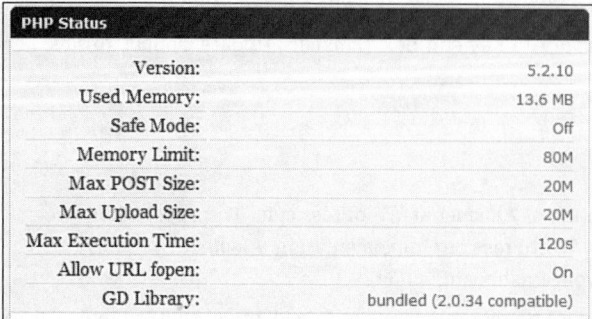

Figure 13.7
GD Press Tools delivers tons of information to your Administration page.

- **Update Notifier**—WordPress makes it abundantly clear when the core application has been updated on the Dashboard every time you log in to WordPress. This is a good thing, because often minor releases come out after a security issue has been found in the wild, and a fix is ready. What happens, though, if you use a third-party editor, or email your posts into WordPress, and just don't visit the site every day? Update Notifier can help. This plug-in checks the WordPress update servers every day and emails you when it's time to update. You're still responsible for applying the update, but you can't say you weren't notified.

- **File Monitor**—As with Update Notifier, this plug-in keeps an eye on the files in your WordPress installation, and emails you when one or more files change. This email represents good news after you've applied some updates, and less than happy news when you haven't made any changes. Once again, File Monitor just tells you what's changed. You're responsible for deciding what to do next. The Troubleshooting Note at the end of the chapter should help.

- **WP Database Backup**—You've heard it a million times. If you value your data, back it up regularly. When you're a blogger, your readers depend on having access to your posts. Those who have linked to your blog posts expect those links to work, too. When you remember that everything in your blog is stored in the database, you'll know to make a point of backing up that database regularly. This tool inserts a Backup page in the Tools menu (see Figure 13.8).

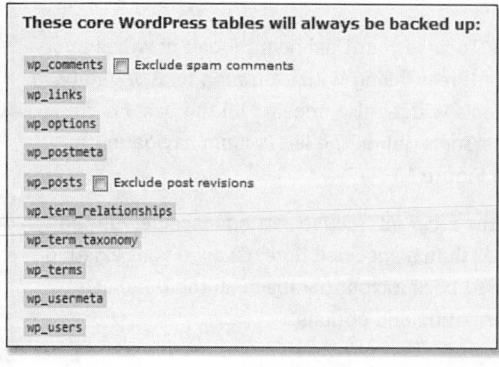

Figure 13.8
Protect your blog with the WP Database Backup plug-in.

On this page, you can specify particular database tables (besides the defaults) to be backed up, choose what to do with the completed backup (store in a location on the server, download to your computer, or email to an address of your choice), and schedule your backups.

- **WordPress Exploit Scanner**—Protect yourself against hacker attacks by running this scanner periodically. Click the Dashboard widget in the navigation bar, then click Exploit Scanner. Click the Run the Scan button. The plug-in searches for hidden links, malicious JavaScript and other possible exploit code, and it provides a fairly detailed report on the same page when the check is complete. You can adjust the default items to scan, but unless you have reason to believe something's wrong and know where the problem might lie, we recommend leaving the defaults alone.

Statistics

Your web hosting company will offer you a detailed statistics package that identifies how many times your pages are being visited by a browser, and an educated guess about who is visiting. These statistics packages are designed to report on static web sites. As a blogger interested in making connections with people, you need a different set of statistics. We've already talked about the WordPress.com Stats plug-in, but there are some other popular and effective plug-ins to give you deeper insight into your audience:

- **Google Analytics for WordPress**—Joost de Valk (also known as Yoast) is one of the bright lights of the WordPress community. This plug-in connects your blog to your Google Analytics account (after you share your account ID) and tracks downloads, AdSense clicks, image searches, and quite a few other relevant statistics.

- **Woopra Analytics**—This plug-in provides yet another free set of analysis tools. Sign up for an account at woopra.com (the plug-in provides a link in the Settings area), and add a bit of JavaScript code to your theme's footer to allow Woopra to track your traffic. Access the analytic report through their desktop client, downloaded from their site.

- **Search Meter**—Ever wonder what your visitors search for when they come to your blog? This plug-in tracks what people type into your search box and what kind of results they get, including terms that generated no results. Go to Settings, then Search Meter to set up your options. Go to Dashboard, then Search Meter to receive your search report.

- **bSuite**—This plug-in provides another way to find out what your audience wants. This plug-in aims to "help surface interesting and relevant posts," among other things. Go to Settings, then bSuite to adjust the default settings. Go to Dashboard, then bStat Reports to view Quick Stats on daily page loads.

 note

If you turned off Related Posts in the General Settings earlier, be aware that bSuite turns this feature back on by default. Uncheck Insert Related Posts Links at Bottom of Each Post to turn off this feature.

Comments

For some people, the ability to interact with readers through commenting is at the heart of the blogging experience. WordPress offers a basic commenting system out of the box, but that may not be enough for you. One or more of these plug-ins can trick out your commenting area more to your liking.

- **IntenseDebate**—This commenting system is now owned by Automattic. This system helps you organize discussions by threading conversations. Commenters can develop a reputation across blogs through comment and user ratings. A nice feature for the site owner (you) is the ability to respond to comments via email. Create a free account at www.IntenseDebate.com, then install and activate the plug-in.

- **Disqus**—This is the other prominent commenting system, presumably if you want your commenting system to be less intense. Disqus (pronounced "discuss") is about connecting traditional blog commenting with other social networking tools. If your audience can tweet with the best of them, this system may be what you need. Commenters can log in with their Facebook or Twitter accounts, along with OpenID (an identity management system supported by WordPress and IntenseDebate). Install the plug-in, sign up and log in at www.Disqus.com, and you're ready to go.

- **GD Star Rating**—Using this plug-in, you can let your readers rate pretty much any element on your site with either stars or thumbs up or down: your posts and pages, along with other comments. Take the ratings statistics and post them in a sidebar. These developers even offer a support forum, so whatever problems you might encounter can be dealt with in a prompt and reasonable manner. This is another plug-in from the same developer as GD Press Tools, listed in the Administration section.

- **Subscribe to Comments**—Using this plug-in, you can generate a separate RSS feed for your comment stream and allow commenters to get an email when someone else replies in the thread. When someone comments on the standard form, the plug-in adds the option to subscribe. Use Settings, Subscribe to Comments in the Administration page to customize your messages.

- **Ajax Edit Comments**—Ever said something in a comment or a blog that you wanted to take back? When you're the blogger, WordPress lets you edit posts and comments at all times, but what about the other visitors? In most cases, those words will haunt them to eternity or at least until the final crash of the last web server on earth—unless, of course, you have installed this plug-in. Ajax Edit Comments lets your commenter edit her own words for a period of time that you (or your admin) can set.

Advertising/Search Engine Optimization

While you may not be into blogging strictly for the income potential, there's certainly no harm in picking up some of the loose change available for bloggers. These tools are about maximizing your exposure and visibility on the web, and turning at least some of that fame or notoriety into supplements to your bank account.

- **Google XML Sitemaps**—Search engines all love highly organized sites. This plug-in generates a new sitemap every time you update your blog, keeping the engines notified that there's something new to index. Generate the sitemap and define the search engines you want to notify in Settings, XML-Sitemap.

- **All in One SEO Pak**—This is the most popular WordPress plug-in ever. This set-and-forget tool aims to raise your blog's profile to get you more visitors and, in turn, a bigger audience. Look for All in One SEO in the Settings area of the navigation bar to set things up.

- **SEO No Duplicate**—Some folks try to game the search engine system by making sure certain phrases appear early and often within their sites. If your blog happens to focus on medical advertising, and every post mentions one drug after another, you could find yourself bounced from search engines entirely. To avoid this, you want to use the Canonical property in your head tag to define your topics. This simple plug-in helps you easily tell the search engine bots the preferred version of a page.

- **Easy AdSense**—Once you have that big audience, Google AdSense could just make your blog economically self-sustaining. This plug-in wants to simplify adding Google ads to your site.

Links

All three of these plug-ins allow your visitors to flag posts on social bookmarking and networking sites:

- **AddToAny**—This plug-in is not kidding when it calls itself AddToAny. Visitors can share your post via email, social bookmarking sites, and more social sites than you're likely to have ever heard of. They also have a Share button for WordPress.com users that functions like a bookmarklet.

- **Sociable**—Thousands of folks download this plug-in every day to put a colorful little ribbon to "share or bookmark this post." It is configurable for dozens of sites.

- **ShareThis**—The familiar green button doesn't paste a million little logos on your page like the others, but instead takes people to the ShareThis site, where they can select the service(s) they want to post to.

Multimedia

These plug-ins simplify and enhance audio/visual aspects of your blog.

- **Page Flip Image Gallery**—Create an Image Gallery that looks more like a presentation, with Page Flip effects. This plug-in is great for photoblogs that document events.

- **Viper's Video Quicktags**—This plug-in is so good and so useful it was incorporated into WordPress v2.9. Consider Video Quicktags as one of the links plug-ins in reverse. Want to include video from YouTube, Vimeo, Blip.tv, or some other popular site in your post? This plug-in relieves you of the obligation to copy an entire block of HTML to embed the player on your site. Just click a site button and paste the URL in the edit box to display the clip.

- **WPAudio MP3 Player**—If you're disappointed with the standard Flash-based WordPress audio player, you might want to upgrade to this relatively new player. It claims better sound, performance, and continuing development.

- **Podcasting**—If you prefer to talk into a microphone than write your blog, podcasting is the way to go. This plug-in helps get your podcast distributed through podcast network sites. Post the URL of your podcast file, and this plug-in will wrap it in an iTunes-compatible feed. Plus, it will slap an appropriate audio or video player on your site for your visitors to use.

Social Networks

Some people think traditional blogging is being displaced by the 140-character microblog, like Twitter. These plugins show that the two formats aren't necessarily at odds; use them to link your blog to various social networks.

- **WP FollowMe**—This is a simple plug-in that allows visitors to connect with your Twitter account. We'll take a closer look at this plug-in in Chapter 15, "PHP Basics: Themes and Plug-Ins."

- **Lifestream**—Consolidate your social networking and microblogging activity in WordPress with this plug-in. Lifestream collects RSS feeds from all of your networks and puts them in one place.

- **WP Greet Box**—You've probably been to a site that welcomed you with a warm greeting, "Hi, looks like you came here from Google. Hope you found what you were looking for. If you like this post, maybe you'd like to subscribe to my RSS feed." Although the more paranoid might wonder how you knew where they came from, many more people probably recognize the warm fuzzy feeling you were trying to generate. This plug-in will generate just such a message.

- **Twitter Tools**—This is Alex King's umbrella for an entire ecosystem of microblogging connections to WordPress. Twitter Tools by itself "allows you to pull your tweets into your blog (as posts and digests) and create new tweets on blog posts and from within WordPress." If you're big into the bird (even if you're not so crazy about the Fail Whale), check this out, and then search the directory for "twitter tools" to discover what other developers have done with this framework.

STYLE SHEETS FOR BUILDING THEMES

Creating Style Sheets

WordPress was designed to simplify the blogging process for people who want to focus on creating content without worrying about design or coding. Surprisingly for some, a lot of people choose to give back to the community by designing themes to enhance the looks of WordPress blogs and coding plug-ins to enhance the core functionality of WordPress, making it easier to use. If that sounds like something you'd like to do, this set of chapters is for you.

In this chapter and Chaper 15, "PHP Basics: Themes and Plug-Ins," we cover the basics of tweaking and creating themes using Cascading Style Sheets (CSS), then look into the guts of WordPress by playing with its underlying language, the self-referential PHP: Hypertext Processor (PHP for short). When we're through, you won't be a professional web developer, but you will know enough to create beautiful themes and write plug-ins to make your site as functional as possible.

Would-be theme developers need to know the basics of standards-based web design. In this chapter, you'll become initiated in the ways of the World Wide Web Consortium (W3C) in designing style sheets and dynamic pages that work the same in all modern browsers.

Sometimes all you want to do is tweak a setting or two in an existing theme. You'll learn more about how to do that here as well.

Introducing XHTML

One great reason to use WordPress is that it takes care of most problems associated with building websites, so you can focus on creating great content. Think about what happens when you visit any website. Chances are good you'll have at least three categories of questions that help inform your opinion about whether it's good or not:

- What's it about? Most of your questions fall under this category, because it's about the *content*. As you've probably heard, content is king!

- What does it look like? These types of questions are about the *presentation* of the content.

- What can I do with it? How can I act on the content? These questions usually focus on interactivity, usability, and (for our immediate purposes) *functionality* of the site.

WordPress tends to the presentation side of things through themes, and between external plug-ins and the core, you can get pretty much all the functionality you might want. Once you've installed and set up WordPress, you never have to think about these pieces again.

Maybe you want to worry about the look of your blog. WordPress clearly does not stand in your way. This is where web standards come into play.

Defining Web Standards

WordPress is developed to give support to, and be compliant with, web standards, but as the saying goes, one of the great things about standards is that there are so many to choose from. As we explained in Chapter 6, "Using HTML in Your Widgets and Blog," there's been a bit of a debate going on among the leading thinkers and practitioners of the World Wide Web. Among the battlegrounds is the question of separating content from presentation. This debate can get a bit tedious, so we'll spare you most of the details, but it might be useful to run through some definitions and relevant organizations. Some of these you might be familiar with; others you might encounter while digging deeper into these issues.

- **HTML**—You know what this is, as described in Chapter 6: the basic language of the World Wide Web. It consists of tagged text. Tags sometimes represent content, sometimes represent presentation, and sometimes are just abbreviations. This standard is at version 4.01, and has been since 1997. Although browser support for the standard has been haphazard at best over the years (adoption levels of HTML far outstripped the ability of standards bodies to agree on much), this standard has been around long enough that browsers pretty much know what to do with every HTML tag. In fact, browsers think they know what to do with HTML tags that aren't even there, but often guess wrong.

- **XHTML**—Extensible HTML (XHTML) "has the same depth of expression as HTML, but also conforms to XML syntax," says Wikipedia. This is HTML that adheres to some of the tagging rules of XML and handles the rules of CSS better than HTML 4.x. WordPress wants its content to conform to this standard, and the visual editor helps you do that.

- **CSS**—Cascading Style Sheets are a major effort to separate content from presentation. Much more detail about CSS can be found later in this chapter in the section, "Introducing CSS."

- **DOM**—The Document Object Model (DOM) from the World Wide Web Consortium (W3C) offers a standard structure for web documents. It defines how style sheets, XHTML, and scripts work together to display a web page. Jeffrey Zeldman has a great analogy in *Designing with Web Standards*: "If your site were a movie, XHTML would be the screenwriter, CSS would be the art director (who decides how a film "looks"), scripting languages (like PHP in WordPress) would be the special effects, and the DOM would be the director who oversees the entire production."

- **HTML 5**—HTML 5 is a newly germinating W3C standard designed to replace both HTML 4 and XHTML. If it's not the real bridge to XML, it could become the final destination. Find the official document describing the differences between HTML 4 and 5 at www.w3.org/TR/html5-diff.

- **XML**—In its earliest days, Extensible Markup Language (XML) was seen as solving the problems of HTML by allowing anyone to create their own tagging language for every type of document. Although that drive has slowed, XML is now, at least in the web context, leading the way toward treating tags as ways of defining objects. There is a solid structure behind how web documents are created. Sir Tim Berners-Lee, the inventor of the Web, believes this will lead to what he calls the Semantic Web (see the entry later in this list).

- **W3C**—The World Wide Web Consortium (W3C) is the governing standards body for HTML and most web standards on this list.

- **OASIS**—The Organization for the Advancement of Structured Information Standards (OASIS) governs standards mostly related to web services and XML documents of all types. These include the new XML-based office-productivity standards, such as the Open Document Format, and two standards for software documentation, DocBook (for printed material) and the Darwin Information Typing Architecture (DITA) for online documentation.

- **Semantic Web**—Berners-Lee defines this as "The Web of data with meaning, in the sense that a computer program can learn enough about what the data means to process it." The Semantic Web is a place where anyone, and any machine, can view the source of a web page and understand both its organization and the type of data it has. The potential to aid human decision making in all fields is staggering, if it could be realized (a big "if").

XML and XHTML

What is XML? Web developers and writers can answer this question in different ways. For WordPress users, think of XML as a standard that does two things: It completely separates content from presentation and enforces a structured approach to writing. That structure is defined in one of two forms: the older Document Type Definition (DTD) or the newer XML Schema. The DTD form is considered as one type of schema, but the practical differences for those of us who are not information architects are few. Both types use the W3C DOM as the basis for the hierarchy. This hierarchy should remind you strongly of the story outlines we all learned in school.

To see what a DTD looks like, go to www.w3.org/TR/2000/REC-xhtml1-20000126/DTD/xhtml1-strict. dtd. This is the Strict XHTML 1.0 type definition. Every WordPress page should refer to this site, and should validate to that standard. Using the WordPress visual editor makes this, well, automattic. (Sorry for the awful pun.) If you use another HTML editor or web authoring tool, you should be able to specify the DTD or DOCTYPE using a project setting or menu item. Check the documentation for your tool.

On a technical level, WordPress blog pages are a terrific example of Extensible Hypertext Markup Language (XHTML). This W3C standard combines standard HTML pages with style sheets and scripting. XHTML offers visitors a dynamic experience, while offering developers a way to quickly create and edit the look and feel of a site with minimal effort.

The XHTML 1.0 standard was created by the W3C to serve as a bridge between today's web, coded in HTML, and tomorrow's web, to be coded in XML. With the introduction of HTML 5 to replace both the existing HTML and XHTML standards, that bridge might be standing in place, unused, for a very long time.

XHTML takes advantage of the DOM. This standard came about after different browsers used different methods to organize and display HTML pages. The two dominant browser companies, Microsoft and Netscape, fought for market share using proprietary scripting languages and tags that only their browser understood and could process. Designers, in turn, had to create pages that looked best in one browser or another. The W3C created the recommendation for DOM Level 1 in 1998 to provide access to each and every part of an XML document, including comments and processing instructions. It was meant to work for any programming language that could parse and manipulate XML documents.

 **note**

It's a small point, but one worth noting in our standards discussion: In XHTML (and XML), tags are in lowercase letters. Many HTML editors still create tags with ALL CAPS, such as <HREF=> and <BODY>. Check your authoring tool's settings to force it to use lowercase tags. The WordPress editor, of course, takes care of this for you.

Essentially, the DOM describes a web page as a tree, with each tag serving as a leaf on the tree, as shown in Figure 14.1. Here you have a page identified through the HTML tag. Every HTML page must have a <head> section and a <body> section. The <head> includes the page title tag and title text. The <body>, in this case, has a single heading tagged <h1>, with text for that heading and a link. The link is composed of the <a> anchor tag and the <href=> tag signifying a hypertext reference outside the page.

With the DOM, theoretically, scripting languages like PHP and JavaScript should be able to access and change properties and content of each item (called a node) in this tree. Until fairly recently, all browsers (especially Internet Explorer) had inconsistent support for the features of the DOM. This has changed with the latest set of browser revisions. Internet Explorer 7 and 8, Firefox 3.x (and any other browser based on the Gecko rendering engine), and Opera 8 and up have better DOM support. The battle for web standards is moving forward!

Figure 14.1
The Document Object Model (DOM)

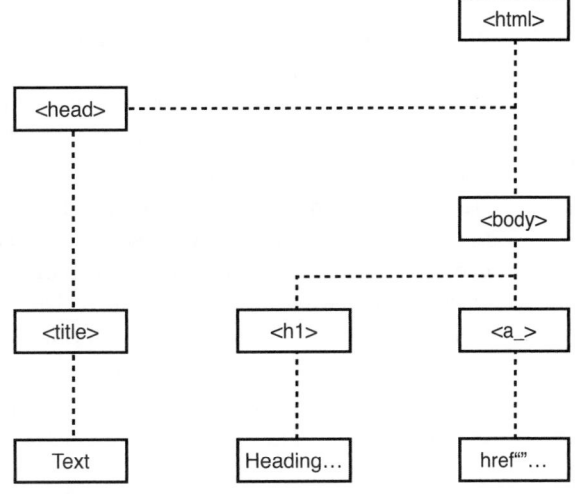

Rendering Engines

A rendering (or layout) engine like Gecko is the power under the hood of a Web browser. A browser provides the toolbars and menus that allow you to see web content in a familiar context, similar to other desktop applications. A layout engine translates all those HTML tags, image files, cascading style sheets and video links into what we think of as a web page.

Layout engines can be used in any application that displays HTML graphically. Gecko is the engine behind all the Mozilla products; not just Firefox, but the Seamonkey browser suite and Thunderbird email client as well.

Other prominent layout engines include: Trident (used in Microsoft Internet Explorer and some versions of Outlook), WebKit (used in Apple Safari and Google Chrome), and Presto (used in the Opera browser).

Writing HTML-Friendly XHTML in WordPress

We described in Chapter 6 some of the ways that the WordPress visual editor takes care of most of the XHTML-specific issues without you having to think about it. Besides handling the proper tagging of italic and bold text, the editor covers some of the housekeeping functions of a well-formed XHTML page:

- Declaring a DOCTYPE and namespace in the page header
- Making sure all tags are closed out with the </tag>
- Using lowercase for tags
- Putting quotes around link URLs and other tag attributes

If you use something other than the WordPress editor to create your blog posts, you should validate all your posts against the XHTML 1.0 standard. Like a debugger does for software programs coded in a particular language, a validator checks the document type declaration (DOCTYPE) you make in your header and flags places where your page doesn't meet the standard.

Even if you haven't posted to your WordPress blog yet—or even created a web page—you can test your tool's default adherence to the standard by creating a page with at least one h1 heading, one h2 heading, a link, and some text. Run this page through a validator and see what it finds. You can probably adjust your tool's settings and defaults to fix the problems. If not, consider getting another tool.

Validating your pages is easily done, and there are several ways to do it. Go to the W3C Validator at http://validator.w3.org/ and test your pages:

- If you have posts already live, use the Validate by URI tab. Copy the permalink of your latest post into the box.

- If the post is saved to an HTML file, use the Validate by Upload tab.

- You can copy and paste all your text directly from your editor into the edit box in the Validate by Direct Input tab. Be sure to include all the header information, as the validator cannot identify your document type if the declaration is not present.

 tip

Many web authoring tools include a built-in validator, or can incorporate the free HTML Tidy validator as a plug-in. Check your tool's documentation to see how to validate your XHTML without leaving your application.

You can always use the W3C Validator (or any other online validator), shown in Figure 14.2 as a substitute or a supplement to your built-in test.

 **note**

The URI in this tab stands for uniform resource identifier. This is an XML designation for any item in the DOM tree, including the more familiar URL, or uniform resource locator, links.

Click the More Options link to give yourself a bit more help in troubleshooting any problems the validator finds. While you're still learning, we recommend checking the Show Source, Validate Error Pages, and Verbose Output check boxes. This gives you the most information. The Show Outline option displays your headings and tells you whether you are using them properly. Check this if you use subheadings in your blog posts. You could check the Clean up Markup with HTML Tidy check box to use HTML Tidy to clean up your mistakes, but the lessons to be taught by the validator just wouldn't be as lasting (see the Troubleshooting Note at the end of this section for more about these lessons).

We ran one of the author's (McCallister's) posts through the W3C Validator, and the results appear in Figure 14.2. Clearly, he needs a more standards-compliant editor!

 **note**

Choosing "Group Error Messages by Type" generates more errors than the default setting, "List Messages Sequentially," but it does help in identifying the nature of a problem.

Many of the errors listed in the validation report shown here should have been easily identified and fixed by the editor. About one quarter were "XML parsing errors," including badly placed closing tags. Some of these were introduced by an imported Text widget. About one tenth involved failing to include closing tags for some paragraphs (a starting <p>, but no closing </p>).

Figure 14.2
Running your
posts
through the
W3C
Validator
at http://
validator.w3.
org can be an
unsettling
experience.

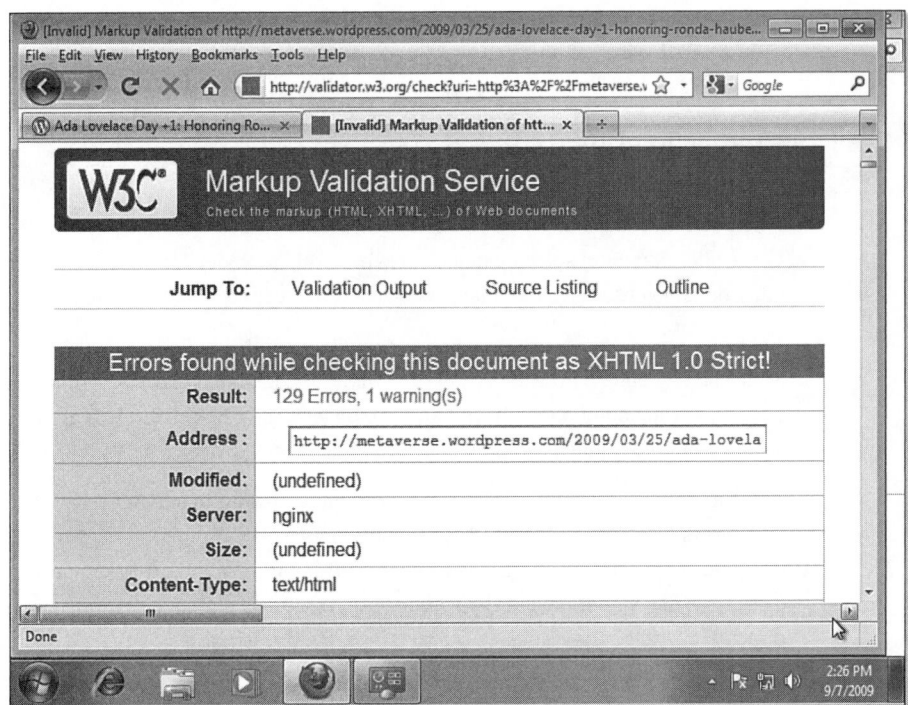

Nearly one third of the errors spotted were the result of pasting in ancient copy from another site. Back in the day, the <font> tag in HTML was the only way to escape having a website written in the Courier typewriter typeface, with <font-size> in there to define a bigger or smaller font for nonheading text. Because this post was about web history, it makes sense that there would be a lot of those tags in there. Had the blogger paid closer attention to his HTML tab, he might have been able to clean those old tags while retaining the same look as his subject displayed at the time.

Another one fifth had an interesting category: "document type does not allow element X here; missing one of Y start-tag." This is a violation of the XML structure. Here, the tag itself was legal, just not its location. This is where the outline structure demanded in XML makes itself felt.

In Figure 14.1, we showed you the basic structure of a web page using the DOM. XML also has rules about what tags can go where. Let's say you have a numbered list describing how to plant bougainvilleas. Your DTD says you have to have the number first, followed by a period. After that, you can have a paragraph explaining the step. After the paragraph, you can do one of these things:

- Go to the next item in the list.

- Include another descriptive paragraph.

- Write a note or sidebar with special formatting.

- Insert a graphic image.

You think the picture of the bougainvillea should go right after the number, so a visitor can see what they are doing before reading the step. A properly setup XML editor won't let you do that, period. In XHTML, you get an error.

Troubleshooting Note

The W3C Validator offers explanations for some error types in its report, and always tells you where the error occurs. When you select the Show Source option, the Validator includes a link to the offending line, so you can look at where this problem lies. Making changes to the code must be done outside the Validator page, in whatever editor you use to create your posts.

As is often true of software debuggers, though, sometimes the real cause of the problem is located a few lines before. So when the Validator complains that you omitted an end tag (such as </p> at the end of a paragraph) and things look right on the offending line, check for an extra opening tag (such as two consecutive <p> tags).

Also, many of the errors flagged in our example appeared in sidebar widgets. In the WordPress.com environment (where the example lives), you might want to alert the theme designer that there are standards problems with widgets, but there's not much you can do directly. When you are using the self-hosted WordPress.org software, you can edit the CSS directly to resolve the issue. A note to the theme developer may still be a good thing, as many of them work hard to comply with the XHTML standard.

As you can see, there is much to be learned in creating standards-based web pages. Wikipedia has a list of some of the more common errors in writing and editing standards-compliant XHTML. Find this at http://en.wikipedia.org/wiki/XHTML#Common_errors.

Introducing CSS

Cascading Style Sheets take all your design decisions and basically put them all in one place, separating content in WordPress from presentation. This allows HTML tags to display differently depending on the context within a page or site.

In this section, we discuss the basic style sheet.

What CSS Is Meant to Do

Maybe you don't think you know what a style is, but you're wrong. In a word processor, you've seen that word Normal or Default or something similar in the upper-left corner. Perhaps you've clicked on the drop-down menu to see what else is there. Maybe you've even clicked on one of the entries to create a heading in a document. If so, congratulations! You've applied a style to a document. That style came from a style sheet, which word processors tend to call a template.

A word processing template is really just a list of names for groups of formatting options applied in a particular circumstance. When you have a list of things to which you want to apply bullets, a style can specify any or all of these, and perhaps many more:

- What the bullet should look like

- How big the bullet (and its accompanying text) should be

- The amount of space between the margin and the bullet

- The amount of space between the bullet and the list text

- The amount of space between items in the list

The same is true for a web document. What CSS does especially well is allow you to define what some text (or nontext area on a page) is (there's that Semantic Web again), and apply particular formatting to all other items on a page—or any other page linked to the style sheet.

In the early days of the Web, site designers had to invent their own navigational tools to allow visitors to roam around the site's content. Although you could just have a set of text links, that got old pretty quickly. People want menus, or something that looks like a menu. Menus imply choices, of course, and you always want an easy way to get back home, too. (Not to start a Beatles sing-along here.)

When designers started creating navigation tools, those tools had to be manually copied to every page on a site. If you wanted to give visitors a visual clue where they were, you had to code that information on a page, with JavaScript or some HTML tag. This was very tedious work, as you can imagine.

 **note**

WordPress themes also have template files that describe the look of the four main areas of your pages—header, footer, index, and sidebar. These are different from a word processing document template in that the latter is mostly focused on text formatting, whereas WordPress templates cover many other aspects of how your page displays.

CSS Levels: A Brief History

As you study CSS, you'll discover two levels, or versions, of the standard. CSS Level 1 (CSS1) became a W3C recommendation in 1996. It covers the basic text and layout functions, such as fonts, general text alignment, background colors, and margins.

CSS Level 2 (CSS2) was adopted 2 years later (lightning speed for the W3C), with an update to 2.1 currently nearing the end of the W3C adoption cycle. (Yes, that's right, more than 10 years later, which is more typical speed for the W3C.) CSS2 adds new capabilities like absolute, relative, and fixed positioning of elements, the concept of media types, support for text that can be read right-to-left, and new font properties such as shadows. V2.1 updates the standard to remove features not supported by the current generation of browsers, and confirms some features that browsers do support.

CSS Level 3 (CSS3) is in the very early stages of adoption, and is not yet substantially supported by current browsers. You can follow this standard's progress at the W3C progress report page at www.w3.org/Style/CSS/current-work#table.

With CSS, you create all your common formatting (headers, footers, navigation, and the like) on your style sheet once, and apply it on every page. Write once, or change once, and you're done. This is why all your WordPress pages have the same general look when you apply a theme to your site.

What Is a Style Sheet?

A style sheet is a reference document for presentation of web pages, such as WordPress blogs. You link to it from the main page and it handles the rest.

Finding a style sheet to look at is easy once you've set up WordPress. Look in your WordPress\wp-content\themes folder. There you'll find your initial two options, the Default (Kubrick) theme and the Classic theme. If you've installed any other themes, these will also be located here. Some themes have more than one file with the `.css` extension (a popular one is `ie6.css`, to specifically address how pages should look in Internet Explorer 6.x), but you will always find `style.css` as your primary style sheet.

Even WordPress.com users can look at (and save) an existing theme's style sheet without the CSS upgrade. Follow these steps:

1. Log in to your account and open the Dashboard.

2. Click on Appearance in the navigation bar on the left.

3. Select Edit CSS. The WordPress.com Style Sheet Editor (Figure 14.3) appears.

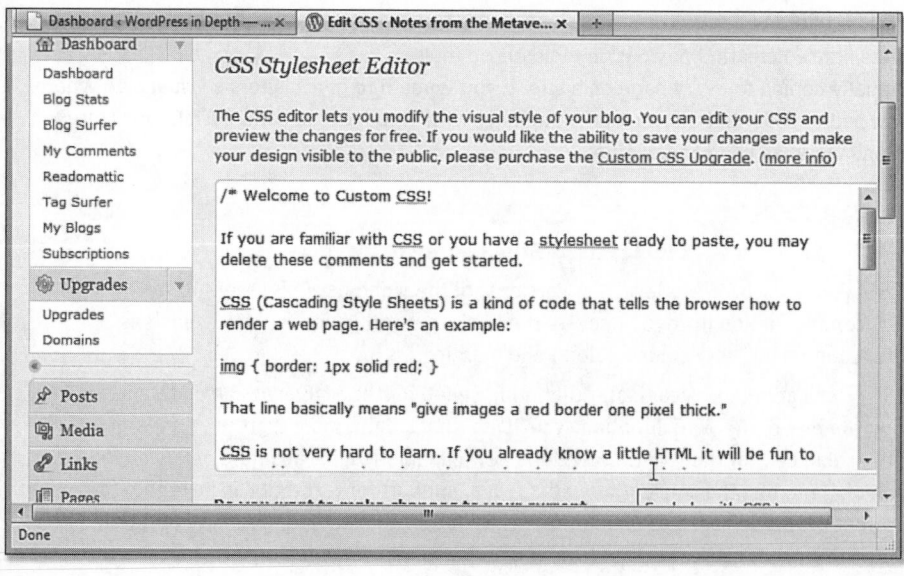

Figure 14.3
WordPress.com users can view the Cascading Style Sheet for their theme, but cannot edit it.

4. (Feel free to read the helpful comments in the editor screen before proceeding.) Below the editor is a line reading "Do you want to make changes to your current theme's stylesheet, or do you want to start from scratch?" Just below that, click the View Original Style Sheet link.

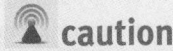
5. Your current theme's style sheet appears. If you want to play with it offline, your browser should have a Save As (or similar) option on the File menu.

As we've noted before, making changes to the CSS in WordPress is restricted to people who pay for the CSS upgrade on WordPress.com and those who perform the work of installing the WordPress.org software on their servers (or on their host's servers).

For now, just open `style.css` in a text editor or HTML editor. You might be surprised at how much of this information a novice can understand. You might not understand all the settings at first glance, but try to pick out some of these items:

- The standard font for ordinary body text

- What size each heading (h1, h2, and so forth) is

- How many pixels from the left edge of the page does body text start (margin)

- Where colors are assigned

If you're more experienced with HTML, you will find more familiar tags and settings. You might be pleasantly surprised at just how much you can do with CSS without much prior knowledge.

Anatomy of a Style Sheet

It is time for some more definitions. Figure 14.4 is a partial view of the CSS behind the default WordPress theme, Kubrick. Looking at `style.css`, you see something similar to a two-column table, with an object on the left side, some braces, and some settings on the right. The whole thing is called a *rule*. The object is called a *selector*, and the stuff inside the braces is a *declaration*. Each declaration has at least one *property* (like `color`, `font`, `margin`, or `border`) and a *value* (that you set the property to).

The first part of Figure 14.4 is a comment that browsers won't read. Comments are designated in CSS by the opening `/*` and the closing `*/` (notice that these two keys are at the top of the number pad on the right side of your standard keyboard).

This comment tells you, the human, something about the theme it describes. This is followed by another comment defining a Typography and Colors section of this site. The functional part of the style sheet follows, with rules for the body text.

You might recall that the W3C Validator threw an error for using `<font>` tags on a website. Yet this first rule in the CSS file defines `font-size` and `font-family`. Is this a contradiction? A resounding "No!" comes from the standards crowd. "Font descriptions belong in CSS, and nowhere else!" The

 caution

Before editing any CSS file, always save a backup copy. Because everything in a CSS file can be changed, simple typos can make your whole design explode. Save the original as `Old_Style.css` or something else, then save the version you're working on under a new name, so you can quickly recover from any serious mistakes.

note

The generic Sans-Serif font is defined by your operating system. In Windows, the Microsoft Sans Serif font is the default; this setting is buried in the Registry under `HKEY_LOCAL_MACHINE\ SOFTWARE\Microsoft\Windows NT\CurrentVersion\ FontSubstitutes\MS Shell Dlg`.

In Linux, the Sans-Serif default depends on your desktop environment. KDE uses Deja Vu Sans as a default, while GNOME uses just plain Sans. The Mac uses Helvetica and Geneva.

font-family defines the basic font for body text on this page. Several font families are named because not everyone has the same fonts on their system. The order is important. Browsers will check the system for each font in order, stopping when it finds one on the computer. 'Lucida Grande' (with single quotation marks around the phrase because it is longer than one word) is a base font for the Macintosh operating system, Verdana and Arial are Windows fonts that have migrated across many platforms; nearly everyone will have one or the other. If a computer has none of the above, the generic Sans-Serif font will display body text.

Selector

Property

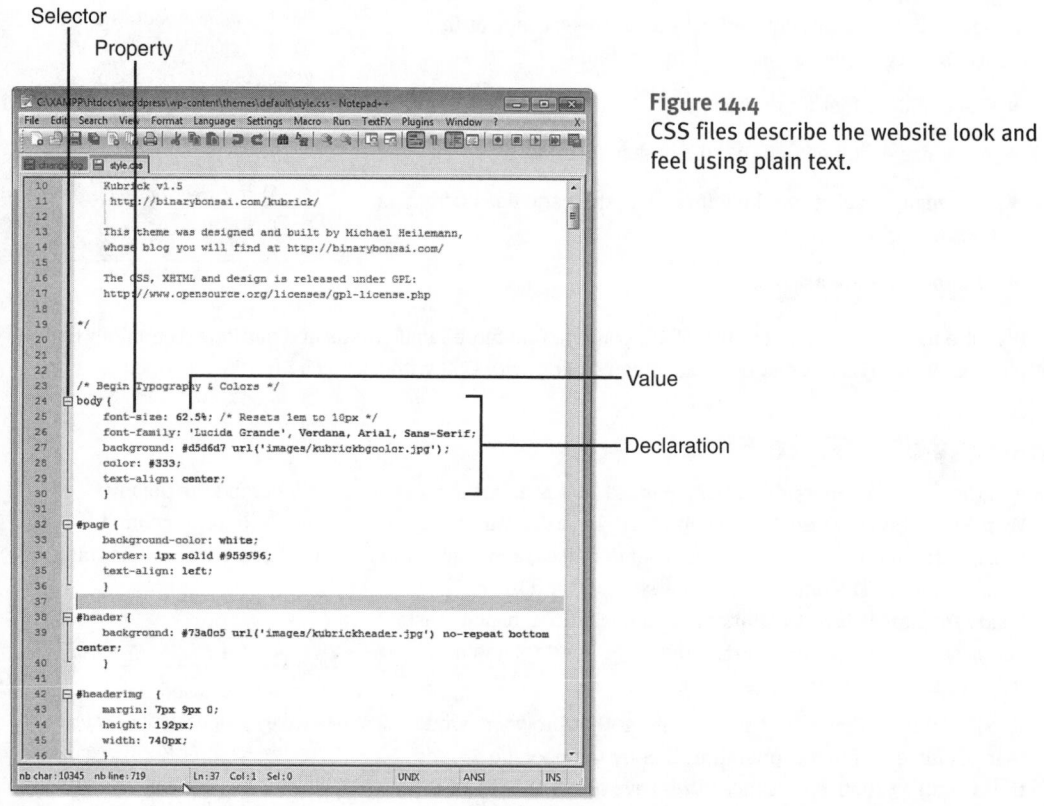

Figure 14.4
CSS files describe the website look and feel using plain text.

Value

Declaration

The Background property here defines a background image for the main body, here with that distinctive shade of blue used by many popular WordPress themes. The #alphanumeric code is a rendering of the color in hexadecimal (Base 16 numbering); there's also a link to a JPEG image. The Color property colors the body text (not the background).

The body descriptor rules end with the text-align property. This sets where the text sits on the page. In Figure 14.4, the text is centered.

The next rule defines some of the page layout. Your Background-Color property defines what goes around the text and shows another way of describing colors in CSS—it's called an English word (white). There's a border around the page, with another hexadecimal color declaration.

The third property in the rule defines the text alignment for the page. Wait a minute. Didn't we use `text-align: center` for the body? Won't that conflict with `text-align: left` here? This is where the "cascading" part of Cascading Style Sheets comes in.

When it comes to rules in a style sheet, the order of the style sheets matters. A rule or property is in effect until another rule takes over. Yet there are some rules that only apply to certain sections or areas of a page. This can get complex, but did you notice that the page layout rule is labeled *#page*, with a pound sign in front? That # (sometimes called a *hash*) symbol indicates one special type of selector. This is a CSS ID area. In web page source code, you'll often find division tags to separate areas of a page. This shows up as a `<div id= >` tag, and it's perfectly legal in XHTML. A division/div is part of the DOM. Guess where that ID in `<div id= >` is defined? Right—everything contained within the "page" div is aligned to the left margin. Outside the "page" div, but within the body of the document, the text is centered.

Another important exceptional selector is the `Class` selector. Scroll down in `style.css` and you'll see `.widecolumn.entry;` where the `<p>` tag gets a new font size. The leading dot in `.widecolumn` indicates a CSS class. Back in XHTML, while some `<div>`s have *ids*, others have *classes*. The primary difference between an ID and a class is that a document can have many classes with the same name in different rules, but each ID name in a single document must be unique.

A few other things to pay attention to while scrolling through this `style.css`:

- Properties and values are always linked with a colon, as in `background-color: white`.

- Every property/value pair ends with a semicolon (;). This is a very important habit to fall into as you write your own style sheets, and also holds true in PHP.

 **note**

We will let you in on a secret, but you have to forget it instantly: The last item in a rule sequence (before the closing brace) does not need a semicolon—the brace serves that function. Trying to remember when you're allowed to omit the semicolon requires too much brain power, and you will leave it out when you need it most. So always put the semicolon at the end! You don't lose any style points for having extra punctuation in this instance.

Enough theory for now—it's time to play with a theme for real. We'll start with small tweaks to existing theme style sheets, and then take a very close look at a popular theme to give you an idea of what you can do with CSS from the ground up.

Tweaking Theme Style Sheets

We've discussed finding themes and getting them installed in both Chapter 3, "Creating Your Blog's Look," (focused on WordPress.com) and Chapter 12, "The WordPress Toolkit: Themes," (focused on WordPress.org). This section is for the idiosyncratic, the dreamers, and the born tinkerers who cannot accept having what everyone else might be using. Their theme must be unique, or close to it. Maybe you've just looked at a few of the featured themes in the WordPress Free Themes directory and found something just about perfect—if only it had...this. Or, after having engaged in a systematic march through the directory, you've shared your vision with a professional theme developer, who didn't quite capture what you need. Because blogging is not all about having the "right" or perfect theme, you have to pick something to use while you search. We'll start there.

When Using an Existing Theme Is Good Enough

At some point in this journey toward your unique theme, someone is going to ask something along these lines: "Do you mean to tell me that there are more than a thousand themes out there, and you don't like any of them?" You should never use the lack of the perfect theme to keep you from blogging, or even from using WordPress. While you continue your search, find something that will suffice for the moment. In WordPress, changing themes is not a big deal. There's even a Change Themes button on the Dashboard that you could click every day for a decade if you're so inclined.

Most WordPress themes can be bent to your will, even at WordPress.com. Just because a theme designer says Theme X is "perfect for a consumer catalog site," with the right vision, you could make it over into a fantasy sports blog, heavy on the trash talk.

If you're particularly averse to delving into CSS, or coding in general, search in the Theme Directory for the Theme Options tag. Many theme developers provide settings pages, where you can customize your theme with a few mouse clicks. Figure 14.5 shows the settings page for the Arclite theme.

 **note**

Scientists have found that it's not enough that someone has done an experiment before you, if you can't find it quickly enough. After a couple of days of seeking and not finding, it becomes cheaper to do the experiment again than to keep looking for it.

It's the same with theme development: It might be quicker and more certain to create a theme yourself than to search, and search, and search for exactly what you want among existing themes. Additionally, if you create a theme yourself, and find it needs one more tweak, you're ready and able to do that tweak yourself. ("Tweak, and ye shall find," anyone?)

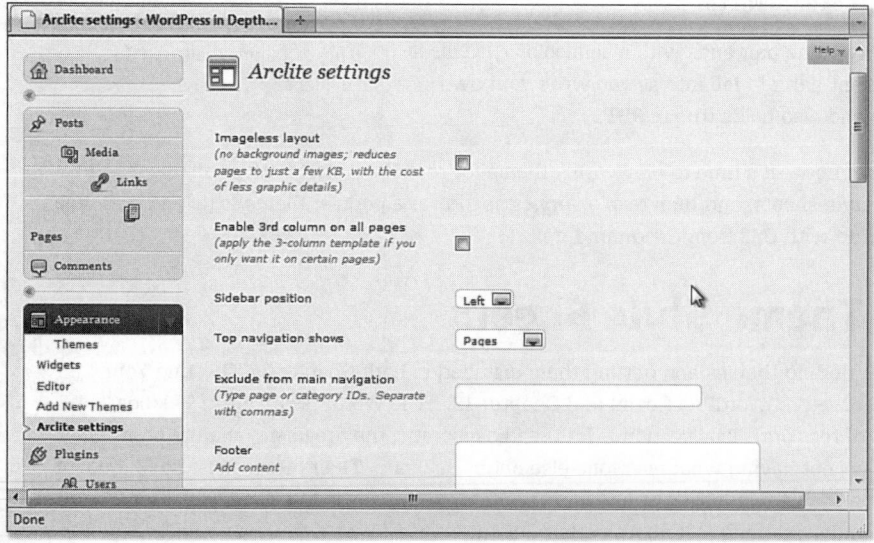

Figure 14.5
The Arclite theme lets you tweak without coding with its own settings page.

The Arclite Theme Settings page handles many common design aspects, and more than a few not-so-common ones. M. Popovici of Digital Nature, the Arclite Developer, does a pretty good job on this page of explaining what each setting does in limited space, but there is more to say about them. This is also good guidance for creating your own themes.

- **Imageless Layout**—Instead of placing an image in the background, the theme uses the standard color options to create a background. This is something to consider if your page is often accessed by mobile devices, where Wi-Fi might be slow. This might be less pretty, but your page will load fast in any environment.

- **Enable 3rd Column on All Pages**—This setting gives you the option to have three columns (more precisely, two sidebars) throughout your site. This promotes a consistent look, but your static pages might not need all the sidebar material.

- **Sidebar Position**—Would you like your sidebar(s) on the left or right of your content?

- **Top Navigation Shows**—This header includes some navigation buttons. Click here to show static pages (covered in Chapter 10, "Adding Upgrades, Audio, and Video") or your categories (covered in Chapter 4, Creating Your First Post").

- **Exclude from Main Navigation**—This setting is good for when you're drafting a static page, but it's not ready for visitors just yet. Perhaps there was a category you used to post heavily to, but have lost interest in. Keep these items out of the navigation bar by adding them here (page names and category IDs) separated by commas. Note that items excluded here are still part of your blog, and visible to search engines (including any search boxes on your site).

- **Footer**—Do you want to include some information at the bottom of each page on your site? Use the edit box provided to add copyright or trademark notices, a link to one (or all) of your other sites, a favorite quotation—whatever fits.

- **Logo Image**—If you have a logo for your blog (or the sponsoring organization), upload that here.

- **Show Search**—This setting lets visitors find what they are looking for on your site. The default is yes; we recommend keeping it there.

- **Show Theme-Default Category Block**—If you don't like the way the categories look in the theme, turn this off. You can then choose a plug-in or code your own way of displaying your categories.

- **Header Background**—Use this drop-down menu to change the header. Choose from one of the many textures, upload your own image (with the option to have one primary, centered image of the size 960 x 190 pixels over a repeating, tiled image; that is, you can display a small photo of a patch of grass that stretches across the header, and then add another big graphic of your favorite animal strolling on this grassy field), or define your own plain background color.

- **Widget Title Background**—Arclite supports widgets and highlights them with a pink title cell by default. The drop-down menu lets you choose Green, Blue, or Gray instead.

- **Content Background**—Here M. Popovici of Digital Nature (the Arclite Developer) gives you a couple of options for changing the background of the theme. For a more radical revision, you'll have to go into the theme template and change it yourself.

■ **Index Page/Archives Show**—We discussed putting excerpts on your home page in Chapter 4. Although "Full Posts" is the default setting, Arclite makes it easy to switch to excerpts.

■ **User CSS code**—This is a free-form CSS edit box, where you can add or change any CSS setting directly. Using the Arclite editor here ensures that your changes will survive the next theme update, as the existing CSS is backed up and restored as part of the update process. This is a very nice favor Popovici does for his users. He includes buttons for some popular tweaks as well.

■ **Use jQuery**—This is a JavaScript library used for a variety of effects. It's included in some themes, but can be added manually as well. At the time of this writing, Popovici was testing this functionality and asking users not to turn this off.

■ **Use Theme Lightbox**—A lightbox highlights images on your blog in a popup when a visitor mouses over the image. Many plugins exist to create this effect in WordPress, but Arclite has its own implementation of a lightbox included by default. Uncheck this box if you prefer another plugin.

■ **Remove Arclite settings from the database after theme switch**—It's so easy to switch themes, you might want to change things up a bit periodically. If you decide to use another theme temporarily, by default you keep Arclite's settings around for easy switching. If you want to dispose of Arclite permanently, however, check this box before switching; Arclite will then remove itself completely from the WordPress database.

When you've made your changes, click the Save button at the bottom and then click Visit Site to examine the results of your handiwork. You can edit further if you choose.

Tweaking an Existing WordPress.org Theme

Not every theme developer offers users a settings page. Even if there is a settings page, you might need to tweak an item other than those the page offers. In this section, we cover some of the standard CSS tweaks to fix common complaints. Going through these will help you understand how to make your own themes better as well. You might be surprised at how easy some of these changes are.

The Theme Editor

By this point, you're probably not surprised that WordPress has its own Theme editor, available to those who run the WordPress.org software. Look around enough, and WordPress might have everything you might ever need for your blog. You saw the WordPress.com theme editor previously in the section, "What Is a Style Sheet?" In WordPress.org you can use the editor without buying an enhancement. From the Dashboard, open the Appearance tab and click Editor. No surprises in that this editor looks very much like the Post editor. Figure 14.6 shows a CSS file from the Arclite theme in the Theme editor.

The primary difference between the Theme editor and Post editor is that the right sidebar contains a list of all files that constitute your theme. PHP templates provide the bulk of the list, with a few CSS style files bringing up the rear. Click each link to display the file in the editor.

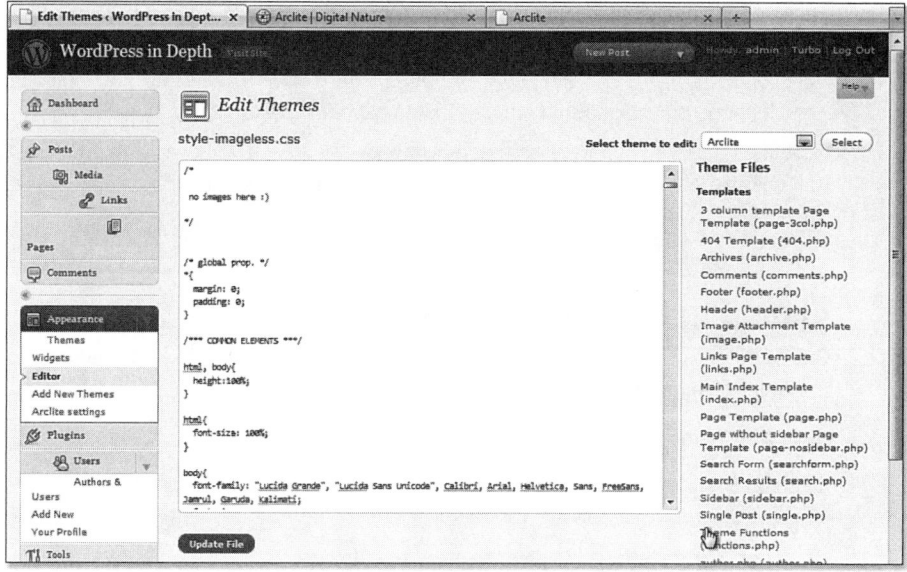

Figure 14.6
The Theme editor lets you play with a theme's CSS and PHP files in the familiar WordPress environment.

The Theme editor displays the files from your currently active theme by default. Use the Select Theme to Edit box in the upper right of the Theme editor to edit a different theme.

There's no formatting toolbar in the Theme editor, as there's nothing to format. There are no drop-down menus as in a settings dialog box. You are expected to know what to do here. As with the Post editor, when you make changes here, they become part of your site the instant you click Update File. For this and many other reasons, take care of your theme files.

 note

Feel free to look at the PHP templates in the editor now. We look more closely at the PHP side of theming in Chapter 15.

Backing Up Themes to Preserve Your Choices

Preferences change. So do ideas of what looks good. For that matter, theme templates change too, to plug security holes or offer more options. This is all to remind you to protect yourself and your choices as you make changes to your theme.

The Theme editor does not allow you to save files with a different name. It only edits and updates existing theme files. Before editing your theme templates and CSS, back up your default files. Use your FTP program to place a copy on your own computer's hard drive. Rename any file on your server you plan to edit (for example, call the original `style.css` file `theme-default.css`).

Continued...

When you've finished editing, back it up again! You can keep separate backup files for every change, or overwrite the last backup. This choice is only limited by your storage limit at your hosting company, or the space on your computer's hard drive. Themes are text files, and don't take up much space, so you should be able to keep as many backups as you want.

The next time you update your theme, chances are good it will overwrite your existing files, and all the changes you made. Compare the new theme files with your backup. Restore rules as necessary.

Changing Background Color

One of the most common theme tweaks is to change the default background color of your site. This is a quick change that is easy to implement.

1. In the Theme editor, open `style.css`.

2. Scroll down to the `body` selector. In the Default theme, it looks like this:

```
body {
  font-size: 62.5%; /* Resets 1em to 10px */
  font-family: 'Lucida Grande', Verdana, Arial, Sans-Serif;
  background: #d5d6d7 url('images/kubrickbgcolor.jpg');
  color: #333;
  text-align: center;
  }
```

Your theme will have something similar.

We want to change the background property. Select everything between the colon and the semi-colon and type in your preferred color.

To stick with valid CSS, use one of these color names: aqua, black, blue, fuchsia, gray, green, lime, maroon, navy, olive, purple, red, silver, teal, white, and yellow. You can also type in a hex code for your preferred color. A short list of some common hex codes is included in Table 14.1. Find lovely charts of hex codes at www.webmonkey.com/reference/Color_Charts and www.w3schools.com/Html/html_colornames.asp.

This property should now look like this:

```
background: purple;
```

4. Click Update File at the bottom.

5. Scroll back to the top and click Visit Site next to your blog title. The background color should be the one you selected.

Troubleshooting Note

You might encounter a message at the bottom of the editor, saying "If this file was writable you could edit it." This indicates that the permissions for your WordPress files are set wrong on your host server.

We talked about permissions in the "Get Permissions First!" sidebar in Chapter 11, "Installing and Upgrading WordPress Software." Briefly, the base file security on UNIX- and Linux-based servers allows—and denies—access to files based on different types of users (Owner, Group, and World).

If you're having trouble with permissions, go to the File Manager application in your host's administration site (what this is called and how it looks depends on your host). You should find the WordPress folder, then the wp-content folder. Both the folder and the files inside should be listed as rwxrwxrw- (or 776). Under the wp-content folder, go to themes. These files should have the same permissions listing. You should be able to edit the permissions directly; if you can't, contact your host (after checking the host's help files) for assistance.

The Owner of these files should be the WordPress user (which may have a different name, depending on what user owns the WordPress database). The Group includes the owner and anyone else you've granted permission to post articles or comments on your blog. Theme files should be group-writable.

Table 14.1 Popular Hexadecimal Codes for Background Colors

Color	Hex Code	RGB Value
White	#FFFFFF	255,255,255
Black	#000000	0,0,0
Red	#FF0000	255,0,0
Yellow	#FFFF00	255,255,0
Green	#008000	0,128,0
Blue	#0000FF	0,0,255
Purple	#800080	128,0,128
Brown	#A52A2A	165,42,42

Replacing Your Header Image

In Chapter 10, we explained the process of adding images to your blog posts. Changing your header image consists of using your FTP client to upload your image to the server, and changing one line in your CSS to point to that image. More precisely, follow these steps:

1. Start your FTP client.

2. Locate the image you want to use on your computer, and upload it to the /wp-content/themes/<*theme-name*>images folder.

3. Log in to your WordPress site.

4. In the Dashboard, open the Theme editor (under Appearance).

5. Your current theme should appear. Check Select Theme to Edit in the upper-right corner to confirm. Use the drop-down menu to change, if necessary.

6. The style sheet listed at the top should be `style.css`. If not, scroll down the Theme Files list on the right side, and click `style.css`.

7. Scroll down the editor window until you find the `#header` selector. If you're using the Default theme, it will look like this:

```
#header {
  background: #73a0c5 url('images/kubrickheader.jpg') no-repeat bottom center;
  }
```

8. To replace the existing header image, change this line to:

```
background: #73a0c5 url('images/<newimage.png>') no-repeat bottom center;
```

Where <*newimage.png*> represents the name of the image file you uploaded earlier.

9. Click Update File at the bottom.

10. Scroll back to the top and click Visit Site next to your blog title. The image you selected should appear.

Creating a CSS-Based Theme from Scratch

A style sheet can be as simple as one line changing a global font characteristic of a website, or it can amount to hundreds of lines guiding the formatting of dozens of classes and types of web content. The WordPress Default theme's `style.css` runs 705 lines, and the complete `style.css` for Arclite is nearly twice that size. Figure 14.7 shows what the Arclite theme looks like when implemented.

The Arclite CSS offers an outline for what you need to create your theme. In this exercise, we are not going to tell you about every line. There are some interesting ideas for your WordPress site, though.

 **note**

See and download all the files for the Arclite theme at http://digitalnature.ro/projects/arclite.

Figure 14.7
Arclite is a
popular
theme, with
a clear style
sheet too.

 **note**

If you want to build a theme from scratch, you need the right tools. As with writing web pages with plain HTML, there are many tools available to you for writing CSS. You can write CSS with any plain text editor, including Windows Notepad. Many web page editors, from Adobe Dreamweaver to the free cross-platform KompoZer application, have specialized CSS editors. There are even a few dedicated CSS editors out there, led by the popular Top Style.

Header Comments

To write a new theme, you have to start with a fresh file. In whatever editor you choose, open a new file, and save it as `style.css`. We will walk you through the Arclite stylesheet as an example.

Start the style sheet with some information about you and the theme. This is done through a comment at the top of the file. In a happy coincidence, in both CSS and PHP, comments are separated by the `/*` start symbol and `*/` to close. In between the start and close symbols, you'll find the following:

- Theme name
- Date last updated
- Author, with link to website
- License under which the theme is released, usually the GNU General Public License (GPL) or another open source license

The comments look like this:

```
/*

  Arclite CSS design
    last update: 17 july 2009

  Author: digitalnature
    http://digitalnature.ro/projects/arclite

  The CSS, XHTML and design is released under GPL.
    http://www.opensource.org/licenses/gpl-license.php

*/
```

Global Properties

This section sets some fonts for sections that aren't otherwise formatted. It also sets the standard margin at zero.

```
/* global prop. */
*{
  margin: 0;
  padding: 0;
}

/* try to use custom fonts through css3 (opera 10+, safari 3.1+ and ff 3.5+) */
@font-face {
  font-family: "Union";
  src: url("fonts/union.ttf") format("truetype");
}

@font-face {
  font-family: "Share";
  src: url("fonts/share.ttf") format("truetype");
}
```

Common Elements

This section covers all the standard formatting issues: body text, headings, lists, tables, forms, and so on.

Some highlights are as follows:

- **Links**—Did you know you could change the color of your links? With CSS, you can:

  ```
  /* links */

  a{
  ```

```
    color: #0071bb;
}


a:hover{
    color: #f44365;
    text-decoration: none;
}
```

A Word About Color Combinations

In using CSS, it's natural to focus on what you can (and can't) do. However, as you move beyond experimenting into actually changing or creating a theme, give some thought to what you should (or shouldn't) do.

Changing link colors is a good example. People are very much accustomed to the HTML standards: a specific shade of blue for unvisited links and purple for visited links.

If you change these, you create a usability challenge for your blog visitors. Depending on the other colors in your theme, there are color pairs that are recognizable to people as replacements for the blue/purple pair—and color pairs that aren't.

Once you learn how to make a change, consider carefully what's right. Try your ideas out on other people. You—and they—will be glad you did.

■ **Tables**—Before CSS got into the mainstream (and, sadly, still for many web developers), the only way to get objects placed properly on a site was through the use of tables. CSS allows you to use tables for their real purpose: displaying data in rows (tr) with headings (th):

```
/* tables */

table{
    margin: .5em 0 1em;
}

table td, table th{
    text-align: left;
    border-right: 1px solid #e8e1c8;
    padding: .4em .8em;
}

table th{
    background: #ab967e url(images/table-header.gif) repeat-x left top;
    color: #fff;
    text-transform: uppercase;
    font-weight: normal;
    border-bottom: 1px solid #e8e1c8;
```

```
}

table td{
  background: #d8ceb6;
}

table tr.even td{
  background: #e1d9c3;
}

table tr:hover td{
  background: #f0eada;
}
```

- **Ordinary Lists**—You can organize and style different types of lists with CSS. Ordinary (numbered and bulleted) lists can be positioned this way:

```
ul, ol{
  margin: .4em 0 1em;
  line-height: 150%;
}



ul li, ol li{
  list-style-position:outside;
  margin-left: 1.6em;
}
```

- **Definition Lists**—If you need to define terms in a post, you have the option of using a specialized and semantic list, called a definition list. This consists of three tags: dl for the list; dt as the term to be defined; dd for the definition:

```
dl{
  padding: .3em 0 .8em;
}

dt {
  float: left;
  clear: left;
  width: 9em;
  text-align: right;
  font-weight: bold;
  text-decoration: underline;
}

dd {
```

```
    margin: 0 0 0 10em;
    padding: 0 0 0.5em 0;
}
```

■ **Fixing Browser Bugs**—This `.block-content` class identifies and repairs a problem Microsoft Internet Explorer 6 has sizing width by percentage:

```
.block-content{
    width: 100% !important;
    width: 960px; /* for ie 6 */
    min-width: 780px;
    max-width: 1200px;
    margin: 0 auto;
    display: block;
}
```

While this `.mask-main` class fixes another bug in a more recent Internet Explorer version:

```
.mask-main {
    position:relative; /* This fixes the IE7 overflow hidden bug */
    clear:both;
    float:left;
    width:100%;
    overflow:hidden; /* This chops off any overhanging divs */
}
```

■ **2-column vs. 3-column layouts**—Setting up columns is really just defining widths for them. Set up classes for your columns (col1, col2, and col3). Define where the column starts in relation to the left or right margin, and how wide it should be:

```
/*** 2 column layout ***/

#page.with-sidebar .mask-main .mask-left {
    right:30%;                   /* right column width */
}

#page.with-sidebar .mask-main .col1 {
    width:70%;                   /* left column width */
    left:30%;                    /* right column width */
}

#page.with-sidebar .mask-main .col2 {
    width:30%;                   /* right column width */
    left:30%;                    /* right column width */
}
```

```
/*** 3 column layout ***/

#page.with-sidebar.and-secondary .mask-main .mask-left {
  right:25%                        /* right column width */
}

#page.with-sidebar.and-secondary .mask-main .col1 {
  width:50%;                       /* left column width */
  left:25%;                           /* right column width */
}

#page.with-sidebar.and-secondary .mask-main .col2 {
  width:25%;                       /* right column width */
  left:25%;                           /* right column width */
}

#page.with-sidebar.and-secondary .mask-main .col3 {
  width: 25%;
  left: 25%;
}

.clear-content{
  height: 1px;
  clear: both;
  display: block;
}
```

We've gone through some of the basic elements of any web page here. You may not use all these elements in your blog (tables come to mind here), but a lot of the tweakable elements are up in the front—always a good thing. Let's move a little deeper into the page.

Header

The header section covers much of the initial impression a visitor has of your blog. It has to look good, be professional, and offer visitors the idea that what you are offering them is worth their time. WordPress does this with a solid graphic image, a bright-looking title (and subtitle), and solid navigational tools. In Arclite, this is all defined in the header section.

Search

Here is a simple method to add search to your blog. It begins with defining the look of the search box with a pair of images, search-bg-png and search-go.png:

```
/* search */
.search-block{
  background: transparent url(images/search-bg.png) no-repeat left top;
```

```
  position: absolute;
  right: 2em;
  bottom: 1em;
}
```

The section above defines the background image with a right and bottom border. The section below makes the box 146 pixels wide and 30 pixels tall.

```
.search-block .searchform-wrap{
  background: transparent url(images/search-go.png) no-repeat right top;
  width: 146px;
  height: 30px;
}
```

The input region of the box is 100 pixels wide, with a dark color to stand out against the standard brown Arclite background. The float property sets the position of the element relative to the search block's margin; here it's on the left side.

```
.search-block input{
  background: none;
  border: 0;
  color: #928a85;
  float: left;
  width: 100px;
  padding: 0;
  margin: 0;
}

.search-block input.searchfield{
  margin: 5px 0 0 8px;
}

.search-block fieldset{
  border: 0;
  padding: 0;
}
```

This section defines the size of the search box as 36 pixels wide, and 30 pixels high. Whatever case you type in the box, the text-transform property turns it into uppercase.

```
.search-block input.go{
  width: 36px;
  height: 30px;
  text-transform: uppercase;
  text-align: center;
  float: right;
  color: #fff;
}
```

Just having content available isn't all you need. The content must be findable. Between categories, tags, and a search engine, you make your blog posts accessible to every visitor. The last piece to making your content findable is navigation.

Navigation

This section handles the navigation for the site. You owe it to yourself and your visitors to give them an easy way to get around your site. There are many ways to do this. Arclite offers such an easy way.

```
/* main navigation */
```

#nav-wrap1 uses absolute positioning to put itself exactly 170 pixels from the top of the browser. A high z-index ensures that this won't ever be covered up by anything else on the page. The z-index property only works when the position is declared (instead of a float).

```css
#nav-wrap1{
    background: transparent url(images/nav-left.png) no-repeat left top;
    padding-left: 25px;
    position: absolute;
    z-index: 100;
    top: 170px;
    left: 1em;
    height: 64px;
}
```

#nav-wrap2 contains the list of elements as 64-pixel high buttons positioned on the left side.

```css
#nav-wrap2{
    background: transparent url(images/nav-bg.png) no-repeat right top;
    padding-right: 25px;
    height: 64px;
    float: left;
}

#nav-wrap2 ul#nav, #nav-wrap2 ul#nav li{
    padding: 0;
    margin: 0;
    list-style-type: none;
}

#nav-wrap2 ul#nav{
    background: transparent url(images/nav-div.png) no-repeat right top;
    padding-right: 2px;
    display: block;
    height: 64px;

}
```

Here, each navigation button floats left relative to each other, so that the buttons appear left-to-right.

```
#nav-wrap2 ul#nav li{
  display:inline;
  float: left;
  position: relative;
  background: transparent url(images/nav-div.png) no-repeat left top;
  padding-left: 2px;
}
```

This defines the label that links to the page. Notice the anchor (a{}) tag at the top.

```
#nav-wrap2 ul#nav li a{
  display: block;
  margin-top: 1px;
  height: 35px;
  float: left;
  color: #b5d1e6;
  text-decoration: none;
  font-size: 120%;
}
```

The button changes color when you hover the mouse over it using a class called fadeThis.

```
#nav-wrap2 ul#nav li a:hover{
  color: #fff;
}
```

```
#nav-wrap2 ul#nav .fadeThis {
  position:relative;
  z-index: 1;
  background: none;
}
```

```
#nav-wrap2 ul#nav .fadeThis span.hover {
  position: absolute;
  top: 0;
  left: 0;
  display: block;
  height: 100%;
  width: 100%;
  background: transparent url(images/nav-active.png) repeat-x left top;
  z-index: -1;
  margin: 0;
  padding: 0;
}
```

```
#nav-wrap2 ul#nav li a span{
  display: block;
  margin-top: 6px;
  padding: 0 8px;
}
```

There is some very cool work on this navigation bar.

Main Content

This section covers the formatting of the essential component of your blog, the post. It includes how post titles look, the font, and how tags appear—both on the main page and on the page where the permalink points.

```
/* post */
.post, .page{
  margin: 1em 0;
}
```

Proving yet again that WordPress is a global phenomenon, Arclite allows several Asian font-families their place in the sun. Jamrul is a Bengali-language font, Garuda is Thai, and Kalimati is Nepali. You'll find references here and in other locations in the CSS.

```
h3.post-title, h2.post-title{
  font-family: "Union", "Lucida Grande", "Lucida Sans Unicode", Arial, Helvetica, Sans,
FreeSans, Jamrul, Garuda, Kalimati;
  margin: 0;
  padding: .8em 0 .1em 0;
  font-size: 180%;
  font-weight: bold;
  letter-spacing: -0.04em;
  text-shadow: #fff 1px 1px 1px;
}
```

Titles for posts can be h2 or h3 headings, and can also change color when you hover the mouse.

```
h3.post-title a, h2.post-title a{
  text-decoration: none;
  color: #000;
}
```

```
h3.post-title a:hover, h2.post-title a:hover{
  color: #df2e56;
}
```

You can see here how easy it is to define a consistent look for all of your posts, with some flexibility for your visitors' operating system and preferred browser.

Rules for Displaying Comments

This section separates out the Comments section from the main post, but still promotes the consistent look of the blog with the same fonts. Comment headings are defined here as level 3, but it appears a little bigger (150%) than the standard h3 heading:

```
h3.comments{
  font-family: "Lucida Grande", "Lucida Sans Unicode", Arial, Helvetica, Sans,
FreeSans, Jamrul, Garuda, Kalimati;

  padding: 0;
  margin: 2em 0 0 0;
  font-size: 150%;
}
```

Comments appear as an unordered list, but there are no bullets. This is courtesy of the list-style-type property.

```
ul#comments{
  margin: .6em 0 1em 0;
  list-style-type: none;
  padding: 0;
}
```

Individual comments also have no bullets.

```
ul#comments ul{
  margin-left: 2em;
  list-style-type: none;
}
```

If someone comments on your post in their blog using the trackback feature, it appears in a distinctive way. The line is a little bit shorter than on a standard comment.

```
ul#comments li.comment, ul#comments li.trackback{
  width: 85%;
  margin: 0;
  padding: 0;
}
```

```
ul#comments li.comment li.comment{
  width: 100%;
}
```

While you can use a plugin to manage your comments (a variety of them exist), sometimes simple is best. Just make some style definitions as is done here, let Akismet handle the spam, and you're done.

Sidebars

The main thing to format in this section is the various menus and lists that make up the sidebar. There is nothing here that we haven't already covered.

Footer

The last substantive section covers the footer. There are styles here for RSS feeds, the copyright notice, and room for up to six widgets.

We begin by defining colors for the footer as a whole...

```css
/*** FOOTER ***/

#footer{
  padding: 1em 0;
  color: #e7e0c7;
  border-top: 1px solid #fff;
}
```

...and links inside the footer.

```css
#footer a{
  color: #a59079;
}
```

This puts the orange RSS icon that allows people to subscribe to your blog feed a little bit to the right of the left margin.

```css
#footer a.rss{
  background: transparent url(images/rss.png) no-repeat left top;
  padding-left: 20px;
}
```

Let your visitors click here to get back to the top of the page.

```css
#footer a.toplink{
  padding: 1px 6px;
  background: #584d43;
  color: #9b856f;
  font-size: 50%;
  text-decoration: none;
  margin-left: 4px;
}
```

The copyright notice is centered, using a little smaller font.

```css
#footer .copyright{
  text-align: center;
  font-size: 85%;
}
```

The next few blocks allow you to add widgets, and define their styling. As you can see, we are mostly concerned with positioning and colors.

```css
#footer .add-content{
  text-align: center;
  margin: .6em 0;
}

/* footer links/widgets */
ul#footer-widgets{
  margin: 0;
  padding: 0;
  color: #726a60;
}

ul#footer-widgets li.widget{
  float: left;
  padding: 0;
  margin: 0;
  width: 50%; /* default  */
  list-style-type: none;
}
```

Don't try to crowd too many widgets into a footer!

```css
ul#footer-widgets.widgetcount-1 li.widget{ width: 50%; }
ul#footer-widgets.widgetcount-2 li.widget{ width: 50%; }
ul#footer-widgets.widgetcount-3 li.widget{ width: 33%; }
ul#footer-widgets.widgetcount-4 li.widget{ width: 25%; }
ul#footer-widgets.widgetcount-5 li.widget{ width: 20%; }
ul#footer-widgets.widgetcount-6 li.widget{ width: 16%; }
/* no point to add more than 6 widgets, unreadable */
```

Widget titles are small, but italicized.

```css
ul#footer-widgets h6.title{
  background: transparent url(images/div-h2.gif) repeat-x left bottom;
  padding: .1em .4em;
  font-style: italic;
}
```

This puts some space around any content in the footer widget.

```css
ul#footer-widgets .the-content{
  margin: 0 1em;
  padding: .4em 0;
}
```

Here we get more positioning for each widget.

```
ul#footer-widgets li.widget ul{
  padding: 0;
}

ul#footer-widgets li.widget li{
  margin: 0;
  padding: 0;
  list-style-type: none;
  padding: .2em .6em;
  display: block;
  background: transparent url(images/div-h2.gif) repeat-x left bottom;
  position: relative;
  margin-top: 1px;
}

ul#footer-widgets li.widget li li{
  padding-left: 1em;
  border: 0;
}

ul#footer-widgets li.widget li a{
  text-decoration: none;
}
```

Like other elements in the theme, you get a consistent pattern of color changes when the mouse hovers.

```
ul#footer-widgets li.widget li a:hover{
  color: #fff;
}

ul#footer-widgets li.widget li span.hover {
  position: absolute;
  top: 0;
  left: 0;
  display: block;
  height: 100%;
  width: 100%;
  background: #403123;
  z-index: -1;
  margin: 0;
  padding: 0;
}
```

That concludes our tour of a theme CSS. There are many fine books and websites to help you learn more about CSS and XHTML. For a complete reference of CSS properties, how they work in various browsers, and examples you can play with, visit the W3Schools site at www.w3schools.com/css/css_reference.asp. You'll find more references in the Appendices.

PHP BASICS: THEMES AND PLUG-INS

Introducing PHP

WordPress is written in the PHP scripting language, and, therefore, much of what users contribute to the software in the way of themes and plug-ins is written in the same language. In this chapter, you'll learn a little bit about the language, along with its relationship to WordPress and the MySQL database. You'll find out where PHP fits in with theme creation. We conclude with writing WordPress plug-ins with PHP and getting them into the WordPress Plugin Directory.

PHP is the result of another lazy programmer's effort to simplify his life. Back in 1994, Rasmus Lerdorf wanted to eliminate some of the drudgery associated with updating his personal web page. Lerdorf wrote some Perl scripts to generate HTML tags based on some code programmed in the C language. In June 1995, he announced the existence of the Personal Home Page (PHP) tools, version 1.0, in a Usenet CGI news-group. Those tools have since evolved into a full-fledged scripting language with a powerful engine, Zend, and a large community of developers hacking the code. You can read more about the history of PHP at http://php.net/history.

Learning PHP

Many people are put off by any kind of programming. However, millions of people who are non–college graduates or liberal arts majors, who don't like math, who would never wear a pocket protector or fix their eyeglasses with electrical tape, or who otherwise consider programming to be something they do not do have learned the necessities to program in WordPress.

It's fine to get a book on PHP or WordPress programming, take a course, and/or find a supportive and knowledgeable friend if you feel the need. However, you might be surprised how far you get with the introduction and orientation given here and with existing WordPress plug-ins as grist for your mill.

The coding might seem intimidating at first, but many who were initially frightened have learned by example and experimentation, supported by the WordPress community. You won't break WordPress—many more talented, and with far worse intentions, than you have tried and failed. Don't be afraid to dive in.

The PHP Home Page at www.php.net defines PHP as "a widely used general-purpose scripting language that is especially suited for Web development and can be embedded into HTML. Much of its syntax is borrowed from C, Java, and Perl with a couple of unique PHP-specific features thrown in." It is open source, so anyone can contribute to its development, and works from the web server to deliver pages. As you'll see later in the chapter, PHP often pulls data out of relational database management systems such as MySQL and PostgreSQL to display web pages that look no different from pages coded in standard HTML.

The core WordPress software is written in PHP. Themes consist of PHP templates and CSS styles. Plug-ins can be written in PHP exclusively, or can include code from other languages (such as JavaScript), but need to be able to hook into WordPress to provide the necessary functionality. That is done using PHP as well.

Extending PHP

Although you really don't need to worry about it to work in WordPress, be aware that PHP has its own plug-in library. As you get deeper into PHP, you'll want to check out the PHP Extension and Application Repository (PEAR) at http://pear.php.net and the PHP Extension Community Library (PECL) at http://pecl.php.net.

The PECL library is a set of modules that can link into the language's core. The new functions they provide are then available as any of PHP's built-in functions.

PEAR is a collection of reusable, open source code for use in your PHP applications. The code is organized as collections of files (or *packages*) that act as wrappers, giving convenient access to various PHP functions or extending PHP in some way.

Both PECL modules and PEAR packages can be installed using the php5-pear command-line utility. Calling pear without any arguments displays a list of commands pear understands. The install argument followed by the package or module name installs it; the uninstall argument similarly uninstalls the component.

Installing PHP on Your Development Server

Because you already have WordPress installed, your web server or your web hosting company has PHP on that server. You should have PHP installed on your local computer to develop plug-ins and themes for WordPress for one simple reason: Your blog visitors should not be the guinea pigs while you test new looks and features.

You installed the core PHP language software with XAMPP in Chapter 11, "Installing and Upgrading WordPress Software," but you can always confirm that you have the latest version at http://php.net. To install the latest package in Windows, follow these steps.

PHP4 versus PHP5

There's a small controversy in the WordPress community about the level of support for older versions of PHP. As of this writing, web servers with PHP v4.3 or later can run current versions of WordPress. Considering that v4.3 was released in late 2002, PHP v5.0 came out in July 2004, and the current version 5.3 came out in June 2009, you might wonder why WordPress has not updated its system requirements.

PHP 5.0 added object-oriented features to make the language more like C++ and included a new interpreter engine contributed by the Zend Corporation. Over three minor iterations, more features have been added.

For a long time, Matt Mullenweg actively opposed moving to PHP5 on the grounds that it failed to improve on the earlier version and that it had been a flop in the marketplace (see his 2007 essay "On PHP" at http://ma.tt/2007/07/on-php). When the PHP developers ended support for the entire v4.x series in late 2008, adoption increased.

The problem for the WordPress team is that a substantial number of WordPress installations are apparently still running on servers with PHP4.x. At the 2009 WordCamp NYC in New York City, Mullenweg said that approximately 12% of all WordPress sites were still hosted with PHP4. That totals to around 2 million WordPress sites based on the older version of the PHP language. Credit this issue to web hosting companies that are reluctant to "fix what isn't broken."

The WordPress development team has indicated that after that percentage dips into single digits, WordPress will likely mandate the language upgrade. With no more security fixes coming for PHP 4, the next security breach against one of these hosts could force the holdout hosting companies to recognize their sites are broken and fix them.

PHP5 also is gaining the feature set to move the v4 laggards to upgrade. Some features included in WordPress 2.9 core run much better on PHP5, like oEmbed and the new time zone support. As a WordPress user, you can appeal to your host to upgrade for these new features.

As a theme or plug-in developer, what does this mean for you? The bottom line is: Don't be afraid to use PHP5 to create scripts for themes or plug-ins. All PHP4 features are included in the current version. For themes, it's not much of an issue. If you want to write a plug-in, know the differences between the two versions, however. You can take advantage of PHP5 features (for example, PHP5 is much better at parsing XML data than PHP4) as long as things don't break in PHP4-based systems.

As a WordPress user, select a host that already supports PHP5. If you have a host that only has PHP4 installed, ask why. Remind them that there won't be any more security patches for PHP4, and you want your visitors to get the full benefit of embedded multimedia on your site.

1. Go to http://windows.php.net/download.

2. Select the `php-<current-version>-Win32-VC6-x86` installer to work well with Apache.

3. Save this file to your hard drive.

4. When the download is complete, run the installer program. After accepting the license, you're asked where to install the software. If you are running XAMPP, choose `C:\XAMPP\php`; otherwise, installing to the default folder is fine.

5. The installer asks what type of web server you are running and how PHP should relate to it. Choose the Apache 2.2.x Module (as shown in Figure 15.1) and click Next.

6. When you do that, the installer asks where the Apache configuration files are located. In XAMPP, this is `XAMPP\apache\conf`. Click Next.

7. Choose the modules you want to install. Accepting the defaults is OK, though you can also install the PHP Manual in the Extras module. Click Next and then click Install to complete this process.

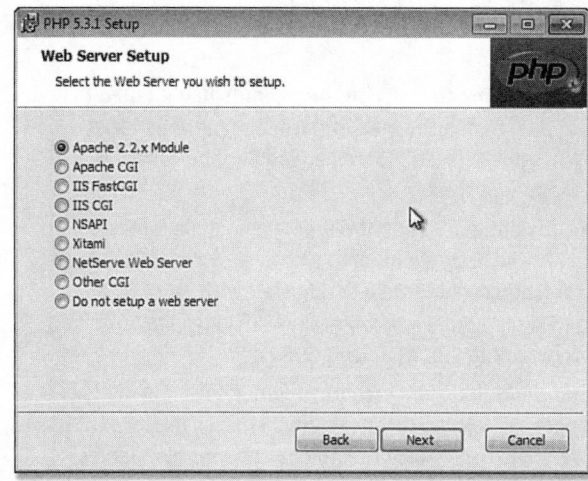

Figure 15.1
Connect your new PHP installation with the Apache server.

It's a simple process to confirm that PHP is properly installed on your system. Open a text editor and write this line:

```
<?php phpinfo(); ?>
```

Save the file as `C:\XAMPP\htdocs\test.php`. Now open your web browser to http://localhost/test.php. The PHP info page should appear. If you don't get the PHP info page, make sure the script was typed correctly, and then see if Apache is running by going to http://localhost.

Look carefully at the info page. You will see which PHP extensions are installed, where your `php.ini` configuration file is stored (XAMPP stores this in `C:\XAMPP\php`), and a fairly detailed configuration report.

Before writing any PHP code, you should also check that your favorite text editor or integrated development environment (IDE) supports PHP code highlighting and the like. With the popularity of PHP, it should not be difficult to find an editor that includes this support.

Integrated Development Environments

If you're new to programming, you might not know what an integrated development environment is. In traditional programming, this is an application that includes:

- a text editor for writing source code
- a language compiler (sometimes more than one) to translate the source code into a form the computer can understand
- a debugger, to find causes for problems in the code
- a tool to automate the build process for programming projects involving more than one program

Microsoft Visual Studio, C++ Builder, and Delphi are well-known Windows IDEs. Eclipse is a terrific cross-platform IDE.

When you're programming in PHP or other web-oriented languages, you can use any one of several IDEs, many of them free of charge and/or open source. These include Adobe Dreamweaver and ActiveState Komodo in Windows, KDevelop, Quanta Plus, and Anjuta in Linux, with NetBeans and Aptana as cross-platform applications.

Writing PHP Scripts: Basic Syntax

You've already written your first PHP script—the one-line `test.php` script you used to test your installation in the last section. There's more to learn, of course, and you will do that in this section.

The PHP interpreter basically treats any documents fed to it as text and echoes back the contents, unless it finds code set between special opening and closing tags. Part of what makes PHP effective in WordPress is that you can embed your code in an HTML page and PHP won't touch your HTML. It will only process your PHP code, and the end result is a final HTML document with the PHP code replaced with the resulting output.

In Chapter 14, "Style Sheets for Building Themes," we talked about the importance of the semicolon in writing CSS. It is equally important, indeed essential, in PHP.

Variables, Strings, and Arrays

Before we begin, let's define three essential types of data used and referred to in PHP. If you think of a programming language as having a grammar, these are the most important nouns in this language.

Variables are used in PHP to store information in memory that the script might need. The way variables work in PHP was basically stolen from another scripting language, Perl. They are identified by a $ and are not strictly typed like variables in other languages. This means a variable can hold a number, a string, or anything else that you might want to alias.

Variables are defined with the dollar sign, the name of the variable, and the value:

```
$color=White
```

Now, every time you include `$color` in your script, PHP will return the value `White`.

In programming, *strings* are collections of words and characters. In PHP, strings are surrounded by quotation marks. Most strings use double quotation marks ("Hello World!"), but if you want the string interpreted literally, use single quotation marks. This becomes useful when you include a variable in a string (yes, strings are often in variables, and variables appear in strings). PHP will return the variable's value only when the string uses double quotation marks. In this command, you complete a sentence:

```
echo "The president of the United States lives in the $color House.";
```

This command, which uses single quotation marks, describes a variable's value:

```
echo 'The $color variable currently has the value 'white', but you can change it
easily.';
```

Variables can only store one value at a time. If the background color for your blog is white, and will always be white, go ahead and define your `$bgcolor` variable as `white`. On the other hand, if you want to change the background color on specific calendar days, you could write a script that draws on a list of colors available for each occasion. In this case, you need something more flexible than a simple variable. You need an *array*.

The easy way to create an array is through the `array()` function (see the "Functions" section later in the chapter for more on functions). To set up a group of background colors to be called on those special occasions, do this:

```
$bgcolor = array ("pink", "yellow", "teal", "green", "violet", "tan");
```

Notice three things about this line:

- You declare arrays using the same dollar sign used in simple variables; an array is really just a variable with multiple values.

- Values are represented as strings, in double quotation marks.

- The statement, as with all lines in PHP, ends with the "instruction terminator" semicolon. The statement doesn't work without the semicolon. Never forget that when writing your PHP scripts.

Arrays are composed of keys and values. Remember that programming languages are about translating what a human wants into something a machine can understand. In the previous `$bgcolor` example, the values are the words in double quotation marks, whereas the key is the sometimes-invisible method the language uses to translate the value.

In this type of array, called an *indexed array*, order is important because that's where the key is. Each element in the array has an index number, starting with zero (0). This format is common to most programming languages, not just PHP. To refer to one item in this array, you point to its index number, as in this code to turn your background color violet (not pink!):

```
$bgcolor(4)
```

It's very easy to forget that the first item is numbered 0, the second is numbered 1, and so on. This problem is not unique to computing; in the United Kingdom, you walk into a building on the ground floor, and have to go up to the first floor; in the United States, the ground floor *is* the first floor. Computing just brings this long-standing confusion to new areas of endeavor (see Figure 15.2).

Figure 15.2
Arrays let you choose a variable's value from a list. When writing your script, reference the number, not the name. Note that the series starts with zero.

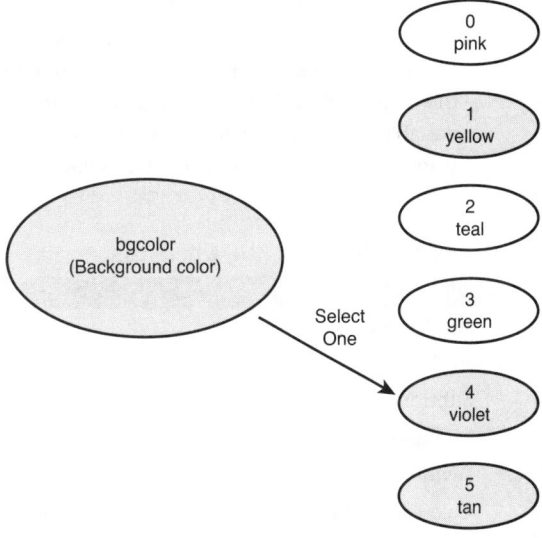

Indexed arrays are just one of three main array types in PHP. *Associative arrays* use named keys, one of the reasons they are sometimes called dictionaries. The third type is called *multidimensional*, and it holds more than one set of key/value pairs, thus they are "arrays of arrays."

As you will see later in this chapter, the $_GET and $_POST arrays are among the most important PHP items in WordPress. These arrays are called *superglobals* in PHP, meaning they are available to you in all PHP scripts and need not be declared. What are they?

We have to backtrack a little bit and remind you that PHP is a language that only runs inside a web server. Looked at another way, PHP has access to any data that passes through the server. The server receives requests that use an assortment of methods, but mostly just two: GET and POST. The superglobal arrays allow any script to obtain data from each of those requests.

The GET method is used most often for search results, and its chief advantage is that it creates a unique URL (that can be bookmarked or otherwise referenced) based on the query string. The POST method passes data invisibly, and does not create a unique URL.

WordPress uses GET to pull in the different parts of a theme into your site.

 **note**

The POST method (and resulting $_POST array in PHP) is not the same as a blog post.

Operators and Control Statements

Continuing the grammar analogy, operators are the verbs that allow you to do things in scripts. PHP offers a variety of mathematical and logical operators to compare variables. By using them with PHP's flow control structures, you can write scripts that follow different paths, depending on the value of the variables.

 tip

Would you rather not think about what method was used to receive data, but just get it from the server to use in your script? Use the $_REQUEST superglobal instead of $_GET or $_POST.

Table 15.1 shows selected PHP operators. The one that causes the most trouble, in PHP and in other programming languages, is the = operator. In PHP, = takes an active role; the value of the variable on the right side is put into the variable on the left. In PHP, = is not a question that returns true or false; it's an action. (To test whether two variable are equal, you use = =.)

Table 15.1 Selected PHP Operators

Meaning	Operator	Example
Assignment	=	$x = $y
Add	+	$x + $y
Subtract	-	$x - $y
Multiply	*	$x * $y
Divide	/	$x / $y
Calculate the remainder	%	$x % $y
Negation	-	-$x
Increment by 1	++	$x++
Decrement by 1	—	$x —
Equal to	==	$x == $y
Exactly equal to	===	$x === $y
Less than	<	$x < $y
Greater than	>	$x > $y
Less than or equal to	<=	$x <= $y
Greater than or equal to	>=	$x >= $y
Not equal to	!=	$x != $y
Logical NOT	!	!$x
Logical AND	&&	$x && $y
Logical OR	||	$x || $y
Group	()	($x = 5) && ($y = $z)

In some other languages, = is a test, and variants on the equal sign are used for assignment. Try to remember that = is an assignment operator, but don't be surprised if you forget sometimes.

In the example below, the script offers a greeting depending on the weather report. It begins with two variables, $weather and $times, with their respective assignment operators. The first if

statement describes the greeting if $weather equals (= =) rain. The second if statement
describes the greeting if $weather does not equal (!=) rain.

```php
<?php
  $weather = "rain";
  $times = 17;
  if ($weather == "rain") {
      echo "I've already told you" ;
      echo $times;
      echo "times... if it's going to rain you should bring your umbrella!";
  }
  if ($weather != "rain") {
      echo "Have a nice day!";
  }
?>
```

Loops

PHP also has looping structures that can be used to cycle through a section of code any number of
times. This saves you the time of having to explicitly write the same section of code over and over.
Here's an example that zips through and writes out all the numbers between 1 and 10,000—each on
a separate line:

```php
<?php
  $x = 1;
  while (x >= 10000) {
      echo $x;
      echo "<br />";
      $x++;
  }
?>
```

As with array indices, it's important to remember that the first time through a loop starts with the
first item, or item 0, unless you specify otherwise. Check loop beginnings and endings carefully
to make sure the count is exactly right; "off by 1" errors are among the most common in
programming. They tend to cause you to miss important information (at the beginning or end of
an array) or to generate garbage (after you go out of the array's boundaries by 1).

What makes a WordPress theme work is the posting loop, which you'll learn more about in "The
Index Template" section later in this chapter.

Functions

Many predefined functions are available in PHP to help manipulate data, explore strings of text, and
even generate graphical images and PDF files. From its simple Perl days, PHP has grown to be a
very useful and robust scripting language. We highly recommend exploring the documentation
available at www.php.net to learn more about the power of PHP.

WordPress themes basically don't exist without PHP's `include` function. It's used to import the contents of another file. This allows you to include other PHP scripts or even other HTML files into your scripts and use PHP to template your website:

```
<html>
<h1>Welcome!</h1>
<?php include "menu.html"; ?>
<img src="img/me.jpg" alt="picture of me" />
<p>Welcome to my website.  Here you'll learn all sorts of neat stuff about
me.  Here are some of the things that are going on in my life right now:</p>
<?php include "events.html"; ?>
<p>Thanks for stopping by!</p>
<hr />
<?php include "footer.html"; ?>
</html>
```

This standard web page incorporates three PHP scripts that use the include function to pull in three separate files, menu.html, events.html, and footer.html. Where at one time these files might display as separate frames with different navigation schemes, PHP allows you to view these elements seamlessly on a single page. A separate style sheet would determine the exact placement of each included element.

Forms

Maybe it's a small exaggeration, but you could think of WordPress as just a big collection of specialized web forms. One has a really big edit box to fill with your thoughts, also known as blog postings. Other forms let you categorize and tag your posts in a free-form manner, link to your favorite sites, and give you a way (RSS) to let your visitors become regular readers. Then, there are the settings forms that let you define what your site looks like and what sort of functionality it should have through plug-ins and widgets. Did we mention the forms that let your readers comment on your posts?

PHP makes it pretty easy to create forms with a small amount of programming and a bit of HTML. You'll see that when we look under the hood of a plug-in in "Examining an Existing Plug-in" later in the chapter.

PHP and MySQL

Before you even installed WordPress, MySQL already knew it was coming. This is how closely WordPress, PHP, and MySQL work together.

Every bit of content in your blog—posts, sidebars, style sheets, comments, graphics, Dashboard, and all the rest—is stored in the MySQL database you set up during your installation (or that WordPress.com set up for you when you launched your hosted blog). What happens when your site has a visitor? In a matter of seconds, all this goes on, as shown in Figure 15.3:

 **note**

There is no shortage of books to help you learn PHP and MySQL together. Julie C. Meloni's *PHP, MySQL and Apache All in One* will get you off to a great start.

1. A visitor's web browser calls on a page from your site.

2. The web server sees a PHP script on the requested page and fires up its PHP interpreter (mod_php5 in Apache) to execute the code.

3. Some of those PHP commands allow the script to connect to the MySQL database as the WordPress user and ask the database for the content that belongs on the page.

4. The MySQL database retrieves the requested content and sends it back to the PHP script (more precisely, to the page it's on).

5. The script, in turn, pours all of this content into a few variables.

6. The script then echoes the content from the variables for display on the page.

7. The script combines the database content with any plain HTML included on the requested page and hands it back to the web server.

8. The web server sends the HTML page back to the browser.

9. The visitor (ideally) becomes enlightened, entertained, enthralled, or some combination thereof. She tells you so on the comments page, beginning the process over again.

Figure 15.3
How PHP and MySQL work together to make a web page.

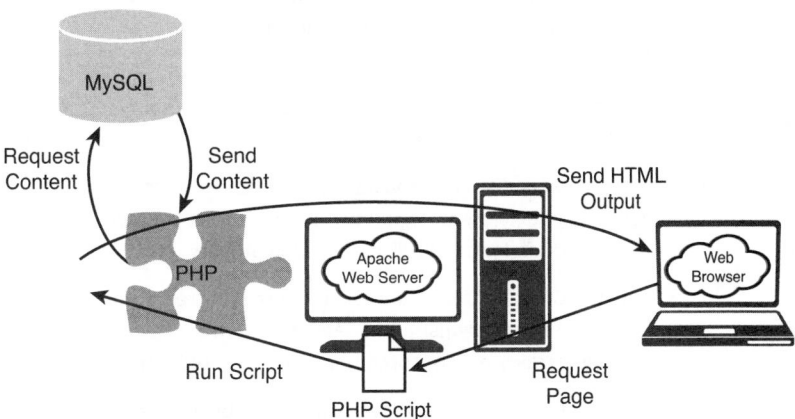

Why store your content in a database when it's just text? Isn't it just easier to have this material surrounded with some variant of HTML or XML tags? When you think about a blog as a moving target, a combination of static and dynamic elements, the answer becomes apparent rather quickly. Maintaining a blog full of static posts quickly becomes a logistical nightmare.

Coming up with enough blog content to keep people visiting can be hard enough without having to continually think about how many posts should be on the front page, making individual permalinked pages for each of your posts, and all the comments people make on them. This is a job ripe for automation, and the best way to automate content delivery is by keeping your data in one easily accessed place.

WordPress creates 10 tables as part of its installation, as follows:

- **wp_comments**—Comments (all of them, including the spam) are stored here. Other information about comments stored here includes the author of the comment, their email and IP addresses, and whether the comment was approved by the moderator. You might want to look into this database table periodically to see where your audience (and your spam) comes from.

- **wp_links**—This basically stores your blogroll and anything else defined in the Links panel.

- **wp_options**—All your settings are stored here.

- **wp_posts**—As you might guess, this is where your posts are stored. You might not guess that static pages and attachments to posts are stored here, too. This table should be the biggest in the database (although it's pretty nice when you have a big wp_comments table too).

- **wp_postmeta**—This table stores optional custom fields you can add to your WordPress.org posts. (Sorry, this isn't available to WordPress.com users.) WordPress also uses this table to lock an existing post while it's being edited—a good thing when a blog has multiple authors. WordPress also stores some information here about attachments to posts, such as the path to the attachment on the server. Plug-ins can also use the table to, among other things, define a custom field.

- **wp_terms**—This table has the list of Category (for posts and links) and Tag names. It works with the next two tables to identify your content.

- **wp_term_relationships**—When you associate a Category or Tag for a post or link, that information is stored here.

- **wp_term_taxonomy**—A taxonomy is a classification of terms. In this table, items in the wp_terms table are classified as Category (for posts), Tag, or Link (category).

- **wp_users**—Critical information about users is stored here, including username, registration date, and permissions. Login passwords are also stored here, in encrypted form.

- **wp_usermeta**—As with wp_postmeta, this table stores information about registered users, including the biographical information you offered up in the Administration area.

 note

Leonid Mamchenkov offers a detailed look at the WordPress database tables, with good advice on working with them, here: http://wpbits.wordpress.com/2007/08/08/a-look-inside-the-wordpress-database/

Find some updated advice, with some hands-on work, here: http://mamchenkov.net/wordpress/2009/06/24/understanding-wordpress-database-in-10-minutes/

PHP Theme Templates

In the previous chapter, we focused on using Cascading Style Sheets (CSS) in creating WordPress themes. Basically, a theme is composed of at least four PHP files, known as templates, plus your CSS. These templates constitute and create your theme. The templates are found in the /wp-content/themes/<theme-title> folder:

- **Main Index (`index.php`)**—This file describes the area where your blog posts appear. As a template, this is also where the other elements of your theme get pulled in to create your blog page(s).

- **Header (`header.php`)**—This is the top of your blog page, with the title of your blog, the tagline, and perhaps an image.

- **Footer (`footer.php`)**—This is the bottom of the page, containing useful, if not always widely read, information about your blog. Your copyright notice, the theme creator, and your hosting provider are among the items that can appear in the footer.

- **Sidebar (`sidebar.php`)**—This includes your recent posts, blogroll, and sundry widgets to make your blog more interesting.

All WordPress themes have these four templates; your theme might have more. The Arclite theme has 19 page templates, covering everything from search results to comments to the message that appears when visitors discover a dead link (`404.php`). We just focus on the four primary templates here.

As with your CSS file, you can use the WordPress theme editor to look at and make changes in your PHP templates. From your Administrative page, go to Appearance, then Editor to open the theme editor. Click any of the Template files in the right sidebar to open that template in the editor.

The Index Template

You probably know this, but just in case: Without an Index page, you don't have much of a blog. You don't even have much of a web presence. When your would-be visitor types in the address www.mycoolblog.com, and there's no Index page (whether that page is called *index* or *home*), the browser does not know what to do, and your would-be visitor gets an error message and a perplexed look on her face. She'll think "Oh no, another dead blog!" and quite possibly never return.

Conversely, if all you have is an Index page, and no header, sidebar, or footer area, you lose many of the aspects of WordPress that make it such an attractive platform. A blog with no headline, or blogroll, or way to access older posts would seem a bit empty too. There is certainly a place for blogs missing one or more of these features, but you might not even recognize it as a weblog with all of them missing.

This scenario is not likely to ever happen with your WordPress blog (unless of course, you don't keep the domain registered), as the Index page pulls everything together in a nice little package. This is done through PHP scripts sitting on your `Index.php` page.

If you open just about any Main Index template, the first thing you're likely to see is a call to the header template. It looks like this, with perhaps a comment and some line breaks:

```
<?php get_header(); ?>
```

This single line of code brings the `header.php` file to your blog's home page. Is this critical? Probably. Is it easy to do? Certainly! It is not, however, the most important item on this

 **note**

`get_header();` is a WordPress template tag. You'll learn more about these in "The Sidebar Template" later in this chapter.

page. That honor belongs to what is commonly referred to in WordPress circles as simply "The Loop."

If you don't have a blog without an Index page, you don't have a WordPress blog without The Loop. This is a PHP function that displays each post in reverse-chronological order on your Index page. It incorporates the styles specified in the `style.css` file associated with your theme, and puts everything in that you want.

As we discussed earlier, loops are functions that basically revolve around a series of dilemmas we ask the computer to solve for us. A loop asks the question "what if" and behaves differently depending on the answer(s) it gets. If something is a pineapple, then we want some ham. If it's not a pineapple, but it's not a pine tree, we want to do something else. If this thing is just an apple, sometimes we want a pie, other times a telephone.

PHP loops also ask the question "what if?" over a period of time. While something exists, we should do that. If it disappears, we should do something else. Most important, it stops asking the question at some point, lest the loop become infinite—a very bad thing.

What WordPress is most concerned within its loop is whether there's a post available. So the basic question it asks before initiating The Loop is another simple one:

 caution

An infinite loop occurs when there is no way for a program to stop, such as when you haven't described what to do in each "what if?" situation. The result of an infinite loop is that the program eats up all CPU time and could cause the computer to freeze up. Avoid infinite loops at all costs when writing your own scripts.

```php
<?php if (have_posts()) : ?>
```

Roughly translated, this means: "Are there posts in this blog?" More to the point, the page wants to know if there's any content in the WordPress database. If the answer is yes, The Loop is turned on:

```php
<?php while (have_posts()) : the_post(); ?>
```

This code says "Oh joy, there's a post in the database! Please, database, put the contents of this post on this page here!"

Once it has its post retrieved from the database, many wonderful things might occur (a place for a thumbnail image, some background color, links to other posts, most anything really) depending on your installed theme or plug-ins. But one thing is guaranteed—The Loop will end, in this fashion:

```php
<?php endwhile; ?>
```

Then the function itself will end, in this fashion:

```php
<php endif; ?>
```

Implementing Post-Thumbnail Support in Your Theme

Before WordPress v2.9, you needed custom field hacks to place a decorative image on every post. It's a lot easier now with the Post-Thumbnails feature, but you have to implement this feature in your theme.

This is actually pretty simple. You need to open the functions.php file in your favorite text editor (or the WordPress Theme Editor). Insert this code anywhere in the file:

```
/* Add support for thumbnail images attached to posts */
add_theme_support('post-thumbnails');
```

For backwards compatibility with older versions of WordPress, use this code to check for the existence of the add_theme_support function:

```
/* Don't break WordPress versions older than 2.9, but add support for thumbnail
images attached to posts */
if ( function_exists( 'add_theme_support' ) )add_theme_support( 'post-thumbnails' );
```

All the previous code adds a thumbnail to posts and static pages. If you prefer one or the other, try these lines that make use of arrays:

```
add_theme_support( 'post-thumbnails', array( 'post' ) ); // Add it for posts
add_theme_support( 'post-thumbnails', array( 'page' ) ); // Add it for pages
```

To define the size of your thumbnails at 50 pixels square:

```
set_post_thumbnail_size( 50, 50 ); // 50 pixels wide by 50 pixels tall, box resize
mode
```

Want to include your thumbnail as part of the site's RSS feed? Add this code:

```
/* Include post-thumbnails in RSS feed. */
function insertThumbnailRSS($content) {
    $content = '<p>' .the_post_thumbnail('medium'). '</p>' .$content;
    return $content;
}

add_filter('the_excerpt_rss', 'insertThumbnailRSS');
add_filter('the_content_feed', 'insertThumbnailRSS');
```

Be aware that a post thumbnail requires two database queries, so each thumbnail slows down your home page. This is yet another good reason to keep your home page to seven active posts.

That is, it will stop asking "what if?"

What happens if there is no post on the page? This can happen if a would-be visitor gets a faulty link to one of your blog posts. The Loop offers something equivalent to a forlorn look, and tells the visitor "Not Found. Sorry, but you are looking for something that isn't here." It also includes a search box so your visitor can find what he was looking for. As we noted earlier, you can include plain HTML inside the PHP code:

```php
<?php else : ?>
<h2 class="center">Not Found</h2>
<p class="center">Sorry, but you are looking for something that isn't here.</p>
<?php include (TEMPLATEPATH . "/searchform.php"); ?>
```

As you get more into plug-ins, you'll notice that some of them will tell you to place the code inside The Loop. Now you know where that is.

Further down the Index page, you will see how the sidebar and footer templates are called into the main page, because what's the point of having a blog page if your blogroll is not on it?

Custom Post Types

WordPress includes four basic post types: Post, Page, Revision, and Attachment. Post types are stored in the wp_posts database table. The ability to add custom post types is included in version 2.9. It doesn't do much in this first iteration, but what a future this option has.

In Chapter 12, "The WordPress Toolkit: Themes," we talked about the Semantic Web and identifying content for what it is, not necessarily how it looks. Custom post types point in that direction and create some new formatting opportunities. Let's say you run a music blog. While most of your posts may just be your thoughts on bands and such, you also review new music. To serve your visitors, you want to include some basic information about the track(s), artist(s), CD title, and the like with links to where people can get the track. You can create a Review post type and include fields for this information in your theme's CSS.

Unfortunately, you can't do this just yet. In v2.9, you get three basic functions to include in a plug-in:

- **get_post_type()**—Returns the current item's post type in The Loop. This function is identical to $post---->post_type.
- **get_post_types()**—Returns an array of all post types.
- **register_post_type($post_type, $args_array)**—Called from within a plugin or functions.php. Only one available argument: "exclude_from_search"

Essentially, all you get to do it register a new type as being searchable or not. For now, you still need to define custom fields and retrieve them in your theme files. The cool stuff isn't built in—yet.

This option is pretty exciting, but is mostly a developer plaything until at least version 3.0.

The Sidebar Template

This template handles the content and placement of your sidebar material. You can drop widgets here, if your theme allows it. Otherwise, you must use tags and parameters to define your sidebar.

Template tags are basically PHP functions inside WordPress. For example, earlier in the chapter we showed you the `phpinfo()` function to display information about your PHP installation on your web server. WordPress has an equivalent template tag called `bloginfo()`. Note the parentheses after the function; parameters are declared inside the parentheses.

Even when there are no parameters at all you want to display, you still have to type the parentheses to show that this tag has no parameters to set.

If a tag has parameters, it will be one of these types:

- **Boolean**—This provides a True or False answer that can be displayed as a binary number (0=false and 1=true).

- **Integer**—This is a positive or negative number. You will sometimes see these inside single quotation marks ('42').

- **String**—This is text, which can range from a single letter to a list of words. Strings, regardless of their length, will always be inside single quotation marks. A string either sets an option for the parameter or displays text on the screen.

> **note**
>
> If you already know PHP, consider whether you want to use other people's widgets (and not have to worry about code) when looking for a theme to use as a basis for your own unique vision. Some themes don't support widgets and only use template tags to create sidebar items.
>
> Look for phrases like "widget-ready" or "supports widgets" in a theme's description.

Let's look at one common template tag to show you how tags and parameters work together in a sidebar item.

Use the `get_archives()` template tag to link to your archive of old posts. The Arclite theme includes a monthly list in its default sidebar. The code looks like this:

```
<?php wp_get_archives('type=monthly&show_post_count=1'); ?>
```

Two parameters are set here, separated by an ampersand (&).

- `type` identifies how much time is represented in these links. Type a string value of `daily` (if you write multiple posts per day), `weekly`, `monthly`, or `postbypost` (for a collection of the most recent items).

- `show_post_count` is a Boolean value indicating that you want to show the number of posts in each archive link. So if you post once a day, your sidebar links as set previously would look like this:

    February 2009 (28)
    March 2009 (31)
    April 2009 (30)

>  **note**
>
> Parameters are similar to (and sometimes called) "arguments" in a command line statement. The list of colors we used in the "Variables, Strings, and Arrays" section would be parameters for a color() function. Generally speaking, function parameters are enclosed by parentheses.

> **note**
>
> Those who cringe at the sight of the words Boolean and integer: Be not afraid, no math is required to use WordPress template tags. Everything you need to know about each template tag and its parameters is waiting for you at the WordPress Codex.
>
> Visit http://codex.wordpress.org/Template_Tags. Scroll down to the Tags section, and click the link of the tag you want to use to see all its parameters and how to use them.

Table 15.2 shows you the most common parameters used with the get_archives tag.

Table 15.2 Common get_archives Template Tags

Parameter and Type	Values	Example
Type (string)	monthly (default) daily weekly> postbypost	`<?php wp_get_archives ('type=monthly'); ?>`
Format (string)	html (default)—Displays each link as a list item option—displays the link choices as a drop-down menu link—Displays list within <link> tags custom—Define your own tags to display the list with. Use this with before and after parameters	`<?php wp_get_archives ('format=option); ?>`
Limit (integer)	() = All posts displayed	`<?php wp_get_archives ('limit=15'); ?>`
before (string)	Used only with html and custom formats; Defines text that appears before the links display.	
after (string)	Used only with html and custom formats; Defines text that appears after the links display.	
show_post_count	Not available with postbypost type. True = 1 False = 0	`<?php wp_get_archives ('show_post_count=1'); ?>`

The Header Template

As we've noted, the header is incredibly important, as it contains the following, among other things:

- Your blog's title and tagline; that is, the first method of grabbing visitors by telling them something of what your blog is about

- The link to your theme's CSS file and, therefore, everything a visitor's browser needs to display your blog the way you want it

- The URL for both your blog and your blog's RSS feed, allowing anyone multiple methods for finding your blog and the golden prose contained within

Header templates might be more or less complex when you encounter them in the Theme Editor, but the basics should be pretty similar, as they contain the same type of information. You might not be entirely surprised to learn this information is awfully similar to the information you gave WordPress when you installed it.

That information is stored in the `bloginfo()` tag we discussed earlier. Table 15.3 shows you some of the more common parameters. The form of the tag is `<?php bloginfo('<parameter>'); ?>`.

Table 15.3 Common `bloginfo()` Parameters

Parameter	Information
name	Blog title
description	Tagline
url	The web address (uniform resource locator) of your site
stylesheet_url	Where your CSS file (`style.css`) is located, as a URL
version	The WordPress version you're using
rss2_url	Where your RSS (Really Simple Syndication) feed is located, as a URL
stylesheet_directory	Where your theme is located

The Footer Template

Default footers are pretty boring, but they don't have to be. Most often, your visitors will see a link to your theme developers (something you should never remove), a link to the RSS feed for your blog pulled from `bloginfo(rss2_url)`, some site information, and maybe a link to the top of the page. Some plug-ins even use the footer as a place to put content that appears elsewhere on the page.

Examining an Existing Plug-In

As we mentioned at the beginning of this chapter, WordPress itself is a PHP application, so it's more than logical that additions to the core software are also written in this language. In the rest of this chapter, we're going to look closely at a popular plug-in, FollowMe.

WP-FollowMe (just FollowMe going forward) is a simple plug-in that adds a badge to your site connected to your Twitter account page. Clicking the FollowMe badge on your blog allows visitors to see your recent tweets, and follow you if so inclined. Besides the basic functionality that we discuss here, FollowMe lets you change the badge's default color of Twitter blue to something more compatible with your existing color scheme, and place the badge where you like.

FollowMe is available through the WordPress Plugin Directory, and at the website of its creator, http://wpburn.com/wordpress-plugins/wp-followme-plugin. Once you've installed it, you can use the Plugin Editor to view and change the plug-in code.

From your Administration page, click Plugins to see your currently installed plug-ins. Click the Edit link under FollowMe to open the plug-in editor (see Figure 15.4). You can also open the file `wordpress\wp-content\plugins\WP-FollowMe\followme.php` in any text editor to view the code.

This file is not as well commented as it could be, but you can clearly see what each section of the code is intended to do.

 caution

Be sure that your plug-in is not activated when you open it in the editor. Any changes you make could corrupt the working plug-in. This would likely be disruptive for your visitors, and could potentially bring your whole blog down until it's fixed.

The script begins with six lines, including the basic information the WordPress Plugin Directory needs from each plug-in.

- **Plugin Name**
- **Plugin URI**—The home page for this plug-in
- **Description**—A brief explanation telling your would-be users what your plug-in does and why they need it
- **Author**—Your name or handle
- **Version**
- **Author URI**—Your home page

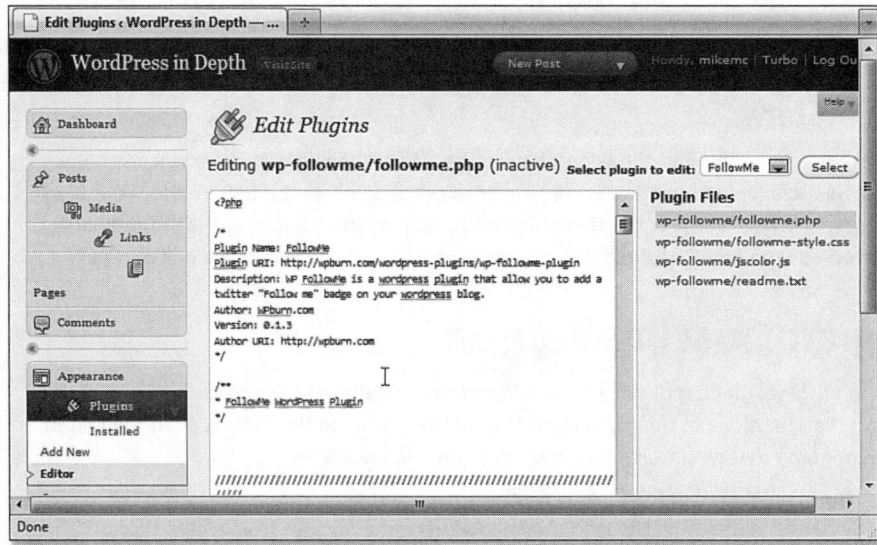

Figure 15.4
Edit plug-ins just like themes in the WordPress plug-in editor.

Even if you don't want to be included in the Plugin Directory, having this information in your plug-in is an excellent practice to follow.

The real program begins with a couple of IF statements that check for special conditions before the program should run. ABSPATH is a constant in WordPress invoked when WordPress is installed to a different directory than the blog URL. The program runs when it finds both the WordPress files, and the plug-in (Class followme) is activated.

```
if (!defined('ABSPATH')) {
    return ;
    }

if (!class_exists('followme')) {
```

 tip

Although not required to be included in the Plugin Directory, it's very good to have explicit licensing information in this initial information section. The directory requires all plug-in code to be released under a free or open source license, compatible with the GNU General Public License—just as the WordPress code itself is.

The bulk of this script creates the `followme` class, with a series of functions that define the badge and set up the administrative settings that make the plug-in useful. The first function adds FollowMe to the Settings menu:

```
Class followme {
    function init() {
        // attach the handler
        add_action('wp_head',
            array('followme', 'wp_head'));
        add_action('wp_footer',
            array('followme', 'wp_footer'));
        // attach to admin menu
        if (is_admin()) {
            add_action('admin_menu',
                array('followme', '_menu')
                );
            }
```

 tip

When you look at the FollowMe code, you will see that each section is clearly marked with dividers, so you can see what's going on. There's no particular standard for dividing things up, so choose a character or other method of clearly marking your code, and stick with it so others can always see what you did.

This code hooks into the built-in WordPress plug-in upgrade system:

```
        // attach to plugin installation
        register_activation_hook(
            __FILE__,
            array('followme', 'install')
            );

        // plugin updated, upgrade it
        //
        if (version_compare(followme::version(), get_option('followme_version')) > 0)
        {
            followme::install();
            }
        }
```

This section puts a function called followmerize in the page footer—see, we told you some plug-ins take advantage of the footer real estate! You'll see what 'snippets' are shortly.

```
    function wp_head() {
        return followme::followmerize(__FUNCTION__);
        }
    function wp_footer() {
        return followme::followmerize(__FUNCTION__);
        }
    function followmerize($tag) {
        $followme_settings = (array) get_option('followme_settings');
        if (isset($followme_settings['snippets'][$tag])) {
            echo $followme_settings['snippets'][$tag];
            }
        }
```

This section is about installing the plug-in and setting up the default settings:

```
function install() {
      // settings
```

This section creates the FollowMe badge, with the default settings configured. Notice the link to FollowMe's own style sheet, which you can also edit in the Plugin Editor:

```
$plug_url = plugins_url('wp-followme/followme-style.css');
$header_cont = '<link href="'.$plug_url.'" rel="stylesheet" type="text/css" />';
            $followme_settings = array(
```

The snippets mentioned in followmerize represent the muscle of the plug-in:

- The background color is defined.

- When a mouse clicks on the top area of the badge, you link to the Twitter page defined in the Settings page, http://twitter.com/wpburn by default.

- When a mouse clicks on the bottom area of the badge, you link to the plug-in home page.

- 'culoare' defines the badge color in hexadecimal code. This can be defined on the Settings page.

- 'twitteracc' is the defined Twitter account.

- 'margintop' and 'leftright' define the badge's position on your blog page.

- 'followmeus' is a setting that allows you to point to the account of your multiauthor blog (Follow Us, not just Follow Me).

Although you can edit this file directly, you can also use the Follow Me Settings page (refer to Figure 15.5):

```
'snippets' => array(
  'wp_head' => $header_cont,
 'wp_footer' => '<div class="followme_r"><div class="followme"
style="background-color:#59B7FF"
onclick="window.open(\'http://twitter.com/wpburn\')"><noscript><center>JS<br
/>is<br />off</center></noscript></div><div class="ili_right"
onclick="window.open(\'http://wpburn.com/wordpress-plugins/wp-followme-plugin\')"
><noscript><a href="http://wpburn.com/wordpress-plugins/wp-followme-plugin">Get
it</a></noscript></div><div class="ili_left"
onclick="window.open(\'http://wpburn.com/wordpress-plugins/wp-followme-plugin\')"
><noscript><a href="http://wpburn.com/wordpress-plugins/wp-followme-plugin">Get
it</a></noscript></div></div>',
                'culoare' => '59B7FF',
                'twitteracc' => 'wpburn',
                'margintop' => '150',
                'leftright' => '_r',
                'followmeus' => 'followme'
                )
          );
```

This section creates the FollowMe Settings page. This function looks like Figure 15.5 when it is displayed.

Figure 15.5
Create this complete settings page with a dozen lines of code.

Add the Follow Me Settings page to the main WordPress Settings area by adding this simple function, add_submenu_page:

```
function _menu() {
    add_submenu_page('options-general.php',
        'followme: FollowMe Settings',
        'FollowMe Settings', 8,
        __FILE__,
        array('followme', 'menu')
        );
    }
function menu() {
    // sanitize referrer
    $_SERVER['HTTP_REFERER'] = preg_replace(
        '~&saved=.*$~Uis','', $_SERVER['HTTP_REFERER']
        );
    // information updated ?
```

When you have a Settings page, don't forget to include a way to save the changes:

```
    if ($_POST['submit']) {
        $_ = $_POST['followme_settings'];
        $_['snippets'] = array_map('stripCSlashes', $_['snippets']);
```

```
// save
//
update_option(
    'followme_settings',
    $_
);
```

Then, once you've clicked Submit, update the snippets:

```
die("<script>document.location.href =
'{$_SERVER['HTTP_REFERER']}&saved=settings:" . time() . "';</script>");
        }
    // operation report detected
    if (@$_GET['saved']) {
        list($saved, $ts) = explode(':', $_GET['saved']);
        if (time() - $ts < 10) {
            echo '<div class="updated"><p>';

            switch ($saved) {
                case 'settings' :
                    echo 'Settings saved.';
                    break;
            }

            echo '</p></div>';
        }
    }

    // read the settings
    //
    $followme_settings = (array) get_option('followme_settings');
```

```
?>
```

This is the end of the PHP script. Looking further down the file, this plug-in isn't finished, though. It includes what appears to be a JavaScript implementation of the plug-in, which is beyond our scope. This is followed by the actual definition of the Settings form, existing of pretty much standard HTML.

Once you've written your plug-in, it's time to show it off to the world. WordPress is, of course, all about sharing.

Submitting to the WordPress Plugin Directory

You want to get your plug-in into the hands and blogs of millions of users, don't you? Perhaps the best and easiest way to do that is to get your plug-in into the WordPress Plugin Directory. You already know how easy WordPress makes it to search for and install plug-ins from the directory, so why wouldn't you want to add your new program to the list?

Why Not Submit to the Plugin Directory?

The main reason you wouldn't want to be in the directory is probably because you want to maintain control over your source code, and/or you want to make money directly from creating your plug-in. The Plugin Directory is explicitly restricted to plug-ins released under a software license compatible with the GNU General Public License (GPL). There are a variety of licenses that qualify, but all of them allow anyone to use, copy, and enhance your code independent of you, though they must return any enhancements back to you, where you can consider adding that enhancement to your code. This is actually what WordPress does when you submit your plug-in to the directory—many plug-ins eventually become part of the WordPress core.

Some people have the misconception that the GPL doesn't allow developers to charge money for code. This is not true, as companies who have written very large checks for copies of Red Hat Enterprise Linux can attest to. Nonetheless, the WordPress Plugin Directory doesn't have a shopping cart page in its workflow, so don't expect to generate income from your directory downloads. Theoretically, you could sell copies of your plug-ins from your website directly, while still being hosted in the directory, but you probably shouldn't expect much income that way.

Also remember that many people with a great deal of programming talent, WordPress knowledge, or both have released plug-ins for free before you. Most people who do charge for plug-ins began by developing plug-ins for free, building up a following of people who liked their work, before charging for their most complex offerings. Even people who do charge for plug-ins often charge less than would be needed to fully cover the time they spend writing and supporting their work. In other words, although a few people might "get rich" from plug-ins, it's not a way to get rich quickly or easily. When in doubt, release your work freely.

If you're writing a plug-in to phish for bloggers and their visitors' personal information, or infect the population with some vicious virus, worm, or Trojan, chances are very good you won't be able to get that into the directory (and you run the risk of being exposed before the world as an evildoer). The same goes for racist, genocidal, pornographic, and similarly objectionable materials.

Most plug-ins, and their authors, don't come under these categories. So let's see what it takes to get into the directory.

Submitting to the Plugin Directory

The process to get your plug-in into the directory is fairly straightforward, and explained at http://wordpress.org/extend/plugins/about.

Briefly, the process goes like this:

1. Create an account at WordPress Plugins.

2. Sign up at http://wordpress.org/extend/plugins/add. You'll be asked for the name of your plug-in, a description, and the URL.

3. To quote directly, "Within some vaguely defined amount of time, some one will approve your request."

4. You will then gain access to a Subversion source control repository to store your plug-in.

5. Write a readme file in the standard WordPress readme format, defined at http://wordpress.org/extend/plugins/about/readme.txt.

6. Upload your plug-in files and readme to the Subversion repository.

You're in! Now you get download statistics, ratings, and comments on your plug-in. Fame awaits—and the satisfaction of knowing you've made a solid contribution to the global WordPress community. It's a good feeling; enjoy it.

V

APPENDICES

IN THIS PART

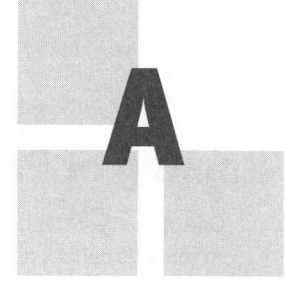

WORDPRESS.COM VERSUS WORDPRESS.ORG

Choosing the Right WordPress for You

Books like this one are about *how*: how to do all the many things you might want to accomplish with a new tool. They're called how-to books for a reason.

Because this book is an *In Depth* book, though, we also include a fair amount of the *why*: why you might want to take on the extra work to add a capability to your blog, for instance, or why you might want to pay for an upgrade (for WordPress.com users) or an extra-cost theme or plug-in (for WordPress.org users).

It's easy to choose WordPress as your blogging platform. It's the most widely used, most capable, best-supported blogging platform out there.

Once you choose WordPress, though, you face a potentially difficult decision: *which* WordPress? WordPress.com, the completely free, easy-to-use version? Or WordPress.org, which requires you to pay for hosting and requires you to do more, but is much more powerful?

Confusing the picture further, upgrades available for WordPress.com bridge much (not all) of the gap between it and WordPress.org. So it's not a black-and-white decision; there are shades of gray in the middle.

Naming of Parts

One of the best things about WordPress, in all versions, is that it's largely a volunteer effort. Automattic only leads the development of the various versions; volunteers handle much of the heavy lifting of software development, technical support, and more.

Automattic makes all its money from the sale of upgrades to WordPress.com and a few other efforts. The company had fewer than 20 employees until recently, and only has about 50 employees as of this writing.

Automattic's light touch is generally welcome; the fact that the company takes on as little as possible directly encourages the volunteer efforts so necessary to the whole effort. The rock group REM once made an album called *Automatic for the People*; Automattic is widely seen as being "for the people" as well.

However, in some ways, the WordPress community could use stronger leadership. The most important example might be the naming of the two main versions of WordPress. Poor naming is responsible for a lot of confusion, a lot of anguished questioning, and, almost certainly, some poor choices by confused users who start with the wrong version for their needs.

The versions of WordPress don't even actually have real names. The versions are as follows:

- The easier version to use, at least at first, is the free version of WordPress software for your blog, hosted for free at Automattic's expense, available on the WordPress.com website. Because Automattic does the hosting, there's not only no cost, but also very little hassle. This version is called WordPress.com, but that's not really a name for the service; it's just where you go to use it.

- The initial, and still more popular, version of WordPress is free software that you download from the WordPress.org site. You have to host the software on a web server you have access to or pay someone to host it for you. (Some hosts do everything you can think of, making this option almost as easy as WordPress.com; others leave it all to you, or offer a variety of options.) Either you or the host have to keep the WordPress software updated, manage the database that powers your blog, and run antispam software. This version is called WordPress.org, but that's not really its name either; it's just where you—or your host, in some cases—go to get the software.

Automattic and its friends in the WordPress community often refer to WordPress.com as the "hosted" version, but this is a useless description; all WordPress blogs are hosted by someone, and many WordPress.org users don't deal directly with hosting at all, except for writing a check. What the description of WordPress.com as "hosted" really means is hosted for free by Automattic. That, however, just begs the question of what Automattic is, and demands further understanding of its relationship with the large and powerful community around WordPress.

This is an example of the myopia that the technically savvy often have with regard to how things look for the rest of the world. It's quite easy for WordPress.org users to understand the split between the versions and to deal with the confusing naming because they spend a lot of time with the software and are technically expert enough to understand the details. However, current and prospective WordPress.com users, as well as outsiders to the WordPress community, often find the difference very confusing.

Automattic does acknowledge that the difference "can cause some confusion for people" by providing a long description of the difference online, as shown in Figure A.1. The Automattic explanation doesn't even mention the ability for you to make money with a WordPress.org blog, but not a WordPress.com one—perhaps the single most important motivation for WordPress.org users.

We like our explanation, in the following two sections, better, and it's shorter to boot. Feel free to use both as needed to clear up any lingering doubts.

Figure A.1
Automattic provides a supportive explanation in Support.

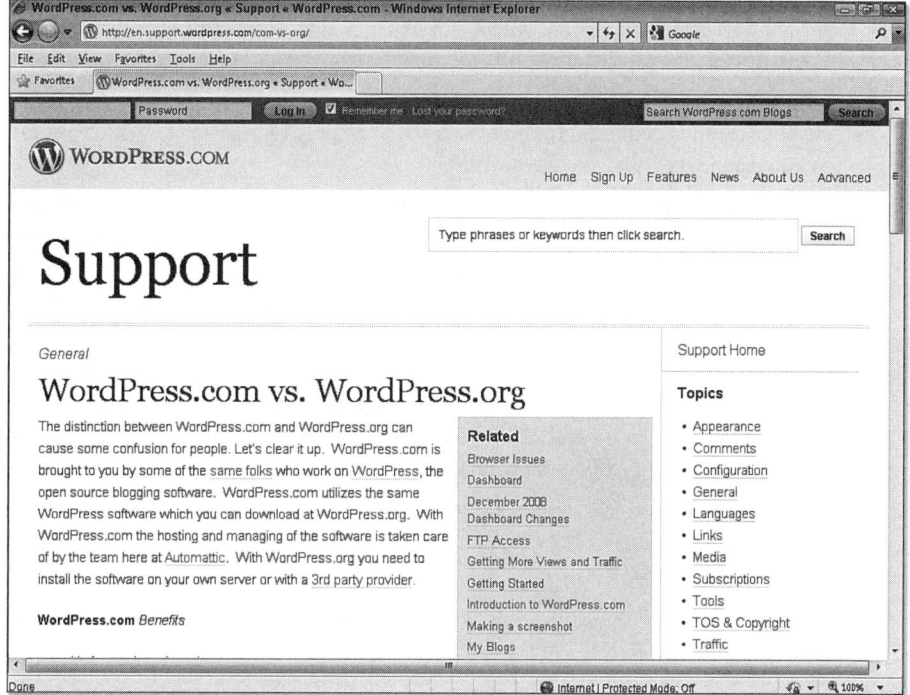

Differences like the difference between WordPress.com and WordPress.org arise in software all the time. AutoCAD, the computer-aided design software, has a "light" version called AutoCAD LT. (AutoDesk, the company behind AutoCAD, is extremely user-oriented, and supports a vibrant community, but still manages to do a bit of branding where needed.)

The lower-cost, easier-to-use version of Microsoft Office is called Microsoft Works. Photoshop Elements does most of what the "full" Photoshop does for about 10% of the price.

In all these cases, good naming, and some hard work on the marketing front to introduce and support both versions, makes it much easier for users to choose the right offering; for the press to talk about both offerings; and for third parties, such as software vendors and, yes, book authors, to help people get the most out of each of the products. Perhaps someday there will be

 note

Ironically, the least-used of the major versions of WordPress (in terms of numbers of installations), WordPress MU, does have its own brand, and even a logo, which you can see at http://mu.wordpress.org.

a simple division between WordPress EZ, for instance, and WordPress Pro—to make up a couple of names—and we'll all be able to communicate with each other more easily.

Until that day, we're all stuck talking about WordPress.com and WordPress.org. No doubt you understand the difference by now—but, also without a doubt, you'll have trouble explaining it to outsiders.

Choosing WordPress.org

In Chapter 1, "Getting Started with WordPress," we provided a brief description of the differences between WordPress.org and WordPress.com. Here, we deal more with why you would want to choose one over the other.

We begin with WordPress.org; it was first, it has many tens of millions of blogs, and it's what most people mean when they say "WordPress."

Wikipedia handles it accordingly; the WikiPedia article on WordPress is entirely about WordPress .org, with WordPress.com handled in a separate entry. At this writing, though, Wikipedia also exemplifies and exacerbates the confusion. The Wikipedia entry calls WordPress.org "self-hosted blog software," which is ridiculous: Software can't host itself; it's hosted on a web server.

In explaining the differences, Automattic focuses on technical aspects—and they are important. WordPress.org allows you to change the code of the WordPress software itself and to upload themes and plug-ins. WordPress.org is also supported by a great community (which has offered so much information, for the better part of a decade now, that it can be hard to find a single, definitive, precise, and relatively up-to-date answer—thus this book).

On the negative side, WordPress.org requires you to pay a web host, to have more technical knowledge, to stop spam (usually by running one or more plug-ins), to back up your database, and to handle upgrades to new versions of the WordPress software.

Inherent in all this you have to understand what hosting is, what a database is, what different kinds of spam are for blogs, and much more. You have to understand these issues not just in a general way, but well enough to make decisions and take action on them.

These are serious issues. You can completely trash, damage, destroy, and delete some or all of your blog, or you can make mistakes that allow spam and malicious software to do it for you. Not only can your blog be lost, but your reputation and, if the blog is for an organization, your organization's reputation can be affected too. (An IT consultant whose WordPress blog is lost forever due to mistakes is not going to find it easy to recover.)

However, this description doesn't cover the four most important issues in deciding to go with WordPress.org: making money with your blog, Automattic's ads on your site, tapping the WordPress community, and getting the right host.

Making Money with Your Blog

You can't make money from a WordPress.com blog. (At least, not directly—you can *promote* your book, for instance, on a WordPress.com blog, but you can't *sell* it there.) Automattic bans e-commerce on your WordPress.com blog as well as Google AdSense ads and extensive links to the Amazon.com partner program and other advertising and partner programs.

You can do all of this and more from a WordPress.org blog, and many very profitable sites do just that.

This is not such a big issue for many people when they first start out. You probably need some time to build traffic before you can, to use that awful word, monetize it. The issue, though, is that you can never do these things from a WordPress.com blog. (Automattic might adjust the anticommerce policies in effect for WordPress.com at some point, but it's unlikely to reverse them completely.)

If you ever want to make money from your blog—or ever think you might—choosing WordPress.com is not only just deferring the day you have to deal with WordPress.org, it's also allowing you to build up traffic to the WordPress.com site—then be faced with the hassle of trying to take that traffic with you to the WordPress.org site. This is an effort that is unlikely to be completely successful, however hard you try.

There are more subtle money-related issues as well. By using WordPress.com, you learn only a subset of what "full" WordPress—and the universe of software changes, themes, and plug-ins that are only available with WordPress.org—can do. Your blog will be worse than it could be, and you'll be trying to learn all the new stuff and revise your blog to take advantage of it, just when your business is starting to take off—a time when you might actually have other things you'd rather be doing.

It's bad enough that WordPress.com prevents you from making money; if WordPress.com sites were some kind of ad-free, commerce-free zone, it might even be acceptable for most people. Depending on the topic of your blog, that's hardly the case, though.

Automattic's Ads on Your Site

Automattic puts ads on your WordPress.com site—the very Google AdSense ads that you would no doubt love to have on your site yourself, if you could.

The problem is not so much your lost revenue (see this section's Tip for details). It's the infuriating thought of random ads being plastered on your site.

Not only do you not control the ads, but you're also not notified of them and, in what would be a classic good news/bad news joke if it weren't so unfunny, you never get to see them. WordPress users never see ads on WordPress.com sites, so you have no way of knowing how many, if any, ads your non-WordPress-user site visitors are seeing, nor even what a WordPress blog ad looks like. (See Chapter 10, "Adding Upgrades, Audio, and Video," for an example.)

No one knows the frequency with which these ads run. Automattic isn't saying, and comments on the topic are all over the map.

Many people find this objectionable enough to either use WordPress.org over WordPress.com, on this ground alone, or to pay for the WordPress.com No-Ads upgrade (see Chapter 10). However,

 tip

Making revenues of a penny per pageview from Google AdSense ads or similar ads is pretty good money for a blogging site. A few cents per pageview is truly excellent, and probably only possible if your blog is about something very popular that sells online for good money, such as computer hardware or cell phones.

With this in mind, unless your blog has many thousands of pageviews, you're not losing much moolah by not being able to run your own AdSense ads. At a penny per pageview, it would take 10,000 pageviews for you to make $100—and much more for you to make much more.

this upgrade costs about $30 per year—about three months' worth of hosting service from a low-cost host for a lower-volume blog (which, despite bloggers' best efforts, most blogs are).

Tapping the WordPress Community

One of the best things about WordPress.org is the WordPress community. However, this is a silver lining that does come with a bit of a cloud.

The cloud is that the WordPress community is a handy target for Automattic to shuffle support issues onto. Automattic doesn't take on the burden of organizing and maintaining all their input.

People are very interested in what's new. So each new version of WordPress, and whatever features are new in it, gets a lot of "ink" online.

The trouble is that when you search for information about a feature, you can find information that was true at one time, but that has since been superseded partly or completely in newer versions.

The WordPress community is almost entirely made up of volunteers. So there's little updating of old posts, understandably. However, this can leave you in the position of archaeologist, digging through comments that have accumulated in layers over the years, trying to make sure that the information you find is accurate and current.

The solution to this is to really engage with the WordPress community—to spend time on a few sites that seem particularly close to what you're trying to accomplish, to find meetings of WordPress people near you, and to get to know people with more advanced knowledge. WordPress people are generally great about this. However, it does take time and effort, and can be a bit embarrassing when you're on the steepest part of the learning curve, always asking for help and rarely able to help others.

Automattic and the WordPress community have engineered a good solution overall, with low costs associated with all forms of WordPress, and a layer of professional support over many layers of informal support from the community. However, when you fall through the professional layer, it can take time and energy to learn your way around the layers below.

Getting the Right Host

The secret to success with WordPress.org is getting the right host. The difficulty is that you need some time, effort, and luck to get this far. Even if you're ready and able to host the package yourself, you might still want to "just say no" to yourself and pay for hosting instead.

WordPress hosts vary in how WordPress-friendly they are. Web hosts generally compete strongly on costs, which makes sense; people doing an online search for a host find cost the easiest thing to focus on. All the other aspects are more or less subjective and require a lot of reading to even begin to evaluate.

However, the old saying, "you get what you pay for," applies. If you can find a host that seems to offer more in terms of WordPress support—especially if you get a personal recommendation for such a host—it's almost certainly worth paying a bit more.

The difficulty here is that there's a chicken-and-egg problem with WordPress hosting. It will probably take you a couple of years of WordPressing to get to know people in the WordPress community, to get to know what you want, and to get to know your blog's volume, use of multimedia, and other key factors, sufficient to choose not only a good host overall, but one that is a really good fit for you. However, you have to choose a host right at the start.

Once you choose a host, you're somewhat stuck, especially if your blog is successful. It's unlikely that a move to a new host will be entirely easy, cheap, and, perhaps most important, successful in maintaining your hard-won search engine ranking as you move to new servers. So, you want to make a good choice up front, which means investing time and effort.

No one wants to be in the position of calling your host about a WordPress problem and having the answer be: "Word-what?" That is, however, the risk you take. Proceed with care.

Choosing WordPress.com

There are more than five million WordPress.com blogs as of this writing. You can't use a WordPress.com blog for online commerce, ads show up on it, and you can't go beyond the 70-plus themes and tame plug-ins that you're allowed. Why would anyone do this?

The answer is just that it's easy. Very, very easy. And completely free. The "limited" version of the WordPress software available on WordPress.com is still very powerful indeed.

If you're trying to decide whether to go ahead with a WordPress.com blog, one approach is to do so, but to make your WordPress.com blog more or less personal. It's less likely that you'll end up wanting to monetize it. In doing your personal blog, you might discover one or more topics that you want to make into a WordPress.org blog.

Don't be afraid to start with a WordPress.com blog. Just be ready to jump to WordPress.org as soon as traffic starts to rise, or as soon as you're ready to get more hands-on with your blog.

What if you really can't decide between the two? The key, to us at least, is people. If you know one or a few people who can help you with advice and tips on a WordPress.org blog, you can probably go ahead with it, knowing that you have some guidance available as you go "onward through the fog."

Even if you don't have friends who are WordPress.org users, this book is another clue. If you find yourself very much interested in the additional themes on WordPress.org and the plug-ins you can find there, or find yourself wanting to mess with code of one type or another, WordPress.org is probably for you.

If all that stuff seems scary, start with WordPress.com. Learn your way around and then, if you choose, move up to WordPress.org.

WORDPRESS DOCUMENTATION

Finding Your Way Through the Online Documents

It's fair to say that WordPress is fairly well documented and supported. It's also fair to say that WordPress is not very well documented and supported.

Huh? Right about now, you might be thinking of the old saying that you can't have it both ways.

Let's start with the optimistic view. For an open source project, WordPress is quite well documented. (Many open source projects lack any end-user documentation at all.) Support is also good, in a sense—there is some!

The pessimistic view is that even expert WordPress users complain about how long it can take to find information or get an answer. For those of us who aren't experts, and bring with us our expectations from working with commercial products, or in a workplace with decent IT support, WordPress documentation and support can look sparse indeed.

And for those of us who like printed manuals, there's nothing; it's all online. This does have the advantages of easy searchability and easy updating. But online documentation usually lacks the coherence, consistency, and high standards of editing of a good, printed document. Anyone in their right mind wants both, so each can support the other; but the official WordPress documentation is online only.

We invite you to spend a few minutes here to learn about the core WordPress documentation elements and what each of them does and doesn't do. This small investment of time now will save you many hours in the future by guiding you to the answers that are out there and by helping you avoid wasting time looking for answers that probably aren't easily found.

WordPress.com Documentation

Strictly speaking, there is no official WordPress.com documentation.

All Automattic offers is a guide to the existing documentation for WordPress—that is, for WordPress.org—with pointers to the parts that are most likely to be helpful to WordPress.com users.

The trouble is, the WordPress.org software has additional screens and additional fields on screens that are shared between the two. The WordPress.com user will find little depth on the relatively simple topics—simple, that is, to most WordPress.org users—that he or she is likely to worry about. At the same time, there's a lot of extraneous stuff that the WordPress.com user doesn't even need to know about.

It's a bit like exploring the moon by starting with a map of the universe, then crossing off all the parts that aren't the moon. In the official WordPress documentation, there isn't actually a map of just the moon.

This book attempts to improve on the situation by providing WordPress.com-specific information along the way. However, there's still a lack of specific information for the WordPress.com user. If you are using WordPress.com, you'll have to learn to wear blinders and ignore WordPress.org stuff that doesn't apply to you while you find the information and support you need for WordPress.com.

The WordPress Codex

The WordPress Codex is the first place to look for information about using WordPress. It's the closest thing to official documentation that WordPress has. Visit the WordPress Codex at http://codex.wordpress.org, as shown in Figure B.1.

Many people use the Codex, though, without realizing it's a wiki. A what, you might say? A *wiki* is an online storage capability for articles from a variety of people. Posting to a wiki is usually pretty much unrestricted, and editing is done by volunteers. The results can be pretty good, especially for broad, complicated topics with fast-changing information.

The best-known wiki is, of course, Wikipedia, the online encyclopedia that takes as its subject, well, everything. Tellingly, Wikipedia has recently had to tighten up its procedures after some people posted opinions as if they were facts. The WordPress Codex still allows absolutely anyone to add to or edit most of the pages in it.

The WordPress community is very strong and does a good job of maintaining the WordPress Codex. However, to have a wiki as the gold standard of a product's documentation, rather than as a supportive element to a professionally written and maintained core, is a bit unnerving.

There actually is an official WordPress document, the WordPress User Handbook. It's worth reading to get a coherent view of WordPress.org—not WordPress.com, sorry—straight from the horse's mouth, so to speak. The Handbook can suffer from versionitis; at this writing, the Handbook is one release behind the current version of the software, making it out of date in parts. Visit the WordPress User Handbook, as shown in Figure B.2, at http://wordpress.org/docs.

Figure B.1
The Codex is near-official WordPress documentation.

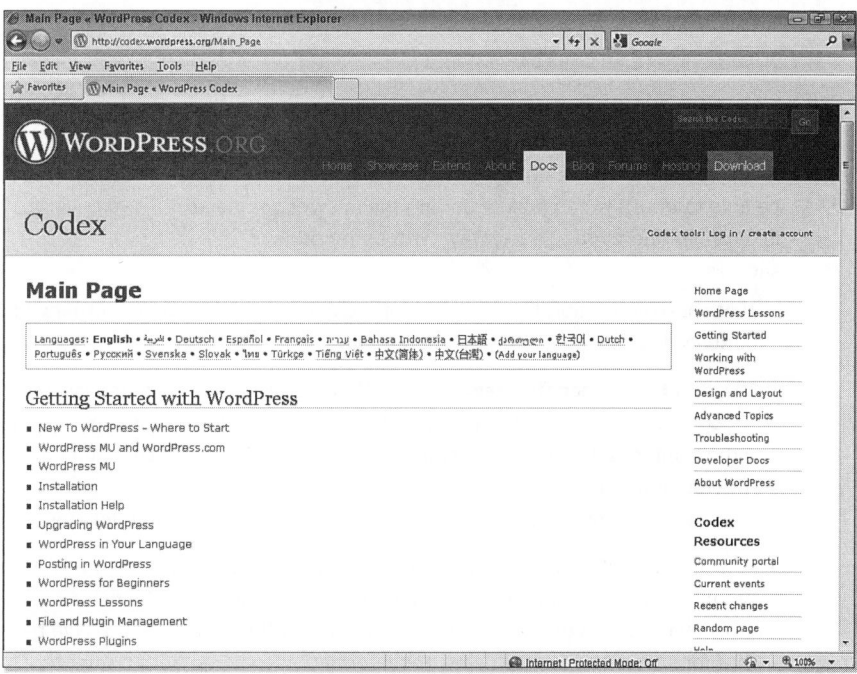

Figure B.2
The Handbook is one coherent, if sometimes out-dated, document.

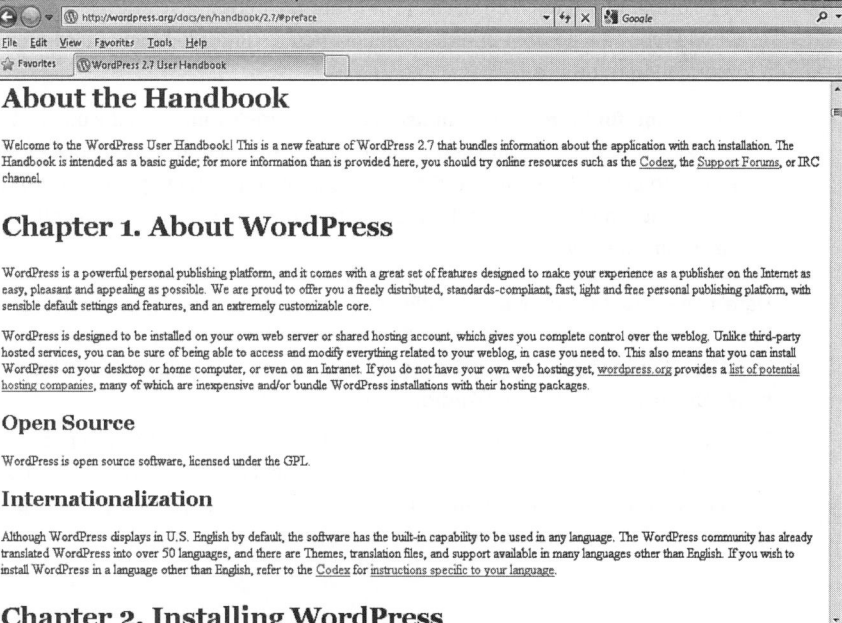

Problems with WordPress Documentation

Sometimes, when you run into problems with something, it's good to know that someone else has had the same problem; it lets you know you're not alone. Thus reassured, you might be able to return to the task of finding the answer you need in a calmer and more relaxed way, with better odds of success.

 **note**
The WordPress Codex is a replacement for a previous wiki, called MediaWiki, that broke down because it was hard to use and disorganized. That's none too reassuring.

In that constructive spirit, here's a list of the main problems we and others whom we know have experienced with WordPress documentation:

- **Hard to find a specific answer**—Most WordPress users search for the answers they need using Google. Because there's so much WordPress information online, finding something resembling official information on a topic can be very difficult. It's quite common to find WordPress-related information that isn't quite what you need—for instance, information about a popular plug-in from a developer when you want information about plug-ins in general.

- **Out-of-date information**—This takes two forms. The first is that the WordPress community might not have gotten around to updating information yet. The more subtle problem is that the documentation might look fine to the many WordPress users who have been around a long time, but for newer and novice users, the information could do with a rewrite.

- **Wrong technical level for many**—The WordPress documentation, along with the vast majority of information online about WordPress and books about WordPress, are oriented to a core audience of longtime WordPress.org users. (There are no longtime WordPress.com users, as it's relatively new.) If you're a newbie of either version, you're going to have a hard time understanding the information out there.

- **Misleading for WordPress.com users**—Automattic's refusal to document WordPress.com properly, along with their confusing naming of the two most-used versions of WordPress, makes it very hard on the beginners and "light" users who mostly populate WordPress.com. (Sorry to be harsh, but WordPress.org is the product that provides most of Automattic's sources of income, so this seems deserved.)

Here's an example of how the WordPress documentation can let users down. Let's say you go to the WordPress.com site and click on the Support link. Now if you're a WordPress.com user, you might have heard or read something about plug-ins—which, you will probably know by this point in this book, are only supported on WordPress.org.

But if you search for help on plug-ins from within WordPress.com, you're not told this fundamental fact; instead, you get links to a bunch of forums, where people who don't know this crucial information repeatedly ask for help on how to do so. (One recent topic is "Yet Another Discussion About Plug-Ins," showing how this repeatedly comes up.)

Using Google to Access WordPress Documentation

Google is a great search engine, but it (and other search engines) can work against you by being so comprehensive. They reach out very broadly—to conversations that might be on a subtly or completely different topic to what you're interested in—and back in time, for instance, to comments about older versions of WordPress.

Here are a few WordPress tricks that might help you get better results on your search:

- **Use the word *WordPress* in your search**—No matter how WordPress-specific a word might seem to you—theme, plug-in, and so on—it almost certainly has many other meanings as well. Include the word *WordPress* in your search to narrow the results.

- **Use *site:wordpress.org*—Along with your Google search, you can include the phrase *site:wordpress.org*. This limits your search to information on the WordPress.org site. This cuts out a lot of unrelated information.

- **Use *site:codex.wordpress.org*—To search only within the Codex, include the phrase *site:codex.wordpress.org*. This limits your search to the Codex only, as shown in Figure B.3.

Figure B.3
You can get straight into the Codex from Google.

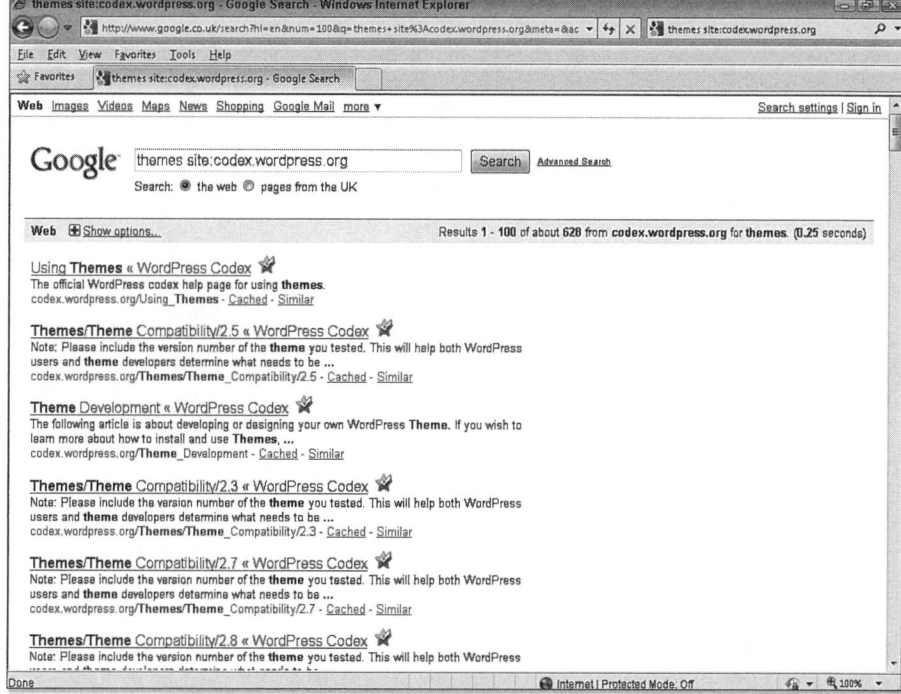

- **Use search within the WordPress.com site**—The WordPress.com site is a good (not great) place to search for information specific to WordPress.com, or even for beginner information for WordPress.org. Just visit http://support. wordpress.com to start your search.

- **Use Lorelle on WordPress**—One of the best blogs and resources about WordPress is the Lorelle on WordPress blog at http://lorelle.wordpress.com. (Yes, wordpress.com!) Additional information can be found at http://codex. wordpress.org/User:Lorelle.

- **Use the Google Toolbar**—Opening up a search window every time you need a little help can be cumbersome, and the built-in search area found in many web browsers can be too small for complex, WordPress-related searches. The Google Toolbar provides more room and is always available in your browser, without opening a new window. (The Chrome web browser from Google allows you to type search querries into the address bar, eliminating the problem of a lack of space.)

 tip

If you're a WordPress.com user, always start any email or message board query by clearly stating that you're seeking an answer for WordPress.com. The same goes for in-person conversations and phone calls. Most WordPress users are very much steeped in WordPress.org; if you don't limit the conversation up front, you're likely to get a confusing answer that doesn't apply to you.

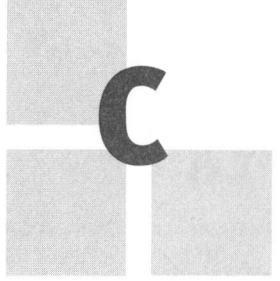

EXAMPLES OF WORDPRESS BLOGS

Why Look at Famous Blogs?

The famous inventor Thomas Alva Edison once said that genius is 1% inspiration and 99% perspiration. Looking at well-known and well-implemented WordPress blogs can help with the inspiration part. Even more important, it can help you put your perspiration into a direction that's likely to be productive.

The WordPress community is not a marketing machine in the usual sense, but it does celebrate and publicize its successful members pretty effectively. For a long list that's got a lot of good examples, visit http://codex.wordpress.org/User:Matt/Famous_Blogs.

Another great place for inspiration is the frequently updated WordPress Showcase site at http://wordpress.org/showcase. Doug Hanna from Automattic links to the blogs of the famous, but also to sites that use WordPress in a unique or innovative way. Ratings are implemented on the Showcase, so you can vote for your favorites, too.

As you spend more time with WordPress, you're likely to pay more attention to the WordPress logo showing up in odd places on the Web. Some business and other websites are entirely WordPress-driven, and show the WordPress logo on the tab of your browser as you go through the site. Other sites have a WordPress blog integrated into a non-WordPress site, and the WordPress logo only appears on the bloggy bits.

Here, we've picked a few blogs that we think illustrate some of the best uses of the capabilities of WordPress. Do your own research to find examples that are inspiring to you—and, perhaps, work on your own blog until it's worthy of someone's "Famous Blogs" list.

XXL

XXL is a "real" magazine—and XXL uses WordPress to host a lively, "real" website. As you visit the site, you'll see fully capable site navigation, a News feed, a Twitter link, and more.

Visit www.xxlmag.com to see the home page of XXL, which receives a constant stream of updates. WordPress also makes it easy for the site to put bloggers front and center. This is vital for a magazine website that can use the blogs to host constant live information, without a lot of hassle—and with a mix, perhaps, of paid and unpaid contributors.

Click the Bloggers link to visit the Bloggers page. You can see a mix of brands, famous and not-so-famous faces and names, and more. Again, XXL doesn't have to invest a lot of money to develop full blogging capability; it's all part of WordPress.

Not to say this kind of effort is cheap—but the money can go into what people see rather than the software back end. And because WordPress is open source, XXL can make changes when they need to.

You probably shouldn't expect to get a look like XXL's, not to mention the same level of interactivity or advertising support, on your own; the XXL site is clearly a big project.

Surfin' Safari

We kind of hoped this was a blog about surfing—and it is, in a way. The topic, though, is web surfing, not waxing down our surfboards and not being able to wait for June.

WebKit, a toolkit for web browser development, is one of the most important open source projects around—not quite as important as WordPress, perhaps. It's used as the core of Apple's Safari browser and many other famous browsers, including several smartphone browsers.

Figure C.1 shows the home page for Surfin' Safari. It's much more a typical blog than the XXL site—far less customization and eye candy. Surfin' Safari is just the facts, but still presented in a clean, attractive style.

Surfin' Safari gives developers, or just interested members of the public, an easy and familiar way to get information and interact with the WebKit team—a great example of what a blog is all about.

 tip

If you want to have a little fun, look up the website rankings for some of these famous blogs at www.alexa.com. Your blog might someday get more traffic than some of the famous ones!

Figure C.1
Surfin' Safari
is the home
for WebKit
development.

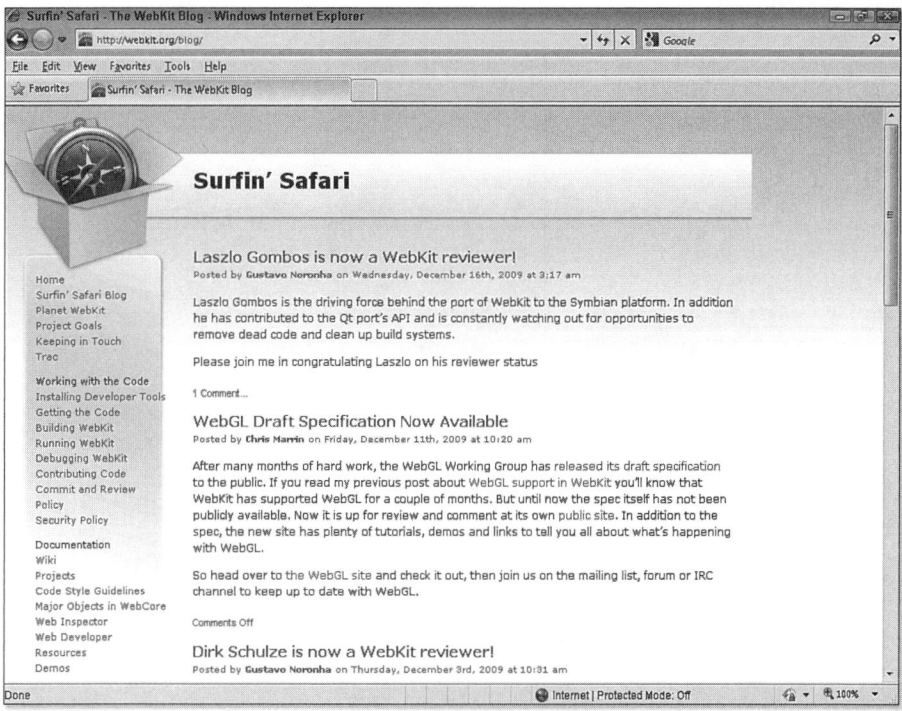

New Kids on the Block

New Kids on the Block are very famous in the United Kingdom and some other countries, less so in some others. They stopped performing for a while but have recently come back.

Their blog is located at http://nkotb.com/blog/—try saying "nkotb" three times fast! The New Kids on the Block blog is a simple WordPress blog. You'll recognize the archives list, similar to hundreds of other WordPress blogs you've seen.

You could put together a blog like this yourself, using the WordPress software or even WordPress.com. Some of the content is of wider interest than most of us could get—for example, video clips with band members and tickets for their upcoming concerts. (I suppose we, the authors of this book, could do a video interview with each other. But if we performed in concert, somehow it's unlikely that TicketMaster would be handling the tickets!)

The formats, though, are familiar. The videos are hosted on YouTube, there's a simple categorization of posts into Blog posts and News posts, and other familiar WordPress blog elements.

So the New Kids on the Block site is a great example of the type of thing you could hope to do yourself—and perhaps even take further than the New Kids have.

EXAMPLES OF WORDPRESS.COM BLOGS

Equal Representation for .commies

Remember how we've said that the WordPress community as a whole tends to neglect hosted WordPress.com blogs in favor of WordPress.org blogs? Not always, it seems. There's a site for WordPress.com Weblog Awards that highlights excellent work on the WordPress.com site. Visit http://weblogawards.wordpress.com/.

Take a look at the blogs highlighted here, and others on the WordPress.com Weblog Awards, to see more of what you can do with WordPress.com, and just how many famous people and organizations don't feel the need to hassle with directly using the software from WordPress.org.

Famous Quotes

The Web is perhaps the single greatest machine for looking up quotes ever invented. It's certainly enriched our writing.

The Quotes Famous Quotes site doesn't even have its own URL—it's at http://quotes.wordpress.com, as shown in Figure D.1. It uses a very ordinary template—the header is even the famous WordPress blue. Yet it's full of life and individuality.

It has integrated Twitter updates, comments with images, and more. You can do all of this yourself on your own blog.

Or, you can just look at the cool quotes. Here's a favorite of ours, from Lisa Hoffman, the wife of Dustin Hoffman and owner of a skin care and fragrance line: "Love is like pi—natural, irrational, and very important."

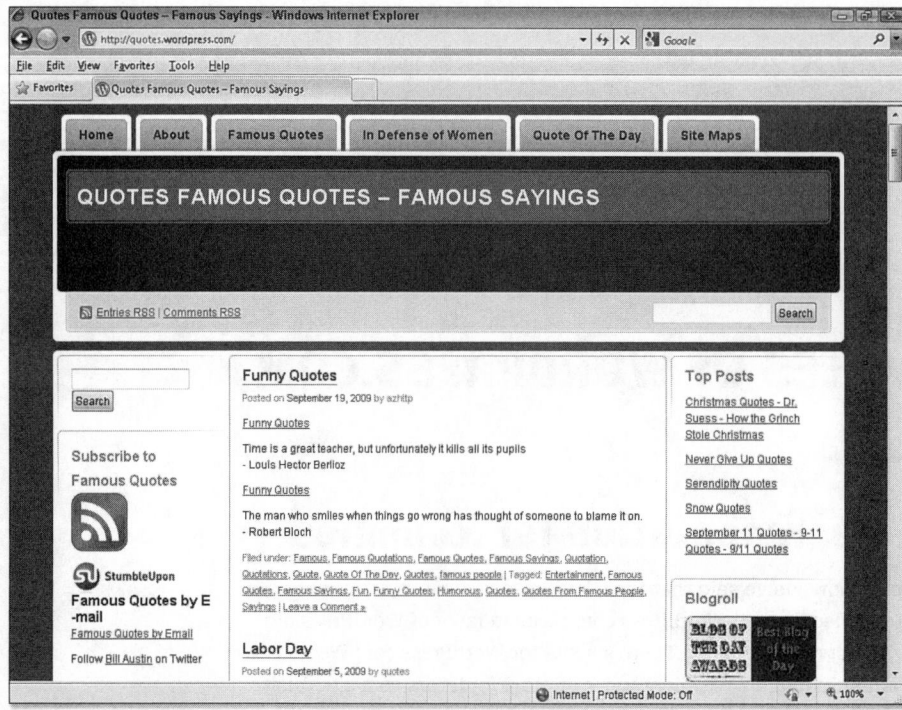

Figure D.1
The Quotes Famous Quotes blog shows off what you can do with WordPress.com.

The Outland Institute

The Outland Institute site is the web home of a famous radio show from Joy 94.9, a radio station in Australia. Figure D.2 shows their award-winning site, which you can find at http://outlandinstitute.wordpress.com.

This site is even more basic than the Quotes Famous Quotes site. Design-wise, it probably represents just a few hours' work, yet it has great stuff on it.

Because the design of the site isn't anything fancy, we have to think that the content tipped the scales in favor of Joy 94.9. Any site that has a story about Great TV Moustaches has something special going for it. Starting, of course, with Tom Selleck as *Magnum, P.I.*, then going on to David Hasselhoff on *Knight Rider*, and others.

 note

We know David Hasselhoff didn't have a moustache as Michael Knight on *Knight Rider*—but he did when he was playing his character's evil twin brother, Garthe Knight!

Figure D.2
The Outland
Institute
blog is, well,
Outland-ish.

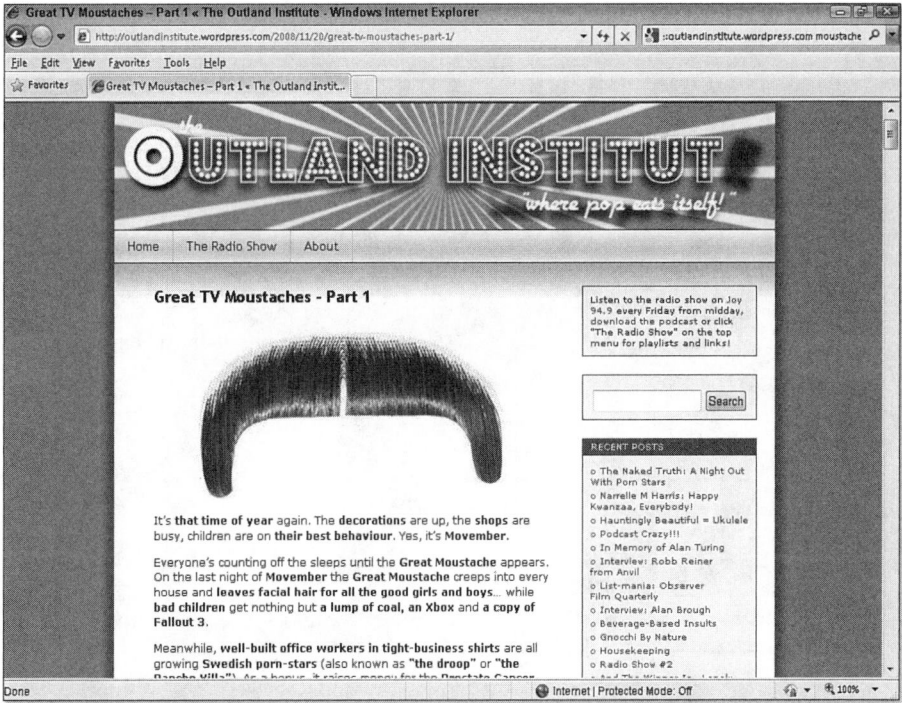

Music at SFSU

One of the early dreams for the Web was the same as the early dreams for television—that it would be a home for science, art, music, and much more that's uplifting.

At a time when I Can Haz Cheezburger, a site hosting captioned photos of cats, is a big hit, perhaps the dream has not been fully dreamt quite yet. But the JPLL Music News site at http://jpllmusicnews.wordpress.com is inspiring, both from a design point of view as well as its content. The site is shown in Figure D.3.

This site is an example of robust use of different design, along with lots of graphics, video, and audio.

The blog bravely uses white on black, and even orange on black, text. We find it a bit hard to read, but it's different and interesting looking.

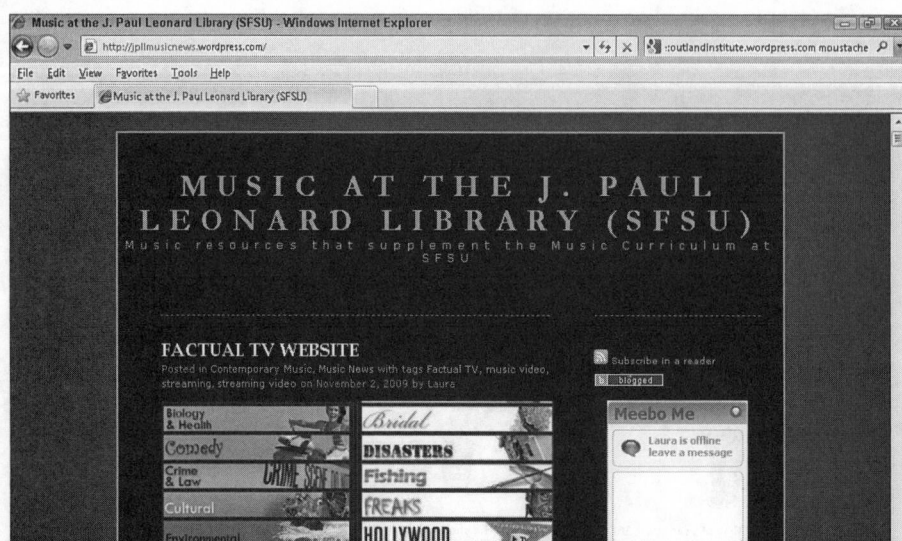

Figure D.3
San Francisco State University strikes the right note.

All of the content is tied to the music curriculum at San Francisco State University, which means it's hardly all classical—punk, rock, jazz, and blues figure prominently.

Enjoy your visit to this site, and use it to inspire your own use of graphics and multimedia.

WORDPRESS SITE MAPS

Navigating the WordPress Sites

WordPress.com and WordPress.org are big sites and it can be difficult to find your way around. We want to save you some time by describing the areas of each site, with an emphasis on where to go for specific problems.

Some of the details might change periodically; WordPress, after all, is a dynamic system.

Navigating WordPress.com

Blogging at WordPress.com is supposed to be easy—and it is, until you try to push the envelope a little. As you become more familiar with WordPress' capabilities, you may run into trouble, and find yourself looking for help more often. Knowing where to look for help is often a critical part of the battle. This section will help you find the assistance you need.

Home Page: http://wordpress.com

As you might expect, the WordPress.com home page is targeted mainly for people interested in blogging and convincing them to do so with WordPress. The site is also for people who just want to browse through blogs. The bulk of the page features 11 "freshly pressed" blog posts representing some of the best of the last 24 hours on WordPress.com. The 12th box offers statistics on the number of bloggers, new posts, comments, and total words on the site. The right column gives visitors reasons to join the blogging party at WordPress.com and the obligatory registration link.

Across the top of the page is a small bar for logging in to your blog and a search box for people to find blogs to read.

Navigation options sit at the bottom of the home page along with links to other official WordPress sites. A rotating set of visual links to auxiliary WordPress sites gets its own box, and links to current posts on the WordPress.com blog round out the page. Our tour focuses on the six links off the home page (see Figure E.1).

ON WORDPRESS.COM
24/7 Support
Forums
Free Features
Premium Features
VIP Hosting
Advanced Services
Popular Tags

Figure E.1
WordPress.com is organized into these sections, located in the lower-left corner of the home page.

Support Options: http://en.support.wordpress.com

The Support page at WordPress.com has a much plainer look than the home page. It's composed almost entirely of links to various help pages. Under the search box at the top, you'll see answers to common beginner questions and a description of the differences between WordPress.com and WordPress.org.

Common support topics are listed in the right navigation column, but save yourself an extra click by scrolling down this page, as links to many common issues can be found here. The navigation column also has a list of recently updated support articles. Look here for answers to new problems.

If the articles in this area aren't solving your problem, and searching the forum isn't working for you either, click Contact Us to work with WordPress.com support directly. There's a simple form to fill out (Figure E.2). Include your name and email address so support can contact you. Point to your blog's URL so the staff can see what's happening. Define your problem briefly in the Subject line. Use the drop-down menu to select the appropriate topic area. Finally, fully describe your problem in the message box. You can erase the default questions ("I did..., I saw..., and I expected..."), but they do help you focus your description. Click the Contact Support button to send the form to the Support team.

When your problem is solved, and if you then feel moved to say something nice to your support staff—many of whom are volunteers—you might find your comment (with a link to your blog) on the Support Hugs page.

Figure E.2
The
WordPress.
com Support
form lists the
questions
you should
answer in
describing
your
problem.

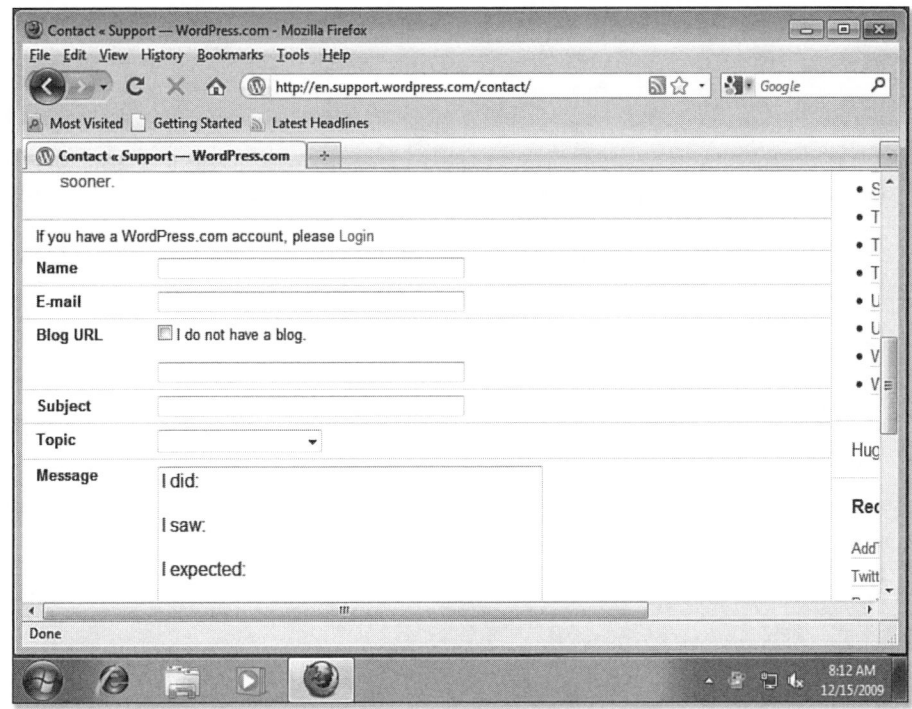

Forums: http://en.forums.wordpress.com/

Click the Forums link in the lower-right corner of a WordPress.com page to find help from other users. Use the search box to find topics relevant to your issue, or dive right in. Log in with your WordPress.com username before posting, then read the "Eight Things to Know Before Posting in WordPress.com Forums" post at the top of the page.

From the main forums page shown in Figure E.3, you can review the latest discussions to see if there's something you can help with, or use the left navigation column to find the correct forum area. Discussions are tagged, so you can find common topics there too.

As you participate in the forums, you can mark discussions as a "favorite." This creates an RSS feed for the topic that you can follow in a feed reader.

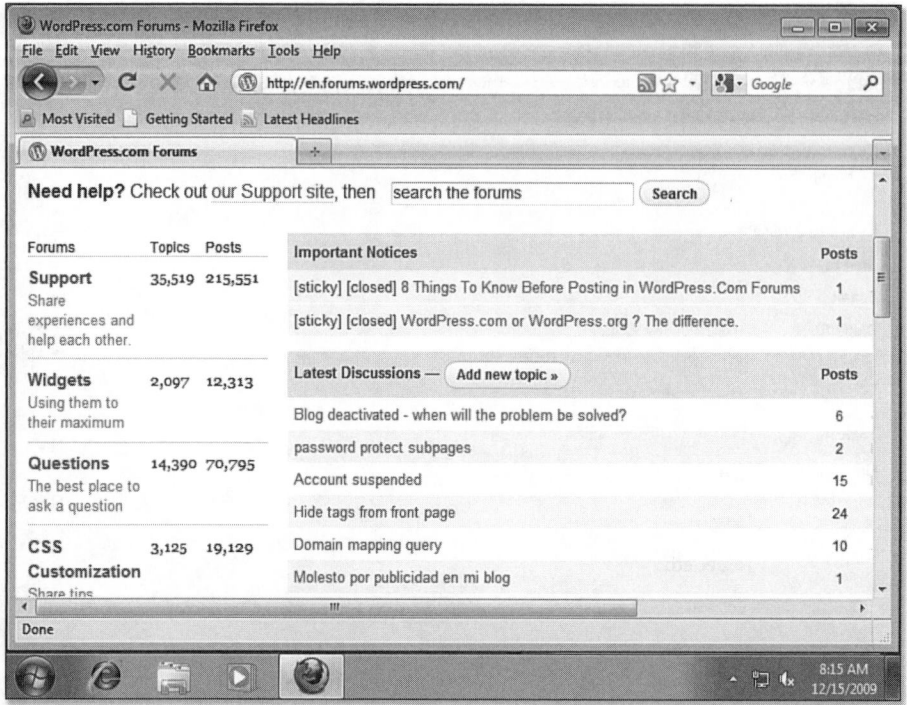

Figure E.3
Visit the
WordPress.com
Forums to get
help from
other users.

Features: http://en.wordpress.com/features

The marketing pages shown in Figure E.4 spotlight the features that come with every free
WordPress.com blog. Some items link to further explanations of some features (such as the tagging
system and Akismet). Other items link to the premium features offered for extra money.

News: http://en.blog.wordpress.com

Find the News page in a tab at the top of the Features, News, Support, and Advanced pages, or in
the bottom navigation. This opens the WordPress.com blog, where WordPress developers highlight
new features (usually ported over from WordPress.org) available to the hosted service.

As you might expect, the WordPress.com blog shown in Figure E.5 includes widgets that search,
display monthly archives, and display a tag cloud. Two RSS feeds, for posts and comments, are also
available. Click Subscribe Me to receive blog posts by email.

Figure E.4
Need more persuasion to start blogging at WordPress.com? Look at all these features!

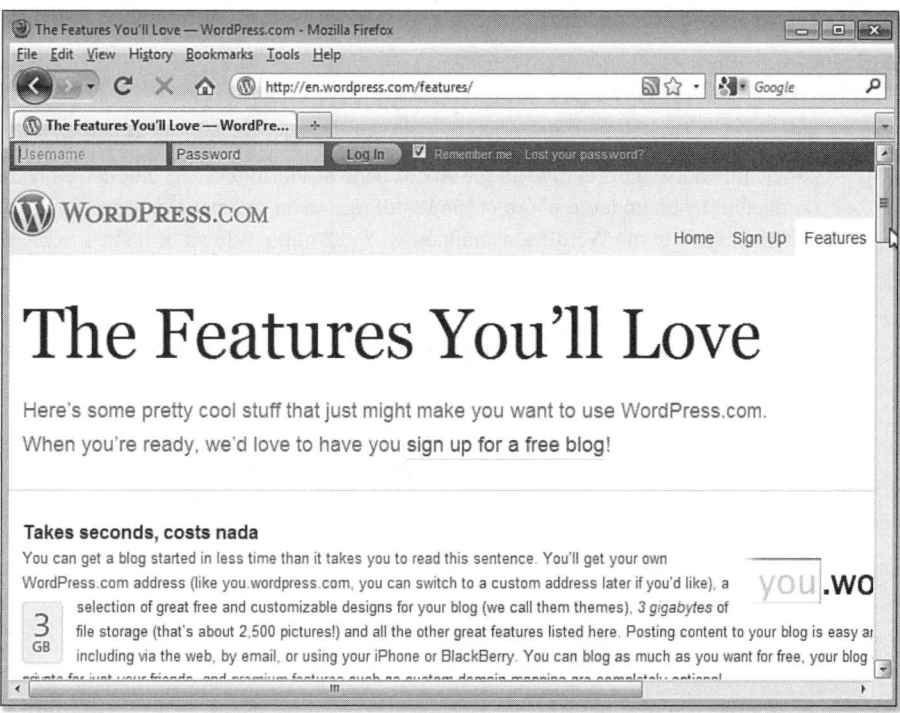

Figure E.5
A blogging platform needs a blog, no? Keep up with what's new at WordPress.com at the News page.

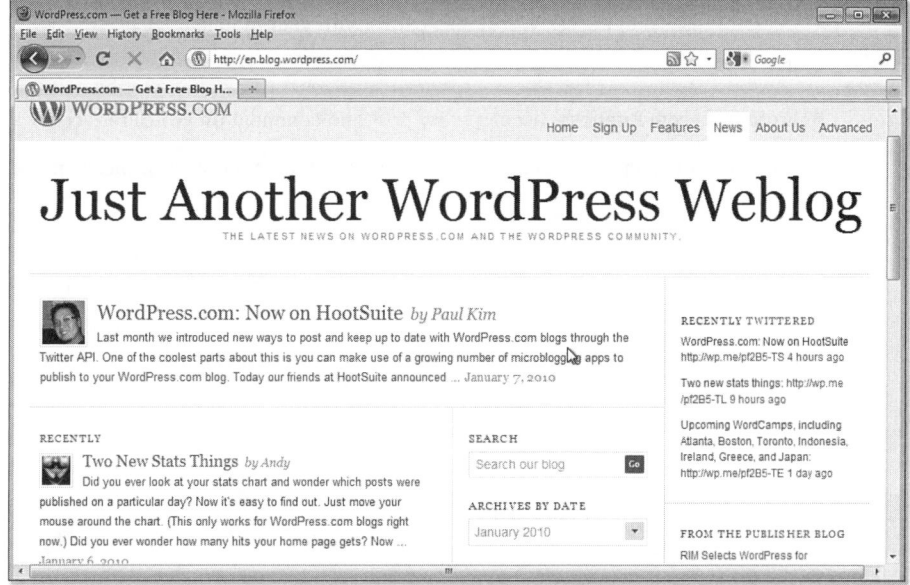

You can also see the recent Twitter feed for the blog and see the latest posts to the WordPress Publisher Blog at Automattic.

About Us: http://en.wordpress.com/about

Find the About Us page only from the tab at the top of the Features, News, Support, and Advanced pages. It is not as informative as the About page at WordPress.org, but certainly more personable. Dominated by an undated photo of the WordPress team, the page explains some of the shared values and norms of the WordPress community. You'll get a little bit of history, some community rules, and philosophy.

Advanced Services: http://en.wordpress.com/advanced-services

Find the Advanced Services page shown in Figure E.6 either from the tabbed interface at the top of the Features, News, Support, and About Us pages, or in the navigation area at the bottom of any page. The page includes links to features used by the more savvy users—like you! Some of these items are free; others have a cost. All of these have been covered in other places in this book. These items include the following:

- WordPress.com premium features

- WordPress.com VIP hosting

- WordPress.org

- Translate.WordPress.com (for people who can help translate English pages to other languages)

- m.WordPress.com; access WordPress pages with your mobile device

- Site stats

- WordPress.com Firehose; access every post and comment on WordPress.com

- IM.WordPress.com; read posts and comments through your instant messaging client

Figure E.6
Get more out of WordPress at the Advanced Services page at WordPress. com.

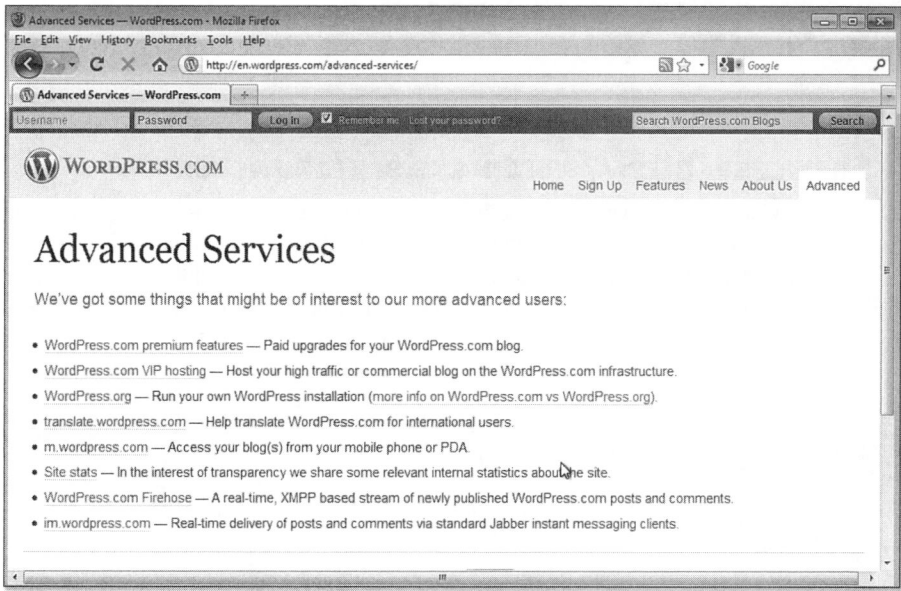

Navigating WordPress.org

Because Automattic largely tends to the administration of WordPress.com, there are far fewer things that can go wrong than with self-hosted WordPress.org software. Therefore, this site has more information and support options. Because people can be a lot more creative with a WordPress.org installation, there are also more demonstrations of that creativity here.

The community ethic that permeates WordPress.org offers you opportunities to become an active contributor. Use the site to submit your best ideas, help other users in the forums, contribute to the Codex—whatever you think you can do.

Home Page: http://wordpress.org

As with WordPress.com, the home page shown in Figure E.7 is targeted mainly for people interested in installing the WordPress software, not current users. There's a prominent download link front and center. At the bottom are links to common places a new or would-be user would like to go: the WordPress Books page, the Development blog, the install process (find a host, install the software, Read the Fine Manual), and the Showcase of unique and well-known WordPress sites.

Across the top is a tabbed navigation bar, which is the focus of our tour. The WordPress.org search engine is also in the upper-right corner. Type your search terms and click Go for a standard, full-text search of the site.

Figure E.7
Navigation for WordPress.org is at the top of the home page.

Figure E.7
Navigation for WordPress.org is at the top of the home page.

Showcase: http://wordpress.org/showcase

The WordPress Showcase shown in Figure E.8 highlights famous, notable, and unique uses of WordPress across the Web. Automattic staff selects the sites to showcase based on things they see and on submissions. This offers potential users a sense of the "big players" who are already part of the WordPress community. It also offers current users some inspiration about the kinds of innovative and creative things you can do with your own site.

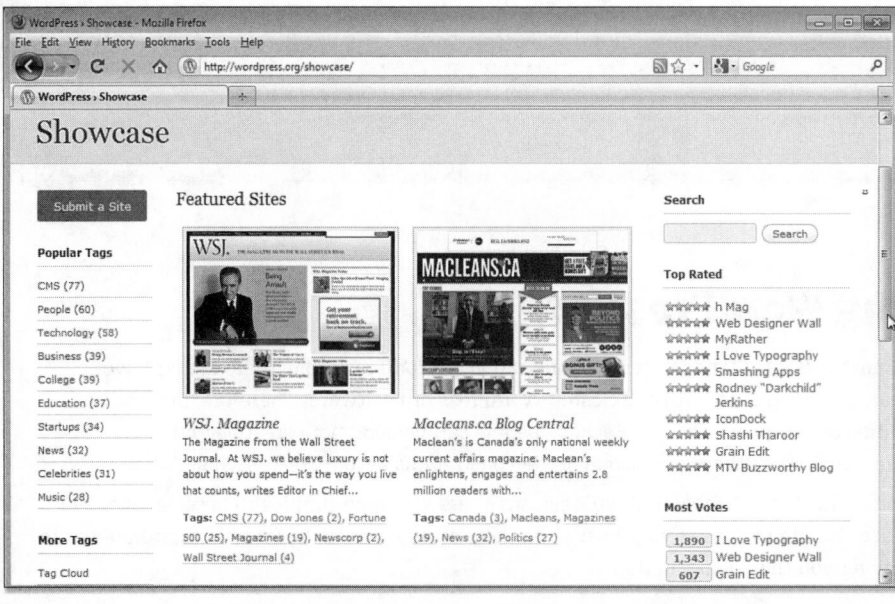

Figure E.8
Inspiration and the chance for fame await you at the WordPress Showcase.

Click on any link in the Showcase to view commentary on why a site was selected. Click Visit Site (or the graphic) to check out the site yourself. When you return, offer your own commentary by giving the site a star rating.

You'll find navigational aids on the left, via the tagging system. Each site is tagged based on the flavor of the software it's using (WordPress, WordPress.com, WordPress MU, BuddyPress) and the type of site it is or area it covers (news, college, technology, personal, and the like).

Featured and Recently Added sites are located in the center of the main Showcase page, offering another entry point into the system. The right column displays the user rating results.

Have you found a WordPress site worthy of including in the Showcase? Do you think your site is especially creative, innovative, or otherwise noteworthy? Click Submit a Site, read the rules for inclusion, and explain why you think the site belongs. Someday you too might see your site among the chosen.

Themes, Plug-Ins, and Places to Complain: http://wordpress.org/extend

This page, shown in Figure E.9, is primarily devoted to the creativity and participation of the WordPress community in developing the platform. It's the place to see (and download) user-contributed themes and plug-ins, the place to offer ideas to the core team for future versions of WordPress, and the place to anonymously complain (or kvetch, for those in a Yiddish mood) about the WordPress software you already have.

Figure E.9
Enhance your site with themes and plug-ins, then offer your own ideas on how to extend WordPress.

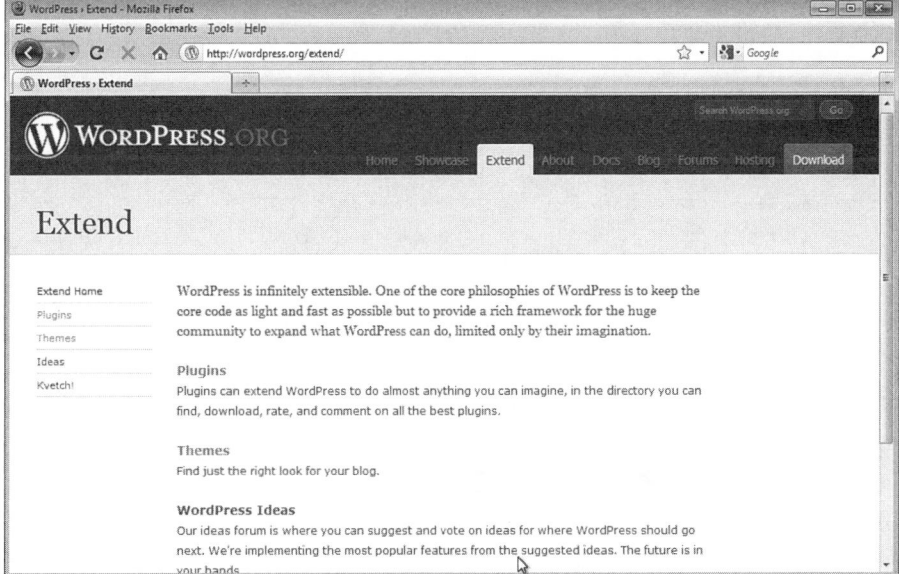

We've devoted large chunks of previous chapters to working with the Free Themes Directory (see Chapter 12, "The WordPress Toolkit: Themes") and the Plug-in Directory (see Chapter 13, "The WordPress Toolkit: Plug-Ins"). Let's look at the other parts of this area here.

WordPress Ideas: http://wordpress.org/extend/ideas

One day, you will wake up with the most brilliant idea for making your blog the best ever. You'll say to yourself "Well, certainly WordPress can do this thing for me," and search through the widgets and settings to see what's there that you can bend to your will. Many times, you will find the right combination to do what you want. But as brilliant and creative as you are, perhaps no one else has thought of this exact thing before. When that happens, it's time to visit the Ideas page. This is a marketplace of proposals and suggestions for WordPress.

When you arrive, you'll see the number of total ideas (2,900 at this writing), the latest ideas, and the most popular ideas on the site (see Figure E.10). To propose your idea, you must first register with the Ideas site. Enter your preferred username and an email address, and some optional information. You'll get a password emailed to you, and then you can both rate other ideas and propose your own.

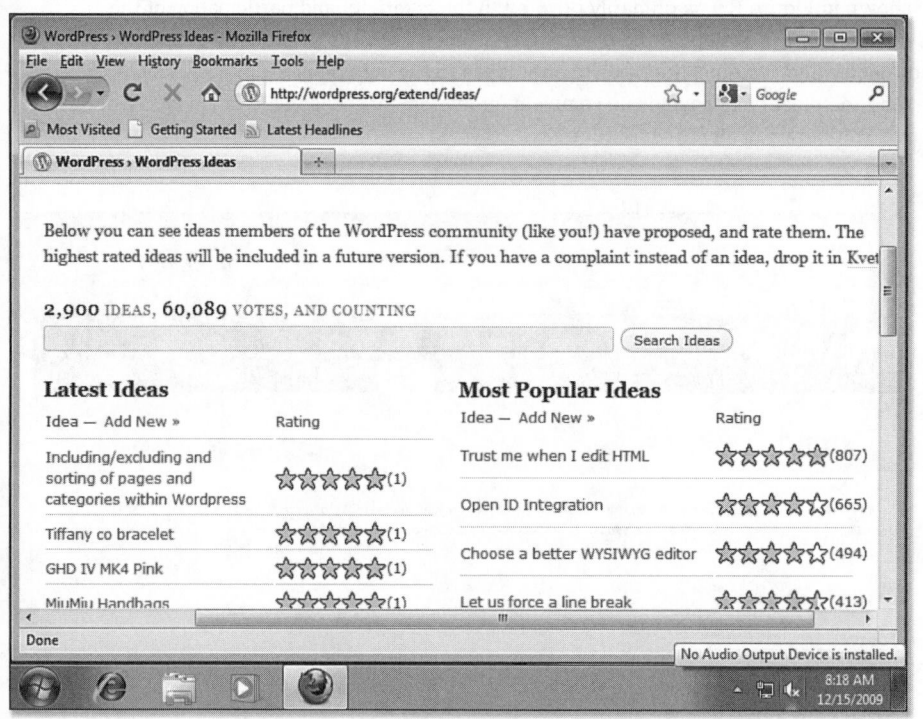

Figure E.10
Do you have a great idea for WordPress? Submit it here, and rate other ideas, too.

Before submitting an idea, use the search to see if others had the same one. Because the site promises that "the highest rated ideas *will* be included in a future version" (emphasis added), it's better that 500 people declare their preference for a "different WYSIWIG editor" in one spot with a high rating, instead of having dozens of separate proposals to change editors, with varying ratings.

Once you've registered and received your password, log in to the Ideas site. Now at the bottom of the main Ideas page, you'll see the Propose an Idea section. Type your one-line summary and then fill up the edit box with additional information about your idea. Try to think of it from the point of view of the WordPress people—don't describe only what you want to do, but also describe, as exactly as you can, what needs to change in the software for you to be able to do it. This not only makes your idea easier to implement if it's chosen, but you also get more respect—and, therefore, more support—from the WordPress community, who will appreciate your clear and complete description. Add some tags at the bottom, and click Submit Idea.

Registered users also get access to four other areas of the Ideas site. Use these to explore other people's ideas and rate and comment on them:

- You haven't rated—This page displays five random ideas that you haven't voted on. Give a star rating to each, and you'll get a new batch.

- Implemented—This is proof the Ideas site works. This is a list of ideas that have become part of WordPress to date. Note that it doesn't always require a massive outpouring of user demand to get something implemented. Sometimes all it takes is a simple, easily programmed idea.

- Under Consideration—This is the category where all new ideas go. Each page contains 18 ideas and their current cumulative rating. Click any idea to add your rating.

- Addressed by Plug-in—Your idea might not be in WordPress core yet, but a plug-in developer has already scratched your itch.

The Ideas site is a great way for ordinary users who don't write software or design themes to give back to the community. Take advantage of the opportunity to shape WordPress' future!

Kvetch! http://wordpress.org/extend/kvetch

Some days are filled with sweetness and light and love for the goodness that is WordPress. Other days, WordPress is just driving you up the wall. The Kvetch! page is here for those less-than-sunny days.

No registration is necessary for this part of WordPress.org; just type in your anonymous complaint about the software. Click Kvetch It! Your complaint flies into the development team's mailbox.

What's more fun for the rest of us is that all the kvetches are stored in another database table. Whenever someone opens the page, a database query asks to display a random kvetch at the top of the page. Click the Load Another link to see another one.

The World of WordPress: http://wordpress.org/about

This area is about background information and promotion (see Figure E.11). It serves to introduce you to the WordPress community. As with any community, there are shared values and norms. You can learn a bit about those here. You'll get a little bit of history, some community rules, and philosophy. Transparency being an important value, there are links to the blogs of each senior member of the development team in the right column.

Be sure to explore the links in the section called "Connect with the Community." You'll find the forums and mailing lists and see if there's a WordCamp coming to a city near you.

Along the left column are pointers to the practical considerations of getting WordPress—the technical requirements, feature list, technical road map for upcoming versions of WordPress, and books to help you along the way. You'll also find statements of philosophy (including the meaning of open source software) and traditional legalisms surrounding privacy, usage of the term "WordPress" in other top-level domains (in brief: Don't), and the required publication of the GNU General Public License (GPL).

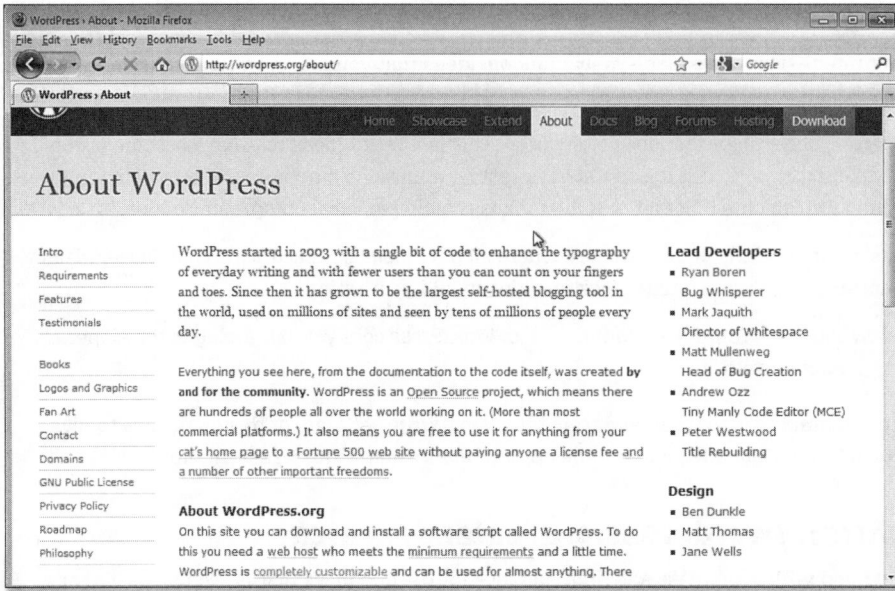

Figure E.11
Learn more about the WordPress community at the About page.

Finally, there is promotional material to be found on this page. There are testimonials from happy WordPressers, fan art, and official logos and graphics to splatter over your digital universe.

We covered the next tab, Docs, in Appendix B, "WordPress Documentation;" so we'll move on here.

Latest From the Developers: http://wordpress.org/development

The WordPress Development blog is located on this site, and its RSS feed is included in the default administration page Dashboard with every WordPress.org software installation. This is where WordPress developers keep the user base informed about new features and other things on the minds of the development team. You'll find requests for input, announcements of new beta versions ready for testing, and many other things directly related to developing the WordPress core. There's also a link to the WordPress Planet, a collection of feeds about WordPress from the team and other prominent WordPress folk.

Get Help From Your Peers: http://wordpress.org/support

If you have a problem, or want to clarify something about your blog, the first place to go is the Codex docs collection (see Figure E.12). If you can't find an answer there, or the problem is with a plug-in, theme, or something else, come to the Support Forums page. You should find help from one or more

 tip

If you're one of those people who prefer getting help via email instead of web forums, sign up for the WPGarage list at Yahoo! Groups. Visit http://tech.groups. yahoo.com/group/wpgarage for information.

of a multitude of helpful folk. Browse through the forum categories, do a direct search, or click a tag in the Hot Topics cloud to begin looking for answers.

Figure E.12 Get help for any issues at the WordPress. org forums.

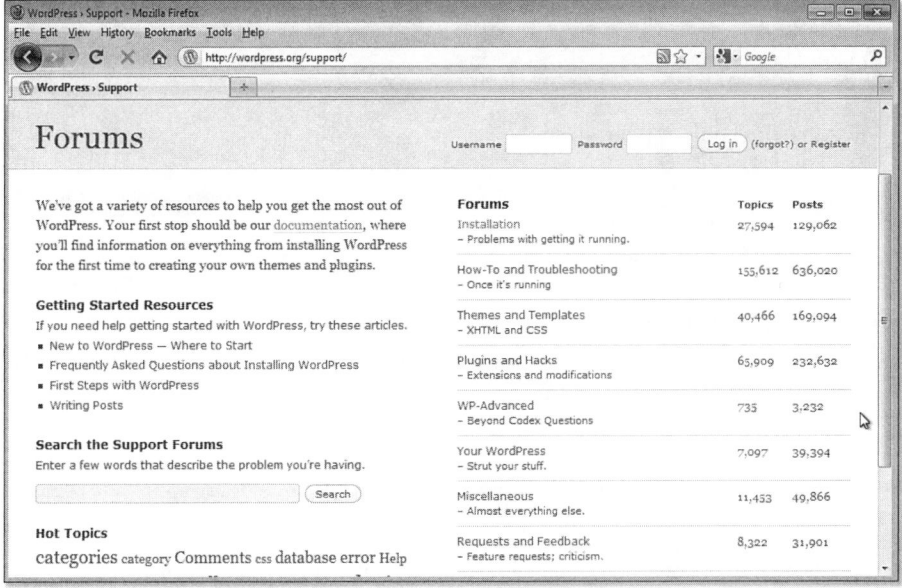

Finding a Host: http://wordpress.org/hosting

This page offers a few Web hosting firms that contribute to WordPress in exchange for a listing here. Learn more about selecting a host for your WordPress blog in "Finding a Blog-Friendly Host" in Chapter 11, "Installing and Upgrading WordPress Software."

Downloading WordPress: http://wordpress.org/download

The Download tab is colored differently than the other tabs on WordPress.org for a simple reason: It's often what people most want to do when they visit the site. This page makes it pretty easy to get the latest stable version, but that's not all. In the left column, shown in Figure E.13, are links for the increasingly adventurous user (or tester, or developer).

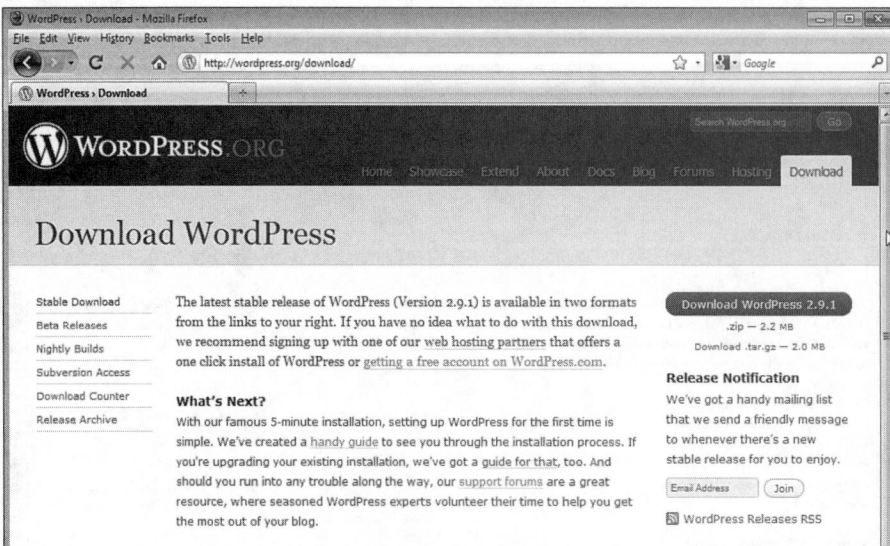

Figure E.13
Download the right WordPress for you, from stable to beyond bleeding edge.

The types of downloads, and who might find them interesting, follow:

- Stable Download—The safest choice. These versions appear every few months, and have gone through a fair amount of testing.

- Beta Releases—The prerelease version of the next release. Should be fairly stable, but some plug-ins might have issues. Use beta releases to test your configuration and help find bugs before installing on your host's server.

- Nightly Builds—The bleeding edge of development. As implied, things break—and get fixed—from day to day in these builds.

- Subversion Access—Beyond bleeding edge, this lets you check out, download, and compile the WordPress source code any time you want. You could, in theory, recompile WordPress each time any WordPress core developer in the world checked in a new file.

The last two items in the left side navigation are more informational. The Download Counter tells you how many times the current version of WordPress has been downloaded. The Release Archive contains links to every WordPress beta, release candidate, and released version, dating all the way back to 0.71. Don't ever put these versions on a production server!

That completes our tour of WordPress.org.

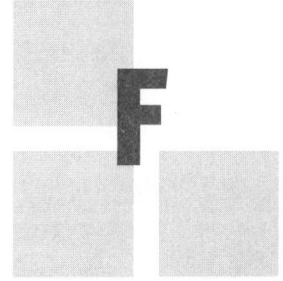

IMPORTING CONTENT FROM OTHER SYSTEMS

In Chapter 11, "Installing and Upgrading WordPress Software," we showed you how to transfer existing content from WordPress.com to WordPress.org. Although WordPress-to-WordPress conversions are pretty simple, you can move your content from most every popular blogging platform—and more than a few more obscure platforms as well—to WordPress.org.

In this appendix, we walk you through two methods of transferring posts and other data from another blogging platform into a self-hosted WordPress.org blog. The first is a direct import, which offers a fairly easy way to import. The second is to import content indirectly using either an RSS feed or (X)HTML files from the old blog.

The same WordPress.org Import tool we showed you in Chapter 11 (shown in Figure F.1) can handle nearly all of the platforms listed here, and a few more. WordPress.com users can generally do the same, with a few exceptions. These are all noted in the following platform descriptions.

If you don't see your platform here, many more are included in WordPress's guide to importing content at http://codex.wordpress.org/Importing_Content.

 caution

Before performing any of these import processes, back up your WordPress database. Back up the data on the other platform as well.

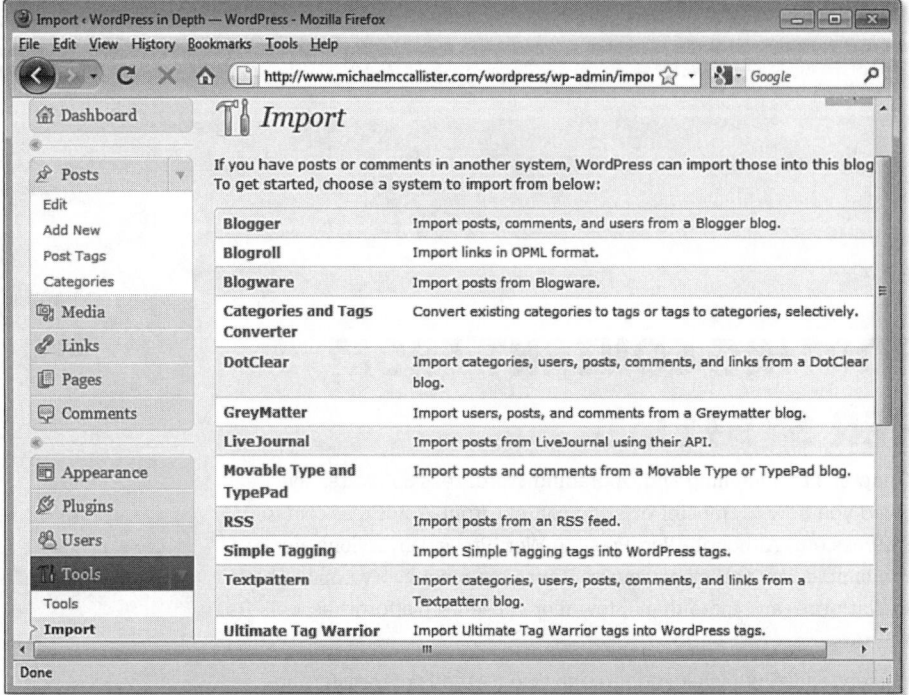

Figure F.1
Use the WordPress Import tool to get your posts from many other blog platforms.

Direct Import into WordPress

Transferring from Blogger/BlogSpot

What you'll get: Posts, comments, and users

WordPress.com: Yes

WordPress Importer: Yes

1. In the left navigation, click Tools, then Import.

2. Click the Blogger link.

3. Click Authorize. Google will ask you to confirm that it's OK for another website (WordPress) to access your Blogger account.

4. Type in the Google/Blogger login information (email address and password) to sign in. Again, Google will tell you that WordPress is requesting access to your Blogger account.

5. Click Grant Access. The WordPress importer will run. Depending on how much content you have at Blogger, this can take quite a long time. When it finishes, you'll be sent back to the WordPress Administration page. You should see the name of your Blogger blog.

6. Click Import. The text on the button changes to Importing…. When it is complete, it reads Set Authors.

7. Click Set Authors. The Blogger username displays on the left side of the page, and a drop-down menu containing your WordPress authors displays on the right.

8. Tell WordPress who is who. Because WordPress can handle multiple authors, and Blogger only gives you one, use this drop-down menu to define the Blogger username with the appropriate WordPress username. If it's just you, the task is easy.

9. Click Save Changes to complete the transfer.

Transferring from LiveJournal

What you'll get: Posts and comments

WordPress.com: Yes

WordPress Importer: Yes

1. In the left navigation, click Tools, then Import.

2. Enter your LiveJournal username and password so the importer can connect to your account.

3. If you have posts on LiveJournal labeled Private, you can include them in WordPress as password-protected posts. Type in the password you'd like for these posts in the Protected Post Password edit box.

4. Click Connect to LiveJournal and Import.

5. The importer will retrieve your posts, then your comments, then will organize comments in threads. When the process completes, click Have Fun! to display your blog with all your imported posts.

> **caution**
>
> The WordPress Importer will post all LiveJournal notes publicly unless you enter the Protected Post Password here.

Transferring from Movable Type/TypePad

What you'll get: Posts, comments, and trackbacks

WordPress.com: Yes

WordPress Importer: Yes

1. Export your content from the Movable Type or TypePad blog. From the Overview menu on your blog, click the Import/Export link.

2. Click the Export link at the bottom of the Import/Export page. Save to your computer as a .txt file.

3. Return to your WordPress Administration page. In the left navigation, click Tools, then Import.

4. Click the Movable Type/TypePad link.

5. Click Browse, and locate the exported text file from your other blog.

6. Click Upload File and Import. The importer runs, and displays a confirmation message when it's finished.

Transferring from Textpattern

What you'll get: Categories, users, posts, comments, and links

WordPress.com: No

WordPress Importer: Yes

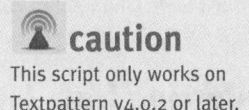

caution
This script only works on Textpattern v4.0.2 or later.

1. In the left navigation, click Tools, then Import.

2. Click the Textpattern link.

3. Enter your Textpattern information: Database User, Database Password, Database Name, Database Host, and Table Prefix (if any).

4. Click Import.

Indirect Transfer

Transferring from an RSS Feed

What you'll get: Posts and comments

WordPress.com: No

WordPress Importer: Yes

Practically all blogging platforms include Really Simple Syndication (RSS) feeds to allow readers to subscribe to and read blogs in a dedicated feed reader. Many of these also create separate RSS feeds for comments. If there isn't a specific import script available for your blogging platform, this is probably the next best thing.

1. Locate the RSS feed page for your blog (often <domain name>/feed). Save this file to your computer.

2. Return to your WordPress Administration page. In the left navigation, click Tools, then Import.

3. Click the RSS link.

4. Click Browse, and locate the saved RSS feed file from your other blog.

5. Click Upload File and Import. The importer runs and displays a confirmation message when it's finished.

Transferring from (X)HTML

What you'll get: Posts

WordPress.com: No

WordPress Importer: Indirectly

If all else fails, you can try rebuilding your posts manually into RSS items, and importing as shown above. The Codex entry shows the proper format for each post.

```
<item>
 <pubDate>Wed, 30 Jan 2009 12:00:00 +0000</pubDate>
 <category>Kites</category>
 <category>Taiwan</category>
 <title>Fun times</title>
 <content:encoded><p>What great times we had...</p><p>And then
Bob...</p></content:encoded>
</item>
<item>...
```

Just be sure the <content:encoded> line is a single long line with no newlines embedded.

Collect all of your posts in a single file, with each post as an item.

There are two other ways to approach this problem:

- If you have well-formed (that is, tagged with standard W3C elements) HTML, the Import HTML Pages plug-in may help.

- Nilayan Sharma of Technetra offers a method to convert HTML to WordPress using the Atom Publishing Protocol, an alternative protocol to RSS: http://www.technetra.com/2009/02/24/migrating-your-blogs-content-to-wordpress.

INDEX

Symbols

! (exclamation point), HTML comments, 136

2-column layouts, themes (CSS), 311-312

3-column layouts, themes (CSS), 311-312

A

a tag (HTML), 127, 136

About the Author(s)/About the Blog, 153-154

About Us
WordPress.com, 376
WordPress.org, 381-382

accessing WordPress documentation with Google, 361-362

accounts (WordPress), creating, 32-33

activating
plug-ins, 277
themes, 268

ad-free service, cost of, 13

Add New Post page, 84

adding
links, 93-94
strategies for, 94-95
new links to blogrolls, 117-119
polls, 160-165
posts, new, 84-86
static pages, 152-153
users to blogs, 149
widgets, 69
new, 71-73

AddToAny, 285

Administration page, WordPress statistics, 170-171

administrators, 149-150

ads, 12
generating revenue from, 14-15
on WordPress blogs, 12
WordPress.com, 353
WordPress.org, 353

Advanced Services, WordPress.com, 376

advertising, plug-ins, 284-285

AdWords, 179-180

Ajax Edit Comments, 284

Akismet, 9, 43, 279
installing, 280-281
running, 281

All in One SEO Pak, 285

ALT text, 199

anchors, 127
in HTML, 136

AOL, 128

Apache Web Server, 248

API key, 35

architecture, modular architecture, 271-272

Arclite CSS, 306

Arclite theme, 300-301

arguments, 337

arrays
associative arrays, 327
indexed arrays, 326
multidimensional, 327

H

h# tags (HTML), 138

Hanna, Doug, 363

Header (header.php), 333

header comments, creating CSS-based themes from scratch, 307-308

header images
creating, 67
replacing, 305-306

header template, PHP theme templates, 338-339

header.php, 333

headers
changing custom headers, 66-67
themes, 57
themes (CSS), 312
navigation, 314-316
search, 312-314

Hello Dolly, 279
installing, 281

home page, WordPress.org, 377-378

hosted solutions, self-hosted solutions versus, 24-25

"hosted" version. *See* **WordPress.com**

hosting
audio, 220-221
video, 224

WordPress yourself, 246-247
editing configuration files, 250-252
installing web servers and MySQL databases on your system, 247-250

hosting blogs, finding blog-friendly hosts, 230-231

hosting options in WordPress, 22-24

hosts
finding, for WordPress.org, 383
WordPress.org, 354-355

hr tag (HTML), 138

href attribute (HTML), 127

HTML (Hypertext Markup Language), 87, 92, 123-125, 288
basic formatting commands, 88-89
browser support, 128
editors, 137
embedded HTML, YouTube example, 138-141
reasons for using, 89
secondary formatting commands, 92-93
tags, 126-128
character formatting, 130-132

comments, 136
links, 135-136
list formatting, 133-135
More tag, 136-137
paragraph breaks, 132-133
in WordPress, 137-138
transferring from, 389
viewing, 126
XHTML
compatibility, 138
XHTML versus, 124

HTML, 5, 289

HTML mode (Post editor), 125
Visual mode versus, 128-130

HTML Tidy validator, 292

HTTP (Hpertext Transfer Protocol), 123

hyperlinks as formatting, 91-92

hypertext, 127-128

Hypertext Markup Language (HTML), 87, 92, 123-125, 288
basic formatting commands, 88-89
browser support, 128
editors, 137
embedded HTML, YouTube example, 138-141

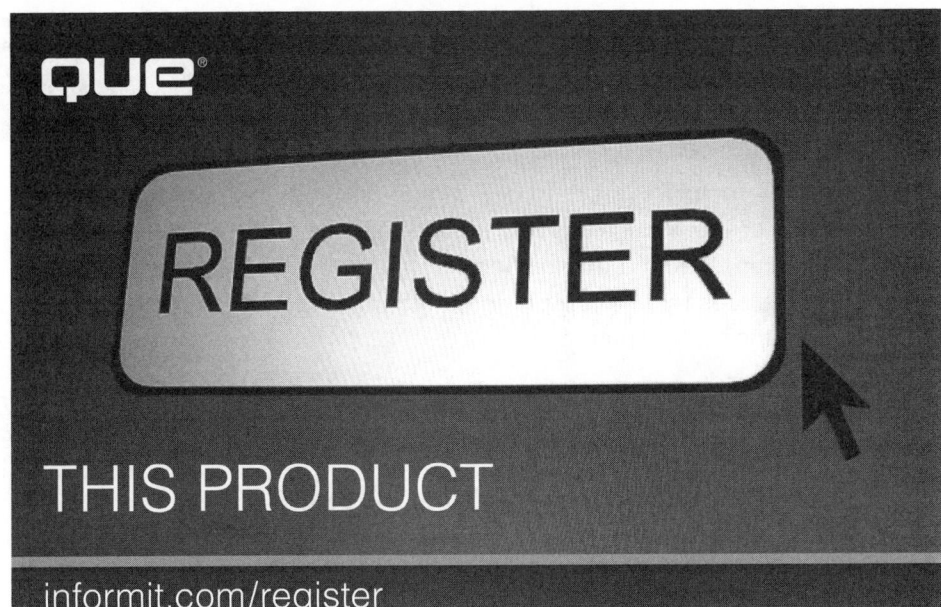

FREE Online Edition

Your purchase of **WordPress In Depth** includes access to a free online edition for 45 days through the Safari Books Online subscription service. Nearly every Que book is available online through Safari Books Online, along with more than 5,000 other technical books and videos from publishers such as Addison-Wesley Professional, Cisco Press, Exam Cram, IBM Press, O'Reilly, Prentice Hall, and Sams.

SAFARI BOOKS ONLINE allows you to search for a specific answer, cut and paste code, download chapters, and stay current with emerging technologies.

Activate your FREE Online Edition at
www.informit.com/safarifree

> **STEP 1:** Enter the coupon code: FNMSSZG.

> **STEP 2:** New Safari users, complete the brief registration form.
> Safari subscribers, just log in.

If you have difficulty registering on Safari or accessing the online edition, please e-mail customer-service@safaribooksonline.com

   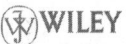